S0-ARG-334

WATCHING WILDLIFE

AUSTRALIA

Jane Bennett
Daniel Harley & Marianne Worley
Bec Donaldson
David Andrew
David Geering
Anna Povey
Martin Cohen

Lonely Planet Publications
Melbourne Oakland London Paris

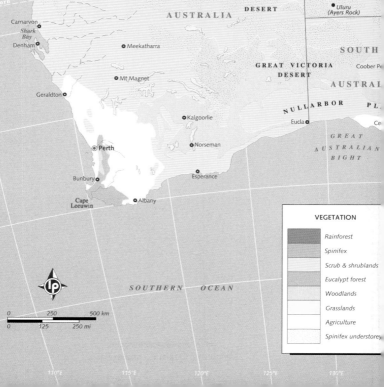

INDONESIA

TIMOR SEA

Melville Island

Bathurst Island

Arnhem S

Darwin

Arnhem Land

To Christmas & Cocos (Keeling) Islands

Katherine

INDIAN OCEAN

Wyndham

Kununurra

Daly Waters

The Kimberley

Lake Argyle

Derby

Fitzroy Crossing

Halls Creek

NORTHERN

Broome

Roebuck Bay

Tanami Desert

Tennant Cre

GREAT SANDY DESERT

TERRITOR

Port Hedland

Dampier

Marble Bar

Onslow

Exmouth

The Pilbara

Tom Price

Newman

WESTERN

GIBSON DESERT

MacDonnell Range

Alice Sprin

Carnarvon

Shark Bay

Denham

AUSTRALIA

Uluru (Ayers Rock)

Tropic of Capricorn

Meekatharra

SOUTH

INDIAN OCEAN

Mt Magnet

GREAT VICTORIA DESERT

Cooper Pe

AUSTRALI

Geraldton

Kalgoorlie

NULLARBOR

PL

Eucla

Ce

Norseman

GREAT AUSTRALIAN BIGHT

Perth

Bunbury

Esperance

Cape Leeuwin

Albany

SOUTHERN OCEAN

0   250   500 km
0   125   250 mi

Watching Wildlife Australia
1st edition – September 2000

Published by
Lonely Planet Publications Pty Ltd ABN 36 005 607 983
192 Burwood Rd, Hawthorn, Victoria 3122, Australia

Lonely Planet Offices
Australia PO Box 617, Hawthorn, Victoria 3122
USA 150 Linden St, Oakland, CA 94607
UK 10a Spring Place, London NW5 3BH
France 1 rue du Dahomey, 75011 Paris

Photographs
Many of the images in this guide are available for licensing from
Lonely Planet Images.
lpi@lonelyplanet.com.au

Front cover photograph
Emu (Mitch Reardon)

Back cover photographs (from left to right)
Daintree River ringtail possum (Martin Cohen)
Buff-breasted paradise-kingfisher (Chris Mellor)
Green tree frog (Jason Edwards)

ISBN 1 86450 032 8

text & maps © Lonely Planet 2000
photos © as indicated (pages 340–1) 2000

Printed by The Bookmaker International Ltd
Printed in China

CONTENTS

AUTHORS

Jane Bennett

Jane grew up on the shores of Sydney Harbour surrounded by beach, bush and disappearing bandicoots. She has worked as a vet with orangutans in Sarawak and ostriches on the Cocos (Keeling) Islands. Nights tagging turtles, and days birdwatching and walking forest transects have balanced a life with too many years at university. She has travelled widely from Madagascar to Macquarie Island in search of wild encounters with weird beasts; and highlights among years of forays into the forests of Borneo have included a face to face encounter with a Sumatran rhino and nearly stepping on a 6m reticulated python. The last decade, she has been based in Tasmania, growing girl babies and practising yoga. She currently lives on Christmas Island in the Indian Ocean.

Daniel Harley and Marianne Worley

Dan majored in zoology at Monash University in Melbourne and after four years of chasing possums through a swamp in the dark, he has started writing up his doctorate examining the ecology of the endangered Leadbeater's possum. He has been involved in a variety of fauna surveys and field studies, covering critters ranging from penguins and owls through to lizards, small mammals, bats and bandicoots. His main interests include the conservation of threatened wildlife and the population biology of birds and mammals.

Marianne was born in the UK, but was promptly whisked away by her family to grow up in Australia. There through regular camping trips she developed a strong affinity with the natural landscape, and its flora and fauna. She completed an honours degree in science, majoring in botany and zoology, and has since spent time on a range of ecological projects, including vegetation surveys and radio-tracking platypuses and possums. She has wandered throughout Australia, Mexico and the UK, and likes to seek out critters, write poetry and sing lots in her spare time.

Bec Donaldson

Researching and writing for Lonely Planet were for Bec (wonderful!) distractions from completing postgraduate research on dolphins, tutoring Aboriginal students and driving trucks for the Army Reserve. Addictions to writing, wildlife and wild places were forced upon her in early childhood when she was home-schooled in the backwoods of Tassie by a mother passionate about creative writing and rehabilitating orphaned marsupials, and a father hooked on bushwalking.

David Andrew

After his father was mauled by a gorilla at Howletts Zoo, David and his family fled the wilds of England to live somewhere safer – Australia. There David revolutionised the face of birdwatching by creating *Wingspan* and *Australian Birding* magazines; edited *Wildlife Australia* magazine; and among other jobs has been a research assistant in Kakadu NP, a birding guide for English comedian Bill Oddie and an editor for Lonely Planet. He is coordinating author for Lonely Planet's *Watching Wildlife East Africa*. David is amassing a bird list to bequeath to the nation.

David Geering

David's passion for birds started early in life and he stumbled into a career as a professional ornithologist in the late 1980s. He has worked in northern NSW and from Darwin to Melbourne on rainforest birds, wetland birds, shorebirds and, currently, honey-eaters (as the coordinator of the national Regent Honeyeater Recovery Effort). But most of all David delights in working on projects where volunteer input is sought and valued. One of the drawbacks of working with birds is that he now has trouble discerning where work finishes and his leisure time starts.

Anna Povey

Anna's work on this book ideally suited her mission of uniting zoology and botany, conducted since her days studying these subjects at very separate departments at university. During her job as Bushcare Support Officer with Greening Australia, Anna continues this mission by telling surprised farmers and timber growers about the sex lives of antechinuses in their bushland. It is her fervent hope that one day all Australians will know more about their own local native plants and animals than they do about European and African ones. In her spare time Anna seeks out the wild places around Tasmania (or further north to escape winter) and is attempting to return her garden to native bushland.

Martin Cohen

Martin has combined a life-long passion for finding and photo-graphing Australian wildlife with research (including a PhD on cane toad ecology), and writing natural history articles that he combines with photographs (in 1999 he won the portfolio section of the Australian Wildlife Photographer of the Year). Martin works as a Senior Conservation Officer with the Queensland Environmental Protection Agency and when not in an office, he is leading scientific expeditions, conducting fauna surveys, guiding ecotours throughout northern Australia, or presenting talks on tropical wildlife. Frogs are his favourite animals and he has been known to be literally knee-deep in muck getting the definitive photo. Martin recently established his own photojournalism and ecotour business (Wild about Australia) in Townsville.

FROM THE AUTHORS

Jane Bennett

Jane would like to thank her mum and dad, corny but true, especially for getting over the bullet wound with the Dragon. Lots of people helped with information, including Peter Brown, Leslie Frost (thanks for enduring the screaming-baby trip!), Stuart Lennox, Steve Smith, Nic Mooney, Steve Johnston and Julia Gibson. More people helped in other important ways, and here the list gets too long: Shauna Cason, Shirley and David Goldsworthy, and Fatimah binte Kassim stand out among many, not least being the Wild Blondes: my husband David Slip and girls, Sacha and Billie. Lastly, that great team at LP, particularly Sue Galley, Chris Klep and Sean Pywell. Thank you.

Daniel Harley and Marianne Worley

We are grateful to the numerous people that gave freely of their time and knowledge – it greatly assisted both our research and travels. In particular, we would like to thank the many national park rangers who were only too happy to share their insight and enthusiasm for their local areas. We would also like to thank Chris Dahlberg and Peter O'Reilly for their lively discussions; Top Tours (and especially Mark!) for their generous support on Fraser Island; Bruce Weir and Greg Knight for their contributions; Ad and Al for putting us up in Sydney; the various local tourist centres that patiently dealt with our list of questions; the countless motor mech-anics along the eastern seaboard who were well and truly put to the test by our vehicle; and our families for their unwavering support. Last (but not least!), we would like to thank all the critters for the memories – they are what it is all about!

Bec Donaldson

Greatest thanks to our editor Sean Pywell for his dedication, encouragement, friendship and light relief throughout the year – Sean it has been an absolute pleasure. Thanks also to Doug Coughran, Colleen Sims, Nick Gales, John Hunter and the many other officers and rangers from the WA Dept of CALM who shared invaluable knowledge and entertaining anecdotes; and to the biologists both in Australia and overseas who revealed inside information about their favourite species – especially Menna Jones for her delightful description of young devils. Bruce and the Rhind family offered heaps of tips and kind hospitality on the road. Special thanks to the Freo crew just for being good mates, and Cain and JJ for being great travelling companions – although unfortunately absent during the feral piglet assault!

THIS BOOK

JANE Bennett wrote the Nature in Australia chapter, the back-bone of the Wildlife-Watching chapter, and the Tasmania section of Parks and Places. Jane also coordinated contributions from other authors. Habitats was written by Anna Povey and Lindsay Brown (the Oceans). David Andrew wrote the Northern Territory section and contributed substantially to many other sections. Bec Donaldson wrote the Western Australia section; and Dan Harley and Marianne Worley zoomed up the east coast to produce South Australia, Victoria, New South Wales and Queensland. The Wildlife Gallery was written by Bec Donaldson (Mammals), David Geering and David Andrew (Birds), Martin Cohen (the sections on reptiles and frogs) and Lindsay Brown (the sections on marine life).

The special sections of the Wildlife-Watching Chapter were written by Jane Bennett (Diving and Snorkelling), David Andrew (Birdwatching), Martin Cohen (Spotlighting), Bec Donaldson (Whale-watching) and Luke Hunter (Photography).

FROM THE PUBLISHER

THIS idea for this series came from David Andrew and was supported by Chris Klep, Nick Tapp and Sue Galley. The idea was initially developed by Sean Pywell and Jane Bennett: Jane left to coordinate the authoring of this book, the first in the series; Sean continued as series editor. Mathew Burfoot designed and laid out the book. Simon Tillema designed and drew the maps, with Chris Klep and Teresa Donnellan tweaking the edges, and Andrew Smith helping with map corrections. Editing and proofing was by David Burnett, David Andrew, Miranda Wills, Thalia Kalkipsakis and Sean Pywell. The LPI team, and especially Fiona Croydon, Valerie Tellini and Brett Pascoe, came up with most of the images; special thanks also to Louise Poultney and Richard I'Anson. Jamieson Gross designed the cover. Mapping was checked by Teresa and Michael Blore; layout by Michael, Lindsay Brown, Nick Tapp and David Kemp.

Thanks also to a great flock of people who helped out, had input or gave support in one way or another, especially Anna Bolger, Paul Clifton, Darren Elder, Richard Everist, Carly Hammond, David Kemp, Glenn van der Knijff, Emma McMahon, Vince Patton, Andrew Tudor, Tim Uden and Tamsin Wilson.

We would also like to thank those outside of LP who assisted with many requests: Jenny Bell and Peter Crawley-Boevey of ANT Photo Library; Chris Coleborn, Chris Dahlberg, Jason Edwards, Bob Forsyth, Murray Lord, Martin O'Brien, John Peter, Jennifer Saunders, Elycia Wallis, Bruce Weir, Mike Weston, Russell Woodford and the many participants on the birding-aus newsgroup.

PREFACE

IT'S been only a few thousand years since all of us were hunters and gatherers – watching over the savannahs of Australia and Africa, and the steppes of Asia, reading the daily weather signs and searching for our next meal. We still have that instinctive connection with wild creatures and the remote places they inhabit. We all hanker to get into the bush and discover our origins, even though the urge is sometimes buried by the complications of modern urban life. And our ancient island continent of Australia is the ideal place to do it.

Australia is blessed with vast tracts of wilderness – from the tropical wetlands of Kakadu to the stunning landscapes of the Centre, from the myrtle forests of Tasmania to the Great Barrier Reef. Every area is inhabited by animals and plants, many found nowhere else on earth, including the platypus, koala, red kangaroo and saltwater crocodile; fish of the coral reefs numbering thousands of different kinds; and hundreds of species of eucalypt.

Over the last 30 years it has been our good fortune to film wildlife in many such areas. We love nothing better than to pack our swags and head off into the wilderness to track and film wild animals through the dramas of their daily lives. One of our most memorable trips was to Raine Island, off the tip of Cape York Peninsula, at the northern end of the Great Barrier Reef. It's the site of one of the biggest breeding colonies of green turtles in the world, where at certain times of year tens of thousands of females come ashore to lay their eggs. At sunrise one morning during our visit we found thousands of turtles stranded on the reef flats at low tide, desperate to reach deep water before they were baked by the tropical sun. Herons fed on newly emerged hatchlings while tiger sharks on the lookout for exhausted adults patrolled the reef edge.

Our job is full of such rare glimpses into the natural world – moments of life and death, and images of animal behaviour never before recorded. It takes time, often months of careful observation, to learn how our subjects think and react to our presence before we can film the revealing moments of their lives.

Much of what we film can be seen by anyone who is prepared to put in a few hours at the right place and time. For all of us, witnessing and recording such events is indescribably rewarding – not unlike the thrill of a successful hunt, except our weapons are not spears but binoculars and cameras.

David Parer & Elizabeth Parer-Cook
Natural History Film-makers

With over 20 years of multi-award-winning experience shooting wildlife documentaries, David and Elizabeth are among the world's most gifted wildlife observers – capturing rare and unforgettable images on film. Seasoned travellers, they recently spent two years filming iguanas and other wildlife in Ecuador's Galapagos Islands.

INTRODUCTION

EVERY experienced traveller knows that getting a feel for a place means getting to know its inhabitants, seeing how they've adapted to life there and picking up the vibes by watching their lifestyle. Local wildlife is part of that picture, although it may not be immediately obvious in some places. For some travellers animals are just part of the landscape, pleasant diversions sparked by the flash of a colourful bird or big 'game'. But for a growing number of ecotourists, wildlife-watching is the main reason to travel. Continuing the tradition of generations of travellers, they are drawn to remote parts of the globe to see citizens of the natural world as unusual and spectacular as any relics of antiquity.

A fleeting glimpse of a wild animal can stimulate the hunting instinct that lurks in most of us, although these days the 'prey' usually ends up on film or as a lasting memory. For some there is that indefinable feeling of being connected with the web of living things that make this planet so special, a reminder that we are just a speck in the universe. Others simply like to 'tick off' on a list every bird or mammal they see. Of course both approaches, and every in between, are valid; and ideally the interest generated by wildlife tourism will create an incentive to preserve wildness and wilderness.

But seeking out wildlife can sometimes take a bit of know-how and this is where the Watching Wildlife series comes in. We provide practical, reliable advice from enthusiastic and veteran wildlife-watchers to help you find wild animals, whether you're on a specialist tour, with a personal guide or on your own. We tell you how to do it, where to go and what you'll see, helping to demystify the process of finding and appreciating wild animals in wild (and not-so-wild) places. It's also your handbook to getting some environmental perspective on the country. And with our Resource Guide we point you in the right direction for getting hold of a ecotour guide, finding a specialist book or joining a volunteer group.

You are holding a treasure map of practical clues that will help you plan an independent wildlife expedition and how to interpret what you see, whatever your mode of travel. You might be an intrepid wilderness bushwalker, a car camper, a coach traveller, a local resident, a novice or a specialist familiar with another landscape looking for an insight into new terrain – this book will give you a wildlife commentary to take on your journey.

From the reef to the forest, eucalypt woodlands to desert dunes, Australia has a unique and fascinating fauna, as you'd expect on an island that has been isolated for 40 million years. Huge, hopping kangaroos; somnolent furry koalas; lizards with ruffed necks; duck-billed, egg-laying aquatic mammals; emerald-green pythons – the list goes on. And, best of all, there are millions of hectares of uncrowded country in which to find them. Read on...

NATURE IN AUSTRALIA

An introduction to Australia's natural history

THE kangaroo is one of the most instantly recognisable animals on earth and one of Australia's most famous icons. The chance to see a kangaroo in the wild often provides the impetus for visitors to Antipodean shores, but once here a previously unsuspected variety of pristine habitats, exceptional birdlife and unusual mammals leave a lasting impression. For most travellers, it is the contrast to their experiences elsewhere that makes Australia memorable.

Australia is only 2% smaller than continental USA (minus Alaska), but has less than a tenth the human population. It is the world's largest island but smallest continent – and often referred to as 'the island continent'. It is a land of extremes, from alpine snowfields to searing deserts, from lush tropical rainforests to coral reefs. It is the lowest and flattest continent, with an average elevation of just 274m; it has the oldest soils (4.2 billion years) and the oldest fossils (3.5 billion years); and only Antarctica experiences a lower annual rainfall.

For biologists, Australia is synonymous with marsupials and monotremes. Although members of these groups also live in New Guinea and the Americas, it is their dominance and diversity in Australia that sets it apart. Reactions to the first specimens of the platypus sent back to England illustrate just how strange the fauna seems to a European eye – it was loudly declared to be a museum fraud.

Modern travellers will be relieved to find plenty of wild places left in Australia, teeming with wildlife. The colours of the fish and coral of the Great Barrier Reef, Kakadu's waterbird-filled wetlands and basking crocodiles, and a red kangaroo against the backdrop of Uluru are probably some of the more famous images of Australian wildlife, but there are countless more to be experienced.

A UNIQUE ENVIRONMENT

Ancient origins

That Australia was once connected to the supercontinent Gondwana is demonstrated by the presence of the same or similar species of plant and animal – both living and in the fossil record – in locations as disparate as South America, New Guinea, New Zealand and Antarctica. Thus, the dripping forests of *Nothofagus* beech in Lamington National Park (NP) closely resemble those in the Patagonian Andes and have changed little since these now widely separated lands broke apart 40 million years ago. Likewise, tiny marsupials still living in southern Chile and Australia probably resemble the ancestral marsupials which diversified so dramatically only in Australia. From this rainforest crucible a whole continent of unique forms and adaptations evolved.

Drying land, retreating rainforests

When Gondwana broke apart, its pieces creating and delineating seas and oceans, the Australian fragment was isolated and remained so for millions of years. The simultaneous isolation of the Antarctic continent created circumpolar winds that gradually desiccated Australia, and the formerly widespread rainforests contracted to the sheltered, damp edges (relict cycads and palms can still be seen in the heart of the arid zone at Finke Gorge NP). A geological uplift on the eastern edge formed the Great Dividing Range, the country's highest landform. Rainfall trapped by these mountains supports the remnant rainforests on the east coast. And when the tectonic plate carrying the land mass of Australia collided with Asia, the northernmost part came under the influence of monsoonal weather cycles characterised by the dramatic oscillations of wet and dry.

Half of modern Australia receives less than 300mm annual rainfall and a further quarter less than 600mm. Much of the country experiences long periods of 'drought' (in fact, such prolonged dry spells are the normal state) that are periodically interspersed with catastrophic bushfires and extensive flooding. Plants that were once a minor component of Gondwanan forests evolved to withstand the drier conditions and spread across Australia – this hardy flora now dominates the natural environment. Among them are the acacias and hundreds of species of distinctive, hard-leaved eucalyptus trees that grow from coast to coast. The farther inland you go, the drier it gets, but inland plants are efficient exploiters of ephemeral water resources and all but the harshest of deserts can be surprisingly densely vegetated. Animals also radiated from the Gondwanan forests; hundreds of species evolved from the ancestral marsupials to exploit niches from tree tops to the forest floor to open plains. Burrowing, carnivorous and other specialised forms arose, and some of the most successful stategies included an ability to withstand the devastation of fire and drought, and to breed and disperse in times of plenty.

From ocean to desert

The Pacific Ocean sweeps up to the fertile but narrow eastern seaboard, where the majority of Australia's highly urbanised human population is clustered around bays and beaches. Away from civilisation the rugged cliffs and sandstone promontories are topped by coastal heaths; in sheltered locations, fringing mangrove forests stabilise the shore. Most of the tropical eastern shore is protected by the Great Barrier Reef, the world's longest reef complex.

Woodlands and coastal forests lead to the slopes of the Great Dividing Range, a series of plateaus that hugs the coast from 50km to 400km inland. Only at its southern end is the spine of this mountain range high enough for alpine snowfields to form, and its apex, Mt Kosciuszko, is only 2228m high. Most permanent waterways run east off these slopes, but the Murray-Darling river system, the country's largest and one of the longest in the world, drains west. Pockets of rainforest remain along the eastern seaboard from Tasmania to Cape York, reaching their greatest diversity in north Queensland.

West of the ranges and escarpments of 'the Divide' the eucalyptus forests become progressively drier and more open, in some places forming distinct stands, such as mallee – these small, hardy trees thrive in the harsh conditions. River red gums and coolabahs line the waterways that extend like green fingers far into the Outback, even where other tree species have disappeared and the surrounding country is dominated by stunted shrubs, saltbushes or grasslands. Extensive fossil deposits show that much of the present-day inland was once a huge sea. Several normally dry riverbeds still drain into salty Lake Eyre, a crusty saltpan 15m below sea level which receives water about once every eight years and has filled only three times in recorded history (two of those occasions were in only the past three decades, and it all but filled again in 2000 – this number of fillings in such a short time may be a result of climate change). When floods do come to the inland, masses of frogs, fish and crustaceans (and birds attracted to the feast) rush into a frenzied breeding cycle before the waters evaporate or drain away.

The western half

Much of central Australia is 'desert', although outcrops such as the MacDonnell Ranges have permanent water and form oases for wildlife. The deserts are some of the most inhospitable places on earth, yet when rains do fall hardy plants flower en masse, and nomadic birds arrive to feast on insects and nectar. West of the dry barrier of the Nullarbor Plain, a vast western plateau covers half the country. Much of it is sandy or stony desert, but the south-west corner is an enclave with relatively high rainfall that supports tall, wet forests; diverse wildflower and heath communities; and many endemic animal species.

Far to the north, vast sandstone outcrops and plateaus form the so-called Kimberley, a remote area with highly diverse and abundant wildlife. Dry seasons in the Kimberley feature intense heat, and deluges in the wet season make much of the terrain inaccessible. Completing the circle, the 'Top End' – the northernmost part of the Northern Territory – is subject to summer monsoonal rains, when floodplains are inundated and animals breed, and a long dry season when wildlife is forced to move on or congregate on drying waterholes until the rains return.

WILDLIFE

The long isolation of the Australian landmass has allowed the survival, evolution and specialisation of several interesting

Rich underwater life

Life in the temperate waters off southern Australia has its origins anchored in ancient Gondwanan seas. But, when the slow drift northward brought the continent into equatorial waters, myriad new life forms spread to form the richest assemblage of marine life on earth – the 2300km-long Great Barrier Reef. 'The Reef' shelters most of Queensland's eastern seaboard from oceanic wave action; and among its complex of large and small underwater ecosystems is an astonishing diversity of life that includes 350 species of coral and 2000 of fish. Dugongs graze sheltered bays, and offshore the movements of whales, sharks, manta rays and pelagic fish fit into a sweeping migration dance of prey and predators in the three oceans circling Australia. Above the surface, rainforest-covered continental islands and sand cays support a wealth of birdlife; and remote cays attract huge numbers of breeding sea turtles. Many of the 2000 individual reef systems are accessible to divers, snorkellers and glass-bottomed boats.

groups of animals. Most famous of these are two groups of mammals, the monotremes and marsupials – best known by representatives such as the platypus, kangaroos and the koala. But among the birds, reptiles and frogs many unique groups are also found.

Fur, eggs and milk

Most Australian mammals are unusual because they are nocturnal, or at best seen around dawn and dusk, and rest-up during the heat of the day. However, one group really stands out. Monotremes are survivors from an earlier age of mammals and two of the world's three species live in Australia (the third lives in New Guinea): the spiny, ant-eating echidna and the aquatic, duck-billed platypus. Like 'conventional' mammals, female echidnas and platypuses produce milk. But unlike other mammals, which bear live young, these extraordinary animals lay eggs, which they incubate until their helpless young hatch.

It is marsupials that dominate the fauna, with 130 species. The red kangaroo is Australia's largest surviving terrestrial native animal – males can stand 2m high when rearing on hindlegs and tail to threaten a challenger. Yet, like all kangaroos, it is born after a very short gestation as a tiny, naked embryo that crawls through a forest of fur into its mother's pouch – the most distinctive feature of marsupials. This loose flap of skin replaces the womb of 'higher' mammals and here the embryo latches onto a teat and develops during the mother's relatively long lactation until it is ready to venture into the world outside. This breeding strategy has served marsupials for 100 million years and they've expanded into nearly all terrestrial niches filled by other mammals elsewhere: mobs of kangaroos graze the plains and follow the rains as antelopes do in Africa; tree-kangaroos browse tropical rainforest foliage like monkeys; Tasmanian devils scavenge and hunt at night like hyenas; gliding possums replace flying squirrels; and quolls have a similar niche to that of civets.

The third group of mammals, the placentals, now dominates most of the earth. But by the time placentals rose to prominence on other landmasses, Australia had been cut off from the rest of the world. Some placentals have since arrived naturally. To seagoing mammals, such as whales, dolphins and seals, water was no barrier. Likewise, the flying mammals – the bats and fruit-bats – colonised Australian night skies when the land mass approached Asia and are now represented by 58 species. And a subtle invasion of rodents (rats and mice) that crossed from South-East Asia some 15 million years ago has evolved into 50 colourful and unusual species that now occupy most Australian habitats.

The isolation that gave rise to such diversity, however, was ultimately the downfall of many native mammals. The arrival of the dingo – a new style of predator – some 3500 to 4000 years ago probably hastened the demise of large native carnivores on the mainland. And when white settlers accidentally or deliberately set loose a host of placentals such as cats and foxes, rabbits and goats; which were adaptable enough to exploit the same niches as many native mammals, the usurpers quickly prevailed.

Scales and feathers

Australia's long isolation is also reflected in its birds. Of the approximately 750 bird species recorded in Australia, more than 300 are endemic (the highest number for any country), and there are many groups that are almost so, such as the honeyeaters and fairy-wrens. There are some 55 parrots, the world's largest array of seabirds and huge numbers of migratory waders. As with mammals, many groups are relics of Gondwana: among them are large ratites (the emu and rainforest-dwelling cassowary); powerful vocalists such as lyrebirds and scrub-birds; and the extraordinary bowerbirds and birds of paradise. More globally distributed groups such as raptors, waterfowl and colourful finches are also well represented. A good selection of colourful, unique and unusual species can be seen near any major population centre.

Ancient and unique families are found right across the country. Many species are widespread but there are many others restricted to relatively small areas of a particular habitat (tropical Queensland supports the greatest diversity). Many groups that are widespread and diverse elsewhere in the world barely make it into Australia (eg, there is only one species of sunbird), reflecting the continent's late contact with South-East Asia, but other bird groups with a wide distribution (eg, crows and ravens) first arose in Australia. In response to cycles of drought and plenty many Australian birds have unusual behavioural traits. For example, a high percentage of waterbirds wander between seasonal floods inland and permanent wetlands near the coast; and communal breeding, a strategy whereby members of past broods help their parents raise subsequent young, is prevalent among many groups, from kookaburras to fairy-wrens.

The gradual drying of this ancient continent has favoured the proliferation of reptiles and Australia has more than 760 species, including giant crocodiles and some famously dangerous snakes. The vast majority, however, are harmless, and range from tiny, jewelled geckoes to goannas topping 2m in length; huge sea turtles to freshwater turtles that aestivate under dry riverbeds until rain returns; and a host of inoffensive snakes from burrowing blind snakes to 7m-long scrub pythons. The diversity of lizards is the greatest in the world and some arid ecosystems support 40 species per hectare.

Revenge of the natives

White settlement was followed by the precipitous decline of many small marsupials which today survive only in isolated patches of woodland in the south-west. Introduced predators, such as the European fox and cat, are largely blamed for their demise and continue to pose a threat to the survival of many species. An ambitious program to wipe out foxes and cats in parts of Western Australia relies on baits laced with a lethal poison known as '1080'. One of the factors that has probably enabled small marsupials to survive in the south-western woodlands is a group of native flowering plants of the genus *Gastrolobium*. Popularly known as poison peas, the leaves of these plants contain a toxin, sodium fluoroacetate – the active ingredient in 1080 – to which native browsers are immune. The poison is retained in the bodies of the marsupials, where it remains active and lethal to any non-native predator that tries to eat them. And whereas baiting in other areas with 1080 can kill as many natives as ferals, and is therefore of limited use in selectively targeting exotic mammals, in the south-west 1080 can be used far more freely and with much greater effect.

The arid centre also supports frogs, most probably a relic of a wetter past (they burrow into moist chambers where they can remain for years until rains stimulate them to break free and join a frantic breeding cycle), but it is the Wet Tropics that supports the greatest number of species.

HUMANS AND WILDLIFE

Aboriginal groups in Australia today are often thought of as desert groups or the coastal and island people of far north Queensland. But, in fact, Aboriginal people at the time of European settlement were far more widespread, if sparsely distributed in places, and had lifestyles that varied to suit the environments in which they lived.

The spread of fire

Since the ancestors of Aboriginal people arrived (opinions vary, but it is thought that humans first arrived in Australia at least 50,000 years ago) volcanoes have erupted, seas have risen by 130m causing the shorelines to shift, and many of the early large marsupials have died out. There has been much debate over the impact of Aboriginal burning and hunting on animal extinctions. Aboriginal hunters almost certainly contributed directly to the loss of megafauna – which included giant kangaroos, wombats, emus and goannas – although the effects varied from region to region. Some argue that these extinctions were inevitable and climate related; overall it was probably a combination of both. However, it is certain that Aborigines altered the landscape through their use of fire, deliberately setting fire to areas to clear undergrowth. This made travel and hunting easier, provided fertile ash for poor soils and stimulated new shoots that were especially attractive to grazing species, which they hunted. Fire had always been a feature of the dry continent, and many plants, such as banksias, hakeas and acacias, have evolved to require burning to stimulate seed germination, or to be fire resistant. The activities of nomadic people most likely favoured the growth of open woodlands where prey such as kangaroos were easier to hunt.

The Aboriginal relationship with the environment eventually settled into one of equilibrium, involving practices which ensured a continual supply of resources. Burning near rainforest was taboo since this habitat is vulnerable to fire and would have been destroyed. And patches of habitat were deliberately left intact, effectively acting as reservoirs of plants and animals that could replenish surrounding areas once drought, flood or a devastating fire had passed. The well-watered Top End and coastal regions where Aborigines made the first landfalls sustained relatively large populations that expanded into marginal land and even deserts in bountiful times.

The invasions begin

When James Cook first landed in 1770, the vicinity of modern Sydney was populated by several roving bands of Aboriginal people who thrived on the abundant oysters, fish and game in the area. Nonetheless, the first settlers found the land hostile and nearly starved while waiting for supplies from England. This inability to learn about the landscape from the people who lived in harmony with it set the tone for colonisation. Livestock and crops were imported for food; exotic animals and plants were established to help overcome feelings of homesickness in the strange new land.

Disease, conflicts with settlers and outright warfare quickly decimated the Aboriginal population. Many tribes disappeared completely and with them their culture, language and understanding of the land. Much of what we know and can learn today comes from isolated groups, like the desert bands and northern coastal people, whose country was less productive, accessible or appealing to white settlers. Non-Aboriginal Australians are slowly beginning to learn about bush food, but much lore is lost forever.

Hoofed animals introduced by white settlers have worn away much of the continent's thin topsoil. Australia's old soils have long been leached of nutrients without being replenished from ash spread by volcanic upheaval. The sinking of wells and the windmills that punctuate the arid interior mark the spread of the erosion, as grazing took over any land with enough water to keep sheep and cattle alive. But improved access to water has been exploited by huge numbers of plains kangaroos – their success means that they are regarded as pests by graziers because they compete with stock for pasture.

CONSERVATION

Since 1840, 66% of Australia's forests have been cleared, 15 vertebrate species – seven of them marsupials – have become extinct and many more are endangered. Major conservation issues include habitat reduction, fragmentation and degradation from land clearing, farming practices and urbanisation. This has reduced the populations of many species reliant on forest or woodland vegetation, resulting in the extinction or rarity of many endemic land and freshwater species.

If it doesn't move, chop it down
A frenzy of tree clearing has occurred over the last two centuries. The exploration of the coast north of Sydney was quickly followed by the extraction of massive trunks of red cedar and kauri pine. This industry continued in north Queensland until 1988, by which time lowland tropical rainforest was virtually extinct. Pockets of rainforest in north Queensland, southern New South Wales and Tasmania remain, but cover only 0.2% of Australia, some protected and some still the subject of pitched battles between conservationists and logging interests.

Mallee woodlands that once swept in a broad band across southern Australia have been cleared almost completely and converted to wheat cropping. Indiscriminate clearing of forest and woodlands for grazing and farming, and the introduction of rabbits have exposed the shallow and fragile soils causing dust

---

Old records yield new clues

Among the large and easily recognised kangaroos, crocodiles and echidnas depicted on some Aboriginal rock-art galleries there are many small animals shown in enough detail to discern different species, eg, fish such as barramundi and catfish, and both long- and short-necked freshwater turtles. Indeed, until recently the pitted-shelled turtle was known to science only from representations at rock-art sites and a few bone fragments. But even more intriguing are ancient depictions of species long extinct – visual records of the fauna of times past. On the Arnhem Land escarpment abutting Kakadu there are depictions of a thylacine-like predator and giant kangaroos that died out millennia ago. And at Carnarvon Gorge in Queensland a representation of a footprint resembles that of no animal known from the area – it too could be another mainland record of the thylacine.

---

storms and floods, resulting in a massive loss of topsoil. The use of superphosphate fertilisers to stem falling productivity raised the acidity of soils. The increased watering of land converted to cropping and orchards has raised the water table, bringing salt from the ancient seabed to the surface and rendering huge areas unfit for agriculture, indeed virtually unable to sustain flora. Tree planting and improved practices, such as contour farming for soil conservation, have become essential aspects of modern farming techniques in response.

Despite rampant forest clearing, bushfires remain a primal feature of life in Australia. Without regular burning undergrowth and leaf litter accumulate in forests, and uncontrollable fires that rage periodically continue to threaten human life and property where fingers of suburbia extend into forested regions around Melbourne and Sydney. In recent years authorities have started to include controlled burns in their management of wooded areas, but their methods remain controversial. Many pockets of bush are fragmented and isolated from refuge corridors; even controlled burns threaten to decimate vulnerable populations of fauna and flora in some areas. And controversy surrounds whether a return to frequent, less-intense burns (similar to that of Aboriginal practice) or infrequent, massive conflagrations (the likely pattern before Aborigines arrived) is best for the environment.

The ferals

The rich mammal faunas of Africa, Asia and the Americas have long had contact with each other. When land bridges formed between these continents and the faunas intermingled, indigenous species either evolved to survive against a new competitor, or perished. Evolution in isolation left much of Australia's wildlife – and, indeed, whole habitats – susceptible to invasion by forms previously absent. When Australia was finally invaded by placental mammals, the results were devastating.

For example, plagues of the introduced rabbit denuded the country during the 1930s. Their numbers have now been reduced by the introduction of diseases such as myxomatosis and the calicivirus, but rabbits irreversibly changed the landscape by contributing to soil erosion through their burrowing habits; by competing with native herbivores for food; and by wiping out native plants by overgrazing. Similarly, hoofed stock gone feral, such as pigs, donkeys, goats and cattle, continue to cut up the ancient friable soil and denude vegetation. Carnivores, such as dogs, cats and foxes kill small marsupials, lizards and birds. Weed invasion is a massive problem in some areas, eg, where water hyacinth chokes waterways in the Top End. Animals other than mammals have also had a devastating impact. The cane toad is a fine example of biological control gone wrong. Introduced in the 1930s to control beetles affecting the sugar cane industry, it has no natural predators in Australia and has since proliferated and spread to take a toll of small animals. The story of Australia's invasions has rarely been a happy one, and there are few other examples of so large an area being devastated by introduced species.

The future

Symptoms of declining environmental health can also be seen in 'dieback' among woodland trees, coral bleaching, algal blooms, declining fish catches and the disappearance of frogs, to name a few. Pitched battles are still being waged between 'greenies' and loggers in old growth forests, and land clearance continues apace in some regions.

But it's not all bleak. In the last 40 years conservation has moved from being a fringe interest to, at times, the centre of political debate on which has ridden the future of governments. Great steps forward have been made in areas of environmental education, management, rehabilitation, energy, design and agriculture. And conservation has moved into the home, with many Australians planting gardens to attract native birds, recycling paper and participating in Landcare and Coastcare programs.

PARKS AND RESERVES

National parks and other reserves

An excellent system of national parks and other reserves protects roughly 7.5%, or 580,000 sq km, of Australia's total land area. This figure excludes marine parks, which cover another 396,000 sq km – some two-thirds of which is the Great Barrier Reef Marine Park. This is a far cry from the situation only 25 years ago, when conservationists were pushing to increase protected areas to cover 5% of Australia's area.

Most national parks (abbreviated in reserve names throughout this book as NP) protect plants and animals from hunting and other disturbances. A few exceptions permit traditional hunting and gathering by Aboriginal landowners, eg, in Kakadu NP. Most native wildlife is also fully protected outside reserves, although limited 'harvesting' of some species is permitted, eg, red kangaroos. Other categories of protected area vary from state to state, and include conservation parks (CP), conservation reserves (CR), game reserves (GR), marine parks (MP), marine reserves (MR), nature reserves (NR), regional reserves (RR), state parks (SP), state forests (SF) and a variety of others.

Icon, pest or barbecue steak?

Kangaroo numbers on Outback properties sometimes exceed those of livestock, and farmers actually pay for 'pest' control; shooting Australia's most recognisable animal is a huge industry, with the carcasses mostly becoming pet food. When an American documentary in the late 1970s exposed the sometimes callous nature of culling, there was a worldwide chorus of dismay. But zoologist Professor Gordon Grigg reasoned that kangaroos are the best-adapted meat for this country, saying they should be harvested for human consumption so we can rid the land of the scourge of cloven hooves – farmers should view roos as a resource, not as pests. Others have endorsed this idea and kangaroo fillets are starting to appear on Australian menus – but there's little sign yet of a reduction in livestock numbers.

Each state has its own parks authority, which manages its 'national' parks. However, a federal agency, Parks Australia, is responsible for Kakadu and Uluru–Kata Tjuta NPs plus a handful of smaller parks; and the Great Barrier Reef MP has its own management authority. The state bodies are not responsible to Parks Australia directly and the arrangement parallels the state governments' relationship with the federal government, ie, usually politically at odds and without cohesive national plans or initiatives. Management styles and priorities vary from state to state, as do budgets, fees and park regulations. Forestry management bodies, water authorities and local councils also have parks and reserves that vary greatly in condition, and private landowners can declare their land as a wildlife reserve or place conservation covenants on the land.

The Australian Bush Heritage Fund, concerned at the rate of clearance of unprotected pockets, is a growing nongovernment organisation that buys and manages land of conservation value – an approach some other organisations are also adopting.

International conservation conventions

Australia is a signatory to the World Heritage Convention and has nominated 13 sites. Some, such as the Great Barrier Reef and Queensland Wet Tropics, stand out for their biological richness. But World Heritage sites are chosen for many reasons. For example, Uluru–Kata Tjuta and Kakadu NPs also have ancient cultural associations; Lord Howe, Heard and Macquarie Islands all support unique ecosystems; and others make up significant archaeological (eg, Willandra Lakes Region, where a human burial site 30,000-yeas old was found) and fossil sites (eg, fossil mammal sites at Riversleigh and Naracoorte).

Australia is also a signatory to the Ramsar Convention on Wetlands, which protects wetlands and wetland wildlife of outstanding conservation significance. Among the 53 designated sites, covering a total area of 5,248,596 hectares, are Roebuck Bay near Broome and Kakadu NP.

Reserves nominated under Unesco's Man and the Biosphere program are designated for many different reasons, including research and conservation. Of the 12 Australian reserves nominated, several are national parks (eg, Croajingolong, Kosciuszko) and others are also World Heritage sites (eg, Macquarie Island, Uluru–Kata Tjuta). ■

WILDLIFE-WATCHING

Tips and hints on the art
of watching wildlife

WATCHING wildlife is rarely the close-up dramatic experience we enjoy on TV documentaries. Those camerapeople sometimes spend weeks or months in difficult conditions to get shots that might whizz across your screen in seconds. But they're the images that have encouraged you to try, right?

The good news is that by bearing in mind a few pointers you can maximise the chances of close-up wildlife encounters in real life. Don't rule out beginners' luck (don't rely on it, either), but watching wildlife is like every other pastime – it requires practice, patience and the honing of a few basic skills. But when things fall into place and you do have a close encounter, it will be etched in your memory with a tag of excitement that's usually missing from the armchair experience.

WHEN TO GO

Possibly the single most important influence on the abundance of Australian wildlife – and therefore your chances of seeing it – is rain. Rain affects plant growth, the seasonal availability of drinking water, the concentrations of water-dependent animals, and factors such as distribution, breeding and migration. And its effects differ from one side of the country to the other.

In northern Australia permanent water is the key to finding animals during the dry season (June to August). Getting around is usually no problem, but the Dry is also peak tourist season and popular parks can get crowded. The first rains are heralded by the arrival of migratory birds, and courtship and breeding activity generally cranks up. Timing can be critical: the period just before the Wet proper is the best time to see the greatest variety of species. By late in the wet season many places are difficult to reach and wildlife has dispersed, although visitors are far fewer in number.

As you move south, the seasons become more distinct, and the difference between winter and summer temperatures can be extreme. Summer (December to February) in the south can range from warm to torrid, with little moving by midmorning on a hot day. In winter, rainfall increases markedly but, except in alpine areas, it's never cold enough to force mammals into hibernation (indeed, only one Australian mammal hibernates – the mountain pygmy-possum). Fine weather in winter can be an excellent time to go spotlighting. Nonetheless, cold and wet conditions on the southern mountain ranges can pose a physical challenge at any time of year and every care should be exercised. Although many species in drier regions are nomadic, following favourable conditions, most birds don't migrate for the winter, so in most places there is a high diversity of birds year-round. And winter gales bring a seabird bounty to southern shores from subantarctic waters. By spring the courtship and nesting of terrestrial birds is back in full swing and nomads arrive en masse to bursts of spring flowering.

Winter is also definitely the time to be in the Centre, but more because of personal comfort than the accessibility of wildlife. Summer is characterised by searing heat and swarms of bushflies; daytime temperatures in winter are pleasant and flies normally absent. Rainforests can be very wet places at any time of year, but don't let it put you off – such an abundance of water means plentiful wildlife year-round, including a high number of species often inconspicuous in other habitats, such as frogs and insects. As rainforested regions become wetter with the arrival of the wet season, wildlife-watching becomes even better with the gearing up of breeding activity.

HOW TO LOOK

Looking at the right time and place

Animals are often not where you want them to be, but the better informed you are of their behaviour, the more likely you are to find what you want to see. There are a multitude of things that can affect your chances of success, and every species is different, but here are just a few hints and examples to consider.

Time of Day A crucial factor in successful wildlife-watching. Learn what time of day your quarry is most active, what it does at other times and how these might vary according to season – and plan your days to make the most of these factors. Birds are most active in the early morning, whereas butterflies and reptiles become more active as things warm up. Activity dies off during the middle of the day for most diurnal species, especially if it's hot; it picks up again in the late afternoon, peaking near sundown as they bed down.

As the diurnal species retire, the nocturnal animals start to stir (some normally nocturnal animals may also be active on overcast days). In the same way that many diurnal animals are most active early and late in the day, many night creatures are crepuscular, being most active at twilight and just before dawn. When seeking nocturnal wildlife, it is worth considering the phases of the moon – a full moon makes you more visible and animals shyer; this applies equally to nocturnal mammals and nesting sea turtles.

Food Sources Food availability can change with each season, and knowing your quarry's food preferences can help. For example, trees in flower attract birds, butterflies and bats; emerging termites are snapped up by lizards, small mammals and birds.

Getting closer

When approaching animals, the idea is not to present a threat. Move slowly and smoothly, with no jerky movements. Be as quiet as possible – avoid cracking dry twigs underfoot – and look for signs of alertness and tension in your quarry, which will indicate that you need to back off or risk it bolting. Keeping low to the ground helps, especially if there is bush cover – lower than the height of the animal in question is probably a good guide. A good technique is to approach in stages, allowing time for the animal to adjust to your closer presence. Even though you might think it is unaware of you, it is usually just tolerating your intrusion until it perceives you as a threat. Sometimes it helps to make very soft noises, as if you are eating or have some other occupation of your own – this can be reinforced by approaching obliquely rather than directly so that your object may be convinced you have something other than it in mind.

Water For many animals daily access to water is essential and during the dry season much wildlife will be close to a ready source. The daily ebbing and flowing of tides affects marine life, and the roosting and feeding of shorebirds on mudflats.

Know Your Habitat Some knowledge of where an animal lives will be of great help in finding it. Learn what to expect in each major habitat, and be patient when watching – sooner or later something will show. Once you make the link between species and habitat, your 'search pattern' will change, and new things will reveal themselves. The area where habitats merge is usually productive, eg, woodland abutting grassland provides food and shelter for grazing mammals. Check likely shelters, such as tree hollows, cliff overhangs or termite mounds, and dead trees and overhanging branches used as perches. Regeneration after a bushfire can shift the balance of plants and animals in a community. For example, new grass after a fire attracts grazing mammals; early stages of regenerating heath attract honeyeaters; and mature banksias attract pygmy-possums and blossom-bats.

Weather Daily and seasonal temperatures and rainfall patterns also make a difference. For example, lizards like to bask in early sunshine. A storm can bring on a flurry of activity – swifts moving through on the front, swarming termites and, in the aftermath, predators snapping up insects blown about.

Searching for wildlife

Most Australian mammals are nocturnal, although many sought-after species, such as koalas and large kangaroos, can also be seen during the day (at least at dusk or dawn). This means that seeing a good variety of mammals involves some spotlighting; fortunately the technique is simple and the results usually worthwhile. In contrast, most birds are diurnal and are by far the most obvious vertebrate group in Australia. With a high diversity and abundance of species in most habitats birdwatching is comparatively easy (at least until you begin to chase grasswrens, venture out on a seabird trip, or try to identify small, brown waders from 100m away). Whatever your quarry, a few basic principles apply.

Walk slowly and quietly, avoiding sudden movement and loud noises. Use the environment to your advantage: stand behind cover and in shadows. The less noise you make, the

Feeding wildlife

Feeding animals is a big tourist attraction at several places, including Monkey Mia (dolphins) and Currumbin (lorikeets). However, there is great controversy about the moral and ecological sense of doing this, and most parks these days have signs asking visitors not to feed the wildlife. Artificial feeding can foster a dependence on handouts and cause unnatural population growth (if feeding lessens, over winter for example, managers may have to cull starving animals). Macropods can develop a sometimes fatal condition called 'lumpy jaw' that is probably caused by eating refined foods such as bread. The young of lorikeets that became dependent on an artificial diet of sugar, water and bread showed growth abnormalities from inadequate nutrition. And animals can come to expect food from all humans and some, such as emus and kangaroos, have the potential to become aggressive if they feel they're not getting enough. Think about it.

more calls and telltale rustles you'll hear. Many animals move when startled, but often quickly stop and check you out; if you also freeze, they may relax and pay you no further heed. Raise binoculars slowly (or wait until your quarry goes behind cover) and if you need to talk, do so in whispers or low voices.

Look in the canopy for silhouettes against the sky; look at the ground and in the trees; look along watercourses; and use your peripheral vision (especially at night). Mammals are particularly sensitive to noise and smell, so be quiet and don't wear perfume.

Many birds, especially small bush birds, can be attracted by 'pishing' or imitating bird noises with kissing noises. These noises can also work on small mammals such as antechinuses. Some shops also sell Audubon bird callers, wood and pewter devices that make a variety of high-pitched squeaks. Some parks have bird hides – covered wooden shelters with horizontal openings through which wildlife can be observed or photographed; these are particularly good for watching waterbirds or if there is a group of you. Bushwalkers in cool closed forests often see more inquisitive birds by the end of their lunch stop than they would have seen in the entire morning's walk, but dawn is traditionally the birdwatching hour.

Reptiles bask to warm up and are often found on rocky outcrops facing the sun. In some areas, roads and open paths serve the same purpose, so always scan the path ahead on warm days. Many reptiles and amphibians in hot climes are attracted to roads, which hold the heat of the sun long after nightfall; birds such as nightjars and button-quail can also be found this way in some areas. The best way to look for frogs is to visit a swamp; listen to their calls and triangulate – two searchers fan out and point their spotlights in the direction of the call till their beams converge on the frog.

Identification

Identification is a natural urge (a manifestation of the instinct to avoid danger or find food, maybe) and you'll soon start to learn the differences in shape and colouring between species. With practice it becomes second nature. Initially you should focus on relative size (which in the field is actually more useful than measured size), eg, 'larger than a pigeon but smaller than a duck'; learn where to look for markings, eg, facial markings on wallabies, so as they bound out of sight you can make the most of your (sometimes short) viewing time. Bill colour and shape, as well as plumage, are important on birds. Note details of habits, since many animals have a diagnostic stance or trait. Browsing through field guides will help familiarise yourself with the wildlife of an area and develop appropriate 'search images'.

Our Wildlife Gallery chapter is not meant to be the last word on identification, but will help you get your head around many of the common shapes and colours you'll encounter. We've recommended field guides in our Resource Guide that will enable you to identify all the birds and most of the mammals you might see (the identification of many reptiles, frogs and invertebrates is only possible in the hand).

Tracks and signs

On sandy beaches, dirt roads and desert sands, tracks often tell the story of an area's wildlife. Tracks after rain or tides can tell you how recently an animal passed by. Likewise, forest floors are littered with variously shaped, dry pellets ('scats') – animal droppings that can reveal which species are present and, sometimes, what they eat. Learning to read such signs can be tricky, but the more you look the more you'll learn. A great book entitled *Tracks, Scats and Other Traces*, by Barbara Triggs, opens up a whole new way of looking for wildlife. Footprints, burrow shapes, scats and skeletal remnants are all described. Some bird books also describe nests and owl pellets. Guano ('whitewash') on coastal rocks indicating the presence of seabirds, and on cliffs signifying raptors; the species-specific tracks of sea turtles on nesting beaches; areas raked free of leaf litter in forests for a lyrebird's display ground; and tiny letterbox-shaped holes in desert dunes made by scorpions – just some of the wildlife signs to look out for.

Beyond looking

This is the best bit. Once you have found your bird or beast, you can just observe. With patience (and sometimes luck) you can see beyond the shapes and colours into wild lives. The less threatening a human presence, the bolder animals become and the more you see. Listening and watching will be rewarded with observations of feeding, social interactions, courtship and play. Watching reveals the personalities of individuals and their positions in a group. Is it a male, female, juvenile, dominant, challenger? There's a soap opera being played out, but it takes patience to interpret – try following an individual as it interacts with others. Watching massed animals in a breeding colony can be especially revealing, as can listening to calls and linking them to particular animals and their activities.

Many people are satisfied with simply watching; others extend their interest into photography, writing or art. But if you become hooked on the thrill of the chase, as many do, 'ticking', 'twitching' or 'listing' is another extension of wildlife-watching – one that is especially popular with birdwatchers. The aim is to see and 'tick off' as many species as possible. This is a competitive way to share the challenges of wildlife-watching. As with any competitive activity, though, some 'tickers' get seriously hooked.

Equipment

Binoculars and Spotting Scopes Binoculars are the most important investment a wildlife-watcher can make. With even a basic pair a rustle in the leaves can become a brilliant fairy-wren, and a distant kangaroo brought close-to. Costs range from $100 to thousands of dollars, but, like cameras, you get what you pay for. Top-shelf binos by Zeiss, Leica, Bausch & Lomb or Swarovski have superb optics, last for years and offer features such as water- and dust-proofing. More affordable brands, such as Bushnell and midrange to upper models from respected camera manufacturers (eg, Pentax, Nikon and Olympus), will be sufficient for most situations. A good-quality compact model is also worth consid-ering, but don't be tempted by supercheap compacts or by 'zoom' optics, which usually have poor light-gathering ability.

Some brands offer models with eye-cups to be used without removing spectacles. Decent models also have a dial (diopter), which allows you to compensate for the focusing difference between left and right eyes. Good binoculars are hinged, al-lowing adjustment for the distance between your eyes.

All binoculars should have a designated magnification and objective diameter stamped somewhere on them, normally as a combination of numbers, eg, 8x20 or 10x50. The first number refers to the magnification. At 10x an object 100m distant will appear 10m away through the binoculars, 14m at 7x etc. The second number (usually between 20 and 50) refers to the diameter (in millimetres) of the objective lenses, ie, those at the end farthest from your eyes.

Larger objectives increase light-gathering ability and hence image brightness. Higher magnification reduces brightness. Not only is a brighter image clearer, it is also more colour accurate – crucial for identification. Light-gathering ability can be *estimated* (it's not a perfect guide) by dividing the objective diameter by the magnification – the higher the result, the more light enters the binoculars. Thus 10x50s and 8x40s perform similarly, but 7x42s often give a brighter image. Special interior coatings can also in-crease image brightness. Having extra light-gathering ability may not be all that useful during the middle of the day (an eye can only take so much light before it starts closing its iris), but in dim conditions, such as at dusk or in a rainforest, you'll want all you can get – up to a point. As your iris can only open so far, and this decreases with age, opting for greater light-gathering power may be a waste. To check, test out different binoculars in dim light.

Larger objectives also mean a larger field of view. Usually in-dicated in degrees, field of view refers to the width of the area that fits into the image you see. It is also traded-off against magnification, ie, higher magnifications reduce the field of view. The narrower the field of view, the harder it is to locate your target, especially if it is moving.

Consider also comfort. Large objectives are bulkier. The type of internal lenses also makes a difference. Most binoculars have porro prism lenses, which are offset from each other and make for the familiar, 'crooked' barrels. Roof prism lenses are aligned directly behind each other and allow compact, straight barrels; the drawback is their expense. Good compromises of all factors

---

Using binoculars

After you've spotted a bird or other animal with the naked eye and it is stationary, or relatively so, lift the binoculars to your eyes without removing your gaze from your quarry. If you're new to using binos, it can take a while to swiftly connect what you see with the same spot through the little circle of light, particularly if the magnification is powerful. But the quicker and more accurately you are able to do this, the less often you will lose sight of your target. Always have a sample look around to set the adjustments of your binoculars before you start looking for critters, as you don't want to be fiddling while you follow a bird in flight.

are configurations such as 7x35, 7x40 and 8x40. Birders tend to favour 8x40 or 10x50, that extra magnification critical when seabirding or peering into a rainforest canopy. The most popular top-shelf binos tend to be 7x42, or 8x40 roof prism models.

Test before you buy (a useful source for reviews can be found at 🖥 www.lightshedder.com/BVD/). Compare the image quality in both low light inside the shop and brighter light outside. Look for distorted colours and peripheral distortion of the image (ie, shapes bending at the edge of your view).

Spotting scopes are more powerful than binoculars. They are mostly used for watching waterbirds and waders and are most useful in open habitat, although some birders carry them even through rainforest. Most scopes start at 20x or 25x magnification, but the increased magnification means they must be mounted on a tripod or monopod to reduce shaking. Higher magnifications also increase image distortion from heat haze – it's surprising how much there is on even an overcast day in Australia. Again, a quality scope will be expensive; excellent brands include Kowa, Nikon, Leica, Zeiss and Bushnell.

Spotlights A spotlight beam needs to be strong enough to reach the upper branches of tall trees, which often means heavy 'D' size batteries. Spotlights are best held next to the head, which is why headlamps are popular and models with separate battery packs that can be worn on the waist are more comfortable.

Clothing Ideal clothing maximises comfort (and safety) and minimises disturbance to wildlife. 'Earthy' colours, such as khaki, are least intrusive during the day (colour doesn't matter when you're spotlighting). Some people prefer the breathability of cotton, some go for quick-drying polypropylene and other high-tech fabrics. Long pants and long sleeves are useful even in the tropics to protect from biting insects. In rainforests with leeches, wear long pants tucked into long socks. When it comes to footwear, leather is not a good idea in the tropics. A wide-brimmed hat offers sun protection, but can also shade binoculars from rain and helps with camouflage by breaking the outline of your head.

Field Guides There are many field guides, but useful features include compactness, distribution maps and concise text describing the salient features of each species (eg, habitat, calls and behaviour). Usually a field guide has either photographs or illustrations. Photos can be helpful in developing a search image, but illustrations have the advantage of being able to show all diagnostic features and (hopefully) lack the potential colour distortions of photos. See the Resource Guide for recommended titles. Field guides to animals are usually presented in taxonomic order, a system that can seem arbitrary, but actually shows evolutionary relationships between species and is thus generally consistent between guides (it is also a source of interest in its own right – who'd have thought that a greater glider is actually an unusual ringtail possum rather than a member of the glider family).

GETTING IN AND AROUND

Doing it yourself

Visiting parks on your own to look for wildlife is easily achieved in Australia and highly recommended. Planning, a bit of know-how and some luck is all you need to see most high-profile wildlife. Hiring a vehicle to visit reserves has lots of advantages, the biggest of which is that you can stay in the field as long as you like. But depending on your time constraints you must factor in the huge distances that may be involved; and heed warnings about weather and road conditions – vehicles regularly get stranded, sometimes for weeks, by floods in the Outback and elsewhere.

Be aware of wildlife when driving. The roads are a war zone for wildlife. Night-time is most dangerous as mammals are more active, harder to see and often freeze when blinded by headlights. Collisions with kangaroos, cattle and others pose a real danger to vehicles on Outback roads, and driving at night must be done slowly or, better, not at all. Most birds are not as dangerous to you, but emus and cassowaries are more than large enough to be serious hazards (and both suffer a heavy road toll). Flocks of galahs have the habit of taking off from the path of your vehicle, only to swerve back at the last second – driving headlong into a flock could easily leave you with dents, a broken windscreen or worse, and leave a trail of dead and dying birds.

Many parks are well serviced and some have what could be called luxury camping grounds (camping gear can be hired in major towns and cities). Quality of information is also generally good, although this varies according to the popularity of an area. Dedicated birdwatchers have published excellent information on where to find nearly all Australian bird species, but there's a chasm between information on where to find birds and where to find other wildlife. Rangers are usually helpful (although some are seasonal workers who may not have in-depth park knowledge) and some parks run interpretive programs during peak visitor months.

Local naturalist groups are terrific sources of information – see the Resource Guide for contacts – and some hold outings that you may be able to attend. There is also a growing number of opportunities to contribute to conservation or research projects.

Roads kill

Anyone driving on certain rural roads will be struck by the number of dead animals littering the verge and the high proportion of vehicles sporting 'bull bars' (often called 'roo bars'). There is a connection. In grazing country most of the victims are roos. In winter, wombats are caught out while feeding on roadside grass exposed when snow is melted by the heat of the traffic on alpine roads. In Tasmania anything from Tasmanian devils to eastern barred bandicoots can be unlucky. The most frequent victims have a couple of things in common: they are nocturnal; and they are in healthy numbers, so the proportion dying on roads is not critical to the survival of the population. Some researchers have exploited this phenomenon by collecting population and diet data from the random sample offered by roadkills. If you see a recently killed marsupial it is worth checking the pouch for young with hair (those too small to have fur will not usually survive hand rearing) and take it to a local vet or ranger.

Guides and tours

The right guide can help you see more in a day than you would in a week on your own. The wildlife tour part of ecotourism is relatively new in Australia, although it is growing rapidly. In some places (eg, Kakadu, Wet Tropics) you will be spoilt for choice, but in others it's a struggle to find anyone with sufficient knowledge of wildlife to guide you. We've made some recommendations in this book (see the Resource Guide and individual park entries) – many are small operators, but ones that we feel know their stuff. Many of the best operations cater specifically for birdwatchers, but often their knowledge of all flora and fauna is exceptional. Consider also that tours are sometimes the easiest way to get to remote areas.

Beware that 'ecotourism' is a popular industry tag, and often misleadingly applied to tours whose guides are more interested in beer and barbecues than finding wildlife. Any ecotourism accreditation should be treated with caution – there are a number of schemes, for which the requirements of accreditation differ enormously. Far better to personally examine itineraries and chat to operators to see if they have a wildlife knowledge.

Parks and reserves

Australia's extensive network of conservation reserves protects hundreds of sites significant for wildlife, scenery and Aboriginal culture. Entry to most parks is free but there are exceptions, such as Tasmanian national parks and big-name attractions like Uluru–Kata Tjuta. The dry season in the north, winter in the Centre and school holidays everywhere are the busiest times.

Independent travellers can camp in virtually all reserves, although mostly only at designated sites. Facilities range from basic to comparatively luxurious. The most popular reserves also have other forms of accommodation, such as lodges, which are usually well run and may have resident naturalists/guides. Most national parks promote 'minimal impact bushwalking', with park regulations on safety, fires, erosion control and waste disposal.

Many reserves are on traditional Aboriginal land and some protect sacred sites; if travelling off the beaten path it is essential to be aware of entry restrictions to such areas. If in doubt, seek guidance from relevant land councils – penalties for flaunting these regulations can be severe.

Zoos and wildlife parks

Standards for keeping and exhibiting animals are generally high and most collections are worth a visit for a close-up look at native fauna. Australian species are exhibited almost exclusively in several state-of-the-art 'wildlife' parks across the country and there are several zoos with good displays of native animals. Smaller, specialised collections of reptiles, birds, butterflies and the like are scattered along the tourist trail, especially on the tropical Queensland coast. Some of these are worth a look, but others are definitely of the 'see-the-big-croc' variety. Some worthwhile operations are listed in the Parks and Places chapter.

LIVING WITH WILDLIFE

Close encounters

Australia is renowned for venomous, biting and stinging wildlife, but your chances of being struck by lightning are greater than succumbing to a native animal doing what comes naturally. However, it is dangerous to swim anywhere with saltwater crocs and it pays to take extreme care near the water's edge in such areas; there are usually warning signs in popular destinations but not always in remote areas. As salties are the only large carnivores that hunt humans (though it pays to keep an eye on young children where dingoes have become used to people), being eaten is not of concern away from northern wetlands. Shark attack is rare and most surf beaches have life-savers, shark patrols or are netted to reduce the danger of attack. But in the tropics do not swim in the sea between October and May, when tropical sea jellies with potentially lethal stings are active.

Mosquitoes can be a pest, especially in the tropics – cover up at night and use repellents. Although malaria does not occur naturally in Australia there are other illnesses, such as Ross River fever, that are carried by mozzies.

Ticks are common in coastal areas – bites are irritating and best avoided. Wear long trousers when walking through long grass, and inspect for ticks nightly. Ticks can be removed with with a lighted match, or with tweezers by grasping the head and pulling gently. Leeches are painless and harmless but can be a pest in wetter forests. Be vigilant, wear long trousers tucked into long socks, and remove them by rubbing salt on them or burning with a match.

Disturbing wildlife

Many animals must frequently respond to the presence of predators and will class you as just one more. But engaging a wild animal's attention may disrupt its normal routine and thus reduce its available feeding time. So it is worth respecting an animal's needs and being sensitive to the level of disturbance you are creating. Look and enjoy, but don't go overboard and if an animal shows signs of distress, leave it alone. With the wildlife-watching industry comes immense benefits – aesthetic, recreational, conservation and financial – and it is important for all concerned, for the animals especially, to ensure it is carried out responsibly. ■

To eat or not to eat?

A question many face on menus listing croc steak, roo sirloin and emu burgers. Such fare could never be regarded as haute cuisine, but wildlife farming and harvesting is a growing industry in Australia. Many of these 'wild foods' come from farms with strict regulations on stocking from wild populations. Any species harvested from the wild is usually regarded as a pest that needs to be culled, but don't be afraid to ask where the meat is coming from and why, before making up your own mind. Crocodiles were once shot on sight in the Northern Territory, but attitudes changed when it was finally recognised they were becoming rare. They are now common again and recognised as a resource rather than a pest – farming crocodiles actually fosters their protection in the wild.

BIRDWATCHING

AUSTRALIA boasts the world's largest number of endemic bird species – approximately 300 – including several unique families such as lyrebirds and regional specialities such as bowerbirds. Widespread groups such as parrots are particularly diverse and abundant, and for those in search of a challenge there's no better place on earth to look at seabirds – some 80 species have been recorded. If this is your first birding trip overseas you'll find it a gentle introduction to some of the most unusual and colourful bird groups on the planet, usually unfettered by restrictions on movement and personal safety. And experienced birders can take pleasure in the fact that most Australian birds don't go into complicated moult sequences that confound identification.

How it's done

When planning your trip prioritise sites according to the species you most want to see; popular targets include parrots and regional endemics, but it's also worth taking at least one seabird trip and spending time on migratory shorebirds, many of which are seen in North America or western Europe only as vagrants. Bear in mind that sometimes vast distances must be covered to reach prime spots and flying between main centres can save you days of road travel. Try to get hold of *The Complete Guide to Finding Birds in Australia* by Richard and Sarah Thomas; this invaluable little book could save you a lot of time and effort. *Where to Find Birds in Australia* by John Bransbury is also worth seeking out – it gives less specific detail but provides good general overviews and covers a greater range of places than Thomas and Thomas. Hook up to an on-line chat group, such as birding-aus (birding-aus@vicnet.net.au), for updates, information and to get in touch with local birders, many of whom will gladly take you for a day's birding if you cover basic costs such as petrol or return the favour some day. A number of bird tour companies (see the Resource Guide for some suggestions) specialise in reaching out-of-the-way birding destinations; most concentrate on the northern half of the country – shop around, but these are definitely worth considering for difficult locations.

Make sure your optical equipment is dustproof and waterproof, since a typical birding itinerary ranges from rainforest to dusty plains (and we mean dusty!). A spotting scope is a good idea if you plan to do some wader-watching, eg, at Cairns Esplanade; 25x or 30x magnification is fine – any stronger and you'll have problems with heat haze on warm days. A useful range of bird call tapes is available from birders' supply outlets – a series produced by the Bird Observers Club of Australia covers most species in systematic order.

Birdwatchers line up their scopes and binoculars to enjoy the waterbirds of a tropical lagoon.

Masked boobies are prized sightings for which seabirders travel great distances to tropical islands.

Top spots to go

An excellent variety of birds can be seen in any state and a number of regional endemics occurs in each; most also have at least one state endemic. Queensland has the greatest number of species (more than 600), but many Australian birds are wide-ranging and if you concentrate on the difficult-to-see birds you're pretty well guaranteed to see the widespread stuff sooner or later along the way.

For a good swipe at the endemics, try to cover sandstone escarpment and tropical wetlands in the Top End (Kakadu NP); rainforest in the Wet Tropics (Daintree NP or Julatten); sub-tropical rainforest (Lamington NP); temperate heath (Croajingolong NP); wet sclerophyll (Yarra Ranges NP); woodlands (Chiltern Box-Ironbark and Warrumbungle NPs); mallee (Hattah-Kulkyne NP); desert (MacDonnell Ranges, Strzelecki Track); and WA's south-west (Walpole-Nornalup NP and Two Peoples Bay NR). If you have time, Tasmania, Lord Howe Island and islands of the Barrier Reef make sensational side trips.

Hard-core birders should make the trek to Cape York Peninsula for Australo-Papuan endemics such as the palm cockatoo; to south-west Queensland (grasswrens and yellow chats); and to Broome (masses of waders in season and gateway to the Kimberley for black grasswrens). If you have time, also try to get on a pelagic seabird trip (seasickness pills essential!), especially in winter or spring, for arm's-length views of albatrosses. Regular trips are scheduled, weather permitting, from southeast Queensland, southern NSW and Victoria; and less frequently from South Australia and Tasmania.

If you want to chase rarities, many Australian birders are not averse to a spot of twitching. Notable 'accidental' visitors that you definitely won't see in your home patch include penguins that regularly come ashore to moult on southern shores, and cyclone-driven South-East Asian pittas and flycatchers that hit the north-west.

Anyone, beginner or expert, can enjoy the spectacle of little penguins around the southern coast.

Field guides

Read as much as possible before you go (see the Resource Guide) to familiarise yourself with new bird families. The identification of most groups is well documented in three main field guides (commonly referred to as 'Pizzey and Knight', 'Slater', and 'Simpson and Day'), although potentially difficult groups such as waders and seabirds are handled with varying success. All guides have their merits and faults. The first-mentioned is probably the most up to date and detailed, but is somewhat weighty; Slater is compact and genuinely pocket-sized; and the third is patchy in quality, although it is frequently updated. Most serious birders opt for either Pizzey and Knight or Slater over Simpson and Day, although many, in fact, own all three. ■

DIVING AND SNORKELLING

AUSTRALIA consists of one huge island and many lesser-known smaller ones, with good diving just about all the way round a 47,000km coastline. From the warm waters of the tropical north to temperate southern waters you will find dive shops dotted around the coast eager to introduce you to the local special spots. These include coral reefs, caves, wrecks, drop-offs, kelp forests, diving with seals or whale sharks – you name it.

It's easy to sketch or take notes with a waterproof drawing board and crayon.

What to bring

Those who travel light need only carry their swimming costume, 'C' card and logbook – most dive shops hire out gear that is well maintained. Mask, snorkel and fins can all be hired at popular centres, but if you're planning to spend a lot of time underwater take your own mask, snorkel and, if you can fit them in, fins, as these add most to diving comfort. The only other consideration is your suit. A 3mm steamer is usually enough in warm tropical waters, but elsewhere you'll need at least a 5mm suit (which is a bit bulky to travel with).

The Australian sun is stronger than it seems, especially when you're wet. It is important to cover up even when in the water for only a short time. Snorkellers should wear at least a T-shirt to cover their back and apply sun block to exposed areas of skin.

What's on offer

Most dive shops offer diving and snorkelling tuition. Many places offer 'introductory dives' or 'dive experiences' – in which people not yet qualified can do an open-water dive to see if they want to complete a full course. Australia is a great place to learn to dive, with high safety standards and great locations to choose from. You will need to have a diving medical examination and a reasonable level of fitness (although even fit women shouldn't dive if pregnant). Dives vary considerably according to the degree of experience required, so your logbook is important. Accidents usually result from divers declining in fitness or attempting dives beyond their experience.

Diving in temperate waters has its own rewards, many of which are not encountered on coral reefs.

Snorkelling

All you need to step beyond the glass-bottomed boat is the ability to swim, and a mask, snorkel and fins. The beauty of a coral reef is that most of the best bits are accessible to snorkellers and offer an astonishing variety of sea life in great visibility at less than 10m depth. Free from cumbersome gear and time/air constraints, breath holders with power fins and some practice can dive deep and stay deep (a technique called free diving). At less than 10m the colours are saturated, unlike the blue tinge that creeps in with greater depth. You don't need to scuba dive to enjoy a reef – by snorkelling you can enjoy one of the great wildlife spectacles of the world. However, after a while you might just be tempted to go that little bit deeper.

Top spots to go

The Great Barrier Reef is a huge drawcard for travellers. Some 600 islands and 2500 reefs stretch 2300km along the Queensland coast. There is a huge variety of spectacular and accessible spots, from drop-offs on the outer reef to shallow waters around sand cays. Western Australia has a smaller tropical reef system, at Ningaloo near Exmouth, where whale sharks, manta rays and dugongs are common; and lots of dive sites in the south-west. Darwin has huge tides and crocodiles, but there is good diving in the harbour on wrecks and artificial reefs, or at a variety of inland (freshwater) locations if spring tides have churned things up at sea. There is also great temperate diving around nearly the whole southern coast. At South Australia's Kangaroo Island you can dive with fur-seals, sea-lions and dolphins; and Mt Gambier has world-famous freshwater sinkholes. Tasmania has spectacular kelp forests and wrecks near Bicheno, where winter visibility can exceed 30m in water temperatures of 12°C. Other southern hotspots include Melbourne's Port Phillip Bay; Wilsons Promontory, south-east of Melbourne; Sydney Harbour and neighbouring inlets; and the temperate/tropical crossover between Coffs Harbour and Byron Bay in northern NSW. Some of Australia's far-flung territories, such as Norfolk and Lord Howe Islands, and Christmas and Cocos (Keeling) Islands also offer excellent diving. Even Antarctica is now opening up to specialist dive trips.

Advice on diving is best sought through dive shops or organisations, and the networks are pretty reliable. Details of dive sites can also be found in Lonely Planet's Pisces series. A couple of useful contacts are Dive Adventures (☎ 1800 222 234; 🖥 www.diveadventures.com), which organises dive tours worldwide; and Aurora Expeditions, which dives Antarctica (☎ 1800 637 688).

Underwater photography opens a whole new world that can be enjoyed in waters warm or cold.

Field guides

There are field guides on everything from sharks to sea slugs, whales to whelks. Some useful starting points include the classic *Fishes of the Great Barrier Reef and Coral Sea* by John Randall, Gerald Allen and Roger Steene, which includes over 1200 species; *The Marine Fishes of Tropical Northern Australia and South-East Asia* by Gerald Allen; *A Coral Reef Handbook: A Guide to the Geology, Flora and Fauna of the Great Barrier Reef* by Patricia Mather and Isobel Bennett; and Graeme Edgar's *Australian Marine Life: The Plants and Animals of Temperate Waters*, describing 1200 of the most common temperate species. ■

SPOTLIGHTING

O F Australia's 300 or so mammal species, few are truly diurnal. Some macropods may be abroad on overcast days, but normally if you do see mammals during daylight they're pretty dozy. Most start to stir at dusk and by far your best chance of seeing them is to venture out at night with a spotlight. In contrast, the vast majority of birds and reptiles are diurnal, but there are some notable exceptions. The small effort required for a nocturnal foray could be repaid with sightings of gliding possums, Tasmanian devils or bandicoots; owls, night-jars and specialised feeders such as night-herons and letter-winged kites; and nocturnal geckoes, snakes and frogs. It doesn't take much equipment or know-how to experience the bush at night and, unlike in many other major wildlife destinations around the world, it is quite safe to do so.

Macropods large and small can easily be seen frozen in vehicle headlights along Outback roads.

How it's done

Research, such as knowing what species to expect and where they might occur, is vital to success. For instance, some possums (such as brushtails and ringtails) are very common in most eucalypt forests and even urban areas; koalas are more restricted in distribution but are still locally common; and some species are restricted to tropical rainforest.

The best equipment is a 30W spotlight connected to a 12V gel-cell battery that can be carried in a pouch on your belt or in a backpack. This is a very efficient combination that will provide plenty of light for up to two hours' viewing. This equipment can be purchased from battery outlets or army disposal and car accessory stores. A powerful torch, such as a Maglite, or a portable cycling headlamp, can also be effective. A pair of binoculars, preferably waterproof, is also recommended to look at animals once they've been located.

Any flashlight is usually sufficient to watch the antics of common brushtail possums in city parks.

There is more to spotlighting than just moving a light around in a forest. Hold the spotlight at eye-level and by looking along the beam you will see blazing reflections – eyeshine – from the reflective layer at the back of nocturnal mammals' eyes (a feature which enhances their light-gathering ability). This is the best way to find nocturnal mammals, but it also works well for birds, reptiles, and many insects and spiders. Eyeshine can be detected reflecting from high above the ground (eg, from possums, gliders and birds) to ground level (eg, kangaroos, wallabies, bandicoots and wombats). Listen for movement among foliage and on the ground, then shine the light in its general direction until you find the source of the sound.

It is important to an animal's wellbeing that you do not shine a bright spotlight in its eyes for too long. Observe it for a couple of minutes and then move on. An animal's feeding routine can be disrupted and repeated disturbance can stress individual animals. Many researchers conducting behavioural studies use a red filter on their spotlight because it possibly reduces any negative effects on the animal. This is not essential if you intend to observe an individual animal only briefly, but it can't hurt to simply put a piece of red cellophane over the spotlight or torch and hold it in place with a rubber band. Research indicates that a semiopaque filter that reduces light intensity by 25% stresses mammals even less than a red filter, and that sightings may increase because fewer animals turn away from the light.

Top spots to go

There are few habitats where an hour's spotlighting will not reward you with a glimpse of some animal or other.

The east coast, from the rainforests of north Queensland to the eucalypt forests of Victoria and Tasmania, supports the highest diversity and abundance of nocturnal mammals – including kangaroos, wallabies, bandicoots, possums and gliders. The highest diversity of possums is in the upland rainforests of the Wet Tropics, where several species of ringtail, including green, lemuroid, Herbert River and Daintree River possums, are reasonably common; rarer species, such as tree-kangaroos and striped possums are occasionally seen; and on the ground pademelons and bandicoots feed along rainforest edges. Mt Hypipamee NP and Julatten offer some of the country's best spotlighting.

Gliders are more abundant in eucalypt forests on the eastern side of the coastal ranges. If habitat contains tall eucalyptus trees that are reasonably spaced apart – not too close, not to far – then gliders are likely to be present. Yarra Ranges and Chiltern Box-Ironbark NPs hold good glider habitat.

In southern Australia arboreal mammals such as gliders, possums and koalas can be relatively common in tall, old-growth forest. Wombats, eastern grey kangaroos and swamp wallabies are also easily visible. Unfortunately, smaller ground-dwelling mammals such as antechinuses, quolls and native rodents are more elusive and rarely seen by spotlighting.

Tasmania offers some of the best spotlighting, largely because – in the absence of foxes – ground-dwelling mammals such as quolls, Tasmanian devils and bandicoots are still common.

Because of its relatively pristine condition, Kakadu NP is a great place for spotlighting. Apart from agile wallabies and bandicoots around camping grounds, northern quolls and brush-tailed phascogales are common, and rock ringtails may be seen in the stone country.

Spotlighting rainforest possums is one of the highlights of a visit to the Wet Tropics.

Field guides

The focus of most spotlighting in Australia is possums and gliders. *A Key and Field Guide to the Australian Possums, Gliders and Koala* by Andrew Smith and John Winter has colour photos and specific ID details, and is designed for use in the field. For night-birds, you can't go past David Hollands' stunning *Birds of the Night: Owls, Frogmouths and Nightjars of Australia*. It's more of a coffee-table book, but in addition to detailed ID and natural history notes, there are superb photos and anecdotal insights into the lives of the birds that the author came to know so well in his quest to photograph all Australian species. Other general mammal and bird guides are listed in the Resource Guide. ■

WHALE-WATCHING

Humpbacks' flukes are distinctively marked and unique for each whale.

Shark Bay, WA, presents opportunities to get very close to bottlenose dolphins.

FEW wildlife experiences are as overwhelming as an encounter with whales and few locations anywhere are as rich in whale-watching opportunities as Australia. Giant baleen whales may seem impossible to find – they're deep-ocean creatures which spend much of their lives far from land. But Australia's east and west coasts are whale highways – major migratory routes for hundreds of giants moving between subantarctic feeding grounds and temperate or tropical breeding sites. All seven rorquals (whales with throat-grooves, including the humpback, minke, sei, Bryde's, fin, pygmy blue and blue – the largest animals ever to exist) are sometimes glimpsed off southern coasts. As for dolphins, they're everywhere; large areas of coastal waters are still relatively undisturbed, so resident populations of several species still use them as nurseries and feeding grounds, though it is bottlenose dolphins that are most commonly seen. Australia is a sanctuary for cetaceans (whales and dolphins), so these animals often show a fearless, friendly interest in vessels and passengers.

How it's done

Migrating whales may be watched seasonally from shore – there are many well-known lookouts which give great views and good chances of sightings. Shore-based dolphin sightings are more opportunistic – again, choose high vantage points. Flights are sometimes available and a few commercial swim-with-dolphin operations exist, but an excellent balance between getting close to cetaceans and minimising the risk of disturbing them is to watch from vessels. Commercial tours are very popular: operators know top places to find cetaceans and have sighting success rates near 100% during peak season. Some tour vessels have hydrophones for listening to whales underwater and tour guides to answer questions – ranging from crew members to qualified, experienced naturalists. Vessels which head out specifically for seabird-watching often also encounter cetaceans.

Strict regulations protect cetaceans from harassment and vessels must operate responsibly around pods. Check with state wildlife departments for details, and do whales a favour by reporting vessels that chase animals (even slowly), divide groups or otherwise disturb them. Whichever way you whale-watch, choose calm seas – animals are difficult to see in choppy water. Brush up on the ID features of cetaceans, eg, size, colour, fin shape and characteristic behaviours. Whales are often located by their 'blows' – white spouts of exhaled breath – particularly on cool, still days. If you're spending some time in Australia, working with a volunteer stranded-whale-rescue organisation can be rewarding – contact wildlife departments for information.

What to take

Binoculars (up to 10x) are invaluable; on commercial tours, check whether any are available to borrow. For best photographic results use an 80–200mm zoom lens (or larger if it's a calm day), plus a polarising filter. On vessels, safety equipment including buoyancy vests should be provided. Don't forget your own comfort – take water- and windproof clothing (even on warm days), nonslip shoes, water, something for seasickness if necessary, and sun-cream, a broad-brimmed hat and sunglasses – go for polaroids for good below-surface vision.

Top spots to go

Whale-watching is most popular during southern migrations (September to November). For information about commercial tours and places to see whales and dolphins, contact tourist information bureaus, state wildlife departments and see this book's Parks and Places chapter and Resource Guide.

Queensland's Hervey Bay, near Fraser Island, is labelled 'the world's whale-watching capital' – humpbacks with calves rest here on their way south and whale-watching vessels do a roaring trade. Tangalooma Resort on Moreton Island has shore-based dolphin feeding. In New South Wales, Cape Byron and Eden are top humpback and southern right whale locations, with tours and excellent lookouts; and Jervis Bay is a hotspot for dolphins. In Victoria, southern rights winter close to shore at Warrnambool and there are several dolphin cruises on Melbourne's Port Phillip Bay.

Kangaroo Island, Eyre Peninsula and the Great Australian Bight, all in South Australia, are brilliant places to see southern right whales with calves hanging out beyond surf breaks from May to October; humpbacks and dolphins are often seen as well. Tasmania's Storm Bay also offers a chance for southern rights.

In Western Australia humpback cruises operate in the Kimberley during winter (watch also for the rarely seen Irrawaddy dolphin). When whales are migrating south, try Exmouth and Ningaloo, Perth and southern towns including Albany (also good for sperm whales). Southern right whales are commonly sighted from southern cliffs such as Cape Leeuwin, and Bremer Bay near Fitzgerald River NP; tours run from Esperance. Bottle-nose dolphins with calves visit beaches at Shark Bay's Monkey Mia.

Flukes of southern right whales are shaped and marked differently to those of humpbacks.

Near Darwin, commonly seen dolphins include bottlenose, spotted, common and spinner. Off all but the northern coasts, whale-watching vessels also provide chances to glimpse killer whales, smaller offshore dolphins, and, during cooler months, the more elusive rorquals – including blue whales. Bottlenose dolphins are likely anytime, anywhere and Indo-Pacific humpbacked dolphins are common around the northern coastline.

Field guides

There are several field guides, but *The Sierra Club Handbook of Whales and Dolphins* by Stephen Leatherwood, Randall Reeves and Larry Foster is definitive and all you need. It's comprehensive, accurate, easy to read and use; covers all known cetaceans; and summarises natural history, including distribution and behaviours. As an ID guide it describes distinctive features for recognising each species and provides dozens of full-colour, technically realistic paintings and 130 photos (black-and-white, but still effective). Plus it's a handy, large-pocket size. ■

PHOTOGRAPHY

WILDLIFE photography is a highly specialised field but the quality of today's equipment – even modestly priced, nonprofessional gear – means that excellent results are possible for anyone. In many destinations, wild animals are so used to visitors that exceptional chances for photography often arise.

What to take

If you're buying your first camera the selection is mind boggling. Canon or Nikon are the choice of most professional wildlife photographers, largely because they offer formidable lens quality, but all established brands are good. Cameras essentially all do the same thing, though with varying degrees of complexity and technological assistance. Most modern cameras have a full range of automatic functions, but you should select a model that also allows full manual operation. Once you've mastered the basic techniques, you'll probably find it limiting if you're unable to begin experimenting with your photography.

Capturing the beauty of birds in flight presents a challenge under any circumstances.

More important than camera bodies are the lenses you attach to them – for wildlife, think long. A 300mm lens is a good starting point, though bird portraits require something longer. Lenses of 400mm to 600mm focal length are probably out of the price range of most, though 'slower' lenses (lenses with a relatively small maximum aperture), such as a 400mm f5.6, are reasonably priced and very useful when a 300mm doesn't quite reach. Dedicated (ie, 'brand name') lenses have superb optical quality and are more expensive than generic brands (eg, Tamron), but unless you're a pro you'll probably notice only a slight difference.

Zooms are generally not as sharp as fixed focal length lenses (ie, lenses which do not zoom), but the difference is only important if you're thinking about publishing your pictures. Many brands offer zooms around the 100–300mm range which, when paired with a short zoom like a 35–70mm, covers most situations for recreational photographers. The recently released 'superzooms' provide a comprehensive range of focal lengths in one lens. Canon's 35–350mm and 100–400mm, and Sigma's 170–500mm are worth investigating. None is cheap, but they yield publication-quality results in one versatile package.

Australia's wealth of frog species offers plenty of opportunity for macro photography.

Hundreds of accessories can be used to enhance shots, but one that's vital is the tripod. Many shots are spoiled by 'camera shake', particularly when using longer lenses. Tripods can be cumbersome to include in your luggage, but sturdy, compact models such as Manfrotto's 190 ('Bogen' brand in the USA) fit into a sausage bag. An excellent alternative for vehicle-based photography is a beanbag. A small cloth bag with a zip opening takes up almost no room and can be filled with dried rice when you arrive at your destination. Simply lay the beanbag on the roof or bonnet (hood) of your vehicle and rest the camera lens on it.

In the field

Before you go anywhere, know how your camera works. Visit the local zoo or park and shoot a few rolls to familiarise yourself with its controls and functions. Many good wildlife moments happen unexpectedly and pass in seconds; you'll miss them if you're still fiddling with dials and settings. For the same reason, when in reserves, leave your camera turned on (and pack plenty of batteries).

Most cameras have shutter- and aperture-priority functions. In shutter-priority mode, you set the shutter speed and the camera selects the appropriate aperture for a correct exposure; the reverse applies for aperture priority. These two functions are probably the most valuable for wildlife photographers – but you need to know when to use them. Shutter priority is excellent for shooting action. If you want to freeze motion, select the highest shutter speed permitted with the available light and the camera takes care of the aperture setting. On the other hand, if you're trying to emphasise depth of field in your shot, opt for aperture priority. Large apertures (low 'f-stops') reduce the depth of field – a useful trick for enhancing a portrait shot by throwing the background out of focus. However, if you're shooting a scene where you want everything in focus, such as a lone red kangaroo against never-ending spinifex, select a small aperture (high f-stops).

Composition is a major challenge with wildlife as you can't move your subject around; try different vantage points and experiment with a variety of focal lengths. If you're too far away to take a good portrait, try to show the animal in its habitat. A 400mm lens might give you a close up of a seabird's face while a 28mm will show the entire colony receding into the background – all from the same position. Try to tell a story about the animal or illustrate some behaviour. A wombat foraging among grey kangaroos might be too shy for a decent close-up, but could make a lovely subject if you include the roos and surroundings.

Watch for portrait opportunities where macropods have become semitame in some national parks.

Unless you're packing a very powerful flash, wildlife photography relies on the vagaries of natural light and the best shots are invariably those taken in the 'golden hour' – just after dawn and just before dusk. Where possible, get into position early, whether it's at a bird hide, waterhole or scenic lookout you noted the day before. Don't always assume front-on light is the best. Side lighting can give more depth to a subject; back lighting, particularly when the sun is near the horizon, can be very atmospheric.

Above all else, when photographing wildlife, be patient. You never know what will appear at the waterhole next or when a snoozing predator will suddenly spot a chance for a kill. You cannot always anticipate when an opportunity will arise, but if you're willing to wait you'll almost certainly see something worth shooting. ■

HABITATS

*Australian environments
and their wildlife*

THE OUTBACK

Perhaps no plant characterises the Outback so much as the various forms of spinifex grass.

IT is surprising how much life and variety there is in the wide, red spaces of the Outback. This is not only the popularly imagined desert of bare sand dunes, but a land of spinifex hummocks, flowering shrubs, saltbush, mallee and mulga woodlands (below: Francis Peron NP). In many places the vegetation is dense enough to give a false impression of fertility, but in fact these are exceptionally nutrient-poor soils. Nonetheless, after rain the earth is covered by a temporary carpet of extravagant wildflowers – a spectacle proportional to the length of the preceding drought – and gorges through low mountain ranges shelter figs, palms and cycads, relict from the times when rainforest covered the interior. Temporary watercourses are lined with river red gums and coolabahs, while eucalypts, casuarinas and the several acacia species known as mulga may dot the plains, especially between high dunes.

Red kangaroos and wallaroos, can be relatively easy to see in the open landscape, and mobs may congregate around favourable sites such as waterholes and ranges. This is the natural home of the budgerigar, darting about in bright-green flocks looking for seeds. And the Outback has the greatest diversity of reptiles in the world – in even the driest parts there are numerous goannas, dragons, geckoes and skinks.

The toughest of the tough

The Outback is the driest part of the driest continent on earth (barring Antarctica). The arid and semiarid inland, which covers 70% of Australia, receives an average of only 250mm rainfall a year (more rain falls in the north, but it is offset by higher evaporation). 'Drought' (in truth, the norm) may last for years. While 'true' deserts, such as the Sahara, receive less rain than this, it falls more reliably. Succulent plants, such as cacti, do not grow naturally in Australia, as even these desert specialists require regular rain. When rain does fall it is unpredictable and can occur in

Opposite page: Seepage and runoff in rocky gorges promotes the growth of taller vegetation, such as these snappy gums in Karijini NP. Ancient plant communities have survived in sheltered sites throughout the inland.

Opposite inset: The widespread yellow-faced whip snake hunts diurnal lizards such as skinks. Dozens of species of reptile shelter under spinifex clumps.

massive dumps that inundate thousands of square kilometres. As the floods drain off or soak into the earth, wildlife goes into overdrive, taking advantage of the few weeks of plenty to reproduce before moving on or adopting behaviour that will help their survival until the next rains (which may be years away). For example, the thorny devil soaks up moisture like blotting paper and burrowing frogs hold water while buried in underground chambers.

About half of the arid-zone birds, including the emu, are nomadic and simply follow the rains to areas which become temporarily flushed with growth. Others live in areas, such as the ranges, with more stable food supplies. Many can do without water – birds of prey, for example, extract all their requirements from their juicy victims – but species that eat dry seeds, such as finches, must find a reliable source of water.

Goannas and other reptiles might be seen sunning themselves during the day, but most animals are nocturnal or active at dawn or dusk. Early morning sunlight casting shadows in tracks shows just how many small animals live in the arid zone; for example, a surprising number of tracks in the dunes around the Uluru camping ground betray the nocturnal activity of spinifex hopping-mice and snakes.

Small marsupial carnivores can live on little; some, such as the fat-tailed dunnart, store fat for lean times. Large mammals, such as the red kangaroo, can move great distances in search of food and reproduce quickly to take advantage of temporary good conditions. Others have a specialised diet: the euro, for example, uses bacteria in its gut and nitrogen recycled from its urea to digest spinifex leaves. There were more medium-sized mammals before European settlement, but many have since become extinct or extremely rare, unable to cope with environmental changes: the change in fire regime after Aborigines were moved off their land; destruction of vegetation by stock and rabbits; and predation by foxes and cats.

After rains life returns to even the most desolate desert landscapes.

Patches of richness

In a poor land small changes have a big effect. Variations in soil, moisture, topography or frequency of fire make the Outback richly patterned and able to support much more life than would be expected by averaging conditions over the whole landscape.

Reptiles and termites rule, OK?

In arid Australia there can be up to 42 different lizard species living together. Reptiles, especially lizards, dominate the arid interior because being ectothermic ('cold-blooded' – using the sun's heat for warmth rather than their own metabolism) they can survive on little food and can virtually 'switch off' during food shortages. However, it is termites that keep the ball rolling because they eat the tough cellulose of hardy desert plants, such as mulga and spinifex. They then become food for lizards, burrowing snakes and insectivorous mammals. The humidity inside the colony's mound allows termites to escape the dryness outside. Termites are so successful in the desert that their combined weight underground equals that of all the kangaroos and cattle on the surface.

Rainfall in the arid zone is seldom predictable, but when it occurs it can trigger a spectacular blooming of wildflowers – demonstrated particularly well in Kalbarri NP.

Even small depressions collect more runoff after rain, encouraging pockets of richness for plants and foraging animals. Animals are often found in mulga groves, along watercourses and in mountain ranges. At waterholes there can be great numbers of colourful finches, parrots, pigeons and honeyeaters; and dingoes, emus and kangaroos arrive cautiously to drink at dawn or dusk. ■

West MacDonnell NP Palms and cycads in gorges, waterhole oases alive with rock-wallabies, reptiles and arid-zone birds. **Uluru–Kata Tjuta NP** Spinifex-covered plains and dunes (and some big rocks) with an enormous diversity of reptiles. **Flinders Range NP** Yellow-footed rock-wallabies, red and western grey kangaroos, euros, desert parrots, emus and ancient fossils.

WETLANDS AND WATERWAYS

A staggering array of waterbirds gathers at shrinking wetlands in Kakadu NP during the dry.

ANY body of water on this dry continent can attract great numbers of wildlife and provide a vital refuge from the seemingly incessant drought. Wetlands and waterways vary enormously: some are permanent, others are ephemeral; and they cover the gamut from clear mountain streams, to sluggish inland rivers, to fresh and saline lakes, and to a great variety of swamps, marshes and bogs.

Generally, the availability of water allows denser, taller and greener vegetation to grow than is possible in the drier surroundings, and the water and vegetation attract and support migrant and local wildlife. Elegant river red gums (below: Murray River, near Mildura) line riverbanks across most of the continent; wet heathlands are often coloured with a rich variety of wildflowers; waterholes may be carpeted with flowering waterlilies; and reedbeds choking wetland margins provide shelter for nesting birds.

Mornings and evenings at a waterhole can be bedlam: screeching cockatoos and flocks of finches arrive for their daily drink, while a platypus may quietly dive to forage on the bottom then return to the surface to eat. Various species of frog can be distinguished by their calls, some resembling banjos, others bleating lambs. The overall impression is of thriving life.

Nomadic waterbirds

Unlike in the northern hemisphere, where waterfowl tend to migrate with the seasons, Australian waterbirds such as ducks, cormorants and black swans can be seen at any time of year. In coastal regions higher rainfall feeds many permanent rivers, lakes and wetlands which support resident populations of waterfowl and other animals.

In general, however, low rainfall and high evaporation mean that there are comparatively few permanent lakes, and many rivers flow only seasonally or intermittently after rain. Particularly in the Outback, wetlands may be dry for years, then fill after heavy rain further up the catchment. Most inland rivers are little more than chains of waterholes and many are completely

Opposite page: Myriad rivers and creeks draining into the Gulf of Carpentaria make an unusual spectacle from the air. Low tide exposes vast mudflats which attract wading birds that feed on abundant crustaceans and small fish.

Opposite inset: The most inhospitable – and unreliable – of all waterways are saline depressions like Lake Eyre, which fill sporadically after major rains inland. But in flood even Lake Eyre attracts thousands of waterbirds to breed.

dry most of the time. Yet, in flood these shallow, broad riverbeds overflow to inundate vast areas of land that may remain underwater for weeks. Such unpredictability would not suit regular migration, so waterfowl tend to be nomadic and gather wherever water has replenished their food supply. As a result, enormous numbers of birds feed and breed during the temporary boom. Lake Eyre, Australia's largest lake, is a spectacular example. It is usually dry, but on the few occasions each century that it fills, hundreds of thousands of waterbirds gather (pelicans and other birds fly hundreds of kilometres from the coast) to feast on a glut of brine shrimp and fish.

The productivity of temporary wetlands, billabongs (floodplain waterholes) and lakes can be greater than that of permanent ones. Nutrients accumulate while the water body is dry and, once rain falls, suddenly become available to animals and plants that are adapted to grow rapidly during the brief wet period.

From crustaceans to crocodiles

An array of bizarre-looking insect larvae, crustaceans and other invertebrates that live in waterways can be caught with a net and inspected in a jar of water. Freshwater crayfish (the well-known 'yabbies') are common, with the world's largest, the Tasmanian giant crayfish, growing to over 6kg. Regarded as good eating by people and many other predators, yabbies can survive for years in dried-out lakes by sealing themselves in deep burrows with water-filled chambers. Other animals, from freshwater turtles to water-holding frogs, employ similar techniques should circumstances dictate. In good times, aquatic invertebrates become food for water-rats and platypuses which live in burrows on the banks; turtles are quite common, although only their nostrils may be visible above the water; colourful kingfishers hunt from trees, diving after small fish and frogs; and water dragons are often seen sunning themselves on a rock or leaping into the water for safety.

About 190 species of freshwater fish live in Australia. Most are small, although the Murray cod can weigh 90kg. The Queensland lungfish, similar to species that existed more than 350 million years ago, has gills like other fish, but can survive in the muddy, oxygen-poor waters of some rivers by gulping air and breathing through a primitive 'lung'. Unfortunately, introduced carp and trout are the most common and obvious fish in many waterways.

Thousands of alpine tarns dot the high plains of Tasmania and the Australian Alps. Crustaceans, fish and frogs survive in these cold waters – the bleating of the Tasmanian froglet is a common sound from August to December in the Tasmanian high country. (Mt Oakleigh in Cradle Mountain–Lake St Clair NP.)

Algal blooms

In natural Australian rivers, occasional floods replenish the water, flush out accumulated nutrients and salt, and maintain the health of the river. However, in many rivers this cycle has been altered because floods are now controlled by dams, and their flow has been reduced by irrigation and other uses. Combined with an additional load of nutrients from sewage and fertiliser runoff from farms, these changes sometimes lead to massive blooms of blue-green algae. A soup of algae forms which makes water poisonous for humans and livestock to drink, and has devastating effects on aquatic animals.

Wetlands of all sorts, from alpine bogs to paperbark and sedge swamps, are a favourite of frogs. Some species can cope with long droughts by holding water and burrowing, while in permanently moist environments, such as rainforests, other species climb trees. Wherever they are, frogs must have water. Wetlands where water, vegetation and abundant insects are readily available are heaven for frogs. Their abundance in turn attracts numerous predators: herons and egrets, of which colonies of hundreds of birds may nest in paperbarks; and snakes, such as the attractive red-bellied black snake and keel-back. And in the northern wetlands and waterways are two of the country's best known residents: freshwater crocodiles and, at the top of the food chain, saltwater crocs. ■

Perched lakes form over a bed of dead vegetation that lines sand depressions and stops water draining away, so that it 'perches' above the water table. Fraser Island's 40 perched lakes include the highest in the world, and sit 130m above sea level on a bed of pure sand. Typical aquatic life includes freshwater fish and turtles.

Myall Lakes NP Paperbark-ringed lakes and wetlands full of fish, frogs, and birds such as ducks, cormorants and pelicans. **Hattah-Kulkyne NP** Red gums in semiarid zone surround permanent billabongs, attracting many waterbirds year-round. **Carnarvon NP** Cool gorges cut by clear creeks where aquatic invertebrates are food for platypuses, turtles and kingfishers.

THE TOP END

Dᴿᴼᵁᴳᴴᵀ, flood, fire and lightning – in the Top End these all happen every year and with great power. Apply them to the numerous, closely adjacent habitats of this vast area and the result is a mind-boggling abundance and variety of wildlife adapted to a most demanding environment. Kakadu NP, for instance, has some 300 bird species, 120 reptile species, 60 mammal species and more than 1000 plant species so far catalogued. Even in Darwin all sorts of wildlife can turn up, from green tree frogs in the loo to crocs in the harbour, while during the dry season the number of birds at Top End waterholes has to be seen to be believed.

Floodplain to escarpment

Behind the mangroves fringing the shore are floodplains whose inhabitants change with the seasons. During the Dry, the gaping cracks in the dried mud of the plains are full of creatures such as dusky rats, olive pythons and tiny, carnivorous planigales. When the rains come these animals are forced into the open, where many are taken by predators, and to higher ground – even seeking the tree tops as the floodwaters rise. Turtles, crocs and huge (up to 60kg) barramundi move out of permanent waters to occupy the filling billabongs, which also support hordes of birds, frogs and snakes.

Fire-resistant eucalypts such as Darwin woollybutts dominate vast swathes of the Top End.

More species are found in the eucalypt-dominated savannah woodlands than in other habitats. Skinks and birds are particularly noticeable, antilopine wallaroos graze on the abundant grass, and frilled lizards may be seen during the Wet. Pandanus trees (below: overlooking the Alligator River, Kakadu NP) and termite mounds dot the landscape, and provide food and shelter for many animals.

Massive sandstone escarpments and outcrops shelter a different group of species again, including several unique mammals and birds. Water is retained in cool, shady clefts year-round and some areas escape dry season fires. Monsoon rainforests along the creeks harbour agile wallabies, fruit-eating pigeons and mound-building scrubfowl.

Opposite page: Torrential rains during the wet season cause rivers and billabongs to burst their banks, inundating the surrounding plains and forcing wildlife to flee to higher ground.

Opposite inset: In contrast, major rivers such as the South Alligator steer a predictable course through the floodplains during the Dry.

Monsoon

Life in the Top End is dominated by a profoundly seasonal climate. Almost all of the annual rain (about 1500mm) falls during the summer wet season, and there is near-drought the rest of the year. Aborigines recognise six seasons, including a 'knock-em-down' season of strong winds. Other Australians generally recognise only the Wet (December to April), the Dry (May to September), and the Build-up (October to December), when humidity builds and thunderstorms gather.

The rainfall is quite reliable, unlike in the Outback, and the lives of animals and plants are tuned to the wet-dry cycle. The Wet, with all its lush tropical growth, is the season for eating as much as possible, dispersing and, for some animals, breeding. Thousands of frogs can be seen on the roads at night, and snakes and northern quolls come out to feast on them.

During the early dry season, a profusion of wildflowers provides food for insects, honeyeaters and insectivorous animals. Many birds breed at this time. Fruits and seeds ripen as the season progresses, but by the late Dry things get difficult for animals as food supplies decline, water dries up and fires burn hiding places. Many trees lose most of their leaves during the Dry to conserve moisture and the landscape looks arid, except for greener patches around water and in rocky gullies.

This is an excellent time to see wildlife, as the ever-shrinking waterholes attract thousands of waterbirds: black-necked storks (jabirus) and brolgas are the largest, and magpie geese are among the most numerous. Predators, such as crocodiles and olive pythons, lurk in wait for animals which come to drink.

As the waterholes dry up some animals move in search of water; turtles and frogs burrow into the mud; some are eaten by predators; and others simply die. But eventually the rains come again and the cycle starts anew.

By the end of the Dry, only cracked mud sheltering small animals shows where sheets of water have lain for months.

Fire every year

Fire is the other certainty in the Top End, and most vegetation and animals are adapted to avoid or exploit it. Most of the land burns at least every three years, much of it every year, either when lightning sets wildfires or when fires are deliberately lit by land managers. Raptors such as black kites fly from up to 20km away to feast on small animals fleeing the flames, and wallabies and stock graze on the new growth that springs up in the wake of a blaze.

Crocodiles

Freshwater and saltwater crocodiles are common in the Top End. Freshies eat fish, live in freshwater, and are not dangerous unless provoked. Salties occur in fresh, brackish and salty water, grow very large (to 7m) and consider humans a natural part of their range of prey. Formerly endangered because of overhunting, both species are now protected and their numbers are increasing. While both can be seen side by side at select sites, such as Litchfield NP, in general salties are more common and readily viewed. Surprisingly speedy when moving on land, they are best seen basking on riverbanks from the safe distance of a sizeable boat.

There is debate about how often fires should be lit. Aboriginal traditional burning is complex, resulting in a mosaic of patches burnt at different frequencies and protecting the fire-sensitive monsoonal rainforests. These practices are increasingly being used in reserves to preserve the variety of vegetation. But before Aborigines arrived, a different fire regime would have reigned – one with which the flora and fauna would have evolved. ■

Fire, either deliberately lit or as a result of lightning strikes, is an important element of grassland ecology in the Top End. Park management strategies now include controlled burns just after the Wet to reduce the amount of flammable vegetation available for dry season fires. A major dry season blaze can be devastating.

Kakadu NP World Heritage Area of floodplains, woodlands and sandstone escarpments overflowing with wildlife, including many endemics. **Litchfield NP** Also floodplains and escarpments, but more compact than Kakadu with termite mounds a feature and freshwater and saltwater crocs side by side. **Nitmiluk NP** Nine gorges carved through the western edge of the Arnhem Land escarpment; freshwater crocs, flying-foxes and agile wallabies.

FORESTS AND WOODLANDS – 'THE BUSH'

Ageing eucalypts develop hollows which are adopted by a wide range of wildlife, such as this galah, for nest sites and shelters.

THIS is the Australia with which most people are familiar – eucalypts (gum trees), koalas, grey kangaroos and a multitude of birds. Brightly coloured parrots and noisy cockatoos are so abundant that it should be no trouble to see several of the 50-odd species just about anywhere. Some of the tallest trees in the world tower up to 100m high in the wet eucalypt forests, while the drier forests and woodlands are dominated by shorter, but subtly and beautifully varied, trees including more eucalypts but also casuarinas (she-oaks) and acacias (wattles). Australian 'flowering' trees (as opposed to the nonflowering conifers) are unusual because they produce colourful flowers with copious nectar.

Numerous species of honeyeater, lorikeet, mammal – such as pygmy-possums – and insect feast on the nectar and pollen of eucalypts and banksias, and in so doing pollinate the plants. Among the grass tussocks below, slow-moving blue-tongued lizards are outpaced by a host of other species, including furtive skinks and large goannas – snakes are generally fast enough to keep out of your way. The well-known call of the laughing kookaburra is often heard at dawn and dusk in eastern states.

As in most Australian habitats, mammals tend to be nocturnal, but at dawn and dusk kangaroos and wallabies may be seen, sometimes in considerable numbers and especially in open, grassy areas. Throughout the bush, and even in suburban backyards, you often hear the birdlike twittering or fearsome growling, respectively, of ringtail and brushtail possums.

Evergreen/grey/blue

The eastern, northern and south-western coasts where eucalypt forests and woodlands (below: ghost gum woodlands in Litchfield NP) grow are reasonably wet by Australian standards, receiving more than about 500mm of rainfall per year. Yet it is not a rich environment and plants can't afford to lose their leaves or waste water. There is no need to be deciduous in the moderate climate; even less so further inland, where woodlands (in

Opposite page: Most of Australia's once-extensive forests and woodlands have been cleared, leaving islands of biodiversity in a sea of agriculture and pastoralism. At best a checkerboard of habitats results (as around Grampians NP, seen from Beroka Lookout, overlooking Halls Gap), but too often vast swathes of rapidly eroding country have been created.

Opposite inset: Looking across the fertile Tweed Valley from the Border Ranges NP.

which trees are more widely spaced than in forests) receive less rain (as little as 250mm per year). The soft, greyish blue colours of the bush come from the waxy coating and oil content of eucalypt leaves – the wax reduces water loss, the oil discourages herbivores. Evaporating eucalyptus oil gives the mountain air its bluish tinge (hence the Blue Mountains west of Sydney) and the bush its distinctive smell. The possums and koalas that eat gum leaves have special adaptations to cope with the toxins and low nutrient content, but possums seize any chance to eat other foods, including domestic rosebuds.

At least half of the forests and woodlands, which once covered a third of the country, have been cleared for agriculture and grazing. This has been a boon for animals that like open country, such as some kangaroos, wallabies, cockatoos and the Australian magpie. However, most of these animals still require at least some natural habitat, and are most abundant where there is a mosaic of bush and farmland. Most animals do not benefit from clearing at all, and large areas of intact bush are still the best places to find a diverse range of wildlife.

Particularly important are 'habitat trees' – those which are old enough (usually at least 100 years old) to develop hollows where branches have broken off. These are used for nests and shelter by possums, parrots, bats and many other animals, and are good sites for birdwatching by day and to stake out at dusk with a spotlight in case a sugar glider or other creature emerges.

Beneath the trees

To avoid water loss, Australian trees tend to have long, thin, drooping leaves which intercept little light. Much light thus reaches the ground and allows the proliferation of a diverse and relatively dense understorey of grasses, shrubs, herbs and sedges (conversely, rainforests are not the matted jungles of popular perception: they receive plenty of water and trees can afford to have broad, horizontal leaves to maximise their exposure to sunlight, creating a gloomy forest floor on which little grows).

The diverse understorey provides food and shelter for wildlife. Echidnas are found wherever there are ants or termites; other

Sherbrooke Forest, just out of Melbourne: higher rainfall promotes the growth of tall, so-called 'wet' forests with an understorey of tree ferns.

So many parrots

Many plants in Australia, such as eucalypts, banksias and she-oaks, store large quantities of seeds in woody fruits until they are opened by the inevitable bushfire. The seeds then drop onto the newly cleared ground, where the nutrient-rich ash and lack of competition makes ideal conditions for them to germinate. This strategy is very common in the fire-prone bush, and this bounty of seed stored in the treetops is one reason that there are so many species of parrot in Australia. Rosellas, for instance, chew away at smaller gum nuts, while the massive beaks of black-cockatoos make short work of hard banksia cones. Discarded gum nuts and pieces of wood on the ground are common signs that parrots have been at work above. The abundance of flowering trees also supports flocks of brightly coloured lorikeets, which have 'feathery' tongues to lap up the nectar and pollen in the blossoms.

The forests of the south-west are dominated by many species of eucalypt and an understorey that often includes a profusion of wildflowers. Several such communities can be seen in Leeuwin-Naturaliste NP.

common small mammals include native rodents and carnivorous marsupials such as antechinuses, although they usually remain hidden in the understorey by day and emerge at night to hunt in the leaf litter. Birds, however, are abundant and easy to see. Various colourful fairy-wrens and finches frequent the undergrowth and vegetation lining streams; uniquely Australian white-winged choughs and apostlebirds forage in open spaces; and myriad pugnacious honeyeaters feed among blossom. ■

Grampians NP Dry eucalypt forest and woodland with grey kangaroos, koalas and echidnas amid spectacular wildflowers. **Dandenong Ranges NP** Huge mountain ash trees scaled by gliders, and understorey ringing with lyrebird and whipbird calls. **The South-West** Tall jarrah forest to diverse heathy woodlands harbouring numbats, honeyeaters and fairy-wrens.

THE HIGH COUNTRY

A short alpine growing season turns on a host of colourful flowers, such as these alpine everlastings.

L ESS than 0.15% of this flattest of continents is alpine – so cold that trees can't grow. But this distinctive habitat supports several unique animals, such as the mountain pygmy-possum and the yellow-and-black corroboree frog. Some of these alpine specialists are difficult to see, and as there is only a short growing season each year the overall species count is not very high. Nevertheless, widespread animals that also live in the alpine and subalpine 'high country', such as wombats and wallabies, may be more often encountered here – when they graze in the sun to soak up some heat – than in other habitats.

The high country is mostly scattered in patches across the Snowy Mountains, the Victorian Alps and Tasmania's highlands. Although some ranges in the Centre were once the size of the Canadian Rockies, limited geological uplift in recent millennia and a long history of erosion mean that Australia's highest mountain, Mt Kosciuszko, rises a mere 2228m above sea level. The alpine terrain is generally smoother than the typical glaciated profile on other continents, because there were only relatively small glaciers – mainly in south-west Tasmania – during the last ice age. The alpine zone (above about 1800m in NSW, but down to about 1000m in Tasmania) has snow cover for one to four months; the subalpine zone for a shorter period. The snow season has generally become shorter in recent years and the already limited alpine habitat is expected to contract further as the greenhouse effect starts to bite.

Snow gums and snowgrass

The high country: stands of colourful, gnarled snow gums, crowned with snowgrass-covered plateaus, heaths and herbfields studded with everlasting daisies (below: the summit of Mt Anne, SouthWest NP, Tasmania). Below are deep, valleys forested with taller eucalypts. Plants and animals are adapted to survive the cold, but also to withstand summer heat, high radiation levels (because of the thinner atmosphere), severe frosts, winds and a varying frequency of fire. The high country has high rainfall, but paradoxically can be a dry environment: in winter the water is

Opposite page: Herbs and grasses disappear under a blanket of snow at Mt Feathertop, Alpine NP, leaving only snow gums exposed above the drifts.

Opposite inset: The hardy snow gum dominates the subalpine zone. In Tasmania, snow gums grow lower on the slopes than in the Australian Alps.

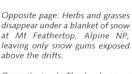

frozen; and in summer the heat desiccates the earth, especially as the shallow soils of some areas hold little water. Vegetation is particularly susceptible to disturbance because plants grow slowly in the cold climate and short growing season.

On the mainland, there is usually a distinct treeline, above which there is an abrupt change from the (subalpine) snow gums and shrubs, to the (alpine) grasses and herbs. The demarcation is usually more blurred in Tasmania. 'Inverted treelines' develop where cold air collects in hollows and causes the trees to end abruptly further down the slope than usual. Conversely, outlying pockets of snow gums can be seen in warmer pockets above the rest of the treeline.

Seasonal animals
Most animals cope with the cold of winter by becoming in-active or by moving down to less hostile altitudes. Reptiles, such as tiger snakes and skinks, hibernate the winter away; they are most likely to be seen during spring when they lie in the open to catch the sun, but are still too sluggish to move quickly from danger. Wombats sleep through most of winter in their burrows, although they can occasionally be seen grazing among winter snow on mild days. Wombats and wallabies have particularly fluffy coats to cope with the cold. Some small mammals, such as the mountain pygmy-possum and the dusky antechinus, are active in runways under the snow during winter. Birds tend to be seasonal visitors: currawongs are the most conspicuous alpine birds, some remaining through the winter; gang-gangs are common alpine cockatoos, although they are not obvious in the trees until their 'creaking-door' call gives them away; and crimson rosellas and flame robins are easily seen. Sphagnum bogs in the Snowy Mountains are the haunt of the spectacular but rarely seen corroboree frog.

Tasmanian cushions
Tasmania's high-country vegetation differs from that on the mainland, with many endemics and many primitive species. Among them are the pandani and the King Billy pine (estimated to live for more than 1000 years). Winters are milder than on the

The common wombat is one of the few marsupials that can live permanently above the snowline, where its burrows can be a hazard to skiers. Wombats are often abroad during sunny weather in winter.

Pygmy-possums and Bogong moths
The only Australian mammal restricted to the high country is the mountain pygmy-possum. It was known only from fossils until one was found alive in a ski hut at Mt Hotham in 1966. It is still rare and its range is contracting as the greenhouse effect reduces its habitat. The mountain pygmy-possum lives among shrubs in boulder fields, moving about during winter under the protection of snow cover, although it can enter torpor ('shut down') when the going gets too tough. One of its favourite foods is the Bogong moth, which was also favoured by Aborigines. This moth migrates from the lowlands in millions during summer, sheltering in, and often filling, cracks between boulders in the high country. Apparently it makes a delicious, high protein food – preferably singed to remove the wings.

high mainland ranges, so there is more rain and much less snow. However, without the protection of deep snow, the plants are subjected to more frost, needle ice and wind, and the soil to more erosion. Tasmania thus tends to have more cushion plants and shrubs, while the mainland has more grasses and herbfields. Cushion plants (there are several kinds) grow in neat, rounded mats that look like green cushions – their shape avoids wind damage and helps them survive extremely low temperatures. ■

The spring thaw reveals the rocky landscape of Kosciuszko NP's highest peaks, where vegetation is stunted and can be buried in snow for months at a time. Even at these heights frogs breed in sphagnum bogs and mountain pygmy-possums inhabit boulder scree. (View of Mt Kosciuszko – the rounded dome in the centre background – from Rams Head Range).

Kosciuszko NP The roof of Australia, stronghold of mountain pygmy-possums with meadows of wildflowers in summer. **Victorian Alps** Snowgrass-covered hills, and colourful snow gum woodlands full of rosellas, currawongs and robins. **Cradle Mountain–Lake St Clair NP** Cushion plants and King Billy pines, plus wombats, wallabies and Tasmanian devils.

RAINFORESTS

Light filters through fan palms in the canopy at Daintree NP.

EVERYONE knows how diverse tropical rainforests are, but it's hard to be blasé about a habitat that covers only 0.3% of the continent, yet supports about half of Australia's plant species and one-third of its bird and mammal species. The rainforests of north Queensland's Wet Tropics are the quintessential rainforest (below: Mission Beach, Queensland), thick with vines, palms, epiphytic orchids and buttressed trees, and supporting an enormous diversity of wildlife.

South of the tropics, there are first subtropical, then temperate rainforests. These become increasingly less diverse in flora and fauna the further south they are, but they offer their own selection of plants and animals, many unique. Subtropical rainforest at first appear very similar to their more northerly counterparts, but a closer look will reveal that whereas the former are often dominated by just a handful of tree species, the latter are far more diverse. Temperate rainforests are strikingly different: they are often quiet, still and dominated by extraordinarily beautiful, lichen-draped beech trees.

As you'd expect, rainforests are wet – they generally need at least 1500mm of rainfall per year, although one site in north Queensland receives up to 7m a year. But the survival of rainforests also depends on soils, aspect and temperature (although cool-temperate species can cope with some snow). Monsoon rainforests occur in areas where rainfall is very seasonal, such as the coastal north-west, and can survive without rain for seven or more months each year, partly by losing leaves during the dry season. But an absence of fire is critical for all rainforests because, unlike other Australian habitats, rainforests are destroyed by fire.

Rainforest occupants

Tropical and subtropical rainforest vegetation contrasts vividly with the eucalypts and wattles that dominate most of 'the bush'; and, not surprisingly, it supports a very different fauna. Instead of grazers (there being no grass) there are browsers of leaves, such as tree-kangaroos, cuscuses and the greatest diversity of possums in Australia, including the distinctive striped possum. There are lots of frogs in this moist environment, some hiding in basket-shaped epiphytic ferns. And invertebrates, such as brilliant

Opposite page: Watercourses fed by high rainfall that percolates through deep leaf litter form highways through dense rainforests. Streams draining North Queensland's Paluma Range support freshwater crayfish and platypuses, while large animals such as cassowaries use them as thoroughfares.

Opposite inset: Tropical reptiles at Cape Tribulation include Boyd's forest dragon, a colourful rainforest lizard.

butterflies and leeches, far outnumber the vertebrates – this is the case with all habitats, but it is more immediately apparent in the tropical and subtropical rainforests. Tropical rainforest contains many New Guinean animals as well as Australian endemics, and many wide-ranging species commonly found in other habitats also exploit this rich biological resource. The subtropical rainforests still teem with many of the same birds and mammals found further north, but lose the New Guinean elements and other northern endemics.

The extravagance and diversity of plant life in the northern rainforests strikes you immediately, but don't expect to see throngs of animals as soon as you enter. Many animals are nocturnal and many that aren't are often hidden some 30m up in the canopy. Nevertheless, patience should uncover green tree frogs and lots of rainforest birds, including bowerbirds and riflebirds; and with a spotlight you're bound to detect bandicoots and possums, and (with a dash of luck) tree-kangaroos. Fleshy fruits are common in the tropics and subtopics, so these forests are major habitats for fruit-eating birds and for flying-foxes. A fruiting tree, such as a fig, is an ideal place to watch for colourful fruit-doves, parrots (including diminutive fig-parrots) and bowerbirds congregating to feed. When flying-foxes are not eating, their camps are easy to find because of the noise hundreds of them make as they spend the day upside-down in trees.

In rainforests the canopy is so dense that very little light filters through to the ground. These forests are consequently relatively open at ground level (belying the popular image of 'impenetrable jungles'), but since most of the vegetation is in the canopy, that is where most of the animals are, too. It is worth straining your neck for a glimpse of the gorgeous eclectus parrot or the huge palm cockatoo. Strangler figs, with their lattice of roots, can form an excellent hide if the supporting tree has rotted away so that it is possible to climb up inside. Some ground animals, such as the cassowary and musky rat-kangaroo, feed on fallen fruits; and fresh scratchings in the litter indicate the vigorous efforts of lyrebirds and brush-turkeys to uncover insects.

Warm-temperate rainforest fringes Greaves Creek in Blue Mountains NP's Grand Canyon Walk.

Ancient history

Rainforests once covered much of the continent, but today grow only in small patches along the east coast from Queensland to

---

Aerial seeding

Animals such as flying-foxes and birds are important agents of dispersal for the seeds of many plants, because they eat fruit then excrete the seeds, sometimes far from the feeding site. The pied imperial-pigeon is probably the major carrier for rainforest seeds in the north – flocks of this black-and-white bird migrate between New Guinea and northern Australia, and travel to offshore islands daily. Some fruits are so large that only cassowaries can eat them; the loss of cassowaries from an area could cause problems for the long-term survival of these plant species. Rodents also disperse the seeds of some plants, such as macadamia nuts, although they do eat a significant proportion!

Three species of Nothofagus beech grow in Australian rainforests. Antarctic beech is the most northerly, found as far north as Lamington NP. Myrtle beech is found in the cool-temperate rainforests of Victoria and Tasmania. And deciduous beech is found only in Tasmania. Nothofagus forests – here in the Mersey Valley, Tasmania – are characterised by dense moss beds and trailing lichens.

Tasmania. Parts of the Wet Tropics have been a rainforest refuge during perhaps the last 60 million years, enabling rainforests to survive climatic fluctuations, a general drying out and increased frequency of fire across the continent. Rainforests harbour many of the world's most primitive flowering plants; even more primitive species of cycads and conifers; and some of Australia's most ancient animal species, such as the cassowary and musky rat-kangaroo. In subtropical and temperate rainforests, stands of southern beech trees (*Nothofagus*) are relics of the supercontinent Gondwana from 50 million years ago – their only living relatives are in New Zealand and southern South America.

Some three-quarters of Australia's rainforest has been lost to clearing and logging since Europeans arrived. The destruction continues in many areas, although some 60% of remaining forests are now secure in conservation reserves. ■

Daintree NP Australia's highest diversity of arboreal mammals plus many birds unique to the Wet Tropics. **Lamington NP** Large tract of accessible subtropical rainforest with many frogs and reptiles, and several unique birds. **Mt Field NP** Cool-temperate rainforest alive with lyrebirds, possums, wallabies and quolls.

SHORES

The towering limestone cliffs of the Nullarbor Plain shear off into the Great Australian Bight.

MUCH of Australia's 30,000km coastline is still in its natural state and, with empty beaches (below: Waterloo Bay, Wilsons Promontory NP) to be found even near cities, makes one of the easiest habitats in which to find wildlife. Rock pools support a wealth of unusual life forms; beaches are swept by seabirds and picked over by oystercatchers; and mangroves, mudflats and saltmarshes form nurseries for fish, and supermarkets for thousands of wading birds that arrive annually from the northern hemisphere. When the tide is in, the shores become a marine environment, but its ebb leaves behind a land environment, and life on the shores has to be adapted to the benefits and hardships of both situations. People have taken advantage of the shores' bounty for millennia – Aboriginal middens ('rubbish heaps' of discarded shells, bones and the like) can be seen behind many beaches.

Hot and salty or wet and dangerous

The (usually twice-) daily routine of high and low tides creates a distinct environment. The sea brings water and food, such as plankton, detritus and dissolved nutrients, that supports a great quantity and diversity of life. But with it comes predators and herbivores, ranging from crustaceans and octopuses to fish and, in the north at least, crocodiles. Low tide brings relief from these threats, but allows land-based predators, such as birds, to move in and creates a new set of risks: dehydration, sunburn and, as seawater evaporates, increasing salinity. Rain and rivers bring an influx of freshwater, which results in a reduction of salinity – just as much a problem.

Rocky shores

Rock platforms and boulders provide a stable footing for many animals and plants in the intertidal zone. Rock pools in particular usually contain sea stars, flowerlike sea anemones, many different kinds of mollusc, and various seaweeds, sponges and colonial animals like bryozoans. These cover the spectrum of colours from bright yellow to pink, and many of what appear to be plants are in fact animals, including the sponges and

Opposite page: The daily tide cycle creates one of the most demanding of habitats, by turns inundating marine life then exposing it to direct sunlight. Temperate, tidal rock platforms support complex communities of molluscs, crustaceans and other invertebrates among waving fronds of weed.

Opposite inset: Animals trapped in rock pools at low tide, such as crustaceans, octopus and fish, can disperse between pools when the tide comes in again.

anemones. Blennies, odd 'horned' fish, reside in the pools, while all sorts of ocean fish can be trapped by the retreat of the tide. Certain species, such as the enormous black elephant snail, prefer to shelter under a ledge, while crabs are common in crevices or under boulders. A visit to the pools with a strong torch at night may reveal octopus and shrimps out hunting.

Beaches

Sandy beaches hide buried worms (some more than 2m long) and hinged shells, such as pipis, for which oystercatchers and plovers probe along the tideline. Washed-up seaweed creates an abundant food source in an otherwise fairly poor habitat, and is rapidly decomposed by sandhoppers (amphipods) and other invertebrates, which in turn form food for birds. Overhead, gulls, sea eagles and brahminy kites keep an eye out for food, while out to sea terns plummet after fish.

Behind the beaches, sand dunes may be riddled with the burrows of a shearwater colony. Vegetation forms a succession from hardy, salt-tolerant grasses and succulents nearest the beach, to wind-sculptured teatree scrub, heath and finally forest further away from the shore. The coastal heaths flower prolifically and often then host enormous numbers of honeyeaters, as well as more cryptic nectar and pollen feeders such as pygmy-possums. The coastal heaths form on poor, sandy soils. In inland and montane areas there are also heaths on similarly poor soils, and there can be strong similarities between the fauna of such otherwise environmentally disparate habitats.

Few animals live permanently on sandy beaches, but many exploit the riches cast up by the waves.

Mangroves, mudflats and saltmarshes

These habitats, which occur on shores sheltered from wave action, are the most biologically rich ecosystems of the coast. The abundant mud makes them less than ideal for exploring, but with binoculars, egrets, pelicans and many waders can comfortably be seen from a distance. Mangroves really must be visited if you are dedicated to your bird list, as many species that are quite common in mangroves (some almost exclusively so)

Living tidemarks

Sea creatures that can survive greater or lesser periods out of water typically live in distinct zones, which are particularly obvious on steep, rocky shores. Those few animals which can survive at higher levels must spend more time uncovered at low tide and thus receive fewer nutrients, but have the advantage of reduced competition for space. The overall effect can sometimes be of overlapping 'stripes' of different creatures at different levels. At the top are tiny snails that can survive on just the splash from waves at high tide. Barnacles can survive below this level and need just a few hours underwater. In the middle zones there are usually numerous limpets, which graze microalgae; and sometimes a miniature 'forest' of seaweeds, such as Neptune's necklace, makes a home for different molluscs. At the lowest zones are more seaweeds and animals like the filter-feeding cunjevois (sea squirts) that cannot survive long out of water.

Different mangrove species grow in a succession from the water's edge, where hardy pioneers are tolerant of tidal inundation, to those that connect the mangrove community to dry land and adjoining terrestrial plant communities.

cannot easily be seen elsewhere; examples include shining fly-catchers and collared kingfishers.

Both mangroves and saltmarshes play a vital role in stabilising the shoreline, provide essential nurseries for many (including most commercial) fish species, and provide habitat for wildlife. Their importance is now generally recognised, but both types of habitat are still being destroyed around Australia to make way for coastal development. ■

Darwin Signboards on the East Point mangrove boardwalk explain ecology, wildlife and Aboriginal lore. Also Charles Darwin NP. **Broome** Mudflats of world significance for migrating birds and user-friendly mangroves with many specialised birds. **Great Ocean Road** Wild beaches with many plovers and oyster-catchers, interspersed with rocky shores full of pools.

OCEANS

Fringing reefs, supporting diverse fish and invertebrate species, grow around cays such as Lady Elliott Island.

THE oceans draw the world map. The readily recognised shape of Australia is merely the latest in a series that began with the island continent's separation from the supercontinent Gondwana some 50 million years ago. In the eons since, changing sea levels have gradually but markedly transformed the shoreline; oceans have invaded low-lying land, including much of the heart of the continent, and in their retreat left behind telltale fossils and a legacy of sand, sedimentary rock and salt.

Australia, the world's largest island, is bounded and shaped by three oceans and four seas. Land and ocean converge along thousands of kilometres of coast on palm-fringed tropical beaches, muddy mangrove forests and storm-wracked rocky shores. An extensive continental shelf, and countless bays and inlets, host an abundance of marine animals and plants in diverse communities, from pearl oysters, dugongs and coral reefs to little penguins, leafy sea dragons and giant kelp forests.

The great wall of coral

Drawing energy from the tropical sun and creating building blocks of calcium carbonate from sea water, the coral polyp and its symbiotic zooxanthellae – an ingenious association of plant and animal – is the basis for all life on a coral reef. Solid ramparts built on ancestral foundations defy ocean swells, and support and shelter an unknowable variety of fishes, worms, crustaceans, molluscs and other forms.

Corals colonised northern Australian waters soon after the continent drifted into tropical climes. Ancient coral reefs grew upwards, chasing the sunlight, only to die and become stranded far inland by a fluctuating sea level; the Great Barrier Reef as we know it is a relatively recent structure. But today 'the Reef' is a magnificent coral community that stretches for 2300km along Australia's north-east coast and covers an area of more than 200,000 sq km. Cays (below: Lady Musgrave Island), rocky islands and atolls make up an interlocking chain of reefs supporting one of the greatest assemblages of living diversity on earth, much of it readily accessible to the casual observer.

There's safety in numbers, and a myriad of small fishes – damselfish, angelfish, butterflyfish and more – can be seen in the briefest of swims along a tropical reef. Bright flashy colours

Opposite page: The distribution of many tropical marine species, such as these trumpeters and red morwongs, straddles subtropical waters – and even stretches to cays and reefs isolated by deep trenches.

Opposite inset: Plantlike invertebrates such as feather stars decorate the underwater landscape of the Great Barrier Reef.

advertise species, sex, maturity or danger. Contrasting colours mask body shape, false eye spots deceive predators and fleshy appendages help conceal those that would be eaten as well as those on the prowl.

Swift currents sweeping through the maze of reefs carry food for plantlike feather stars and sea cucumbers. Large predators such as barracuda, sailfish and sharks are an ominous sight in the deeper channels through which wing majestic manta rays – huge but harmless plankton feeders. Ancient-looking sea turtles also feed and breed in these waters – two of the largest are the carnivorous loggerhead and the green turtle.

Under Capricorn

South of the tropics, mudflats and mangroves give way to sandy beaches and rocky headlands. Offshore, cool temperate waters nurture colourful sponge gardens, and rocky reefs support masses of red, green and brown seaweeds. Spiny sea urchins, bristling crayfish, huge stingrays and poisonous octopus thrive in the cool, often cold, water, but for divers the extra effort is often rewarded, especially when cryptic benthic fauna reveal their diversity and colour during a night dive.

But you don't need to enter the depths to observe the great whales and their smaller cousins, the dolphins. Bottlenose and common dolphins can be observed in coastal waters right around the continent: great pods herding schools of fish, bunching and corralling the prey into a tight ball, individuals dashing in to snatch a meal. Humpback whales migrate from summer feeding grounds in Antarctic waters, skirting the eastern and western shores to give birth and mate in subtropical and tropical waters. Southern right whales similarly migrate to nursery grounds off the southern coast where, from cliff-top vantage points, they can be seen with their newborn calves.

Southern coastal waters are also home to the little penguin, the smallest penguin species. Penguins spend their days at sea hunting small fish before returning at dusk to selected beaches where downy chicks with enormous appetites are hidden in burrows. These colonies, vulnerable to terrestrial predators, are

The rough leatherjacket is a temperate representative of a family also found in the tropics.

Trading places

Lifestyles of reef-dwelling creatures are incredibly varied: some behaviours and roles are familiar, but there are also extraordinary acts that challenge our preconceptions. At nightfall many of the reef's diurnal creatures retreat into caves and crevices; some fish change colours as they hide, others secrete a mucous blanket to smother any scent that would attract a nocturnal predator. At night a different array of species emerges and, in many cases, the ecological niche temporarily deserted by one is adopted by another. 'Cleaning stations' are fascinating examples: these stations operate day and night with different species working separate shifts. Large, normally voracious cod become patient recipients to the attention of small wrasse or tiny shrimp that swim or crawl through their cavernous, teeth-lined mouths to extract parasites and 'floss' away debris from recent meals. But outside the cleaning zone, it's back to 'bigger fish eats smaller fish'.

Thick leathery kelp fronds are attached to rocky reefs and platforms by a holdfast. Individual kelp fronds can be massive, measuring 20m in length, and the waving kelp forests provide shelter for a rich array of temperate marine life.

mostly confined to islands but the daily procession is easily observed at certain localities. Offshore islands are also the favoured retreat for fur seals and sea-lions, where small bachelor groups or great, noisy breeding congregations seasonally crowd the rocky beaches and headlands.

Even more goes on beyond the gaze of the nature-cruise passenger or the deepest scuba diver. Hundred-year-old fish, bright orange and large eyed, hover over peaks of submerged mountains. Beyond the reach of sunlight, enormous squid with arms several metres long capture fish and, in turn, are the prey of deep-diving sperm whales. The Southern Ocean's depths are one of the richest hunting grounds for species 'new' to science – as well as being the latest larder to be raided by fishing fleets.

The diversity of marine habitats around Australia underlies one of the richest assemblages of flora and fauna on earth. Couple this with the relatively unpolluted waters of the southern hemisphere and it is a unique and priceless asset to be enjoyed, understood and protected. ■

Great Barrier Reef Huge cod, spectacular corals, giant clams and diverse fish. **Jervis Bay NP** Sponge gardens, colourful invertebrates, dolphins and occasional whales. **Bicheno** Towering kelp forests, crayfish and sponge gardens. **Kangaroo Island** Sea-lions, fur-seals, ascidians and temperate corals.

PARKS AND PLACES

The best wildlife-watching destinations in Australia

INTRODUCTION TO PARKS AND PLACES

POSSUMS scamper over suburban roofs, bright flashes of rosellas and lorikeets punctuate city gardens and you just can't ignore the green tree frogs in the toilet bowls at Fogg Dam. Some creatures know no boundaries and can be seen in some of the most unlikely places, but it's worth making Australia's superb network of national parks and other reserves the focus of your wildlife-watching trip.

Australia has more than 850 national parks and 13 World Heritage sites; 7.5% (ie, 580,000 sq km) of the total land area is under some form of natural heritage protection; and those figures don't include marine parks, which cover 396,000 sq km – two-thirds of which is the Great Barrier Reef. With such a choice, and distances in Australia as expansive as the landscape, it helps to do some planning before you set out – and that's where this chapter comes in. The parks and other special places it points you towards have been chosen largely for their wildlife value and accessibility, rather than simply their scenic landforms or popularity.

This mainstay of the chapter are wildlife profiles of destinations renowned for wildlife-watching – a rundown on what is there, what's special and, importantly, where to find it. It is certainly not meant to be a complete listing of an area's fauna, and indeed the vast majority of species ('the other 99%' that aren't 'charismatic megafauna') cannot be done justice in such a short space. But you will get a good feel for what mammals, birds and other large animals you can reasonably expect to see, and with the many inside tips you will often be able to go that step further and see or appreciate something that might otherwise remain hidden.

We also mention sites in the capital cities worth visiting if you have only a few hours to spare; and summarise a swag of other sites ranging from enormous parks offering a huge range of wildlife, to small hotspots renowned for particular specialities. The maps give you an idea of where things are located and highlights where some of the wildlife can be found, but are not intended for precise navigation. To cap it off, we've briefly suggested travel itineraries for each state that will fit into typical holiday durations and show a good cross section of wildlife. As in any voyage of discovery, local knowledge is always worth seeking out.

The destinations included here are great stages on which to view the dynamic habitats, plants and animals of Australia. Animals move around, seasons change, weather varies. There is no guarantee that you'll see absolutely everything you're after, but with the right directions you should see something amazing in just about any part of the country. We wish you a rewarding journey. ■

Suggested itineraries – Australia

One week You can make the most of a short stopover by heading for Cairns (instant access to the Great Barrier Reef and Australia's best birdwatching) or Darwin, where Kakadu and other nearby NPs showcase Top End wildlife. Check the state sections for suggestions on how to spend a week near other capital cities.

Two weeks Combine highlights near Cairns and Darwin, or do one then jet down to the Centre for desert wildlife at Uluru-Kata Tjuta or MacDonnell Ranges NPs. Again, the state itineraries suggest how to spend a fortnight based at other capital cities.

One month Time and distance are still against you, but you could do a long drive up, say, the east or west coasts and take in (on the east coast) Royal, Warrumbungle and Lamington NPs, Fraser Island and the Great Barrier Reef; Atherton Tableland and Daintree NP; or The South-West, Dryandra Woodland, Rottnest Island, Shark Bay and The Kimberley (west).

There are any number of variations, but a no-expense-spared trip could fly from Darwin and the Top End to Uluru-Kata Tjuta NP, across to Cairns for the Wet Tropics and Great Barrier Reef; on to Brisbane for access to Lamington NP and Fraser Island; a side trip to Lord Howe Island or Tasmania; then cross the continent to work the South-West from Perth; and finish in the Kimberley.

NEW SOUTH WALES AND AUSTRALIAN CAPITAL TERRITORY

State faunal emblems

Platypus An aquatic, egg-laying mammal (monotreme) with dense, waterproof fur and a sensitive, electroreceptive bill. It is common in creeks and rivers east of the Great Dividing Range.

Laughing kookaburra A large kingfisher known for its loud, cackling call. It eats large insects and small vertebrates and is common around picnic areas in forest areas of eastern Australia.

MAKING up the larger portion of Australia's south-east, NSW and the ACT encompass a broad spectrum of habitats – beaches, rivers and lakes to the east; subtropical rainforests in the north; arid plains to the west; and alpine peaks in the Snowy Mountains, which include Australia's highest – Mt Kosciuszko (2228m). In summer the coast can be humid, while a blistering, dry heat pervades the inland (the ACT – in the foothills of the Snowy Mountains – is generally cooler).

The NSW National Parks and Wildlife Service (NPWS) runs the state's 76 national parks; Namadgi NP is the ACT's only national park. Most flank the east coast and encompass the high tablelands or forested eastern slopes of the Great Dividing Range – a mountainous chain running north–south, parallel with the coastline. The forests provide habitat for koalas, platypuses, quolls, gliders, wallabies and a rich birdlife. The western slopes of 'the Divide' grade into the vast arid plains that make up about two-thirds of NSW; the Warrumbungle Range showcases the overlap between dry-country animal and plant communities and those of the wetter coast. Red kangaroos and western grey kangaroos can be found on these plains, in parks such as Sturt NP, and the only NSW population of the endangered yellow-footed rock-wallaby lives among the rocky hills of Mutawintji NP in the far west.

There are also three World Heritage Areas in NSW: the Willandra Lakes Region in the south-west, the Central Eastern Rainforest Reserves in the central-north, and the Lord Howe Island Group 500km off the coast.

The rockwarbler, NSW's only endemic bird, lives on the sandstone escarpments of the Sydney Basin, while rainforest birds can be found in coastal rainforest at Bundjalung and Myall Lakes NPs, and in the subtropical rainforest of Washpool and Royal NPs. Australian brush-turkeys and red-necked pademelons feed in the open at Washpool NP. The magnificent display of the superb lyrebird can be seen during winter in many parks, but perhaps most famously in Royal and Blue Mountains NPs.

The Pacific Ocean is home to dolphins and migrating humpback whales, while estuaries provide habitat for wading birds. The coastal heaths around Sydney attract diverse nectar-feeding birds, mammals and a large number of endemic reptiles. ■

Highlights

- Watching superb lyrebirds display during winter in the Blue Mountains
- Birdwatching along the creeks of the Warrumbungle Range
- Spotting koalas and dingoes near Mungo Brush at Myall Lakes
- Coming face to face with a euro in a red-walled, sandstone gorge at Mutawintji
- Following the soaring of elegant brahminy kites at Bundjalung
- Seeing pods of bottlenose dolphins surfing the waves at Myall Lakes
- Catching up with seven species of macropod in Gibraltar Ranges, Washpool and nearby Mann River

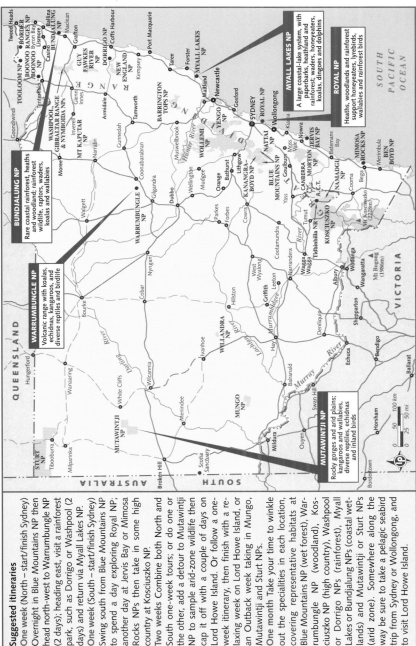

BUNDJALUNG NP
Rare coastal rainforest, heaths, heathland and woodland; rainforest wildlife, raptors, waders, koalas and wallabies

WARRUMBUNGLE NP
Volcanic range with koalas, echidnas, kangaroos, and diverse reptiles and birdlife

MUTAWINTJI NP
Rocky gorges and arid plains; kangaroos and wallabies; diverse reptiles, echidnas and inland birds

MYALL LAKES NP
A large coastal-lake system, with paperbarks, heathland and rainforest; waders, honeyeaters, koalas, dingoes and dolphins

ROYAL NP
Heaths, woodlands and rainforest support honeyeaters, lyrebirds, wallabies and rainforest birds

Suggested itineraries

One week (North – start/finish Sydney) Overnight in Blue Mountains NP then head north-west to Warrumbungle NP (2 days); heading east, visit a rainforest park, such as Dorrigo or Washpool (2 days), and return via Myall Lakes NP.

One week (South – start/finish Sydney) Swing south from Blue Mountains NP to spend a day exploring Royal NP; another day at Jervis Bay or Mimosa Rocks NPs then take in some high country at Kosciuszko NP.

Two weeks Combine both North and South one-week tours; or do one or the other, add a detour to Mutawintji NP to sample arid-zone wildlife then cap it off with a couple of days on Lord Howe Island. Or follow a one-week itinerary, then finish with a relaxing week on Lord Howe Island, or an Outback week taking in Mungo, Mutawintji and Sturt NPs.

One month Take your time to winkle out the specialities in each location, covering representative habitats at Blue Mountains NP (wet forest), Warrumbungle NP (woodland), Kosciuszko NP (high country), Washpool or Dorrigo NPs (rainforest), Myall Lakes or Bundjalung NPs (coastal wetlands) and Mutawintji or Sturt NPs (arid zone). Somewhere along the way be sure to take a pelagic seabird trip from Sydney or Wollongong, and to visit Lord Howe Island.

SYDNEY

A city walled by forest

SYDNEY sprawls across a coastal plain bounded to the east by the Pacific Ocean and to the west by the Blue Mountains. Despite being the oldest and most populous city in Australia, early achievements by local conservation groups, and the steep slopes of the Great Dividing Range, have served to create a city surrounded by 12 national parks and a number of other parks, reserves and rugged wilderness areas. Over half of Australia's bird species have been recorded in the Sydney region and an array of native creatures visit the gardens of Sydneysiders. **New Holland honeyeaters, yellow-faced honeyeaters** and **wattlebirds** are some of the common nectar feeders. **Silver gulls** are the most common bird along the beaches, and flocks of **rainbow lorikeets** feed in flowering eucalypts. **Common brushtail possums** are noisy residents of urban roofs, and the smaller **common ringtail possum** can often be seen at night running along fences or telephone wires. The city's large fruiting fig trees provide food for fruit-eating birds and grey-headed flying-foxes.

Hundreds of **grey-headed flying-foxes** camp during the day in the *Royal Botanic Gardens* on the edge of the city centre, dispersing at night to feed; their main camp is at Gordon, 15km north. More than 100 bird species have been recorded in the gardens, and eels, **eastern snake-necked turtles** and waterbirds can be found in and around the ornamental ponds. The warmer months bring **sacred kingfishers** and **tree martins**; **figbirds** and **tawny frogmouths** breed here regularly.

Centennial Park, 5km south of the centre, has gardens, woodland, forest, ponds and paperbark swamp. There is a good variety of bush birds and a wide array of waterbirds including **black swans** and a colony of breeding **Australian white ibis**. **Common brushtail possums** are also easily seen here.

Sydney Aquarium (☎ 02-9262 2300) at Darling Harbour is excellent, with a seal pool, a touch pool and tanks simulating the open ocean, the Great Barrier Reef, the northern rivers, the Murray-Darling River and Sydney Harbour.

Sydney Harbour NP (☎ 02-9247 5033) protects the last of the native vegetation of Port Jackson – North and South Heads

The botanic gardens adjoining the world-famous Sydney Opera House are home to flying-foxes and a variety of birds, while little penguins breed and fish in the picturesque harbour.

are two of the best spots in Sydney to watch for **seabirds**. Botany Bay and the Kurnell Peninsula are well-known sites for watching **migratory waders**.

Taronga Zoo (☎ 02-9969 2777) on the shores of Sydney Harbour has more than 3000 animals from around the world with a large variety of native animals, including koalas and Tasmanian devils. It also has Sydney's only platypus exhibit, a nocturnal house, a reptile and amphibian exhibit, an aquarium and a wide range of bird exhibits, including a walk-through rainforest aviary. Many wild birds can be seen in the zoo grounds including **nankeen night herons** (near the seal display). *The Australian Wildlife Park* (☎ 02-9830 9187) exhibits many native animals, and includes a nocturnal house and rainforest aviary.

Ku-ring-gai Chase NP (☎ 02-9472 8949), 30km north of Sydney, is a large park comprising heath and woodland. Plant diversity is extremely high; the heaths especially attract honeyeaters and wrens, **eastern pygmy-possums** and **feathertail gliders**. The endemic **rockwarbler** is found around sandstone outcrops, and **superb lyrebirds** in moist, forested areas such as Garigal

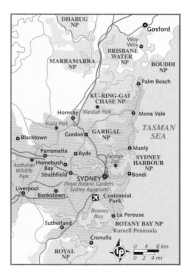

picnic area and West Head. **Swamp wallabies** are also occasionally seen at Garigal. **Crimson** and **eastern rosellas** flock around the feeding area at Kalkari visitor centre and **lace monitors** visit picnic areas throughout the park. **Echidnas**, **long-nosed bandicoots** and **antechinuses** are occasionally seen, and the **New Holland mouse** lives in burnt heaths. The waterways support many fish species and birds such as the **striated** (or mangrove) **heron**, **azure kingfisher** and **white-bellied sea-eagle**.

North of Sydney lies *Dharug NP* (☎ 02-4324 4911), a rugged region of sandstone cliffs and ridges, heathlands, eucalypt forests, rainforest, and mangroves along the Hawkesbury River. **Wombats** and **lace monitors** are often seen at Mill Creek camping ground. Rainforest birds including **Australian brush-turkeys**, **wonga pigeons**, **brush cuckoos** and **satin bowerbirds** can be found here, as well as **glossy black-cockatoos** in stands of she-oaks. Dharug is also a good spot to spotlight for **greater gliders** and **powerful owls**, and in summer, for **white-throated nightjars**. Adjacent *Marramarra NP* (☎ 02-9457 9322) has some of the best mangroves in NSW.

Around *Gosford*, the rainforests are full of wildlife. Rainforest birds, **platypuses**, tame **swamp wallabies** and **red-necked pademelons** can be seen at the *Forest of Tranquillity Rainforest Bird Sanctuary* (☎ 02-4362 1855). A colony of **grey-headed flying-foxes** roosts in Wambina Reserve; **glossy black-cockatoos** and **koalas** inhabit Strickland SF; and the mangrove boardwalk in Carawah Reserve is worth a wander. A diverse collection of reptiles and other wildlife can be seen at the *Australian Reptile Park and Wildlife Sanctuary* (☎ 02-4340 1022) west of Gosford. **Koalas**, **platypuses** and **echidnas** are found in nearby *Brisbane Water NP* (☎ 02-4324 4911), and **white-bellied sea-eagles** patrol the cliffs and beaches of *Bouddi NP* (☎ 02-4324 4911). ■

WASHPOOL AND GIBRALTAR RANGE NATIONAL PARKS

Diversity at the crossroads

Wildlife highlights

This region is a biological crossroads, with a number of species reaching or nearing the limit of their geographical ranges here, eg, superb lyrebirds and powerful and sooty owls occur no further inland. In total, 33 coastal species are at their western limits, and eight inland species at their eastern limits. Many species are also nearing their northern or southern limits. The diversity of macropods is high and among them is the rare parma wallaby. Koalas, possums, and gliders are common. The diversity and abundance of birds is also high, especially of rainforest species and of honeyeaters, which are attracted to spring wildflowers in Gibraltar.

PERCHED on the edge of a plateau 1200m above the coast, Washpool protects extensive eucalypt forests and NSW's largest area of rainforest, containing warm-temperate, subtropical and dry rainforest. The boulder-strewn landscape of adjacent Gibraltar Range is dominated by drier forest and woodland, heathland and subalpine swamps. Both parks are part of the Central Eastern Rainforest Reserves World Heritage Area.

Red-necks and long-noses

Much of the area is wilderness, but good examples of the rainforest and its wildlife are easily seen around Coombadjha Creek. The birdwatching is excellent, with a high diversity of rainforest species. **Superb lyrebirds** (near the northern limit of their range here), **Australian brush-turkeys** (the males have more prominent neck wattles) and **satin bowerbirds** (and their bowers) are easy to see around the Bellbird camping area; **king-parrots**, **crimson rosellas** and **pied currawongs** are present here and elsewhere in high numbers. **Logrunners** can be seen on the short Lyrebird Walk that links the Bellbird camping area to the Coachwood

The rainforest edge can appear as a wall of vegetation. But this is actually one of the most productive areas in which to observe wildlife. Sunlight fosters abundant plant growth which in turn attracts insects and birdlife.

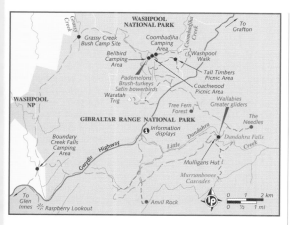

Location Approximately 70km north-east of Glen Innes.

Facilities Information displays at the turn-off to Mulligans Hut on the Gwydir Hwy.

Accommodation Washpool has several camping grounds. Gibraltar's main camping ground is at Mulligans Hut. Full range at Glen Innes and Grafton.

Wildlife rhythms Spring and early summer for wildflowers and associated birds in the heathlands of Gibraltar.

Contact Rangers: Glen Innes (☎ 02-6732 5133), Grafton (☎ 02-6642 0613).

Ecotours NPWS Discovery Tours during most school holidays.

picnic area: pairs or family groups of these hyperactive rainforest birds are constantly on the move, raking through leaf litter, dashing across the forest floor and calling loudly, often in unison.

At night, **mountain brushtail possums** descend upon the Bellbird camping area. Other nocturnal, arboreal mammals include **common ringtail possums**, **sugar gliders** (listen for their repeated *yap*) and **greater gliders**. To see the latter, walk from the Bellbird camping area back along Coombadjha Rd and scan the eucalypt canopy with a spotlight for their bright-yellow eyeshine; you may also see **tawny frogmouths** perched in prominent positions. During the day, the road is a good place from which to hear **eastern whipbirds** and **superb lyrebirds**, and to see **koalas** – they are reasonably common in some eucalypt areas.

The Coombadjha Nature Stroll, starting from the Coombadjha camping area, follows Coombadjha Creek and delves into warm-temperate rainforest dominated by coachwoods. At dusk, watch for **platypuses** from the decking at the Coachwood Pool and in other quiet stretches of the creek. **Red-necked** and **red-legged pademelons**, and **red-necked wallabies** can all regularly be seen late in the day around the picnic areas or other open grassy areas.

Scratching around

The rainforest floor is damp and covered with leaf litter. Everywhere, there are patches which have been raked away – the work of Australian brush-turkeys and superb lyrebirds (inset). Both have huge feet that they use to dig into the leaf litter in search of small animals.

At night, bandicoots and potoroos dig holes in their search for food. In digging up the soil these animals are also aerating it, which speeds up the decomposition of the plant material by invertebrates, fungi and bacteria. The release of nutrients in this manner is especially important in rainforests because the underlying soil may not be particularly fertile. Rainforest trees have adaptations that increase the efficiency of nutrient uptake from the surface layer. Buttress roots are one such adaptation, enabling the tree to spread its roots through the rich but shallow surface layers of soil.

Take a day to do the Washpool Walk. It passes through warm-temperate and subtropical rainforest, and tall eucalypt forest. It is a good place to start searching for sought-after rainforest birds that you haven't encountered around the camping areas. Expect to see or hear **noisy pittas**, **paradise riflebirds**, **wompoo** and **rose-crowned fruit-doves**, **regent bowerbirds** and perhaps the endangered **rufous scrub-bird** – good numbers of which occur in the warm-temperate rainforests. On the walk near the Tall Timbers picnic area you'll hear **bell miners**; and don't miss the Twin Cedars – they are thought to be around one thousand years old. The shiny, black **land mullet**, an impressive lizard up to 65cm long, commonly basks on logs alongside tracks in the rainforest. **Carpet** and **diamond pythons** are also sometimes seen basking, but are mainly nocturnal.

The tall flowering spikes of grass trees are an important source of nectar for many animals.

The emblem for these wilderness areas is the **powerful owl**. It hunts in the open eucalypt forests but roosts in denser areas, often in rainforest; there is always a chance of seeing one by day perched high in a tree, perhaps with the remains of a possum or glider in its talons, but you are more likely to hear its deep, drawn-out *whoo-hoo* at night. Rare **parma wallabies** (until 1967 they were presumed extinct on the Australian mainland, and this is as far north as they are found) also inhabit the wet eucalypt forests; they are sometimes seen at dusk feeding on the grassy verges of forests.

Deeper in the forests at night, **long-nosed potoroos** and bandicoots (there are both **long-nosed** and **northern brown bandicoots** here) dig for underground fungi, tubers and grubs, leaving telltale conical holes – the bandicoots make a distinct sneezing sound.

From Atrichornis to Zoothera

The less fertile habitats of Gibraltar Range provide a totally different experience from that of Washpool's rainforests. **Euros** – solid, shaggy, dark-grey kangaroos – inhabit the woodlands around the granite outcrops. **Wedge-tailed eagles** are sometimes seen soaring above the ranges – keep an eye out on the way to Waratah Trig. **Eastern water dragons** bask along the waterways. And **platypuses** are occasionally seen in Little Dandahra Creek.

Greater gliders are relatively easy to observe around Mulligans Hut, where numerous tracks dissect the low, open eucalypt forest; the grassy areas here are also good for **whiptail and**

Bowers of blue

It was late afternoon when we were setting up camp at Bellbird Rest Area. In the fading light something caught our eye near the forest edge – it looked like litter. Upon closer inspection, we found an assortment of blue: pegs, a plastic spoon, flagging tape, string, straws, key tags, pen lids and an empty chip packet – the work of a male satin bowerbird. In the middle of it all was his display bower of twigs – like a stage.

Next morning the male fly past a few times. Once he even came and checked out our camp. We thought we would test his speed and laid the bait – a blue pen lid and key tag – in a prominent place near the bower. In the next two hours nothing happened, so he missed out – we took them back. What on earth did they use for decoration before humans provided coloured plastics?

Dan Harley & Marianne Worley

The boulder-strewn hilltops of the Gibraltar Range overlook rain-forested valleys in adjacent Washpool NP.

red-necked wallabies, and **red-necked pademelons**. The nocturnal **spotted-tailed quoll**, the largest marsupial carnivore on the mainland, is generally difficult to see, but around Mulligans Hut your chances are better (the northern section of Washpool is also good). In spring and summer the heathlands and woodlands flower profusely, attracting hordes of **honeyeaters** – the Anvil Rock Track is a good place to start.

There are also pockets of rainforest in Gibraltar: they can be seen on the walks to the Needles and 240m-high Dandahra Falls; and along the Atrichornis Track to the Murrumbooee Cascades. The walk to the falls is a good place to look for **red-necked pademelons** and **parma wallabies**. The **rufous scrub-bird** also occurs in these rainforests; a likely spot is on the Atrichornis Track (the track's name comes form the scientific name of the scrub-bird).

Another reasonably common rainforest bird is the **Bassian thrush**. Similar to a blackbird in size, shape and habits, but golden brown in colour overlaid with a striking pattern of black crescents, this thrush extends into Queensland before being replaced by the very similar **russet-tailed thrush** (they were only recently split into two species: *Zoothera lunulata* and *Z. heinei*). The two overlap around the NSW–Qld border, with the Bassian the more common in Washpool/Gibraltar Range. The easiest way to tell them apart is by call: the Bassian most commonly gives sharp *seep* calls or warbling; the russet-tailed has a strong, two-note *thea-thoo*.

At nearby Mann River NR (turn right off the Gwydir Hwy 36km east of Glen Innes) you can find **glossy black-cockatoos** feeding in casuarinas and **brush-tailed rock-wallabies** on rocky outcrops – Tommys Rock is the best place for rock-wallabies. **Whiptail wallabies** are quite common on the grassy, forested slopes leading to the picnic area. At the main picnic/camping area, you should have no trouble seeing **eastern grey kangaroos** and **euros** on the grassy flats; and the Mann River itself is worth trying for **platypuses**. ■

Watching tips

Coachwood picnic area is one of the best areas for a good look at red-necked pademelons; however, unlike those in Lamington NP, just over the Queensland border, these red-necks are timid and flighty, so don't try to get too close – sit quietly and be prepared to wait a while. Little brown birds can be hard to tell apart until you get your eye in: a good place to start is with two of the common LBBs foraging through the leaf litter around Washpool's picnic areas – white-browed and yellow-throated scrubwrens. At night, with a torch and a bit of luck, southern leaf-tailed geckoes can be detected on rainforest tree trunks by their red eyeshine.

KOSCIUSZKO NATIONAL PARK

Pygmy possums and corroborees

> ### Wildlife highlights
> The mountain pygmy-possum is rare, but various native rodents are often encountered in snow-bound huts. Bogong moths arrive in huge numbers every summer. Other wildlife includes echidnas, wombats, kangaroos and wallabies, and the endangered corroboree frog.

Location 450km to the south-west of Sydney.
Facilities Several visitor centres; Kosciuszko Education Centre, Sawpit Creek (☎ 02-6450 5666).
Accommodation Roofed accommodation at Charlotte Pass, Sawpit Creek, ski resorts and surrounding towns; camping grounds and bush camping.
Wildlife rhythms Summer for birds and Bogong moths. Winter to see wombats in the snow and perhaps small native mammals in huts.
Contact NPWS visitor centres at Jindabyne (☎ 02-6450 5600), Tumut (☎ 02-6947 1849), Perisher (☎ 02-6457 5214), Khancoban (☎ 02-6076 9373) and Yarrangobilly (☎ 02-6454 9597).
Ecotours NPWS Discovery Tours (Christmas and Easter).

Spring exposes Kosciuszko's rocky spine and a profusion of plants.

PROTECTING Australia's largest alpine area, the gently sloping plateau of NSW's largest national park stretches for almost 200km across the highest peaks of the Great Dividing Range. Wet eucalypt forests grow on the lower slopes and snow-gum woodlands clothe subalpine areas. At the highest elevations it is too cold for trees to grow (the alpine areas are blanketed with snow for one-third of the year) and instead there are alpine heaths and herb fields which flower prolifically in summer.

Swamp wallabies (widespread in the Thredbo Valley), **red-necked wallabies** and **eastern grey kangaroos** inhabit subalpine habitats during summer; in winter they descend into the lower forests. **Common ringtail possums** inhabit the snow gum woodlands, as do **common wombats**, which are often seen along roads during winter; **common brushtail possums** are more likely in the taller forests. Sawpit Creek camping ground is a good area to see most of these mammals. **Echidnas** are found throughout the subalpine zone; they hibernate for much of the winter and are more likely to be seen in spring and early summer. You could try watching for **platypuses** at dusk in still pools along the Thredbo River or Perisher Creek, which runs through Perisher Valley; however, the creeks in the wet eucalypt forests at lower elevations are probably a better bet.

Kosciuszko's most special mammal is the threatened **mountain pygmy-possum**. It is the only Australian mammal restricted to the Australian Alps and in NSW it is found only in this park – including at Australia's highest point (2228m), the summit of Mt Kosciuszko. Less than 10 sq km remain of its preferred habitat – boulder fields with mountain plum pines (it feeds on the pines' red berries and seeds). During winter the pygmy-possum goes into periods of torpor (normally no more several days at a time) before rousing itself to join **antechinuses**, and **bush** and **broad-toothed rats** foraging in runways beneath the snow. Usually none of these species are likely to be seen, but in winter keep an eye out for them in the ski lodges and mountain huts – this is how the first living mountain pygmy-possum was discovered in 1966.

Moth migration

The diversity of birds is relatively low, but from spring to summer several species are very common. Brown, streaked **Richard's pipits** are everywhere in the alpine herb fields, running across the ground or flying in short bursts which reveal their white outer tail feathers – watch for males performing high aerial display flights. In subalpine woodlands, **flame robins** are conspicuous summer migrants – the male's orange-red breast is striking – along with **crimson rosellas** and **gang-gang cockatoos** (gang-gangs are often unobtrusive, but listen for their distinctive, creaking calls). **Emus** are often seen along the Alpine Way between Jindabyne and Khancoban.

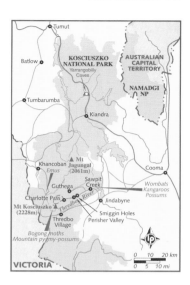

Some of the most unusual alpine creatures are invertebrates. Arriving over spring and summer, **Bogong moths** migrate from the plains of NSW and southern Queensland to Kosciuszko's highest peaks, where they aestivate (ie, go into torpor) in rock crevices before leaving in February. Large flocks of **little ravens** and **pied currawongs** feed on the moths, and they were once feasted on by many Aboriginal peoples. You should be able to find large clusters of the moths quite easily in caves and crevices on the windward side of the peaks; at night many will be on the move and huge clouds of them are often seen at dusk.

Four species of *Kosciuscola* grasshopper are endemic to the area, living at altitudes above 1200m. One of these, the **alpine thermocolour grasshopper**, changes from a dark blue-black colour on cold mornings – the colour assists heat absorption – to a light greenish blue as the temperature rises. ∎

Sexual segregation in a living fossil

The mountain pygmy-possum is the only alpine-dependent mammal in Australia and the only marsupial that hibernates. This relict from the Pleistocene ice ages has another unique feature – its social organisation. Females occupy the best quality habitats, found at higher elevations, while males are relegated to more marginal habitats on the lower slopes. During the breeding season the males move uphill to the females, only to retreat again when the season ends. It is probably female aggression that forces the males to leave for suboptimal habitat. Fewer males survive the winter in these poorer conditions, resulting in an adult population with more females than males. Roads, buildings and ski trails pose a potential barrier to the movement of males; the solution on Mt Higginbotham in Victoria has been to construct the 'Tunnel of Love' – a possum highway of boulders linking male and female habitats.

Watching tips

In summer, have a close look at the grasshoppers in the alpine grassland – some of them have striking markings. Both red-necked and swamp wallabies are smaller than eastern grey kangaroos: red-necks have a distinct reddish nape and a black muzzle, paws and feet; swamp wallabies are darker in colour, but often have a little white on the muzzle. The yellow-and-black patterning of the endangered corroboree frog makes it Australia's most striking frog; it is restricted to some of the wet heaths and sphagnum bogs near Smiggin Holes and Mt Jagungal.

MYALL LAKES NATIONAL PARK

Pelicans, penguins and petrels

Wildlife highlights

Pods of bottlenose dolphins are common along the coastline and a major attraction. The birdlife is prolific and varied: the lakes are home to many waterbirds, including Australian pelicans, egrets and cormorants; a large variety of honeyeaters are found in the heaths; and whistling kites and white-bellied sea-eagles soar above the beaches. The coastal rainforest of Mungo Brush shelters grey-headed flying-foxes, rainforest birds and lace monitors. Koalas are common in the swamp mahogany and paperbark forest. Dingoes and echidnas are regularly seen; gliders and bandicoots less easily observed.

MYALL Lakes is a vast system of coastal lakes behind a 40km stretch of dunes and beach. Waterbirds are prolific on the lakes, especially around Bombah Point. **Australian pelicans** gather on Bombah Broadwater at the edge of the Mungo Brush camping ground. **Black swans** are also common, reaching their highest numbers when it is dry inland. **Black-necked storks** regularly turn up – about as far south as they ever venture.

From the high dunes, pods of **bottlenose dolphins** can be watched as they surf the inshore waves. There are plenty of them, but the best time to look is around noon, when they tend to come very close to the beach. They can also often be seen at night from the Singing Bridge between Hawks Nest and Tea Gardens, swimming with the change of tide in the mouth of the Myall River.

A few **Australian fur-seals** occasionally rest offshore on Seal Rocks off Sugarloaf Point. **Humpback whales** are also sometimes seen from the point between June and August as they migrate north. Seal Rocks is also a good spot to go scuba diving and **grey nurse sharks** are commonly seen in the underwater caves beneath Sugarloaf Point, especially from May to November. For snorkelling, visit Little Gibber, Jimmys Beach (especially at the western point around Barnes Rock) or the lower Myall River.

Whistling kites and **white-bellied sea-eagles** soar above the vegetated dunes along the coastline. Sheltered behind the dunes are diverse heathlands, rife with honeyeaters: **New Holland honeyeaters**, **white-cheeked honeyeaters**, **little wattlebirds** and

Heathland honeyeaters

The area between the dunes and the lakes is rich in nectar-producing plants from the pea, heath and Proteaceae families. Honeyeaters feed here in tremendous numbers, and 17 species have been recorded in the park. Red wattlebirds are the largest, and loudly and aggressively defend nectar sources from other species. Red wattlebirds, blue-faced honeyeaters, Lewin's honeyeaters, noisy miners, eastern spinebills (inset) and white-eared honeyeaters live and breed in the heathlands all year. Others, such as white-cheeked and New Holland honeyeaters, follow the flowering of heathlands and visit in spring.

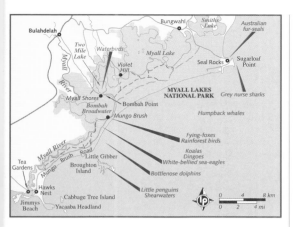

Location 240km north of Sydney.
Facilities Mungo Brush rainforest walk; Hawks Nest Koala Reserve.
Accommodation Many camping grounds and caravan park; wide range in surrounding towns.
Wildlife rhythms Spring–summer for seabirds, waders, and heathland and rainforest birds; winter for humpback whales and grey nurse sharks.
Contact Ranger, Raymond Terrace (☎ 02-4987 3108).
Ecotours Numerous cruises on the river, lakes and ocean (including dolphin-watching); numerous dive operators.

eastern spinebills are just a few of the species that drink nectar from the heaths and banksias.

Offshore are several islands, including Broughton and Cabbage Tree Islands, spring-summer nesting grounds for hundreds of **wedge-tailed** and **short-tailed shearwaters** (and a few **sooty shearwaters**). **Little penguins** also nest on Broughton and the rare **Gould's petrel** nests on Cabbage Tree (its only known nesting site). Access is restricted to the islands, but some good seabird-watching can be had from various ocean outlooks, especially Yaccaba Headland. Besides the shearwaters, penguins and petrels, **terns** and **Australasian gannets** are common. Waders also visit in summer. The tidal flats and wetlands around the mouth of the Myall River host large flocks of **eastern curlews**, **bar-tailed godwits**, **red-necked stints** and several other waders.

Coastal rainforest

A stroll along the 1.5km loop through the rare coastal rainforest of Mungo Brush reveals **wonga pigeons**, black-and-gold **regent bowerbirds** and plenty of smaller bush birds. **Lewin's honeyeaters** and **eastern whipbirds** call constantly, skinks rustle in the leaf litter and **lace monitors** are commonly encountered. **Grey-headed flying-foxes** sometimes make camp in the rainforest; if they're not present, you'll still be able to smell their musky odour.

On the outer edges of the rainforest along the Mungo Brush Rd, swamp mahogany forest supports a healthy population of **koalas**. Koalas can also be seen in the koala reserve in Hawks Nest. **Dingoes** are sometimes seen during the day resting among vegetation on the leeward side of dunes near Mungo Brush.

Other animals to look for are **eastern grey kangaroos** in open areas near eucalypt woodland, **swamp wallabies** in the wetter areas, and flocks of **yellow-tailed black-cockatoos** over the heaths and woodlands. At night, **common brushtail possums** are abundant and it's possible to find **common ringtail possums**, three species of **glider** and three of **bandicoot** – the rainforest and adjacent woodlands are good places to search. ∎

Shorebirds such as oystercatchers probe the tideline while ospreys and sea-eagles patrol overhead.

> **Watching tips**
> The sea-eagles nest in large trees along the banks of the Myall River. A great way to see wildlife on the lakes is to hire a canoe or houseboat. Dolphins calve on the southern side of the Yacaaba Headland, near Jimmys Beach. If you have no luck with bandicoots in the national park, try the golf course in Hawks Nest.

ROYAL NATIONAL PARK

Sydney's sandstone refuge

> **Wildlife highlights**
> Around one-quarter of all Australia's bird species have been recorded here, including superb lyrebirds (almost guaranteed), catbirds, satin bowerbirds, powerful owls and fruit-doves in the rainforest; honeyeaters, wrens and finches in the heathlands; and shorebirds and waterbirds in the waterways. Both mountain and common brushtail possums, common ringtail possums, echidnas, swamp wallabies, koalas, antechinuses and lace monitors are all common in eucalypt forest and woodland. White-bellied sea-eagles, seabirds and humpback whales can be spotted from cliff tops. One of relatively few reliable locations for the rockwarbler.

SWEEPING south from the tidal mudflats of Port Hacking, the second oldest national park in the world has beaches, heathlands, rainforest and 300m-high coastal cliffs. Royal is dominated by a heath-covered sandstone plateau, but the slopes and ridges are topped with dry eucalypt forest, and the gullies and creeks are lined by wet forest and subtropical rainforest. Even with Australia's largest city sprawling right up to the park, the abundance and diversity of wildlife is remarkable.

Gullies, gliders and glow-worms

The easiest place to see rainforest wildlife is along the Forest Path from the Bola Creek picnic area. **Green catbirds** and **satin bowerbirds** are common, while eucalypts on the hillsides feature **eastern whipbirds** and **golden whistlers**. Flocks of **topknot pigeons** sometimes pass overhead and in the late afternoon listen for **brown antechinuses** rustling alongside the track.

Lady Carrington Drive is one of the best places in the state to see **superb lyrebirds**. They often cross this track and forage in the open, and you could see up to a dozen in a morning. During winter they sometimes display close to the track, affording good

Fire and biodiversity

In January 1994 bushfires swept through more than 90% of Royal NP. Studies into their effect on biodiversity have shown that because the park has no connections to nearby bushland there has been no recolonisation by animals completely dependent on forested habitat, such as koalas and greater gliders. Smaller animals were also affected, but perhaps the severity of the effects was lessened as they are able to escape by sheltering underground or beneath rocks, and because they need only small areas of habitat in which to survive..In any case, small mammals are bouncing back. From 1996 to 1998 the numbers of native rats, antechinuses, dunnarts and pygmy-possums increased dramatically and some animal species – such as the endangered New Holland mouse (inset) – have actually benefited from the fire.

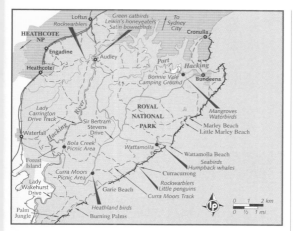

Location 30km south of Sydney.

Facilities Audley visitor centre.

Accommodation Full range in Sydney; camping ground and bush camping.

Wildlife rhythms Honeyeaters August–October; superb lyrebirds display during winter; humpback whales migrate north May–July.

Contact Ranger, Audley (☎ 02-9542 0648).

Ecotours Ranger-guided tours and activities (☎ 02-9542 0649). Keane Bush Tours (☎ 02-9545 4955).

views if approached quietly. By spotlighting through tall, wet forest along Lady Carrington, Sir Bertram Stevens and Lady Wakehurst Drives, you should see **mountain** and **common brushtail possums**. There's also a good chance at **swamp wallabies, sugar gliders, tawny frogmouths, powerful owls** and **southern boobook; sooty owls** and **Australian owlet-nightjars** are more rarely encountered. **Greater gliders** once had a stronghold here, but haven't been seen since bushfires in 1994; it wouldn't hurt to keep an eye out just in case. While out at night, look for **glow-worms** in the trackside embankments.

Audley picnic area offers an introduction to birds of moister areas: **Lewin's honeyeaters, satin bowerbirds** and **green catbirds** are common; **azure kingfishers** and **waterbirds** frequent the river; and **sulphur-crested cockatoos** regularly fly through.

The origma enigma

The Curra Moors track and the track from Engadine to Audley give good access to the sandstone heaths. The most conspicuous wildlife here are the nectarivorous **little wattlebirds, New Holland honeyeaters** and **yellow-faced honeyeaters**. **Eastern pygmy-possums** are occasionally spotlit feeding on flowering banksias in unburnt areas of heath near Heathcote. Between Engadine and Audley, there is a good chance of seeing the **rockwarbler** (or origma), a sandstone specialist and NSW's only endemic bird – it wags its tail sideways as it hops across the sandstone faces.

Echidnas are common in drier areas and may be seen in any of the heaths, as well as grasslands and woodlands. **Lace monitors** are also relatively common in wooded areas.

Little penguins are sometimes sighted in the water below the cliffs at Curracurrong; the cliff tops are also good for **rockwarblers**. The cliffs over Wattamolla and Garie Beaches are great places to watch for **seabirds, white-bellied sea-eagles** and migrating **humpback whales**. Port Hacking's mudflats and mangroves are rich in **waterbirds** and **waders**. ∎

WARRUMBUNGLE NATIONAL PARK

Kangaroos and crooked mountains

Wildlife highlights

Birds are a prominent feature of the park, with a high number of parrot and cockatoo species, and raptors such as wedge-tailed eagles and peregrine falcons. Koalas and common ringtail possums are occasionally seen, while common brushtail possums are abundant. Echidnas, eastern grey kangaroos, euros and red-necked wallabies are common while swamp wallabies are less frequently encountered. A small number of brush-tailed rock-wallabies inhabit remote, rocky areas. The park also has a diverse reptile fauna.

THERE are not many places where you can find rainforest plants a stone's throw from the Outback, but this park is one of them. Similarly, wildlife from inland and coastal regions converges here. Yet not only is the wildlife of the Warrumbungle Range an unusual and diverse mix, it is extremely abundant; and although this is terrific bushwalking country, much of the wildlife can be seen without moving far.

The mobs

Wildlife encounters start on the road in. **Eastern grey kangaroos**, **euros** and **red-necked wallabies** feed in the open alongside Wambelong Creek and around the visitor centre; Camp Blackman is the best place to see eastern greys. The park's other macropods are **swamp wallabies**, which stay close to thickly vegetated areas; and small, isolated groups of **brush-tailed rock-wallabies** in the rocky ranges (although the chances of seeing them are low). **Echidnas** are common throughout the park. By night at Camp Blackman and other camping grounds

The east-west divide

The diversity of flora and fauna found in the Warrumbungle Range today is a result of interactions between geology and climate change. The range was formed by the Warrumbungle Volcano about 17 million years ago. A gradual change after the last ice age to hotter and drier conditions forced the then prevalent rainforest to retreat towards the wetter eastern seaboard, leaving remnant pockets of moist vegetation among the slopes and along the waterways of the eastern side of the range. Today's distribution of fauna in the range echoes these vegetation patterns. Parrots demonstrate the east-west divide as well as any animal group: the western plains and foothills are home to galahs (inset), red-winged parrots, Australian (mallee) ringnecks, cockatiels, budgerigars and blue bonnets; the moist eastern forests harbour crimson and eastern rosellas, rainbow lorikeets, sulphur-crested cockatoos and, along the waterways, turquoise parrots.

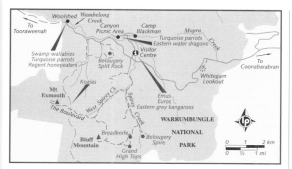

common brushtail possums search their territories for food; **common ringtail possums** are present in smaller numbers.

The Wambelong nature walk from the Canyon picnic area takes no more than 30 minutes, but is likely to turn up plenty as it winds through tall river she-oaks and follows Wambelong Creek – one of the few permanent water sources. **Grey kangaroos** and **swamp wallabies** drink from the creek; and **eastern water dragons** are common on its banks, but drop into the water when approached. The highlight of the walk though are the **koalas** – keep an eye out for them asleep in the river red gums along the creek. Other good places to look for koalas are along Spirey and West Spirey Creeks, and 'the Boulevard' on the Burbie Track – scratch marks in bark and fresh, cigar-shaped droppings at the base of trees are telltale signs of their presence.

The flocks
The park is well known as a top birdwatching spot. **Emus** are easily seen from the main road and **pied currawongs** flock around the visitor centre. When the large ironbark eucalypts flower at Camp Blackman, great numbers of **little lorikeets**, **noisy friarbirds** and a dozen or more other honeyeaters arrive to feed – the noise is constant and tremendous. Keep an eye out in the riot for the rare **regent honeyeater**. Birdwatching is excellent along the banks of Mopra and Burbie Creeks, with **red-rumped parrots**, **galahs** and many small bush birds, including honeyeaters, readily seen. Watch for **willie wagtails** and **restless flycatchers** – both black-and-white – hawking insects stirred up by the kangaroos. On the walk around the Woolshed, **regent honeyeaters** and **turquoise parrots** are sometimes seen (another good area for turqs is the Wambelong nature walk).

Raptors are easily spotted along mountain walks such as those to the Grand High Tops, Bluff Mountain and Mt Exmouth. The summit of Bluff Mountain is a good place to look for **wedge-tailed eagles**. **Peregrine falcons** are also occasionally seen; they nest in recesses along the face of Belougery Split Rock. At night you should see, or at least hear, **southern boobooks**, and usually also **tawny frogmouths**. To see inland birds such as **apostlebirds**, **blue bonnets**, **Australian ringnecks** and **cockatiels**, head west of the park on Tooraweenah Rd. ■

Location 490km north-west of Sydney.

Facilities Visitor centre; wheelchair access to Whitegum Lookout and Gurianawa Track near the visitor centre.

Accommodation Camping; full range at Coonabarabran.

Wildlife rhythms Wildlife is easiest to see in spring and autumn.

Contact NPWS ranger/visitor centre (☎ 02-6825 4364).

Ecotours Coona Country Tours (☎ 02-6842 8245). Bunyip Bush Safaris (☎ 02-6255 1472) runs a four-day tour with a base camp.

Watching tips
Lace monitors are easily seen in camping grounds; in drier areas, the common monitor is Gould's goanna. While walking among stands of smooth-barked scribbly gums, look for the brown, zigzag scribbles on their trunks – tunnels made by moth larvae. Behind the visitor centre is a natural rock birdbath that attracts many birds, especially in dry weather. Stubble quail can be seen in the patch of long grass along the walk around the Woolshed.

BLUE MOUNTAINS NATIONAL PARK

Echoes and imitators

Wildlife highlights

One of the best sites anywhere for superb lyrebirds. Laughing kookaburras, pied currawongs, satin bowerbirds and sulphur-crested cockatoos are also common. In spring, heathland wildflowers attract honeyeaters. Mammals include possums, gliders, wallabies, wombats, and platypuses in the creeks.

Location 60km west of Sydney.
Facilities Several tracks and lookouts have disabled access.
Accommodation Bush camping and camping grounds; full range in nearby towns.
Wildlife rhythms Spring for heathland birds; winter for displaying lyrebirds.
Contact NPWS Blue Mountains Heritage Centre (☎ 02-4787 8877), Glenbrook visitor centre (☎ 02-4739 2950).
Ecotours NPWS (☎ 02-4787 8877).

FAMOUS for its spectacular sandstone cliffs and gorges, Blue Mountains is the most visited park in NSW. Nonetheless, the park, together with the more remote Wollemi and Kanangra-Boyd NPs, is part of a massive complex with plenty of wildlife.

Superb lyrebirds are common throughout wet forest areas, including Leura Forest, Dardanelles Pass at Leura, and the rainforest on the track to the Ruined Castle. The walk to the Grand Canyon and Evans Lookout, Den Fenella and the Valley of the Waters nature track (both near Wentworth Falls) are all good for a variety of birds, including **satin bowerbirds**, **eastern whipbirds**, **laughing kookaburras** and **wonga pigeons**. At Echo Point visitor centre, beside the Three Sisters (the park's most famous landmark), **Australian king-parrots**, **crimson rosellas** and **gang-gang cockatoos** flock to bird feeders.

During spring and summer, **yellow-tailed black-cockatoos** are also common in Blue Gum Forest in the Grose Valley. In spring, heathlands flower profusely and attract **eastern spinebills**, **New Holland honeyeaters** and **red wattlebirds**. The **rockwarbler** (the only bird restricted to NSW) inhabits the rocky outcrops of the park and of the nearby Jenolan Caves, where the Grand Arch and the track that passes Blue Lake are good spots to search.

Marsupials among the gum trees

Eastern grey kangaroos can be seen at Euroka camping ground near Glenbrook. In the late afternoon you may see **swamp wallabies** or **antechinuses** by the edge of tracks just about anywhere. At night, **common wombats**, **greater gliders**, **common ringtail possums** and **common brushtail possums** are active through the park's eucalypt forests.

Kanangra-Boyd NP is less visited and largely a wilderness rich in birds and reptile life, yet it is still readily accessible from Mount Victoria. Along the road from the famous Jenolan Caves to the Kanangra Walls is a good place to see **wombats** and **swamp wallabies**, especially at dusk; the road passes the Boyd River camping ground, where **kangaroos**, **possums** and **gliders** can also be seen. ∎

Watching tips

In rainforest such as at Dantes Glen (near Lawson, 6km east of Wentworth Falls) birdwatching is difficult; rather than walking, sit and see what shows itself. The Blue Mountains swampskink occurs in swampy heath and areas of tussock grass on the plateau around Leura and Wentworth Falls.

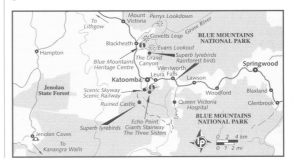

BUNDJALUNG NATIONAL PARK

Rare rainforest and raptors

BEHIND the foredunes of Bundjalung's 38km-long beach between the mouths of the Evans and Clarence Rivers, lies a diverse mosaic of heathland, paperbark swamp, eucalypt forest, mangroves and rainforest. Adjoining Bundjalung, Iluka NR protects NSW's largest and most diverse coastal rainforest.

One of the main wildlife hotspots is around Woody Head, where flowering eucalypts attract **blue-faced honeyeaters** and flocks of **rainbow lorikeets**; **white-bellied sea-eagles** hunt fish along the coastline; **crested terns** and **silver gulls** gather on the beach; and **black-necked storks** feed and breed in the wetlands behind the sand dunes at Shark Bay.

Close by, Iluka NR shelters bird species more often found in Queensland, such as the **barred cuckoo-shrike**, **white-eared monarch** and **varied triller**. When fig trees bear fruit in summer, **olive-backed orioles**, **figbirds** and **regent bowerbirds** are easily seen. Other rainforest birds found here include **noisy pittas** and several species of pigeon and dove. **Eastern whipbirds** and the rapid-fire call of **Lewin's honeyeater** are commonly heard along the rainforest walk. A colony of **koalas** lives in eucalypts near Bundjalung's border with Iluka.

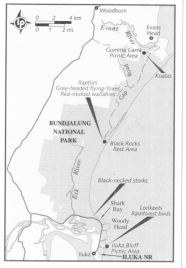

Map: Woodburn, Evans River, Evans Head, Gumma Garra Picnic Area, Koalas, Raptors / Grey-headed flying-foxes / Red-necked wallabies, Gap Rd, BUNDJALUNG NATIONAL PARK, Black Rocks Rest Area, Esk River, Black-necked storks, Shark Bay, Lorikeets / Rainforest birds, Woody Head, Iluka Bluff Picnic Area, Iluka, ILUKA NR. Scale 0–4 km / 0–2 mi

Raptors on patrol

Further north, the Black Rocks rest area blazes with **honeyeaters** in the banksia heathland. It is also one of the best places in the park for raptors, with a continual stream of **ospreys**, **brahminy kites**, **whistling kites** and **white-bellied sea-eagles** scouting the shore.

Red-necked wallabies visit Black Rock's grassy camping ground at dawn and dusk; **grey-headed flying-foxes** arrive at night to feed on banksia and paperbark flowers; and the usually cryptic **brush-tailed phascogale** has also been seen here.

Australian pelicans are frequently seen on the Evans River, while **pied** and **sooty oystercatchers**, **red-capped plovers** and occasionally **little terns**, feed and nest along the beach. The forest near Gumma Garra supports another **koala** colony. ∎

Wildlife highlights
Prolific birdlife, with many coastal raptors, waders and honeyeaters. Eastern grey kangaroos, red-necked wallabies and swamp wallabies are the common macropods. Grey-headed flying-foxes are common and koalas are often seen in forested areas.

Location 55km south of Ballina.
Facilities A rainforest walking track.
Accommodation Several camping grounds and a caravan park; wide range in nearby towns.
Wildlife rhythms Spring and summer for honeyeaters and lorikeets.
Contact Ranger, Lismore (☎ 02-6628 1177).
Ecotours Check with state- and national-based operators.

Watching tips
Watch for eastern grey kangaroos, ibises and egrets in the fields along Gap Rd, before entering the park. The diving around Iluka Bluff is excellent. The caravan park at Woody Head is a good spot for rainforest birds when the fig trees fruit in summer.

DORRIGO NATIONAL PARK

A walk across the sky

Wildlife highlights

Some of the most scenic rainforests in the country. Birds are the most conspicuous wildlife. Common in the subtropical rainforests are fruit-eating pigeons, superb lyrebirds, Australian brush-turkeys, logrunners, eastern whipbirds and noisy pittas. Other wildlife includes pademelons, wallabies, pythons and lace monitors.

Location 60km west of Coffs Harbour.
Facilities Dorrigo Rainforest Centre; tree-top Skywalk; some walks wheelchair accessible.
Accommodation Camping; wide range at Dorrigo and Bellingen.
Wildlife rhythms Summer for fruit-feeding birds and flowering flame trees.
Contact NPWS Dorrigo Rainforest Centre (☎ 02-6657 2309).
Ecotours NPWS guided tours and discovery program include rainforest walks and spotlighting.

Watching tips

Just after dark watch for tawny frogmouths on prominent perches above the road to the Never Never picnic area. The land mullet, one of the world's largest skinks, often basks in sunny spots on the Satinbird Stroll and other tracks; the arboreal southern angle-headed dragon is more difficult to spot on woody perches.

RAINFOREST dominates this World Heritage Area 900m above sea level, and rainforest birds dominate the fauna. Around The Glade and Never Never picnic areas **Australian brush-turkeys**, **king-parrots**, **pied currawongs** and **crimson rosellas** are conspicuous. The Wonga Walk is one of the best for exploring the subtropical rainforest around The Glade, while the Rosewood Creek track from Never Never passes through warm-temperate rainforest.

Spectacular birds that you are likely to see in the rainforest – and almost certainly hear – include **superb lyrebirds**, both **satin** and **regent bowerbirds**, **paradise riflebirds** and **noisy pittas**. Less flashy but equally audible species include the **logrunner**, **eastern whipbird** and **green catbird** – the calls of the latter two are unmistakable.

Many of the birds of the rainforest can be difficult to see, because they mostly remain high in the canopy, but the Skywalk – a boardwalk through the forest canopy – puts those

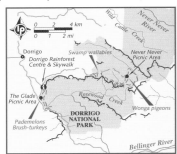

with a head for heights on their level. Rainforest pigeons and doves are a feature and some spend a lot of time in the tree tops: expect to see at least some of **wompoo** and **rose-crowned fruit-doves**, **white-headed** and **topknot pigeons**, **emerald doves** and **brown cuckoo-doves**. **Wonga pigeons** are also common, but are most likely near forest edges. Flocks of topknots arrive in winter, but the diversity and numbers of pigeons and doves is greatest in summer, when most trees fruit, and in the subtropical rainforest, which has more fruiting trees.

Red-neck wonderland

In the late afternoon, **red-necked pademelons** feed along the forest fringes around the picnic areas, and **swamp wallabies** are often seen along the road to Never Never. Watch for **platypuses** in Rosewood Creek around dusk.

After dark, **common brushtail** and **ringtail possums**, and **sugar** and **greater gliders** are active in the eucalypt forests – try the Cedar Falls and Blackbutt tracks from Never Never – and rainforest fruits lure **grey-headed flying-foxes**. Common smaller mammals include **fawn-footed melomys** – an actively climbing rainforest rodent – **bush rats**, **brown antechinuses**, **northern brown** and **long-nosed bandicoots**, and **long-nosed potoroos**; a torch may reveal some of these as the cause of the numerous rustlings you'll hear in the forests at night. ■

MUTAWINTJI NATIONAL PARK

Red roos and rock pools

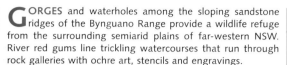

GORGES and waterholes among the sloping sandstone ridges of the Bynguano Range provide a wildlife refuge from the surrounding semiarid plains of far-western NSW. River red gums line trickling watercourses that run through rock galleries with ochre art, stencils and engravings.

The most conspicuous mammals are macropods: **red kangaroos** (white fur on their chest and underparts) and **western grey kangaroos** (darker with doglike muzzles) dot the plains throughout the park. During the day, they rest beneath mulga shrubs and eucalypts, moving out to graze at dawn and dusk – look for their footprints in the red, stony earth. Another large kangaroo, the **euro**, is found in rockier areas such as Mutawintji Gorge. A small colony of endangered **yellow-footed rock-wallabies** also inhabits the escarpments: the only surviving colony in NSW, they number fewer than 100 individuals.

Splendid birdwatching

There is a good Outback birdwatching to be had. **Emus** are common and obvious, feeding in grassy and shrubby areas. River red gums at Homestead Creek camping ground shelter **galahs** and **Major Mitchell's cockatoos**. On the plains among the mulga scrub and woodlands (the area across the creek behind the camping ground is a good starting point) **mulga parrots** and the mallee form of the **Australian ringneck** dart in bright, green flocks; families of dumpy, grey **apostlebirds** hop and glide across the ground; stunning, brilliant-metallic-blue male **splendid fairy-wrens** dazzle; and **chirruping wedgebills** sing incessantly from the tops of bushes.

Along Old Mutawintji Gorge walk, **white-browed babblers** – also in family groups – prise insects from beneath bark and logs, while **red-capped robins** flit between the ground and deadwood.

Keep an eye out for raptors in Mutawintji Gorge and the gorges along the Homestead Creek. **Wedge-tailed eagles** are the commonest and occasionally fly low through the ravines. **Nankeen kestrels**, and sometimes **peregrine falcons**, nest in crevices of the red rock walls. ■

Wildlife highlights

Red kangaroos, western grey kangaroos, euros and emus are easily seen. The only colony of yellow-footed rock-wallabies in NSW inhabits the area. Echidnas are common, as are reptiles and arid-zone birds.

Location 130km north-east of Broken Hill.
Facilities Visitor centre; Thaak-altjika Mingkana walk is wheelchair accessible.
Accommodation Basic camping ground at Homestead Creek.
Wildlife rhythms Very little wildlife can be seen during the scorching summer; come in spring or autumn.
Contact Ranger, Broken Hill (☎ 08-8088 5933).
Ecotours Ranger-guided nature walks and other activities. Twice-weekly Mutawintji Aboriginal rock-art tour (April to November).

Watching tips

Sit quietly by one of the many rock pools and wait to see what shows up. Central bearded dragons and Gould's goannas often roam about the camping ground by the Homestead Creek.

OTHER SITES — NSW AND ACT

Barrington Tops National Park

World Heritage rainforests and alpine woodlands provide a refuge for many rare animals. Swamp wallabies, red-necked pademelons and fawn-footed melomys live in the rainforest; and superb lyrebirds, yellow-tailed black-cockatoos, greater gliders, eastern grey kangaroos, mountain brushtail possums and koalas are common in the eucalypt forest. Common wombats and broad-toothed rats occur in alpine woodlands, and streams support platypuses and eastern water dragons.
320km north of Sydney,
☎ *02-4987 3108*

Ben Boyd National Park

This stretch of coastal heath and woodland was once a base for whaling operations. Southern right whales are now returning

and are often seen offshore, as are humpback and killer whales. Superb lyrebirds display around camping grounds at Bittangabee Bay. Little terns and pied oyster-catchers nest on beaches and seabirds can be seen from shore. Other features are yellow-tailed black-cockatoos, eastern grey kangaroos, common wombats, red-necked and swamp walla-bies, common ringtail possums, sugar gliders and lace monitors.
35km south and 8km north of Eden, ☎ *02-6495 4130*

Boonoo Boonoo National Park

Brush-tailed rock-wallabies bask among granite boulders at The Falls camping ground; possums

and gliders inhabit forest near The Falls. Whiptail wallabies, eastern grey kangaroos, euros, red-necked wallabies and swamp wallabies can all be seen, and yellow-tailed black-cockatoos, rosellas and robins are common. Look for the rare glossy black-cockatoo in she-oak stands.
22km north of Tenterfield,
☎ *02-6732 5133*

Border Ranges National Park

This diverse area includes World Heritage subtropical rainforest with an extremely high diversity of birds, frogs, mammals and butterflies. Rainforest birds in-clude as the logrunner, Aus-tralian brush-turkey, Albert's lyrebird, rufous scrub-bird and various fruit-doves. Red-necked pademelons and bandicoots forage along forest edges, and mountain brushtail possums and koalas live in eucalypt forest.
140km south-west of Brisbane,
☎ *02-6628 1177*

Guy Fawkes River National Park

A rugged wilderness of gorges, woodland, forest and gullies with dry rainforest. Several rare and endangered species occur here, including glossy black-cockatoos, brush-tailed rock-wallabies and

parma wallabies. Dry rainforest shelters pademelons, potoroos, and birds such as the Australian brush-turkey, wonga pigeon and superb lyrebird. Squirrel gliders and masked owls inhabit forest areas. Euros and whiptail walla-bies range the hillsides, while eastern grey kangaroos graze

grassy flats by the Guy Fawkes and Henry Rivers. Platypuses, catfish, turtles and eels are found in these rivers.
100km north-east of Armidale,
☎ *02-6657 2309*

Jervis Bay National Park

A number of endangered and vulnerable species are protected along this undisturbed coastline, including the little tern, hooded

plover, broad-headed snake, ground parrot, white-footed dunnart and eastern bristlebird. Eastern grey kangaroos, red-necked wallabies and swamp wallabies are common, as are grey-headed flying-foxes, ech-idnas and various honeyeaters. Powerful owls occur around Green Point and Bristol Point camping grounds. The Telegraph Creek nature walk is good for woodland and heathland birds; and waterbirds congregate at Ryans Swamp. The bay has a resident pod of bottlenose dol-phins, and cuttlefish and Port Jackson sharks visit in winter. Green Patch Beach is good for snorkelling, and there are sponge gardens and underwater caves in the bay for scuba divers to explore. Humpback whales pass through in early winter and little penguins are often seen. Watch for white-bellied sea-eagles and seabirds from the lighthouse.
180km south of Sydney,
☎ *02-4423 9800*

Lord Howe Island

The lagoon of this World Heri-tage island 700km off the east coast shelters the world's southernmost coral reef, and two mountains on the southern rim of an extinct shield volcano have developed cloud-forest. This is an almost pristine environment, with 105 endemic plant species. Endemic animals include earthworms, a leech, 50 species of spider, many coral fish and the

Lord Howe woodhen. Close encounters with seabirds are a feature: sooty terns, Kermadec petrels, red-tailed tropicbirds, wedge-tailed shearwaters and many others breed here (including the providence petrel – Lord Howe is its only known breeding ground). Only 400 visitors are allowed on the island at a time.
700km north-east of Sydney,
☎ *02-6563 2066*

Mimosa Rocks National Park

This coastal park features the giant, volcanic Mimosa Rocks. There are headlands from which seabirds can be watched, rock pools to explore, beaches where pied oystercatchers and hooded plovers nest, and lagoons lined with mangroves and paperbarks. This is also a good spot for snorkelling and scuba diving. In the rainforest, sooty owls hunt by night and topknot pigeons feed by day. Honeyeaters and lorikeets visit heaths and flowering eucalypts. Look for swamp wallabies, koalas and lace monitors in forested areas.
22km north-east of Bega,
☎ *02-4476 2888*

Mungo National Park

A semiarid area of saltbush, dunes, mallee and the World Heritage-listed, dry Lake Mungo – where there are fossils of

ancient megafauna and an archaeological record showing

40,000 years of human occupation. Red and western grey kangaroos are common, and bearded dragons and shingleback lizards occur around camping grounds and along roads. There are many snakes and geckoes, plus birds such as emus, Major Mitchell's cockatoos and Hall's babblers.
110km north-east of Mildura,
☎ *02-5023 1278*

Namadgi National Park

This mountainous park covers the northern part of the Australian Alps and almost half the ACT. Eastern grey kangaroos, red-necked wallabies and common wombats graze clearings. Sphagnum bogs support the endangered corroboree frog; superb lyrebirds display in winter; and Bogong moths aestivate at Mt Kelly in summer. Wedge-tailed eagles and nankeen kestrels are common over peaks and grasslands. Possums, owls and gliders can be found in forests where diurnal birds include parrots, currawongs, robins and the grey goshawk.
40km south of Canberra,
☎ *02-6237 5222*

Scotia Sanctuary

An electric fence keeps this sanctuary predator-free, and preserves mallee and sand dunes where the rare malleefowl, and other dry-country birds and reptiles, make their home. Natural history, birdwatching, photography and bushwalking tours are available. You can camp, or stay in a homestead or bunkhouse.
216km south of Broken Hill,
☎ *03-5027 1200*

Sturt National Park

This Outback park is a desert of mulga, gibber and sweeping red dunes. Hot summers dry up watercourses and send animals deep into burrows or under shady trees. Red kangaroos are common on the plains; euros inhabit rocky hillsides; and emus roam in large groups. Bearded dragons, shingle-back lizards and Gould's goannas bask on roads. Wedge-tailed eagles soar over the plains, and dingoes and echidnas are occasionally seen. During periods of flooding waterbirds flock in huge numbers. At other times Major Mitchell's cockatoos, budgerigars and cockatiels are common.

330km north of Broken Hill,
☎ *08-8091 3308*

Tidbinbilla Nature Reserve

At Tidbinbilla emus will find you around the picnic areas, and eastern grey kangaroos, superb lyrebirds, satin bowerbirds, rosellas and cockatoos are all common. Spacious enclosures hold koalas, brush-tailed rock-wallabies, wallabies and waterbirds. There's a visitor centre and many walking tracks.
40km south-west of Canberra,
☎ *02-6205 1233*

Tooloom National Park

A walk loops through luxuriant World Heritage subtropical rainforest, where notable species include long-nosed potoroo, red-legged pademelon, black-striped wallaby, Albert's lyrebird, and powerful and masked owls. Much wildlife is difficult to see, but it's worth a visit just to experience the forest.
86km north-west of Kygole,
☎ *02-6628 1177*

NORTHERN TERRITORY

State faunal emblems

Wedge-tailed eagle Australia's largest bird of prey and one of the largest of all eagles is common in the Outback. Excellent hunters, wedgies are nonetheless often seen feeding on roadkills.

Red kangaroo The world's largest living marsupial is abundant in the arid zone. It is capable of speeds of 60km/h, but can't always evade speeding vehicles.

Highlights

- Hundreds of thousands of of waterbirds congregating on Kakadu wetlands
- Easily finding elusive rock-wallabies and grasswrens at Simpsons Gap
- You're no longer top of the food chain – 5m salties on the Mary River wetlands
- Termite mounds towering 6m above the savannah grasslands
- Frilled lizards throughout the Top End erecting their ruff at any provocation
- The howling of dingoes over floodplains at dusk as thousands of flying-foxes stream across the sky
- Desert dunes after rain at Uluru–Kata Tjuta blooming into a sea of desert peas, poached egg daisies, hakeas and grevilleas
- Drifting on your back in a crystal-clear tropical pool at Litchfield while bee-eaters dart overhead and turtles paddle below

MOST of the Northern Territory (NT) lies within the tropics and can be divided into two distinct climatic zones, although the demarcation is indistinct and can vary with flood and drought. The vast arid region features stony and sandy deserts broken by low, rocky ranges and intermittent waterways which drain into large, shallow lakes. Wildlife in this zone is adapted to extremes of heat and cold, and much can survive for long periods without rain. Despite the low rainfall, most of the NT's deserts are well vegetated and after rain bloom with colourful wildflowers.

A variety of reptiles inhabit spinifex-covered sand dunes, while many desert birds – such as honeyeaters, finches and parrots – are nomadic and periodically flourish when food is abundant. Large mammals such as dingoes, red kangaroos and euros are also common. Arid-zone wildlife can be seen in reserves such as Uluru–Kata Tjuta and MacDonnell Ranges NP.

In contrast, heavy rain falls from December to March in the Top End (the north of the state). Here, 'the Wet' is interspersed with a long 'Dry'. The so-called Wet-Dry Tropics support habitats ranging from vast swathes of woodland to dense monsoon rainforest to fertile plains to rocky plateaus. Wildlife is abundant and generally easy to see: it includes crocodiles and concentrations of waterbirds at billabongs during the Dry; several species restricted to sandstone escarpments; and a startling diversity of birds, reptiles and insects in tropical woodlands. Among the excellent system of Wet-Dry reserves are the famous Kakadu and Litchfield NPs, and many smaller reserves close to Darwin.

The NT's Parks and Wildlife Commission (PWC) manages over 90 parks and reserves, not including Kakadu and Uluru–Kata Tjuta NPs, which are managed by the Federal government.

The Territory is at its best overall between June and October, when temperatures in the deserts are lower and wildlife in the north gathers around shrinking waterholes. It is oppressively hot and humid in the Wet-Dry zone during the build-up to the Wet – October and November – but wildlife then is even better, with migratory birds returning; reptiles such as frilled lizards at their most active; and breeding commencing for many animals.

Perhaps the Territory's most famous wild creatures are its saltwater and freshwater crocodiles, which inhabit the coasts and major waterways of the Top End. Large salties must be treated as a potential danger whenever near water in these parts. ■

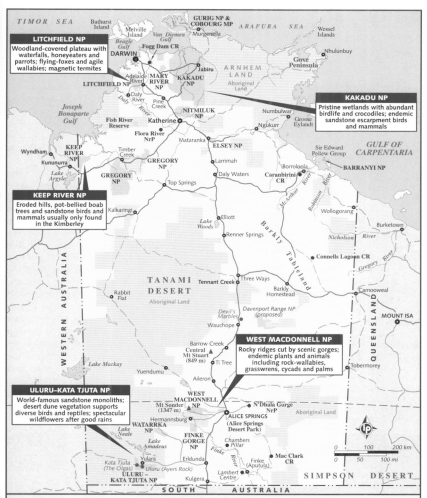

KAKADU NP
Pristine wetlands with abundant birdlife and crocodiles; endemic sandstone escarpment birds and mammals

LITCHFIELD NP
Woodland-covered plateau with waterfalls, honeyeaters and parrots; flying-foxes and agile wallabies; magnetic termites

KEEP RIVER NP
Eroded hills, pot-bellied boab trees and sandstone birds and mammals usually only found in the Kimberley

WEST MACDONNELL NP
Rocky ridges cut by scenic gorges; endemic plants and animals including rock-wallabies, grasswrens, cycads and palms

ULURU–KATA TJUTA NP
World-famous sandstone monoliths; desert dune vegetation supports diverse birds and reptiles; spectacular wildflowers after good rains

Suggested itineraries

One week (North – start/finish Darwin) Visit Fogg Dam en route to Kakadu NP for 3 days to take in Gu-ngarre, Mamukala, Yellow Waters, and Ubirr or Nourlangie. Overnight at Nitmiluk; return via the Territory Wildlife Park.

One week (South – start/finish Alice Springs) Walk around the rocks at Uluru–Kata Tjuta NP (3 days). Visit Watarrka NP (1 day), then Ormiston Gorge and Simpsons Gap in MacDonnell Ranges.

Two weeks (North) As for the one-week tour, but spend 4 days at Kakadu NP and take in Gunlom. Swing west after Nitmiluk to Keep River NP (2 days). On the return, overnight at Litchfield NP and cruise the Reynolds River.

Two weeks (South) Add Trephina Gorge (1 day) to the one-week itinerary and return via Alice Springs Desert Park, then take a 4WD into Finke Gorge and Chambers Pillar.

One month (start Darwin/finish Alice Springs) An easy plan is to follow the two-week circuit for the Top End then fly or drive to Alice and follow the southern two-week itinerary.

Alternatively, add Elsey and Gregory NPs (or plan ahead for permits and take a 4WD or flight to Gurig NP) to make a grand three-week Top End circuit, then fly to Alice Springs and pick the eyes out of the Centre with the one-week trip.

DARWIN

Daily and seasonal rhythms in tropical suburbs

JUST by looking up into the trees that shade Darwin's streets you can tell you're in the tropics: feeding **lorikeets** and **fig-birds** shower blossom onto the pavement, and frangipani and jacaranda blooms drench the air with fragrance. As evening descends **black flying-foxes** crash-land in mango trees and hundreds of finger-sized **geckoes** hunt insects under the lights. In the peace of early morning, **bar-shouldered** and **peaceful doves** poke about for crumbs under footpath tables. Nature is never far away in Australia's largest tropical city.

The *Darwin Botanic Gardens* are easily reached on foot from the city centre. Native trees – including some giant figs – frame grassy parkland, a small creek feeds a rainforest gully, and exotic plantations add an ornamental element. In the early Wet, **frilled lizards** enter their most active season and at night you may see a **common brushtail possum** ambling across open ground. The gardens are a particularly good place to get acquainted with common Top End birds. Watch for flocks of **red-collared lorikeets** – noisy, garish parrots that feed on blossom and fruit. The **pied imperial-pigeon**, a common wet-season migrant to the Top End, is striking in black and white; a few have taken advantage of the gardens' ready food supply and can usually be seen there at any time of year. On the edge of the rainforest gully, **orange-footed scrubfowl** scratch about in the leaf litter, their prominent orange feet in contrast to their sober brown-and-grey plumage. With careful searching the **rufous owl**, Australia's largest (and rarest) tropical owl, can sometimes be seen roosting in shady rainforest trees. Self-guided walks describe the uses to which the Larrakiah people put local plants, and across Gilruth Ave is a mangrove boardwalk that leads to the Museum and Art Gallery of the Northern Territory.

Wading birds can be seen along Darwin's foreshores at low tide; pigeons, figbirds and lorikeets feed in city parks and tree-lined streets; and the mangroves in the background, part of Charles Darwin NP, are home to a specialised suite of birds, reptiles and invertebrates.

Darwin Harbour is a shallow extension of the Timor Sea, with mangrove-fringed fingers which spread right into the suburbs. At low tide the turquoise water races out to expose mudflats which are picked over by armies of colourful **soldier crabs**. Small, goggle-eyed fish called **mudskippers** check that the coast is clear – **eastern reef egrets** are always ready to snap them up – before leaving their burrows to flip about between puddles in search of food. Wading birds such as **eastern curlews** and **whimbrels** probe the mud for small crustaceans before the tide races in again, while chestnut-and-white **brahminy kites** patrol overhead for fish. Authorities pull a **saltwater crocodile** out of Darwin Harbour nearly every week.

Charles Darwin NP protects a large stand of the harbour's mangroves 6km east of the city centre. On any of its walking tracks you may see the scarlet flash of a **red-headed honeyeater**. The braying call of the **chestnut rail** – a hen-sized bird in rich-brown and grey, much sought after by birdwatchers – may be heard here and with patience and luck may be glimpsed as it feeds among the mangrove roots.

North of the city centre is *East Point* recreation reserve. Late in the day **agile wallabies** – lots of them – graze in the open near the tip of the reserve. During the early Wet this area is favoured by migratory waders, especially **little curlews** and **oriental plovers**; they feed in the fields for a few weeks before dispersing across the Top End. Low cliffs with adjoining mud flats and mangroves (through which there is a boardwalk) make an ideal vantage point for birdwatching. The main access road passes through tangled monsoon vine forest, also good for birding.

Holmes Jungle is the best patch of monsoon rainforest in Darwin, and there are also wetlands, woodlands and grassed areas. The large range of habitats makes for a high diversity of birds, including **rainbow pittas** in the rainforest. A better place for **rainbow pittas** is *Howard Springs Nature Park*, 30km east of Darwin; here you'll almost certainly get good views of this normally cryptic and wary species. There are also plenty of **agile wallabies**, freshwater turtles and fish to be seen at Howard Springs, and it is a terrific spot for floating on your back in the pools while watching rainforest birds overhead.

For an introduction to the Top End's wildlife, including a look at lesser-known species, the *Territory Wildlife Park* (☎ 08-8988 7200) at Berry Springs, 58km south of town, is a must. State-of-the-art enclosures and interpretive displays make it easy to spend an absorbing half day here. The choice includes several aviaries, a reptile and invertebrate section, and an aquarium that gets you nose to nose with freshwater fish, turtles and, of course, crocodiles. A display of free-flying birds of prey occurs daily. If you don't have time to look for wild crocodiles you can learn more about these prehistoric survivors – and see some mighty specimens – at *Crocodylus Park* (☎ 08-8947 2510) on the city's outskirts. ■

KAKADU NATIONAL PARK

The Top choice

Wildlife highlights

Agile wallabies and antilopine wallaroos are common in woodlands. Most other mammals are nocturnal, but spotlighting can be productive and could reveal northern quolls, brush-tailed phascogales and bandicoots. Abundant birdlife – more than 280 species – includes tropical finches, parrots and honeyeaters, plus migrant waders and cuckoos in the Wet. Expect to see a dozen or more species of duck and long-legged wading bird at waterholes during the Dry, and tens of thousands of magpie geese in places. Saltwater crocodiles inhabit large waterways; freshwater crocs live in escarpment streams; and frilled lizards, turtles and several types of goanna are among other possible reptilian encounters.

KAKADU is the largest national park in Australia and has the largest range of wildlife in the Territory. The problem is knowing where to start: there is much to see on the river systems and their extensive floodplains, the large tracts of tropical woodlands and the adjoining monsoon rainforest – all bounded by a vast sandstone escarpment up to 200m high. Take as long as you can to enjoy the park: the weather, wildlife, vegetation and landforms are inextricably linked and an understanding of one involves at least some appreciation of the others. The longer you stay the better it gets, and every day is different as a great array of wildlife responds to the changing seasons.

Life on the edge

Looming above the eastern edge of the park is a vast, weathered sandstone plateau scored by deep gorges – the Arnhem Land escarpment – where several species restricted to this habitat live among the spinifex and hardy gum trees. Some of these specialities can be seen at Nourlangie and Ubirr, outliers of this 'stone country'. **Chestnut-quilled rock-pigeons** wander through the Nourlangie car park and **short-eared rock-wallabies** can be seen above the rock-art galleries at Ubirr. But to enjoy

Kakadu under fire

The smoke from grass fires – either deliberately lit or caused by lightning – is a feature of Kakadu during the Dry. The fires pass quickly with little lasting damage to the woodland and many animals profit by the burns. With the first clouds of smoke Australian bustards fly from miles around to pick over the burnt ground. Aerobatic black falcons sweep in to snatch fleeing quail, and black and whistling kites wheel over the leaping flames to pounce on large insects. Black kites have been known to drop a burning twig ahead of a fire, although nobody has proved whether they are trying to start a new blaze or just pick insects off a burning twig in midflight. After the blaze, redtailed black-cockatoos feed on seeds cracked by the heat, goannas scavenge for carrion and agile wallabies feed on new shoots.

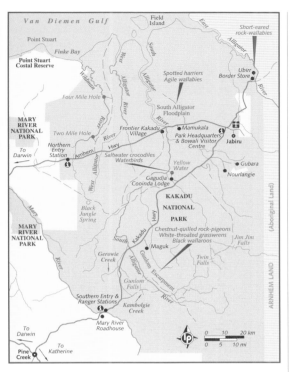

Location 170km east of Darwin (260km to Jabiru).

Facilities Excellent visitor centre (Bowali); Warradjan Aboriginal Cultural Centre; walking trails with interpretation boards; observation hides at Mamukala.

Accommodation Camping at designated sites throughout the park; camping grounds and resorts at Jabiru, Gagudju and the South Alligator River crossing; hostel at Ubirr.

Wildlife rhythms Birds, crocodiles and some mammals concentrate on drying waterholes during the late Dry (September and October); during the Build-up frilled lizards and Leichhardt's grasshoppers emerge and migrant birds arrive.

Contact Bowali visitor centre (☎ 08-8938 1121).

Ecotours Yellow Water Cruises (☎ 08-8979 0111) runs several cruises daily throughout the year – bookings are essential. Gondwana (☎ 1800 242 177) and 4WD Wilderness Adventures (☎ 1800 808 288) have knowledgeable guides.

the wildlife uninterrupted by tourists, you're better off heading further south and climbing the track next to Gunlom Falls to the top of the escarpment. Here **white-lined honeyeaters** feed along the creek and you should have no difficulty seeing rock-pigeons catching the early sun on ledges. This is rugged terrain, but follow the creek and watch for **banded fruit-doves** feeding on sandstone figs – this is one of the best locations for this Arnhem Land endemic. The calls of white-lined honeyeaters and **sandstone shrike-thrushes** echo around the heaped boulders.

Two other prizes here are the **black wallaroo** – the sooty tones of its coat blend into shadowy overhangs – and **white-throated grasswrens**; you'll need an early start to flush the former (the Barrk Sandstone Walk at Nourlangie is also a good place to look) and patience to locate the soft, metallic contact calls of the latter.

Spotlighting in escarpment country (Bardedjilidji Sandstone Walk, by the East Alligator River just below Border Store, is easier terrain for night walking) could yield **rock ringtail possums** and **northern dibblers**: the possums have strong eyeshine, and favour fruiting and flowering trees around large rock crevices and boulders; the dibblers are often seen late in the day, especially on slopes covered with large boulders, eucalypt trees and tall grass.

As the wet season approaches, the nymphs of **Leichhardt's grasshopper** moult into orange-and-blue adulthood. They are

Freshwater crocs live and breed in the pools at the foot of mighty Jim Jim Falls.

Aldjurr, the Lightning Man's children, and at their appearance the brooding sky bursts into violent electrical storms which dump masses of water over the land.

Surface tension

In the Dry, water is the focus of all life and the best way to appreciate it is to take a cruise on the permanent billabongs at Yellow Water. Early morning is best, although any time of day is worthwhile. Silvery shapes in the depths could be **barramundi** or **saratoga**; **spotted archer fish** swim near the surface; and **Arafura filesnakes** sometimes nose along in the shallows. **Azure kingfishers** perch on branches of paperbarks overhanging the water; and the **little kingfisher**, Australia's smallest, perches lower down and is most common at the southern end of Yellow Water. **Darters** sit drying their wings on large branches while another great fish-hunter, the **white-bellied sea-eagle**, watches from tall snags. **Green pygmy-geese** paddle among a waxy carpet of floating lotus lilies – home for **comb-crested jacanas**. Ranks of egrets, herons, **magpie geese** and **brolgas** feed in the adjacent flooded grasslands, where **black-necked storks** hunt in pairs.

Kakadu's wetlands support the world's largest concentration of magpie geese.

Saltwater crocodiles are abundant at Yellow Water and some mighty specimens are usually seen on the cruise; other reptiles include **Gould's goannas** patrolling for carrion, **brown tree snakes** in the foliage of waterside trees and **northern snapping turtles** basking on logs. **Bar-breasted honeyeaters** are a paperbark speciality, **blue-faced honeyeaters** and **little friarbirds** throng in flowering eucalypts, and flocks of **little corellas** wing overhead – watch for the all-white phase of the **grey goshawk** among them.

Walks at other wetlands are definitely worthwhile. You'll see most of the same birds, and probably crocodiles, but won't get quite so close to either, on the floodplain at Mamukala, at Anbangbang Billabong (beside Nourlangie) and on the Bubba or Iligadjarr Walks (both just off the Kakadu Hwy near Nourlangie).

Woodland sights and sounds

The tropical woodlands that cover huge parts of Kakadu ring with the screeches of flocking **varied** and **red-collared lorikeets** and **little** and **helmeted friarbirds** feeding on blossom. **Red-tailed**

Snake charming in Kakadu

As a frog biologist, it was very unusual that I should end up travelling from Townsville to Darwin with an ornithologist to attend a conference on birds. Even more surprising was the interest shown by all attending 'birdos' when I suggested a drive along the South Alligator floodplain in search of frogs and reptiles. After dark, I led a convoy of six or seven vehicles slowly along the main road through Kakadu, frequently stopping and grabbing whatever I could to show the group.

One incident, however, typified my luck when it came to handling harmless snakes in front of nervous novices. A 3m olive python lying on the middle of the road had obviously been injured by a car. With the whole group gathered around, I went to move it off the road. The python did not appreciate my help, and struck. My reflexes were good enough to avoid the snake's first attempt, but not the second. It wrapped its jaws firmly around my hand, drawing blood in a 5cm-long semicircle. I do not know whether the group were impressed with my 'bravery' or just had a good laugh at my expense.

Dr Martin Cohen, herpetologist

black-cockatoos winging slowly through the trees are a common sight; local Aboriginal people say their tails caught fire in the 'sickness country' – the uranium-rich area in the south of the park.

The Gu-ngarre Walk, just near the resort at the South Alligator River crossing, passes through woodland with **agile wallabies**, and a patch of monsoon forest where **orange-footed scrubfowl** and the aptly-named **rainbow pitta** are resident. Check the huge fig trees at the edge of the rainforest for **rose-crowned fruit-doves** and, in season, **koels**, **channel-billed cuckoos** and **pied imperial-pigeons**. Man-ngarre Walk opposite Border Store offers a similar wildlife selection. Another macropod, the **antilopine wallaroo**, can usually be seen where woodlands adjoin floodplains at South Alligator, or grazing on the golf course at Jabiru township.

Spotlighting in woodland is a must to see **northern quolls**, **sugar gliders**, **northern brown bandicoots** and birds such as **bush stone-curlews**, **southern boobooks** and **barking owls** (barking owls are also often seen during the day perched in tree canopies and often also give their *wroof-wroof* call by day); the camping grounds at Merl, Gunlom and Jim Jim–Twin Falls are good places to start looking.

Darwin woollybutts dominate huge areas of woodland; the lower trunk is covered with bark that insulates it against fire; its branches, hollowed by termites, are the basis of the didjeridu. **Frilled lizards** spend the Dry high in the trees, but are commonly seen when they climb down in the early Wet; watch for them all over the woodlands, pretending to be a tree stump or trundling along on their back legs.

The early Wet is a great time to be in the park: courting resident birds are joined by migrant **koels** and giant **channel-billed cuckoos**, calling stridently to attract a mate; and migrant waders, such **little curlew** and **oriental plovers**, fan out across the floodplains. At the peak of the Wet access can be difficult, although the park remains open. ∎

Looking over the floodplains from Ubirr at dusk you'll see a host of waterbirds and hear a chorus that can include dingoes, barking owls, coucals and bush stone-curlews.

Watching tips

Kakadu is a stronghold of several rare or endangered birds including red goshawks (although seeing one is very much a matter of luck), spectacular Gouldian finches (frequently seen in the vicinity of Black Jungle Spring after the breeding season) and hooded parrots – turquoise with a black crown and golden 'shoulders' (regularly sighted between Kambolgie and Gerowie Creeks from the early to late Wet, when they breed in hollows they dig in large termite mounds). Nowhere as numerous as salties, freshwater crocs can sometimes be seen at Maguk and Jim Jim Falls.

KEEP RIVER NATIONAL PARK

Birds and mammals of sandstone country

Wildlife highlights
Excellent range of birds, mammals and plants of the sandstone country. Extreme heat means that the majority of the park's birds are most active at dawn or dusk. Some 50 or so mammals have been recorded, although most are nocturnal. Sandstone outcrops are home to sandstone specialists such as short-eared rock-wallabies, sandstone shrike-thrushes and white-lined honeyeaters. The orange-and-blue Leichhardt's grasshopper, known elsewhere only from the Kakadu escarpment hundreds of kilometres to the east, was recently discovered in the park.

KEEP River's starkly beautiful sandstone ridges, eroded into battlements and weird pinnacles, are among the easiest places to see **short-eared rock-wallabies** and other sandstone specialities such as **white-quilled rock-pigeons** and **white-lined honeyeaters**. The spinifex-covered hills feature abundant birdlife and billabongs support waterbirds, freshwater turtles and crocodiles. In the Dry the heat can be punishing, while in the Wet many of the park's roads are impassable.

The birds line up

Keep River's wildlife is best appreciated by walking the tracks such as those at Keep River Gorge or Jarrnarm. From the observation hide at Cockatoo Lagoon you'll have a good chance of spotting **black-necked storks**, **magpie geese**, **comb-crested jacanas** and other Top End waterbirds, and maybe also the head of a **northern snapping turtle** poking up through the lilies. The

Drunken bottle trees

Related to the baobabs of Africa, boabs are the most distinctive trees in the north-west and many fine examples grow in the park. Their swollen, bottle-like trunks lean drunkenly over the spiky spinifex and can grow to an immense girth – up to 25m. Boabs don't actually hold water, although their pithy flesh has a high moisture content which helps them to survive the long Dry. Boabs are deciduous, dropping their leaves during the rainless months to reduce moisture loss. Then their bare, twisted limbs give a wintry look to the landscape despite the intense heat.

track along the floor of Keep River Gorge passes some of the park's only permanent water and by waiting quietly near the bank you may see an assortment of birds drinking: **rainbow bee-eaters** and **white-breasted woodswallows** scooping up mouthfuls midflight; parties of **little friarbirds** and other honeyeaters lining up on partly submerged branches; and **star** and **double-barred finches** breezing in and out. **Red-backed fairy-wrens** live in the tall cane grass by the river (the male is jet black with a red 'saddle'), **great bowerbirds** forage among the boulders, and **echidnas** dig for ants in open areas.

The Gajerrong and Miriwoong people gathered snapping turtles, waterlilies and yams from Jinumum, the permanent waterhole at the northern end of the gorge, and felt in the mud with their toes for mussels; their middens – piles of discarded shells – can still be seen along the banks. In still pools the green-and-white plumage of **green pygmy-geese** contrasts with a red carpet on the water's surface where freshwater mangroves have dropped their flowers. The blooms last only one night and provide food for the pygmy-geese; the Gajerrong and Miriwoong knew of the mangrove bark's narcotic qualities and used it to stun fish.

A well-preserved rock-art gallery at Nganalam features painted images of *Gurrimalam* the rainbow snake, echidnas, kangaroos, turtles and crocodiles; and fairy martins build their bottle-shaped mud nests under the overhangs. Further north, **saltwater crocodiles** inhabit Policemans Waterhole.

Pipers and yahoos

In the dawn stillness the weathered turrets and crags above Gurrandalng camping ground echo with the clear piping of **pied butcherbirds**. Another melodious singer, the **sandstone shrike-thrush**, seems to compete with the butcherbirds, although its rusty-brown plumage can be difficult to spot among the rocks; both can be seen along the narrow walking track at Gurrandalng. **Grey-crowned babblers** *yahoo* from their look-outs on pot-bellied boabs and parties of **variegated fairy-wrens** fuss among the clumps of a soft, aromatic spinifex that dominates the slopes, hopping up to look as you pass.

There are several species of finch in the park, including the stunning **Gouldian finch** (bright green above with violet breast and yellow belly); you could come across mixed parties of finches just about anywhere, but especially in grassy areas.

Short-eared rock-wallabies bound across boulders and up seemingly pathless cliffs when disturbed. **Euros** also occur in the park: they are twice the size or more of the rock-wallabies and favour slopes and plains rather than cliffs and gorges. The Gurrandalng Trail is also the best place to see a **white-quilled rock-pigeon** take off with a loud clattering that sounds like falling pebbles, its white wing-patches flashing in flight. Like the rock-wallabies, these pigeons shelter under rock overhangs during the heat of the day. ∎

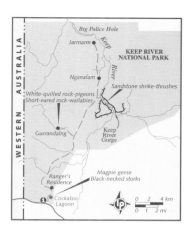

WESTERN AUSTRALIA

KEEP RIVER NATIONAL PARK

Big Police Hole

Jarmarm

Keep River

Nganalam

Sandstone shrike-thrushes

White-quilled rock-pigeons
Short-eared rock-wallabies

Gurrandalng

Keep River Gorge

Magpie geese
Black-necked storks

Ranger's Residence

Cockatoo Lagoon

0   2   4 km
0   1   2 mi

Location 468km to the west of Katherine.
Facilities Walking trails; interpretive signs; information kiosk; observation hide at Cockatoo Lagoon.
Accommodation Two camping grounds in the park; motels at Kununurra, WA.
Wildlife rhythms Birds concentrate on drying waterholes from August to October. Migrant birds arrive during the build-up to the Wet and Leichhardt's grasshoppers emerge early in the Wet.
Contact PWC, Katherine (☎ 08-8973 8888).
Ecotours Check with state- and national-based operators.

Watching tips
Spotted nightjars sit on the park's access roads after sundown and may be seen by driving slowly at night. In the early Wet, Leichhardt's grasshoppers feed on the pungent *Pityrodia* shrubs growing at the base of the escarpment west of Jarrnarm camping ground.

ULURU–KATA TJUTA NATIONAL PARK

Dunes come alive at night

Wildlife highlights
Although largely nocturnal, common desert mammals include red kangaroos, dingoes, and smaller species such as spinifex hopping-mice and desert dunnarts. Some 180 species of bird have been recorded: parrots are well represented by noisy flocks of galahs and Major Mitchell's cockatoos, and resident and nomadic honeyeaters are sometimes abundant. The thorny devil features among the 70-odd reptile species.

LITTLE grows on Uluru – still widely known as Ayers Rock – or the eroded domes of Kata Tjuta (the Olgas) that dominate the surrounding dunescape, but this park is an excellent location to see otherwise inaccessible arid-zone wildlife. **Red kangaroos**, **euros** and **dingoes** can be seen along roads at night (they are less often seen during the day), and many smaller mammal, reptile and bird species are resident in the dunes between Uluru and Kata Tjuta. Plants and animals play an important part in the traditions of the Anangu people, and their knowledge is now being used in park management.

Burrowers, high-fliers and nomads

Rainwater pools at the foot of Uluru attract **painted finches** and parties of twittering, bright-green **budgerigars** (wait at a quiet part of the Circuit Walk). White splashes of guano below favoured roosts are a giveaway when looking for **peregrine falcons** and other birds of prey perched high on the Rock. Among their victims could be the **little woodswallows** or **welcome swallows** that commonly soar in updraughts. **White-backed swallows** and **red-backed kingfishers** dig nest tunnels where the sealed road cuts the dunes east of Yulara. **Crested pigeons**, **galahs**, **Major Mitchell's cockatoos** and **yellow-throated miners** are

Calling birds

In high temperatures small birds quickly lose water. Insect eaters, such as red-backed kingfishers, obtain most of their moisture from their prey, but many species must remain within flying distance of drinking pools. Seed eaters such as finches drink regularly during the day when a permanent source of water is available. Anangu trackers know this and follow zebra finches (inset – they are abundant around Yulara) to pools. The Anangu name for this common finch, *nyii-nyii*, mimics the birds' nasal buzzing, and the names of several other birds important to the Anangu are interpretations of the birds' calls: diamond doves are *kukuku*, Torresian crows are *kaanka* and the musical chimes of crested bellbirds – a distinctive desert sound – are translated as *panpanpalala*.

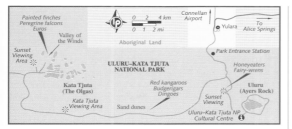

found throughout the park, and at Yulara they are common garden birds. Resident **singing**, **grey-headed** and **spiny-cheeked honeyeaters** – all common in the surrounding dunes – are joined by nomadic **pied** and **black honeyeaters** to feast on nectar-laden desert grevilleas and other shrubs that bloom after heavy rain; good areas in which to look are at the tourist lookouts and near the war memorial at Yulara. It's much harder to pin down insect-eating nomads such as the several species of **chat** and **woodswallow** that pass through in sometimes huge, loose flocks; but if they're about, you'll probably see them. **Western bowerbirds** and their bowers can be found in the woodlands.

After good rainfall, poached-egg daisies – with white petals and pale yellow centre – and dozens of other wildflower species spring up and **water-holding frogs** break out of their burrows to breed (during dry times the Anangu dig them out and squeeze them for a quick drink).

Tracks in the dunes

The dunes are thick with wrens and their Anangu name, *miri-lyirilyi*, imitates their reeling song. Listen for soft contact calls and wait until the birds show themselves – parties of **splendid**, **white-winged** and **variegated fairy-wrens** can all be readily found, and **striated grasswrens** run across the sand like stout mice. The best-known spot for the striated grasswrens is in the spinifex around the Uluru sunset viewing area. The park also has **dusky grasswrens**, a bird of rocky gorges: duskies are more difficult to find, but try the Valley of the Winds.

Spinifex roots stabilise the dunes and make a firm foundation for the burrows of small animals. Many are active only at night and in the morning their tracks tell stories – fine indentations show where scorpions have wandered from their burrows; stalking geckoes leave tiny footprints; and the tails of **spinifex hopping-mice** drag grooves through the sand. The hopping-mice and other small mammals such as **sandhill dunnarts** can usually be spotlit in dunes around Yulara.

The day shift leaves a new record and it's worth following a set of prints: you may catch up with a **thorny devil**, a spiny ochre-and-brick-red harlequin, tucking into a meal of ants; or **crested pigeons** searching for seeds. **Crested bellbirds** chime in stands of desert oaks growing between high dunes; listen here also for **Australian ringnecks** cracking open seed cones among the needle-like leaves. ∎

Location 441km south-west of Alice Springs.
Facilities Information centre situated at Yulara. Aboriginal Cultural Centre interprets wildlife through Anangu eyes.
Accommodation Hotels, hostel and camping ground at Yulara.
Wildlife rhythms Winter rains (unpredictable) promote plant growth and animal breeding, and attract nomadic birds and mammals.
Contact Visitor centre, Yulara (☎ 08-8957 7377).
Ecotours Anangu Tours (☎ 08-8956 2123).

The dunes surrounding Kata Tjuta support many small animals, such as hopping-mice and lizards.

> ### Watching tips
> Reverse the usual routine – visit the sunset viewing areas at dawn and the sunrise viewing areas at dusk and you'll have them virtually to yourself; birds will then emerge from the dune vegetation and nobody will get in the way of your photos. Walk the Valley of the Winds at Kata Tjuta at dawn for a chance of seeing euros.

LITCHFIELD NATIONAL PARK

Magnetic attractions

Wildlife highlights

Dingoes hunt agile wallabies on floodplains studded with the mounds of magnetic and cathedral termites. Excellent birdwatching includes many parrots, cockatoos and honeyeaters. Reynolds River supports both species of crocodile, an assortment of waterbirds, and camps of flying-foxes along its banks. Short-eared rock-wallabies frequent escarpment edges.

Location 115km south of Darwin.
Facilities Boardwalks through rainforest (including flying-fox colony) at Wangi Falls and past termite mounds; excellent interpretation boards.
Accommodation Full range at Batchelor; camping grounds in the park .
Wildlife rhythms Crocodiles and birds congregate at drying waterholes during the late Dry, August–October; migrant birds arrive during the build-up to the Wet.
Contact PWC, Batchelor (☎ 08-8976 0282).
Ecotours Coo-ee Tours (☎ 08-8981 6116). Goanna Eco Tours (☎ 08-8927 3880). Book river cruises at Wangi Falls kiosk.

Watching tips

Spotlighting along roads is likely to turn up nightjars soaking up the roads' heat, and bush stone-curlews.

RISING from almost unbroken tropical woodland, Litchfield's Tabletop Range is an isolated sandstone plateau with stands of monsoon rainforest growing in the folds of its escarpment. Easily accessible from Darwin, the park is a great introduction to tropical woodlands.

Ranks of vertical, 2m-tall slabs like cemetery headstones cover the floodplains near Litchfield's eastern boundary. These concrete-like structures are built by **magnetic termites**, which align their mounds roughly north–south. Nearby, massive buttressed mounds with fluted columns, built by **cathedral termites**, tower 6m high. **Agile wallabies** graze on these floodplains at dusk, ever watchful of **dingoes**; both species can also be seen at dusk anywhere along access roads, and around paperbark-ringed Tabletop Swamp – where egrets, **comb-crested jacanas, black-necked storks, pied herons** and **magpie geese** feed in the lily-covered waters.

To see crocodiles, take a cruise on Reynolds River, where **saltwater** and **freshwater crocs** live side by side. **Agile wallabies** and waterbirds feed on the river's floodplains.

The park's rainforest pockets have good numbers of birds, but it is in the woodlands that birdlife can be most prolific – look for flocks of **red-collared** and **varied lorikeets, red-tailed black-cockatoos** and **honeyeaters**. Birdwatching in both habitats is excellent around Florence Falls.

Tropical fruits

What appear to be fruit swaying in the monsoon forest to the right of the foot of Wangi Falls are actually **black flying-foxes**, squabbling and fanning their wings to keep cool. Here too, **Gould's goannas** and both **black** and **whistling kites** frequent the picnic ground, and **sandstone antechinuses** and **northern quolls** are sometimes seen by spotlighting around the foot of the escarpment.

A deep cavern behind Tolmer Falls is an important breeding site for the **orange leafnosed-bat**, though they are generally only seen as they streak out at dusk – watch for **olive pythons** waiting to ambush the bats by the cave entrance. **Short-eared rock-wallabies** can be seen on the cliffs near Tolmer Falls and elsewhere along the escarpment.

Take a mask and snorkel to look for aquatic life – fish, turtles and crayfish – in the park's crystal-clear pools and streams. ∎

WEST MACDONNELL NATIONAL PARK

Buried fish and clockwork pigeons

THE rugged MacDonnell Ranges form an arid, glowing land-scape of red soils and pink cliffs. Dramatic gorges harbour relict plants and arid-zone animals. To the Arrernte people this area is the Caterpillar Dreaming, and the hills silhouetted against the late afternoon sun look exactly like a line of cater-pillars marching across the landscape.

Ormiston Gorge features some of the park's best wildlife. **Black-footed rock-wallabies** shouldn't be hard to find brows-ing among jumbled boulders (Simpsons Gap is also a good spot), but you'll need to look carefully as their black-slashed ginger-and-brown coats are good camouflage against the cliffs'

fractured planes. **Dingoes** that lurk near the foot of the cliffs may take an adult rock-wallaby attracted to greenery near water. Rare mammals such as the **long-tailed dunnart** are rediscovered in the park from time to time – spotlighting the gorges and tracks could pay dividends. The pads (pathways) of **euros** weave among the spinifex on the hills that flank the various walking tracks, and the animals themselves should be readily seen.

Inland birdlife is abundant. **Spinifex pigeons** – one of Aus-tralia's most striking pigeons – are as approachable as city pigeons and run about the Ormiston Gorge camping ground like clockwork toys. **Major Mitchell's cockatoos**, **Australian ringnecks**, **budgerigars** and other parrots are common, while **western bowerbirds** scout for items to decorate their bowers. Even in the driest times permanent waterholes in the boulder-strewn floor of the gorge support **waterbirds**.

Some of the more sought-after inland birds include **dusky grasswrens**, **painted finches**, **spinifexbirds** and **rufous-crowned emu-wrens**. The grasswrens are almost ridiculously easy (for grasswrens) to find on rocky slopes, especially at Simpsons Gap, and the finches can usually be seen coming to water. The other two species will take a little more work but shouldn't pose a problem for serious birders – the tall spinifex along Ormiston Gorge Pound walk and in Ellery Creek Reserve are good bets. ∎

Wildlife highlights

Euros and black-footed rock-wallabies should be seen, and there's a chance of seeing dingoes and spotlight-ing smaller nocturnal mam-mals. It's one of the best parks for sought-after inland birds such as desert parrots, western bowerbirds, dusky grasswrens, rufous-crowned emu-wrens and spinifexbirds.

Location 3km to the west of Alice Springs.
Facilities Simpsons Gap visitor centre; interpretive signs.
Accommodation Camping areas; full range in Alice Springs.
Wildlife rhythms Winter rainfall promotes breeding of wildlife.
Contact Rangers: Simpsons Gap (☎ 08-8955 0310), Ormiston Gorge (☎ 08-8956 7799).
Ecotours No local wildlife tours, but Alice Springs Desert Park (see Other Sites) is excellent.

Watching tips

Wildlife can be very in-active in the heat of the day, so an early start is almost es-sential. The spangled perch, which can lie buried in mud for many months before rain prompts it to emerge, can be seen in Ormiston Gorge's waterholes. Relict MacDon-nell Ranges cycads survive in moist gorges.

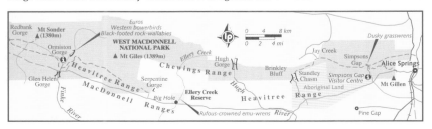

OTHER SITES – NORTHERN TERRITORY

Alice Springs Desert Park
A modern fauna park that makes full use of its setting at the foot of the MacDonnell Ranges to exhibit flora and fauna of the arid zone. Walk-through enclosures show wildlife of the red dune country, gorges and riverine woodlands. It provides excellent opportunities to observe and photograph desert wildlife such as the princess parrot and, in the noctarium, the bilby and greater stick-nest rat. There are daily displays of free-flying birds of prey.
3km west of Alice Springs,
☎ 08-8951 8788

Caranbirini Conservation Reserve
'Lost city' formations – 25m-high sandstone spires – and a semipermanent waterhole that attracts pigeons, finches, ducks and brolgas in the dry months. The reserve also protects the western flank of the Bukalara Range, home to the rare Carpentarian grasswren.
46km south of Borroloola,
☎ 08-8975 8792

Connells Lagoon Conservation Reserve
A flat, isolated reserve in the heart of the Barkly Tableland protecting one of the few remaining areas of undisturbed Mitchell-grass habitat. Grassland birds include Australian bustards, flock bronzewings and pictorella mannikins; and among large mammals red kangaroos and dingoes are common. Long-haired rats form plagues after good rains and feed on abundant grass seeds.
220km north-east of Three Ways, *☎ 08-8975 8792*

Davenport Range
This proposed national park will protect the ancient Davenport and Murchison Ranges – some of the oldest hills on earth – in the transition zone between the

Top End and the Centre. Marks the northern limit of several arid-zone species, such as rufous-crowned emu-wren. Access is by 4WD only.

90km south of Tennant Creek,
☎ 08-8962 4599

Elsey National Park
Elsey's most famous attraction is the Mataranka Hot Springs, popular with travellers and a camp of black flying-foxes alike.

Less-frequented parts of the park protect the pandanus- and paperbark-lined headwaters of the Roper River. Freshwater crocodiles and freshwater fish such as archer fish, barramundi and chequered rainbowfish may be seen from a riverside walking track. A botanical walk explains the Aboriginal uses for various plants, and the solitary great-billed heron sometimes feeds along the river's lower reaches.
100km south-east of Katherine,
☎ 08-8973 8888

Finke Gorge National Park
Sheltered crooks in eroded sandstone ranges cut by the ancient Finke River harbour relict stands of red cabbage palms and Mac-Donnell Range cycads. Good for arid-country birds such as western bowerbirds and the desert

form of the grey fantail. Excellent camping ground but accessible by 4WD only.

138km west of Alice Springs,
☎ 08-8956 7401

Flora River Nature Park
A modest and little-visited park that protects a 25km stretch of the Flora River, its adjacent floodplain and woodland. The river is lined with extensive stands of cabbage palms, paperbarks and river pandanus; fauna includes the pitted-shelled (or pig-nosed) turtle, saltwater crocodiles and a variety of freshwater fishes.
86km west of Katherine,
☎ 08-8973 8888

Fogg Dam Conservation Reserve
One of NT's best birdwatching sites. Once the water supply for a failed rice plantation, it is now

a waterlily-covered bird haven with observation platforms for photography and birdwatching. Large numbers of herons, egrets, magpie geese, ducks, white-browed crakes and comb-crested jacanas are all usually present; agile wallabies feed on grassy margins; and water pythons may

be seen hunting rats in the evening. Adding to the wetland wildlife, there are walking tracks with interpretive signs leading through paperbark woodland, and monsoon forest adjacent to the wetlands – look for rainbow pittas and rose-crowned fruit-doves here.
52km east of Darwin,
☎ *08-8988 8009*

Gregory National Park
The second-largest national park in the Territory yet one of the least visited. The eastern section features glowing sandstone escarpments which run with small cascades after wet-season storms; and cabbage palms lining the foot of cliffs where walking tracks provide stunning views. The much larger western sector stretches south of Timber Creek and most is accessible only by 4WD. Among the 140 bird species recorded are the white-quilled rock-pigeon of rocky escarpments; the reddish-flanked race of the white-browed robin in thick waterside vegetation; and rare Gouldian finches. Both saltwater and freshwater crocodiles inhabit the various gorges and river systems of the park.
165km west of Katherine,
☎ *08-8975 0888*

Gurig National Park and Cobourg Marine Park
Cobourg Peninsula juts into the Arafura Sea from north-western

Arnhem Land, and is protected within Aboriginal-owned Gurig NP and the adjoining marine park. Bali banteng (wild Indonesian cattle) were introduced

in the 1840s and today Gurig supports the world's last remaining wild herd. Marine animals include Indo-Pacific hump-backed dolphins (common), dugongs and six species of marine turtle. Accessible by 4WD and permit only.
550km east of Darwin by road,
☎ *08-8979 0244*

Mary River National Park
A chequerboard of small reserves protecting tropical woodland, floodplain and wetlands bounded by the Mary River. It is an uncrowded alternative to Kakadu. Shady Camp is a popular fishing spot which supports the world's highest concentration of saltwater crocodiles, as well as freshwater crocodiles and, in the Dry, most species of Top End waterbirds. There are observation hides at Bird Billabong and Mistake Creek. Tours run from Darwin.
90km east of Darwin,
☎ *08-8988 8009*

N'Dhala Gorge Nature Park
Several thousand petroglyphs (Aboriginal rock engravings) are the main attraction in this narrow gorge which also supports rare dry-country plants as well as honeyeaters, budgerigars, dusky grasswrens and peregrine falcons.
90km east of Alice Springs,
☎ *08-8951 8211*

Nitmiluk (Katherine Gorge) National Park
A series of nine gorges carved through the western edge of the Arnhem Land escarpment is one of the Territory's biggest scenic attractions, but also supports varied habitats and wildlife. The gorge and tributaries are lined with stands of paperbarks and pandanus where Mertens' water monitors hunt and freshwater crocodiles may be seen in the quieter reaches. Boat cruises visit Aboriginal rock-art sites and offer good oppurtunities to see

cliff-dwelling birds including fairy martins and peregrine falcons.

Black and little red flying-foxes feed in fruiting trees at night. Walking tracks lead through shady pockets of monsoon rainforest, tropical woodland and sandstone plateaus dominated by spinifex and hardy shrubs. In the camping ground, agile wallabies are approachable and Gould's goannas scrounge for scraps; at the park headquarters look out for great bowerbirds, blue-faced honeyeaters and small birds drinking at sprinklers during the Dry. Gouldian finches are sometimes seen in the park's farther reaches.
30km north-east of Katherine,
☎ *08-8972 1886*

Watarrka (Kings Canyon) National Park
Ranks of weathered sandstone domes line the rim of a dramatic, sheer-sided gorge cutting

into the George Gill Range. Water seepage supports a stand of native figs, gums and relict plant species not otherwise found nearby. Little woodswallows feed along cliff faces and spinifex pigeons inhabit rocky slopes.
330km south-west of Alice Springs by road,
☎ *08-8956 7460*

QUEENSLAND

State faunal emblems

Koala Queensland is the stronghold of this most recognisable of marsupials and it is particularly common in the south of the state, although it is mostly nocturnal.

Brolga Common in wetlands and pasture from Rockhampton to the Gulf, the brolga is known for exuberant dancing displays that feature in Aboriginal folklore.

Highlights

- Spotlighting for possums and tree-kangaroos in the Atherton Tableland rainforest
- Peering from hides for black-necked storks and brolgas at the Townsville Common
- Sitting only a metre or two above platypuses foraging in the Broken River at Eungella NP
- Breakfasting with striking yellow-and-black regent bowerbirds feeding at dawn in Lamington NP
- Combing the beach on Fraser Island with just a lone dingo for company
- Standing on the rim of the crater of Bromfield Swamp as hundreds of brolgas and sarus cranes fly in below you at dusk to roost
- Being splashed by humpback whales breaching only metres away from your boat in Hervey Bay
- Snorkelling among the immense variety of colourful fishes and corals of the Great Barrier Reef
- Stopping traffic to give way to a southern cassowary on the road to Mission Beach

THERE is no better state than Queensland to watch wildlife. It has 80% of Australia's bird species, 70% of its mammals, 60% of its frogs and at least half its reptiles. There are more than 200 national parks and 150 conservation parks (under the control of the Queensland Parks and Wildlife Service – QPWS) protecting some six million hectares of deserts, rainforests, coral reefs and rugged sandstone gorges. World Heritage Sites include Fraser Island, the Wet Tropics and the Great Barrier Reef.

The Great Dividing Range runs up the entire east coast, rising to 1657m in the rainforest-shrouded Wet Tropics and petering out near the tip of Cape York, 2200km from Queensland's southern border. The majority of the state lies in the tropics, but only on the eastern seaboard is there sufficient rainfall to allow the proliferation of rainforests. West of 'the Divide' vast plains stretch through tablelands of Mitchell grass, spinifex and mulga to the Simpson Desert in the far south-west. The Great Barrier Reef, the largest coral reef system in the world, shelters 2300km of coastline, much of which is fringed with mangroves.

North Queensland experiences just two seasons – the Wet (summer) and the Dry. December to March is both the wettest and hottest time of year, and is when most wildlife is most active and sees the return of migrant birds. Inland Queensland is best experienced in winter, when temperatures are bearable. The southeast is temperate (even cool) in winter and humid in summer.

Most human activity is concentrated on the coast, which is also the focus for much wildlife-watching and conservation effort. Dugongs graze seagrass beds; humpback whales migrate to calve in shallow bays; sand cays support breeding seabirds and sea turtles; and underwater the Great Barrier Reef is one of the greatest wildlife spectacles on earth.

Queensland is rich in endemic species, and birds and mammals are strong suites in the Wet Tropics and the rainforests of Cape York Peninsula. The Wet Tropics is Australia's most biologically diverse area – covering only 0.1% of the land area, it is home to approximately half the country's bird species and one-third of its mammals.

Sadly, not all is so pristine. Only 4% of this huge state is protected; most of the state's lowland rainforest has been cleared for sugar cane plantations; and Queensland still has one of the highest rates of land clearance in the world. ■

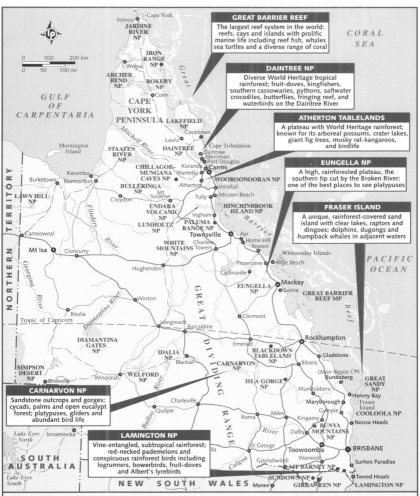

GREAT BARRIER REEF
The largest reef system in the world: reefs, cays and islands with prolific marine life including reef fish, whales sea turtles and a diverse range of coral

DAINTREE NP
Diverse World Heritage tropical rainforest; fruit-doves, kingfishers, southern cassowaries, pythons, saltwater crocodiles, butterflies, fringing reef, and waterbirds on the Daintree River

ATHERTON TABLELANDS
A plateau with World Heritage rainforest; known for its arboreal possums, crater lakes, giant fig trees, musky rat-kangaroos, and birdlife

EUNGELLA NP
A high, rainforested plateau, the southern tip cut by the Broken River; one of the best places to see platypuses

FRASER ISLAND
A unique, rainforest-covered sand island with clear lakes, raptors and dingoes; dolphins, dugongs and humpback whales in adjacent waters

CARNARVON NP
Sandstone outcrops and gorges; cycads, palms and open eucalypt forest; platypuses, gliders and abundant bird life

LAMINGTON NP
Vine-entangled, subtropical rainforest; red-necked pademelons and conspicuous rainforest birds including logrunners, bowerbirds, fruit-doves and Albert's lyrebirds

Suggested itineraries

One week (North – start/finish Cairns) Head straight to the Atherton Tablelands (2–3 days, taking in Mt Hypipamee and Jullatten); do Daintree NP and the cruise (2–3 days), and finish with a day at Michaelmas Cay.

One week (South – start/finish Brisbane) Spend 2 days at Lamington NP then back-track to spend 2 days on Fraser Island or whale-watching at Hervey Bay; finish at Lady Elliott Island.

Two weeks (North – start/finish Cairns) Spend an extra day on the Atherton Tablelands or visit Undara Volcanic NP; overnight on a Reef island; and after Daintree head up to Lakefield NP.

Two weeks (South – start/finish Brisbane) Spend an extra day at Lamington NP, watch whales and visit Fraser Island; see the reef at Lady Elliott or Heron Islands then nesting turtles at Mon Repos before going inland to Carnarvon NP.

One month (start Cairns/finish Brisbane) Follow the two-week northern itinerary or combine the one-week trip with Lakefield and Iron Range NPs, then drive down the coast to Eungella NP, taking in Hinchinbrook NP on the way, before heading into the two-week southern circuit.

A variation would be to skip Cape York and do an inland loop via Lawn Hill NP and other arid-zone parks.

BRISBANE

The koala capital

ALTHOUGH Brisbane is Australia's third-largest city, many areas rich in wildlife, including patches of rainforest and eucalypt forest, have been preserved by forward-thinking councils. The *City Botanic Gardens* (☎ 07-3403 7913), between the Brisbane River and the south-eastern edge of the CBD, has small patches of rainforest with **flying-foxes**, **common brushtail possums** and a variety of birds including **waterbirds**, **lorikeets**, **figbirds** and, in the warmer months, **sacred kingfishers**. As in much of urban Australia, brushtails coexist with people and are the most conspicuous of Brisbane's possums.

While small insectivorous bats such as the **eastern broadnosed bat** are often found roosting in suburban roofs, the larger, fruit-eating flying-foxes are a familiar sight at dusk throughout the city. Brisbane's most common species, **greyheaded** and **black flying-foxes**, camp on *Indooroopilly Island* in the Brisbane River (7km upstream from the CBD). Hundreds of thousands may be present during summer and they are sometimes joined by groups of the nomadic **little red flying-fox**.

The **koala** population in the Brisbane region is probably the largest in Queensland and sightings are frequent in suburban gardens. The catchment between the *Leslie Harrison Dam* and *Daisy Hill SF* supports one of the largest local populations. **Swamp wallabies** and **red-necked wallabies** can still be found in moist, densely vegetated areas – try *Venmans Bushland NP* and Daisy Hill SF – but **whiptail wallabies** are more commonly seen because they feed in open, grassy hillsides.

About 400 bird species have been recorded in the greater Brisbane area and there are dozens of good birdwatching spots. The mudflats of *Moreton Bay* are one of the most significant areas for waders in the country. Up to 24 species of **migratory wader** can be seen between September and April; some of the best sites are Wellington Point and where Queens Esplanade at Thorneside looks out over Waterloo Bay, and the nearby Manly Yacht Club and Raby Bay. The mangroves of the Fisherman Islands and adjacent Lytton area are also well-known

Dolphins, waders, herons and kingfishers are commonly seen by commuters taking ferries along the meandering Brisbane River to the CBD; and flying-foxes leave their vast camp upstream to wing along at dusk in search of fruiting figs.

birdwatching spots, while urban gardens are visited by **Australian brush-turkeys** and flocks of **topknot pigeons**.

Brisbane Forest Park (☎ 07-3300 4855) stretching between Mt Coot-tha and D'Aguilar NP, comprises state forest, council reserves and five national parks. The park's subtropical rainforest is most accessible from the towns of Mt Nebo and nearby Mt Glorious; **mountain brushtail possums** are relatively abundant near Mt Nebo. Maiala NP, near Mt Glorious, and Manorina NP, near Mt Nebo, are great places to see **rainforest birds**, **red-necked pademelons**, **mountain brushtail possums**, **greater gliders** and **common ringtail possums**. The forest near Mt Nebo is particularly good for **frogs**. Boombana, part of the D'Aguilar NP is also known for **rainforest birds**. *Walk-a-bout Creek Wildlife Centre* (☎ 07-3300 4855) in Brisbane Forest Park has a freshwater study centre with displays of aquatic life, including frogs, lungfish, platypuses, water-rats, crocodiles and other reptiles. There's also an aviary and nocturnal mammal display, such as bandicoots, gliders and brush-tailed phascogales. Wild **platypuses** can be seen in *Enoggera* and *Moggill Creeks*, and at *Karawatha Forest Park*.

Humpback whales, **bottlenose dolphins**, **manta rays** and several species of **seabird** are often seen from Point Lookout on *North Stradbroke Island* (☎ 07-3409 9555), a sand island with a diverse array of habitats and rich birdlife. *Blue Lake NP* (☎ 07-3227 7111) is a freshwater lake surrounded by eucalypt forest in which **eastern grey kangaroos**, **agile wallabies**, **swamp wallabies** (a golden subspecies peculiar to North Stradbroke Island), **echidnas** and **koalas** can be seen.

Bribie Island NP (☎ 07-3408 8451) covers one-third of Bribie Island, 65km north of Brisbane. The eucalypt forest and heathlands of this sand island support large numbers of **honeyeaters** and nine **frog** species. Intertidal mangroves and mudflats attract many **migratory waders** and **raptors**. A large wetland in the centre of the island is also worth visiting for **waterbirds**.

The seagrass meadows of *Moreton Bay* are feeding grounds for the world's southernmost population of **dugongs**. *Moreton Island NP* (☎ 07-3408 2710) is a sand island renowned for dusk feedings of **bottlenose dolphins** at Tangalooma – usually eight to nine animals come in. While only guests of Tangalooma Wild Dolphin Resort (☎ 07-3408 2666) can feed them, there is nothing to stop others watching; for more information on the dolphins contact the resort's Dolphin Education Centre. The southern end of the island is one of the region's best area for **waders**, particularly around Mirrapool and north of Kooringal.

At *Daisy Hill Koala Centre* (☎ 07-3299 1032) and *Lone Pine Koala Sanctuary* (☎ 07-3378 1366) you can see koalas close-up and learn more about them. A bit farther afield, the *David Fleay Wildlife Park* on the Gold Coast (☎ 07-5576 2411) and the *Australian Zoo* at Beerwah (☎ 07-5494 1134) are also worth a visit. ∎

GREAT BARRIER REEF

A diverse marine realm

STRETCHING for 2300km along the Queensland coast, the Great Barrier Reef is the largest network of coral reefs, cays and islands in the world. It is not one, but a disjointed chain of 2600 individual reefs and 300 coral cays along the edge of the continental shelf. It is a World Heritage Site and the largest living structure on earth, visible even from the moon.

The Reef is based on hard corals, colonial polyps with a hard limestone skeleton and single-celled algae – zooxanthellae – that live in their tissues and photosynthesize to provide them with food. The two most common types of reef are ribbon reefs and fringing reefs. The linear **ribbon reefs** on the outer edge of the continental shelf, between Cairns and Cape York, have the highest biological diversity but take the longest to reach; and are generally only visited by diving boats. **Fringing reefs** form along the sloping shelf of the mainland and continental islands. Visibility is lower here than on the outermost reefs, because of run-off from the land, but fringing reefs are the most-visited reef type.

Coral grows best on sheltered reef slopes, and highest as '**bommies**' (isolated coral outcrops) on the outer edges of fringing reefs, where porites coral can form outcrops up to 8m tall – bommies are often great sites for diving. In deeper waters, divers can see **fan gorgonians**, corals with flexible skeletons that don't need light but face the current and filter plankton out of water. On the exposed outer edge of the Reef, corals are buffeted by wave action. Here **staghorn coral**, which grows long and upright in calm waters, takes on stunted finger- or plate-like shapes.

Reef flats, the inner section of fringing reefs, are easily walked across at low tide and are a great way to see the Reef without snorkelling or diving. **Sea cucumbers** and **shrimp gobies** – small fish that guard and share a burrow maintained by a species of blind shrimp – are abundant in the sandy sections closest to shore.

All sea creatures great and small
The most usual way to see the Reef is to take a day trip to snorkel or dive – dozens of sites are commonly visited by boat

Sex change
The sex lives of fish are fascinating and varied. While many, such as butterflyfish, form permanent partnerships, others not only change partners they change sex. Those that under sexual reversal includes conspicuous species like parrotfish and wrasses. Juvenile parrotfish are all born as dull-coloured females. Over time some turn into males, becoming so brilliantly coloured that for a long time males and females were considered separate species. Male cleaner wrasse hold small harems of juvenile females, of which one female is dominant and has the greatest access to mating opportunities and food. If the male dies the dominant female immediately and irreversibly transforms into a replacement male. This situation is reversed in the pink anemonefish (inset) – a female holds a harem of juvenile males and one dominant, mature male. If the female dies, the dominant male becomes the new female.

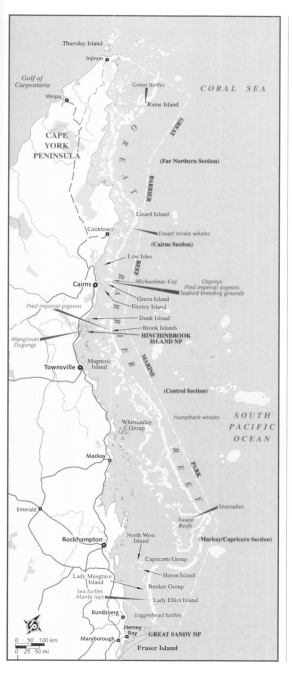

Location The Reef can either be reached by plane or boat from many towns, eg, Cairns, Townsville, Airlie Beach, Rockhampton and Bundaberg.

Facilities The Great Barrier Reef Aquarium (☎ 07-4750 0800) in Townsville is a marine aquarium and information centre.

Accommodation Every variety of accommodation along the coast; resorts and camping grounds on many islands, cays and pontoons.

Wildlife rhythms Humpbacks calve during winter; sea turtles nest between November and February; marine stingers are present October to May; and corals spawn after the full moon in November.

Contact Great Barrier Reef Marine Park Authority (☎ 07-4750 0700). Queensland Department of Environment and Heritage, Gladstone (☎ 07-4972 6055).

Ecotours Innumerable snorkelling and diving cruises visit the Reef between Bundaberg and Cooktown. Operators going to Michaelmas Cay and Hastings Reef include the MV Seastar (☎ 07-4033 0333), Ocean Spirit Cruises (☎ 07-4031 2920), Compass Outer Barrier Reef Trips (☎ 07-4050 0666) and Noah's Ark Outer Barrier Reef Cruises (☎ 07-4050 0677).

operators from major centres. There are also 24 island resorts, most of which have fringing reefs that can be snorkelled and dived – Lady Elliott, Lady Musgrave and Heron Islands all offer excellent conditions for viewing reef life.

The best way to snorkel is to go slowly – focus on the smaller things and let the larger animals come to you. An endless and dazzling variety of corals, on and among which live a myriad of colourful sponges, sea stars, crustaceans, molluscs and other invertebrates; the longer you look the more you'll see and the more likely you are to make sense of it all. You may see gobies, shrimps, crabs and tiny, colourful **Christmas tree worms** attached to hard corals, but flamboyantly-patterned fish are the star attractions. Small **damselfish**, including **anemonefish** and **chromis**, are the most common fishes, but mixed schools of **wrasses**, herbivorous **parrotfish**, **surgeonfish**, **angelfish** and **butterflyfish** will be seen virtually everywhere.

Larger animals seen while snorkelling include sea turtles, sharks, rays and **giant clams**. **Sea turtles** are often encountered; if you don't chase them they are likely to approach and check you out. **Manta rays** are common inhabitants of the outer Reef, often seen flying birdlike through the water as they filter zooplankton; Lady Elliott Island and Manta Ray Bommie at Lady Musgrave Island are good places to see them. **Seasnakes** live throughout the Reef, most commonly in the southern Swain Reefs. Most of the Reef's **sharks** are small, and rarely aggressive to divers and snorkellers. Small, bottom-dwelling species include the harmless **epaulette shark**, the **black-tip reef shark** – probably the most frequently-encountered shark in shallow waters on reef flats – and **white-tip reef sharks**, which feed on the sea floor and rest by day under coral ledges. **Grey reef sharks** live in deeper waters and are usually seen only by divers. The **silver-tip shark** is larger and, like the **tiger shark**, the largest shark on the Reef, usually inhabits the seaward edge of reefs and deeper water.

Dolphins and other whales aren't often encountered while snorkelling or diving; instead, they are best seen by boat. **Dwarf minke whales** are common in the Far Northern Section of the reef. **Humpback whales** gather in the central Reef area every summer to breed; they and their calves are best seen around the Whitsunday Islands and Hervey Bay between August and October.

Giant clams thrive on the Reef, where they are protected from the depredations of the tourist trade.

Coral orgy

The annual mass spawning of coral has been described as the biggest orgy in the animal kingdom. Yet, even after travelling to Heron Island with biology students regularly for 15 years, it remained something I had only heard about and seen on documentaries. Finally, one summer when the moon and tides were just right, I got to see the aftermath of this sexual explosion. Early one morning the students and I noticed a lot of pink slime washed up on the beach. After much discussion as to its cause, we decided to invoke some science and have a look under a microscope. Lo and behold, there on the microscope slides were cells dividing before our eyes. Each cluster was a new fertilised embryo on its way to becoming a new coral polyp – those that survived would form a new part of the Great Barrier Reef.

Bruce Weir, biologist

Continental islands – partially submerged peaks once part of the mainland before sea levels rose – are often cloaked in rainforest and support fringing coral reefs.

See sea turtles and seabirds

Six of the world's seven species of sea turtle live on the Great Barrier Reef, including a rare Australian endemic, the **flatback turtle**. Only **green**, **loggerhead** and **hawksbill turtles** are common and green is the most widespread. Raine Island is the largest green turtle rookery in the world, but the best places to see nesting sea turtles are southern islands, eg, Heron, Curtis, Lady Elliott and Lady Musgrave Islands, and the readily accessible, but strictly controlled, mainland beach of Mon Repos, near Bundaberg. Between November and February female sea turtles – predominantly loggerheads – come ashore at night to lay their eggs; hatchlings emerge between January and March.

The Reef is much closer to the mainland in the north than in the south. Green Island, a rainforested coral cay off Cairns, is probably the most visited cay on the Reef. Like other vegetated cays, it was built up from coral sand, vegetated from the seeds brought by visiting seabirds and fertilised by their guano. **Rose-crowned fruit-doves**, **emerald doves** and **ospreys** breed here, **pied imperial-pigeons** visit in summer, and **eastern reef egrets** and **waders** can be seen on the very accessible reef flats.

One of the best places to see **nesting seabirds** is Michaelmas Cay off Cairns, where more than 30,000 cacophonous **sooty** and **bridled terns**, **common noddies**, and **brown boobies** breed in summer. In the pisonia forests of Heron, Lady Musgrave and North West Islands, up to 90,000 **common noddies** nest between October and March, thousands of **wedge-tailed shearwaters** also have their nesting burrows here.

The densely vegetated 'high' continental islands, like Dunk Island and those of the Whitsundays, harbour populations of reptiles (including **saltwater crocs**), frogs, butterflies, birds and mammals similar to those on the mainland, and **dugongs** feed in their sheltered bays. ■

Watching tips

Go diving at night to see a whole suite of animals that shelter in the reef by day. The Cod Hole, north of Lizard Island, is one of the few places where large potato cod can be fed and touched by divers. Be around for the week following the first full moon in November to witness the incredible spawning of corals all along the Great Barrier Reef.

ATHERTON TABLELAND

Stronghold of Wet Tropics endemics

THE Atherton Tableland is the best place to appreciate the endemic wildlife of the Wet Tropics and is a must on any wildlife-watching itinerary. Over 90% of the original vegetation has been cleared on this crater-pocked plateau, but much rainforest is now protected in the Wet Tropics World Heritage Area.

Crater critters

Mt Hypipamee NP (also known as 'The Crater') offers some of the tableland's best high-altitude rainforest. **Spotted catbirds, grey-headed robin** and **Lewin's** and **bridled honeyeaters** are common (and tame) around the picnic area. Wet Tropics endemics such as **Atherton scrubwrens, mountain thornbills, fernwrens** and **chowchillas** are usually seen along the short walk to the spectacular crater. And keep an eye out too for **Victoria's riflebirds** and **golden bowerbirds**; from October to January the male bowerbirds spend considerable time at their bower – if you find a bower you'll find the bird.

At night, the rainforest from the car park back to the main road is famous for rainforest possums – seven species live here, including the **striped possum, lemuroid** and **Herbert River ringtail possums**. However, apart from the **common brushtail possums** around the car park (these are 'coppery brushtails', a distinctive tropical subspecies), they can be difficult to see – the easiest way to experience the nightlife is on a spotlighting trip run by one of the many ecotour companies. Other things to seek out at night

Rainforest stranglers

The Curtain and Cathedral Fig Trees are giant examples of strangler figs. Tree-kangaroos sleep among their branches; antechinuses live among their roots; and birds, butterflies and flying-foxes feed on their fruits and flowers. Instead of germinating on the ground, where they must compete for light with other plants, strangler fig seeds excreted by flying-foxes and fruit-doves germinate in the canopy of other trees where enough nutrients have accumulated in the pockets of forked branches. The roots grow downwards until they touch the ground and can draw nutrients from the soil. Rather than being strangled in a mesh of thickening roots, it is more likely that the host tree simply ages and dies before the fig is large enough to be serious competition.

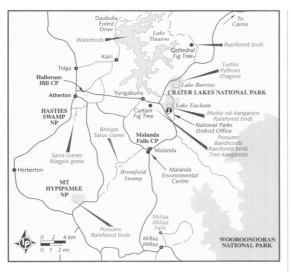

Location 50km south-west of Cairns.
Facilities Malanda Environmental Centre (☎ 07-4096 6957).
Accommodation A full range throughout the Tableland. Naturalists catered for at Chambers Wildlife Rainforest Apartments (☎ 07-4095 3730), Fur'n'Feather Rainforest Tree Houses (☎ 07-4096 5364), Cassowary House (☎ 07-4093 7318) and Kingfisher Park Birdwatcher's Lodge (☎ 07-4094 1263).
Wildlife rhythms June–December for brolgas and sarus cranes; much wildlife most active during the Wet.
Contact Atherton Forest Service (☎ 07-4091 1844). Ranger, Lake Eacham (☎ 07-4095 3768).
Ecotours Nocturnal tours (mostly ex-Cairns) with Wait-a-while Environmental Tours (☎ 07-4033 1153), Carrowong Fauna Sanctuary (☎ 07-4093 7287) and Wildscapes Safaris (☎ 07-4057 6272). Kirrama Wildlife Tours (☎ 07-4065 5181) offers bird-watching trips and spotlighting.

include luminescent fungi (turn off your lights), fireflies during the Wet; and the falling-bomb screams of **lesser sooty owls**.

Bromfield Swamp is the largest crater on the tableland and contains a huge swamp. Access to the crater floor is impossible, but there is a viewing platform on Upper Barron Rd. From June to December **sarus cranes** and **brolgas** – sometimes in their hundreds – fly in to roost at dusk. Sarus cranes also roost at Hasties Swamp, a temporary wetland where large numbers of **whistling-ducks** and **magpie geese** congregate during the wet season.

Enter the dragons

Crater Lakes NP includes Lake Barrine and Lake Eacham; both have circuit tracks through surrounding rainforest which are great for birdwatching. Walkers may also encounter **red-legged pademelons**, **musky rat-kangaroos** (one of the few marsupials active by day) and camouflaged **Boyd's forest dragons**. There's a good chance of seeing **eastern water dragons** and **saw-shelled turtles** on the morning boat cruise on Lake Barrine.

You could also encounter the ground-dwelling **Australian brush-turkey** and **orange-footed scrubfowl** in virtually any patch of rainforest; and watch for two spectacular butterflies – the bright blue **Ulysses butterfly** and the massive **Cairns birdwing**. Along the 28km Danbulla Forest Drive, watch for **southern cassowaries** during the day and **northern bettongs** at night. Lake Tinaroo is a huge reservoir that attracts waterfowl such as **wandering whistling-ducks** and **cotton pygmy-geese**.

The rainforest around the Curtain and Cathedral Fig Trees is great for rainforest birds. **Lumholtz's tree-kangaroos** are occasionally seen at night along the road that passes Curtain Fig, and the car park here is good for **long-nosed bandicoots** and **green ringtail possums**. ■

Watching tips

Rainforest birdwatching can be difficult and frustrating. Start early, as most birds call at dawn, and look for fruiting or flowering trees – hotspots for bird activity. Flowering trees in the main street of Atherton township lure scarlet honeyeaters. Fruiting fig trees offer the best chance of good views of rainforest pigeons and the rare double-eyed fig-parrot – Yungaburra state school is good when the figs are fruiting.

CARNARVON NATIONAL PARK

Cycads and sandstone

Wildlife highlights
Deep, sheltered sandstone gorges (the main attraction) harbour platypuses and relict plant communities; macropods include eastern grey kangaroos, swamp and whiptail wallabies, brush-tailed rock-wallabies and rufous bettongs; and by spotlighting you should easily track down common brushtail possums and yellow-bellied gliders. Attractions among 170 bird species include abundant lorikeets, honeyeaters and fairy-wrens, and less common species like the squatter pigeon and powerful owl. Lace monitors are the largest of the three monitors present, and many frog species inhabit watercourses.

OF the four sections that make up Carnarvon NP the most accessible is Carnarvon Gorge, where Carnarvon Creek has eroded a 200m-deep passage through sandstone. The gorge is a refuge for pockets of subtropical palm rainforest, forests of spotted gum, ancient cycads, and numerous easily-seen birds and mammals.

On the trail of the platypus

There are many side gorges and remote areas to explore, but most wildlife is easily seen at the camping ground or on walks along Carnarvon Creek. **Whiptail wallabies**, **pied currawongs** and social groups of grey **apostlebirds** are prominent during the day at the camping ground, and several **eastern grey kangaroos** usually graze by the creek.

There are plenty of **rainbow lorikeets**, **friarbirds** and **blue-faced honeyeaters** (young ones have greenish faces) when eucalypts are in flower. **Squatter pigeons**, generally uncommon elsewhere, are frequently seen here. **Laughing kookaburras** are always present, eyeing the food of campers for an easy meal. At nightfall, **common brushtail possums** emerge from the shelter of tree hollows and take over from the kookaburras.

Tracks in time

A mammal track engraved on Carnarvon Gorge's Aboriginal rock-art gallery matches no known animal, but it does closely resemble a footprint found in 1871 north of Cardwell and attributed to the legendary Queensland tiger. Scores of people claim to have sighted the 'tiger' and describe it as big as a medium-sized dog, fawn-coloured with dark stripes, semi-arboreal and very aggressive – the North Queensland Aborigines called it *yarri*. Despite no hard evidence of its existence, it was included in two classic early texts on Australian mammals. Norwegian zoologist Carl Lumholtz was convinced the animal was a large marsupial predator. We may never know what the Carnarvon engraving depicts, but it is possible that modern mammal texts have overlooked one native animal.

The nature track which begins at the camping ground is best walked during the early morning or late afternoon for a chance of seeing a **platypus** in the creek. There is a healthy population here and they are often seen from platypus viewing areas along the track. During the day, **azure kingfishers** perch above the water. **Wedge-tailed eagles** soar above the gorge and the white-wash of **peregrine falcon** guano can be seen on the rock walls.

Birdlife is rich along most tracks; the place is alive with the chattering of lorikeets, friarbirds and parties of **Australian king-parrots**. A soft creaking overhead is likely to be from **yellow-tailed black-cockatoos** feeding in she-oaks. **Red-browed finches** and fairy-wrens, including the striking **red-backed fairy-wren**, live among grass and bracken.

Rock pools and moss gardens

A night walk along the nature track can be rewarding. In the eucalypts there is a good chance of spotting **yellow-bellied gliders**, and a lesser chance of **greater** and **sugar gliders**. Yellow-bellies communicate across the tree tops with gurgling shrieks and collect sap by chewing V-shaped incisions into tree trunks – several smooth-barked eucalypts on the Boolimba Bluff track bear incision scars. Yellow-bellied gliders tend to move out of the light beam but can be seen well if spotted low in a tree. Greater gliders do not to move much when spotlit but stare with bright, reflected eyeshine. Sugar gliders betray their presence with a *yap-yap-yap-yap* call; you may also hear the *mo-poke* of a **southern boobook** or the deep *hoo-hoo* of a **powerful owl**.

During the day, keep an eye out for **echidnas** along the main track and on the way to the Rock Pool. **Lace monitors** are also likely, particularly along the watercourse near large trees. The Rock Pool itself is home to **eastern snake-necked turtles** and **platypuses**, and in the morning or late afternoon you may see **swamp wallabies** along the track to the pool.

At the Moss Garden a wet sandstone wall harbours a micro-forest of mosses, liverworts and ferns. This jumble of rock and moss is a haven for dragonflies, spiders, frogs and skinks. **Brush-tailed rock-wallabies** have been seen at dusk on the grassy area behind the Moss Garden toilet; a few are also occasionally seen at the Rock Pool. Small **bats** roost in the caves around Wards Canyon and a rare rainforest relic, the **king fern**, is found here. ∎

Location 750km north-west of Brisbane. Road sometimes impassable after rain.
Facilities Information on wildlife is displayed at the ranger station.
Accommodation Camping; cabins Carnarvon Gorge.
Wildlife rhythms Excellent year-round. Summer (wet season) is best for frogs and invertebrates.
Contact Ranger, Carnarvon Gorge (☎ 07-4984 4505).
Ecotours Sunrover Expeditions (☎ 07-3203 4241): six-day camping trips into Carnarvon Gorge, ex-Brisbane. Why Not Tours (☎ 07-4128 0774 or 1800 353 717): six-day camping trips through Carnarvon Gorge April–December.

> **Watching tips**
> If you are driving into the gorge at dusk or after dark you may see rufous bettongs foraging along the sides of the road near open areas with long grass. These small macropods were once much more common and widespread than they are now.

DAINTREE NATIONAL PARK

Rainforest, crocodiles and kingfishers

Location Daintree River ferry 110km north of Cairns.
Facilities Daintree Environmental Centre has excellent boardwalks, displays and audio-visual presentations. The Bat House – rehab centre for flying-foxes
Accom. Camping at Noah Creek and Snapper Island; other accommodation at Cape Tribulation and Daintree.
Wildlife rhythms Wet season for migratory birds and breeding activity; chances of great-billed herons and basking crocodiles better during winter.
Contact Rangers: Cape Tribulation (☎ 07-4098 0052), Mossman (☎ 07-4098 1305).
Ecotours Chris Dahlberg's Specialised River Tours (☎ 07-4098 7997): informative cruises along the Daintree River. Cooper Creek Wilderness Cruises (☎ 07-4098 9052): day and night mangrove cruises. Crocodylus Village Backpackers (☎ 07-4098 9166): excellent guided night walks.

TROPICAL rainforest, mangroves, woodland, rivers and beaches make up this World Heritage Area. The flanks of rainforested Thornton Peak, usually shrouded in cloud, meet the Great Barrier Reef north of the Daintree River. Although most of the park consists of inaccessible, rainforest-clad mountains, the region's abundant wildlife can be experienced at Daintree River, Mossman Gorge and Cape Tribulation.

Cruising for crocs

The best way to see the Daintree River is to take a cruise. Most focus on viewing **saltwater crocodiles**, but one or two specialise in birdwatching and offer good chances of seeing sought-after species including the **Papuan frogmouth**, **great-billed heron**, **black bittern** and **little kingfisher**. On any cruise you can expect to see **white-bellied sea-eagles**, **ospreys** and **waterbirds**; and riparian reptiles including **eastern water dragons**, **common tree snakes** and **amethystine pythons**. Listen for the *clack* of **snapping shrimp** among the mangrove roots.

Of several bird species that migrate here from New Guinea during summer, the most spectacular are **buff-breasted paradise-kingfishers**, easily distinguished by two delicate white tail streamers. It nests in termite mounds and is easily seen in gardens around Daintree township. **Pied imperial-pigeons**, another migrant, are abundant in coastal forests during the Wet.

At Mossman Gorge an interpretative walk through lowland rainforest identifies more than 100 species of plant and their uses by the local Kuku Yalangi people. **Freshwater turtles**, **platypuses**, and **jungle perch** live in the pools; **white-rumped swiftlets** pursue insects over the river; and **Ulysses butterflies** and **Cairns**

birdwings are common. A colony of migratory **metallic starlings** nests in a large tree near the car park every summer. At night luminescent fungi glow in the forest.

Serpent's home, wildlife cradle

The Cape Tribulation section of the park stretches between the Daintree and Bloomfield Rivers. These rainforests are thought to be a centre of evolution for Australian fauna and a refuge for many ancient plants, including ancestors of the flowering plants. To the Kuku Yalangi, the two rivers are the home of Yero, the Rainbow Serpent.

Arboreal marsupials are particularly well-represented in the rainforest, although it is necessary to go spotlighting to see them. There's a good chance of the **giant white-tailed rat** and **fawn-footed melomys**, both handsome native rodents, and other possibilities include the **striped possum,** several species of **ringtail possum** and the rare **Bennett's tree-kangaroo.**

Spectacled flying-foxes wing across the open sky over the Daintree River at dusk. They roost in the rainforest during the day – try the fan palms along the Marrdja botanical walk at Oliver Creek. This boardwalk passes through lowland rainforest and mangroves, and is a good place to see rainforest birds, including colourful **wompoo fruit-doves** in the canopy, **Victoria's riflebirds** feeding on fruits along the track, and **orange-footed scrubfowl** scratching among the leaf litter. When you reach the mangroves, look for **little** and **sacred kingfishers**, perching on the mangroves' snorkel-like roots, and for **freshwater turtles** in the water.

Several companies run bush walks on which an enormous variety of invertebrates and frogs can be seen, including **New Guinea tree frogs**, **crickets** and **net-casting spiders**. Boyd's **forest dragons** can be seen both day and night, camouflaged at head height on slender trunks – although they'll move round to the other side of their tree at your approach.

A single **southern cassowary** is often seen in the early mornings around the Daintree Environmental Centre. The centre conducts informative botanical tours along a short boardwalk past strangler figs hundreds of years old. The Bat House is a bat-rehabilitation centre where you can view and even hold **spectacled flying-foxes**. ∎

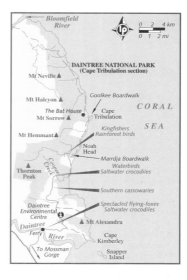

Bloomfield River

0 2 4 km
0 1 2 mi

DAINTREE NATIONAL PARK
(Cape Tribulation section)

Mt Neville ▲

Mt Halcyon ▲
Goolkee Boardwalk

The Bat House ● Cape
Mt Sorrow ▲ Tribulation   *CORAL*

Mt Hemmant▲   Kingfishers   *SEA*
Rainforest birds

Noah
Head

Marrdja Boardwalk
▲   Waterbirds
Thornton   Saltwater crocodiles
Peak

Southern cassowaries

Daintree   Spectacled flying-foxes
Environmental ❶   Saltwater crocodiles
Centre

Daintree   ▲ Mt Alexandra
Ferry River

Cape
To Mossman   Kimberley
Gorge   Snapper
Island

Watching tips

When walking through the rainforest at night, turn off your torch to see luminescent fungi on rotting sticks and leaves on the ground. Look for hollowed-out, round, hard candlenuts on the rainforest floor – each has been gnawed through by a native rodent, probably a giant white-tailed rat. Northern brown bandicoots visit the dining area at Crocodylus Village Backpackers.

Idiots worth preserving

More than 1000 plant species from 95 families – 90 of which occur in lowland areas – have been recorded in the Daintree region. The rainforests of the Daintree have had little disturbance for millions of years, preserving the highest number of ancestral flowering-plant families in the world. Much of the lowland rainforest – the most visited area in the Daintree region – remains unprotected and many forest types of this low-lying coastal area are considered endangered. Among the ancient relics is one of the earliest known flowering plants, the idiot fruit; it is toxic to modern animals but was once eaten and dispersed by dinosaurs. The idiot fruit is now highly endangered, but you can see specimens at the Daintree Environmental Centre.

FRASER ISLAND

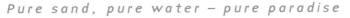

Pure sand, pure water – pure paradise

Wildlife highlights

An astonishing diversity of plants and animals for what is really an over-sized sand bar. Shorebirds and bottlenose dolphins can be seen along the coast, but undoubtedly the island's star attractions are dingoes and humpback whales (it's probably the best place in Australia to see both species). Birdlife includes waders and fish-eating raptors along the coast; honeyeaters flocking in the heaths during spring and summer; and rainforest dwellers such as noisy pitta, fruit-doves and rainbow lorikeets. Freshwater turtles and native fish in pure lakes.

Location 190km to the north of Brisbane; accessible only by plane or ferry.
Facilities Eurong information centre (☎ 07-4127 9128).
Accommodation Many camping grounds; some beach camping permitted; a variety of accommodation at the Kingfisher Bay Resort, Eurong, Happy Valley and Dilli Village.
Wildlife rhythms June–October for whales and seabirds; freshwater turtles, fish and others are more active over the warmer months.
Contact Rangers: Central Station (☎ 07-4127 9191), Rainbow Beach (☎ 07-5486 3160).
Ecotours Kingfisher Bay Resort (☎ 07-4125 5511) conducts spotlighting walks. MV *Discovery One* (☎ 07-4124 7247) and MV *Seaspray* (☎ 07-4125 3586) run whale-watching tours daily out of Hervey Bay between mid-July and late October.

APPROXIMATELY 120km long and averaging 15km wide, Fraser Island is the largest sand island in the world. Known as *K'gari*, meaning 'paradise', by the indigenous Butchella people, its diverse habitats include mangroves, heathlands, eucalypt forests and subtropical rainforest – all growing on sand. Fraser has a World Heritage listing and, after a long history of logging and sand mining, most of the island is now protected by the Great Sandy NP.

Fraser's most famous inhabitants are **dingoes**, thought to be the purest surviving strain because they have been isolated from interbreeding with domestic dogs. Dingoes are quite common, and are often seen padding along beaches; their tracks can be found around camping grounds and dwellings at places such as Happy Valley.

Bottlenose dolphins are common offshore and can usually be seen by watching from vantage points – Indian Head is a great spot – on the east coast; **dugongs** also occasionally pass by, and between June and August **humpback whales** heading north are a common sight. From August to October the humpbacks enter Hervey Bay, which has become Australia's most famous whale-watching destination. Daily boat trips from the mainland take visitors out to watch the humpbacks' spectacular, exuberant breaching behaviour.

Ospreys, **white-bellied sea-eagles** and **brahminy kites** soar above the beaches, ready to drop on a beach-cast fish or seasnake. On the crossing from Hervey Bay watch out for **brown boobies** and **cormorants** perched on buoys. Mudflats at Kingfisher Bay are great for **migratory waders** in summer; Hook Point, at the island's southern tip, and Inskip Point on the mainland opposite, are also legendary wader hangouts – worth a look at high tide. The area's mudflats are the world's most important site for the rare **eastern curlew** (Australia's largest wader); the species is readily seen and easily recognised by its distinct *cur-loo* call.

Treading water

Fraser has more than 40 freshwater lakes, known as perched dune lakes, renowned for their purity. Many support large populations of **freshwater turtles** – you virtually can't miss them in Lakes Bowarrady and McKenzie. In Lake Wabby, the deepest perched dune lake, large **catfish** are often seen in the eastern corner (along with the turtles). Your chances of seeing catfish and turtles are even better during the warmer months, when they are more active.

The '**acid' frogs** of Fraser Island are adapted to the highly acidic waters of the low-lying swampy lands. They are a favourite food of the **keelback** – a small, harmless semiaquatic snake. Watch for it in the swamps and lagoons near the coast, particularly around dusk when it is most active. **Jungle perch** can be seen from the wooden boardwalk that loops around Eli Creek.

In places, rainforest towers 60m high and supports a good variety of birds. Among the more colourful are **wompoo fruit-doves**, **emerald doves** and **noisy pittas**. **Eastern whipbirds** (you'll immediately recognise their whip-crack dueting) and **eastern yellow robins** are both common. The rainforest walk at Central Station is not to be missed: **azure kingfishers** provide splashes of vivid colour above the exceptionally clear waters of nearby Wanggoolba Creek, and look for **eels** floating downstream like pieces of bark.

Scarlet honeyeaters are common in the canopy of the eucalypt woodlands, such as those between Lake Wabby and the east coast; and flowering banksias provide food for other nectar feeders, such as **sugar gliders**, **common blossom-bats**, **honeyeaters** and **lorikeets**. Other birds you are likely to see while travelling around the island include **white-cheeked honeyeaters**, **bar-shouldered doves**, **white-breasted woodswallows**, **figbirds** and **rainbow bee-eaters**. Sugar gliders and **frogs** are frequently seen on spotlighting walks run by Kingfisher Bay Resort. ∎

Watching tips

The north end of Fraser Island marks the most northerly distribution of two rare birds: the ground parrot and black-breasted button-quail. Look for the ground parrots at Wathumba Swamp, near Orchid Beach, and Wocco Lagoon; and for the button-quail around Sandy Cape Lighthouse. Another rarity, the red goshawk, sometimes strays across from adjacent Cooloola NP (winter is the best time to look). Beachcombing after winter storms can be repaid with sometimes amazing wrecks of seabirds.

Bustin' the hump – why migrate?

The 15m-long, 40-tonne humpback whale is one of the world's largest mammals. Yet these massive animals sustain themselves largely on krill – small crustaceans which they sieve from the water. Antarctic waters provide the richest source of krill, but humpback young are born without insulating blubber so adults migrate north to calve in warmer waters. Each winter and spring at least 2000 whales migrate more than 5000km from Antarctica up the east coast of Australia to give birth in the warmer waters of the Great Barrier Reef. Many stop in Hervey Bay on their return trip. One theory is that the whales rest there after the breeding season; another is that the calves need extra time to put on blubber.

LAMINGTON NATIONAL PARK

Rainforest birds and bowers

Wildlife highlights

Easily-observed mammals of subtropical rainforest include both red-necked and red-legged pademelons, and dingoes, but Lamington is most famous for birds and 150 species have been recorded. Common and colourful species include regent and satin bowerbirds, Australian brush-turkeys, and various fruit-doves and parrots; and among the many regional specialities are the noisy pitta, Albert's lyrebird, paradise riflebird and rufous scrub-bird. Koalas and whiptail wallabies inhabit adjoining eucalypt forest; and greater and squirrel gliders, northern brown bandicoots, and several frog species can be encountered on spotlighting walks.

SUBTROPICAL rainforest covering a high plateau that drops precipitously to the caldera of a vast, extinct volcano makes a sensational setting for an introduction to this wildlife-rich region. Major attractions include moss-cloaked Antarctic beech forests – Gondwanan remnants – growing on misty heights and excellent birdwatching attracts visitors from around the world.

Colourful extroverts

At the camping grounds **red-necked pademelons** are virtually always present at first light and in the late afternoon. **Australian brush-turkeys** examine empty breakfast dishes, and in the early morning gather with **crimson rosellas**, **Australian king-parrots** and **rainbow lorikeets** at the bird-feeding area outside O'Reilly's guesthouse at Green Mountains. **Grey shrike-thrushes** fossick for food scraps; and if you sit still an **eastern yellow robin** may even alight on you. **Satin** and **regent bowerbirds** perch in the tops of hoop pines and in spring, particularly when the moon is full, the *walk-to-work* call of **noisy pittas** rings out. **Dingoes** sometimes wander through the camping grounds, and **grey goshawks** (both the grey and pure white forms) are relatively common.

Along rainforest tracks **red-legged pademelons** bound away as you approach. Allow time to walk the 22km Border Track between Green Mountains and Binna Burra. The Binna Burra section has the same type of rainforest and associated fauna as Green Mountains, but also areas of tall, wet eucalyptus forest – watch for **koalas** along the Caves Circuit from Binna Burra.

The high life

The Canopy Walk at Green Mountains allows you to examine enormous ferns and strap-leaved orchids that normally festoon the branches far above your head. The broad-leaved canopy allows little light to reach the floor, so some rainforest plants have evolved strategies for growing in the canopy where they can obtain the sunlight they need to photosynthesize. For example, epiphytes such the bird's nest fern release spores that land and germinate on a branch or trunk; the basketlike fern catches dead leaves and water to nourish it. Other plants produce seeded fruits which are eaten by fruit-doves and flying-foxes then excreted high in the canopy. Vines also use trees for support – the wait-a-while vine, or 'lawyer cane', has tiny barbs that hook into other plants.

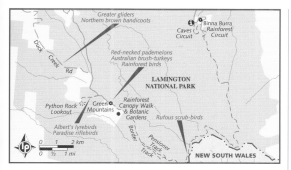

A number of birds can be seen along any of the well-marked tracks: **logrunners** scratch through leaf litter; parties of **yellow-throated** and **white-browed scrubwrens** hop around your feet; and ever-present calls in the understorey are the whip crack of the **eastern whipbird**, the **green catbird's** drawn-out *mee-oow*, and the staccato bursts from **Lewin's honeyeaters**. Listen for the loud, whirring buzz of male **satin bowerbirds** courting females at their bowers. The **regent bowerbird**, in stunning yellow-and-black livery, is conspicuous against green foliage; several are fed at 6.45 each morning at O'Reilly's. **Fruit-doves** wander in search of fruiting trees and are more common in summer. **Topknot pigeons** flock in their hundreds during spring and **emerald doves** can be seen from January until April.

Glowing in the dark

The less popular tracks are best for more elusive birds. **Albert's lyrebird** is best seen at dusk or dawn, or on clouded, rainy days; at Green Mountains, try the Python Rock and Wishing Tree Tracks or the botanic gardens. Male **paradise riflebirds** can sometimes be seen displaying along the Python Rock Track. The powerful song of **rufous scrub-birds** can be heard throughout the Antarctic beech forests, but seeing the bird requires great patience – the Border and Pensioner Tracks are good places to look.

At night there's a new suite of wildlife to see. In the rainforest, the highlights are two rare and rarely seen, nightbirds – the **sooty owl** and the **marbled frogmouth**. You are more likely to see the eyeshine of **northern leaf-tailed geckoes** on a rainforest tree. The warm, rainy weather of summer brings out many frogs, including the tiny, **mountain stream tree frog**, **pouched frog** and **barred frogs** – up to a dozen species can be heard calling at once. **Glow-worms** and fungi luminesce in the gloom and the **Lamington spiny cray**, a large blue crayfish, is commonly seen in or near creeks during summer.

Greater gliders and **northern brown bandicoots** are sometimes spotlit in the eucalypt forest along Duck Creek Rd. Lower down Green Mountain, **koalas** can be found in the drier eucalypt forest and **brush-tailed phascogales** are occasionally glimpsed in headlights. ■

Location 115km south of Brisbane via Canungra.

Facilities Canopy Walk at Green Mountains; Binna Burra Senses Trail lead you – eyes shut – along a track with a rope for guidance.

Accommodation Motel at Canungra. Camping ground and guesthouses at Green Mountains and Binna Burra.

Wildlife rhythms Albert's lyrebirds breed in winter; regent bowerbirds more common near guesthouses August–December; fruit-doves flock in summer.

Contact Rangers: Green Mountains (☎ 07-5544 0634), Binna Burra (☎ 07-5533 3584).

Ecotours O'Reilly's Rainforest Guesthouse (☎ 07-5544 0644) has guided walks, information sessions and wildlife weeks. Binna Burra Mountain Lodge (☎ 07-5533 3758) has guided walks, information centre.

Walking tracks to scenic waterfalls are ideal for birdwatching.

Watching tips

Whiptail wallabies are common in the grassy woodland along the winding road up to the park, especially in the early morning. Land mullets – large, black skinks – are commonly seen along the Wishing Tree Track at Green Mountains in sunny weather. The Green Mountains section can get very crowded on weekends and public holidays; try the Binna Burra section instead.

BUNYA MOUNTAINS NATIONAL PARK

Red-necks and flying colours

Wildlife highlights
Australian brush-turkeys, crimson rosellas, king-parrots, and red-necked wallabies are highlights. Rainforest birds include paradise riflebirds, bowerbirds, fruit-doves, grey goshawks and Pacific bazas. Mountain brushtail possums and koalas occur in eucalypt forests; red-legged pademelons, bandicoots, fawn-footed melomys and ringtail possums in the rainforest; and lace monitors, carpet pythons and frogs along streams.

Location 230 km north-west of Brisbane.
Accommodation Wide range at Dandabah. Camping grounds at Dandabah, Burtons Well and Westcott.
Wildlife rhythms Wildlife is abundant year-round; weather can be cool at any time of year. Rainforest birds are more obvious in the warmer weather.
Contact Ranger, Dandabah (☎ 07-4668 3127).
Ecotours Bunya Mountains Eco-Tourism Holidays (☎ 1800 637 657 or ☎ 07-4668 3131) offers slide shows, guided nature walks and tours (ask at kiosk at Dandabah).

Watching tips
The open, grass-tree area at Mt Kiangarow summit is a good spot to see raptors and flocks of fruit-doves.

A checkerboard of habitats covers an old, eroded volcano, an area conserving the last remaining stand of bunya pines in Queensland. Wildlife is conspicuous in rainforest, vine thickets, open eucalypt forest and grassy 'balds' that have some of the tallest grass-trees in Queensland.

The first place to visit is Dandabah, at the park's south-eastern end. Domed silhouettes of bunya pines poke above a moist rainforest canopy, a backdrop to the hordes of **red-necked wallabies** grazing the camping ground and picnic area. The red-necks are a constant presence, scattered across the grass during the day, many with young, and quietly grazing around the kiosk and cabin doorsteps during the night. One or two darker **swamp wallabies**, a species usually shy of open areas, are known to graze with them. Red-necked pademelons can be seen bounding through the forests alongside the walking tracks.

During the night, **long-nosed bandicoots** regularly forage along the edge of the lawns and **mountain brushtail possums** conduct feeding patrols. Elsewhere, **koalas** are occasionally seen in the tall eucalypt forests, such as those at Burtons Well.

Kings and regents

Throughout the day, waves of brightly coloured **king-parrots** and **crimson rosellas** descend to feed outside the Dandabah kiosk on seeds provided by the proprietors at 10am and 4pm. Around midmorning, the pavement seethes with tiny **red-browed finches** feasting on smaller seeds left by the parrots. **Brush-turkeys** wander about, chasing each other and pecking at morsels left by picnickers; at dusk, these large birds fly up to roost in the bunya pines, staircasing up the spirally arranged branches.

A number of rainforest birds can be seen along the Scenic Circuit through the rainforest. **Green cat-birds** cry constantly from the understorey and flocks of **topknot pigeons** fly above the canopy. **Eastern whipbirds** rummage through leaf litter and green, female **satin bowerbirds** fly through in groups. Bowers of both **satin** and **regent bowerbirds** are hidden on the forest floor, some can be seen along the Bunya Bunya track. ■

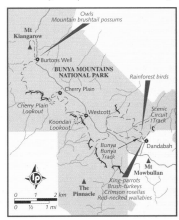

Owls
Mountain brushtail possums
Mt Kiangarow
Burtons Well
BUNYA MOUNTAINS NATIONAL PARK
Rainforest birds
Cherry Plain
Cherry Plain Lookout
Westcott
Scenic Circuit Track
Koondaii Lookout
Bunya Bunya Track
Dandabah
Mt Mowbullan
The Pinnacle
King-parrots
Brush-turkeys
Crimson rosellas
Red-necked wallabies
0 1 2 km
0 ½ 1 mi

EUNGELLA NATIONAL PARK

Platypus pools and an endemic honeyeater

MUCH of Eungella NP is inaccessible, mountainous wilderness, but around Finch Hatton Gorge and the Broken River a number of walking tracks penetrate the luxuriant rainforest.

The Broken River is perhaps the best place to view wild **platypuses**, and these normally shy monotremes are easily observed around the viewing deck – the best time to look is in the early morning or late afternoon. But around the viewing deck is not the only place in the river that platypuses are found; other still pools are also likely to have one or two resident – the large pool 150m downstream from the ranger station is definitely worth checking. Patience and silence are a must – watch for the circular ripples created by the platypuses when surfacing.

It's been claimed by some naturalists that **azure kingfishers** perch above feeding platypuses, diving for scraps left over from their messy eating.

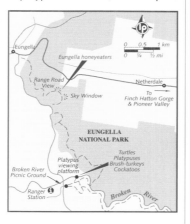

Unbroken views

From the platypus viewing deck, **northern snapping turtles** are a common, but often unappreciated, sight in the river below. Once the light begins to fade, it is worth waiting on the deck a while longer. Soon you may see **Australian brush-turkeys** hopflap upwards from branch to branch to their roosts high in trees on the opposite bank and huge numbers of **sulphur-crested cockatoos** come screeching in, displaying dogfightlike aerobatics before settling at their communal roost; at dusk, tiny **insectivorous bats** emerge, flitting over the water. **Long-nosed bandicoots** sometimes forage around the ranger station at night, and **rufous bettongs** are occasionally seen in the grassed area along the edge of the Broken River picnic area.

Noisy pittas, fruit-eating **wompoo** and **superb fruit-doves**, and **regent bowerbirds** inhabit the rainforest (the latter is sometimes seen in Eungella town during winter), and there's a nesting colony of **white-rumped swiftlets** at Finch Hatton Gorge. However, most birders are keenest to track down the endemic **Eungella honeyeater**. Good places to search for it are along Dalrymple Rd, running north out of the town; at the end of Chelmans Rd; and at Range Road View, particularly when umbrella trees are flowering in summer. ■

Wildlife highlights

Platypuses are the star attraction and can be seen at a number of sites along the Broken River. Brush-turkeys, regent bowerbirds and other rainforest birds are common, and birders know this as the home of the endemic Eungella honeyeater.

Location 80km west of Mackay.

Facilities Platypus viewing platform and Rainforest Discovery Walk at Broken River.

Accom. Camping at Broken River and Fern Flat; caravan park at Finch Hatton; lodge just outside the park at Broken River.

Wildlife rhythms Platypuses are more likely to be seen by day May–September.

Contact Ranger, Broken River (☎ 07-4958 4552).

Ecotours Spotlight walks by park rangers during school holidays. Spotlighting also run by Broken River Mountain Retreat (☎ 07-4958 4528).

Watching tips

In the Pioneer Valley, keep an eye out for the Pacific baza – a medium-sized hawk with a strongly barred breast. In November, a symphony of frog calls starts up with the first rains of the wet season.

HINCHINBROOK ISLAND

Island of mangroves and rainforest

Wildlife highlights
Dugongs occur in significant concentrations and are frequently seen from boats; other common large marine animals include dolphins and sea turtles. Mangroves support saltwater crocodiles, flying-foxes and numerous birds (140 species have been recorded for the island). Land mammals include agile wallabies, bandicoots and native rodents.

Location 120km to the north of Townsville.
Facilities Thorsborne Trail; mangrove boardwalk.
Accommodation Wide range at Cardwell. Camping grounds and resort on Hinchinbrook.
Wildlife rhythms Pied imperial-pigeons breed over summer; dugongs calve in spring.
Contact Cardwell Rainforest and Reef Centre (☎ 07-4066 8601).
Ecotours Hinchinbrook Island Ferries (☎ 07-4066 8270) for day tours, walkers' transport and snorkelling tours. Hinchinbrook Wilderness Safaris (☎ 07-4777 83 07).

Watching tips
Near dawn in summer, pied imperial-pigeons fly in flocks from nesting grounds on the nearby Brook Islands to feed on Hinchinbrook's rainforest fruits.

THE world's second largest island national park, Hinchinbrook is a jumble of granite peaks, vine-entangled rainforest, beaches and mangroves. A day trip by boat from Cardwell or Lucinda makes a great introduction, but if you have more time walk the Thorsborne Trail, a three- to five-day hike along the east coast.

Mangroves fringe the western coastline, a rich habitat for molluscs, fish and crustaceans. Some **saltwater crocodiles** still inhabit the waterways but are shy of boats. Birds are far more obvious: **egrets** and **striated herons** poke among the roots; **little** and **azure kingfishers** dive for prey; and the **great-billed heron**, prized by birdwatchers, is sometimes seen on boat tours from Lucinda. Many **black flying-foxes** visit from the mainland at night, crossing the channel to feed on mangrove flowers. Beneath the mangrove boardwalk between Ramsay and Missionary Bays (the day tour takes you there), **mud whelks** trail across the surface and **burrowing crabs** carry yellowed mangrove leaves down their burrows to eat.

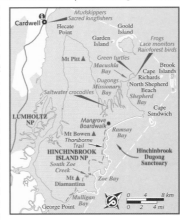

Domain of the dugong

Herds of **dugongs** feed on underwater seagrass meadows in the shallow waters of Missionary Bay. They are often sighted, nose or tail breaking the water, from the Cardwell boat. **Bottlenose dolphins** are most commonly seen in Missionary Bay and Hinchinbrook Channel. **Green turtles** feed around the rocks off Macushla Bay, **mudskippers** flip across the surface of adjoining mudflats and **hermit crabs**, in pre-used mollusc shells, trundle through shallow pools. Hundreds of tiny **ghost crabs** excavate the sand of North Shepherd Beach, and **soldier crabs** parade across the mouth of South Zoe Creek. There are even **fossilised crabs** at Ramsay Bay.

Rainforest birds are common at Cape Richards and **lace monitors** can be seen almost anywhere. Walkers can expect to see **agile wallabies**, and campers will probably encounter **giant white-tailed rats** (notorious for chewing through anything, including metal) and **fawn-footed melomys**. **Water-rats** and **bandicoots** are also common, and **giant tree frogs** emerge at night. ∎

LAKEFIELD NATIONAL PARK

Crocodile waters, termite plains

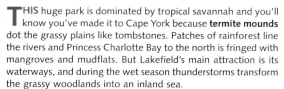

THIS huge park is dominated by tropical savannah and you'll know you've made it to Cape York because **termite mounds** dot the grassy plains like tombstones. Patches of rainforest line the rivers and Princess Charlotte Bay to the north is fringed with mangroves and mudflats. But Lakefield's main attraction is its waterways, and during the wet season thunderstorms transform the grassy woodlands into an inland sea.

During the dry season flood waters retreat, and birdlife congregates at the swamps and lagoons. The selection includes at times thousands of **waterfowl** – radjah shelducks and both species of whistling-duck are prominent – plus **sarus cranes, brolgas** and **black-necked storks**.

Both **freshwater** and **saltwater crocodiles** inhabit the extensive system of creeks and rivers. Most active during summer, in winter they spend considerable time basking on riverbanks – wide mud slides show where they haul themselves out. Kalpowar Crossing is a good area to look for saltwater crocodiles, particularly at night when their red eyeshine can be seen by spotlighting along the Normanby River. Freshwater crocodiles are sometimes seen in Little Kennedy Creek behind New Laura.

Parrots common and endangered

Agile wallabies are common throughout the park's grasslands and woodlands, and **northern nailtail wallabies** graze on the airstrip. Stately **Australian bustards** strut about the plains; **black** and **whistling kites** are conspicuous over the grasslands; and thousands of **little red flying-foxes** take to the air at dusk from one of northern Australia's largest camps near the Mary Valley Homestead, just west of the park boundary.

Golden-shouldered parrots nest in termite mounds, but this endangered bird is usually only seen in the dry season, when it visits waterholes in

the early morning to drink; a good place to search for it is on the plains around Musgrave Station to the west of the park. You should have no trouble seeing other common woodland birds, such as **red-winged parrots, red-tailed black-cockatoos, banded honeyeaters** and **great bowerbirds** – especially if you wait by a waterhole at dawn during the dry season. ■

Wildlife highlights

Agile and northern nailtail wallabies are common, but abundant saltwater and freshwater crocodiles are the park's raison d'etre. Waterbirds congregate at dry season lagoons; savannah birds include brolgas, bustards, red-winged and golden-shouldered parrots, and red-tailed black-cockatoos.

Location 300km to the northwest of Cairns.
Facilities Information boards.
Accommodation Bush camping; camping ground at Kalpowar Crossing.
Wildlife rhythms Crocodiles breed early Wet; golden-shouldered parrots most likely seen April–November.
Contact Rangers: Lakefield (☎ 07-4060 3271), New Laura (☎ 07-4060 3260).
Ecotours Some birding tours pass through the region to see the golden-shouldered parrot. Lotus Bird Lodge (☎ 07-4059 0773) specialises in wildlife ecotourism.

Watching tips

Look at butcherbirds perched on telephones wires – there are two types: pied butcherbirds have black across the chin and upper chest; black-backed butcherbirds, a Cape York endemic, have the white of the chest extending up to the beak.

OTHER SITES – QUEENSLAND

Bowen Area

Horseshoe and Murray Bays have coral reefs – hire snorkelling gear from the caravan park. At night unadorned rock-wallabies come down to feed behind the Horseshoe Bay Café (inquire within), and over the summer Children's pythons are common around the caravan park.
200km south of Townsville

Cairns

A great launching pad for exploring the Great Barrier Reef and Atherton Tableland, with several wildlife attractions close to the town centre. More than 200 bird species have been recorded along the Esplanade alone: world famous for migratory waders probing the mudflats September to March, the Esplanade is worth a look at any time of year. Flecker Botanic Gardens on Collins Ave has a boardwalk that passes through swamp forest. Centenary Lakes and Mt Whitfield Environmental Park are good for rainforest birds, including orange-footed scrubfowl and noisy pitta; and Pioneer Cemetery on Little St is a great place to search for bush stone-curlews. Two mangrove boardwalks have been constructed along the road to the airport.
Queensland Department of Environment and Heritage Information Centre,
☎ 07-4052 3096

Chillagoe–Mungana Caves National Park

Renowned for its many limestone caves, which are important as roosting and nesting sites for bats and white-rumped swiftlets. Dry-country birds include apostlebirds, red-winged parrots and red-tailed black-cockatoos.
210km west of Cairns via Mareeba, ☎ 07-4094 7163

Girraween National Park

A spectacular park of sculptured granite, adjoining Bald Rock NP in NSW, where eastern grey kangaroos, euros, swamp wallabies, red-necked wallabies, common brushtail and ringtail possums

and common wombats are all abundant. Gliders by night and honeyeaters by day feed from the nectar of flowering plants in heaths and woodlands. Dry-country birds include turquoise parrots, laughing kookaburras, wedge-tailed eagles, rosellas, fairy-wrens and diamond firetails; superb lyrebirds are found in wetter forests.
260km south-west of Brisbane,
☎ 07-4684 5157

Granite Gorge

A great spot to see semitame Mareeba rock-wallabies.
12km south-west of Mareeba,
☎ 07-4093 2259

Hervey Bay

Probably the best spot on the east coast for whale-watching – and certainly the most popular. More than 25% of Australia's humpback whales enter Hervey Bay on their return journey to subantarctic waters and adults are often seen with calves. Sightings are almost daily from August to mid-October with numerous tour boat operators.
285km north of Brisbane,
☎ 1800 649 926

Iron Range National Park

This remote park on Cape York Peninsula conserves Australia's largest remaining area of lowland rainforest. Wildlife has strong affinities with that of New Guinea; famous highlights includes the green python,

spotted cuscus, and a host of sought-after birds such as the palm cockatoo, eclectus parrot, red-cheeked parrot, red-bellied pitta, yellow-billed kingfisher and magnificent riflebird – to name but a few.
Approximately 500km north of Cairns, ☎ 07-4060 7170

Julatten

Legendary among birdwatchers, the remnant rainforest at Kingfisher Park Birdwatcher's Lodge is a wildlife oasis. Macleay's, blue-faced and bridled honeyeaters squabble at feeders a few feet away; noisy pittas and orange-footed scrubfowl wander the grounds; and a host of rainforest birds includes pied monarchs and Victoria's riflebirds. Red-necked crakes are often seen at dusk by a pool in the orchard and a pair of buff-breasted paradise-kingfishers nests at the park over summer. At night, long-nosed bandicoots, red-legged pademelons and giant white-tailed rats emerge; the shower block is hopping with giant tree frogs; spectacled flying-foxes feed in the orchard; barking owls, lesser sooty owls and Papuan frogmouths also live on the property. In the early morning or at dusk platypuses can be seen in the creek. This is also a great base for exploring the upland rainforest of nearby Mt Lewis – home of rare, white lemuroid ringtail possums, golden bowerbirds and blue-faced parrot-finches, and where nightjars, owls, possums and leaf-tailed geckoes can all be seen at night.
95km north-west of Cairns,
☎ 07-4094 1263

Kuranda

A tourist village in the hills behind Cairns with a number of wildlife attractions, including the Australian Butterfly Sanctuary

(☎ 07-4093 7575) and Kuranda Wildlife Noctarium. Watch for cassowaries along Black Mountain Rd (drive slowly!). The Carrowong Fauna Sanctuary (☎ 07-4093 7287) runs nocturnal wildlife tours where a host of critters may be seen, including tree-kangaroos, rainforest possums, bettongs, owls and frog – all profits go towards conservation rainforest rehabilitation.
34km north-west of Cairns,
☎ 07-4093 7570

Mission Beach

If you want to see a southern cassowary, this is the spot. The best time to look is in the early morning along roads and forest tracks, particularly in October and November when the males are leading chicks around. Ask locals for recent sightings or

inquire at the information centre set up for cassowary conservation on Porters Promenade.
150km south of Cairns

Mon Repos Conservation Park

This mainland beach near Bundaberg is the largest live turtle rookery on the east coast. Loggerhead turtles come ashore at night to nest here every year between November and February, and hatchlings can be seen from January to March.
15km north-east of Bundaberg,
☎ 07-4159 1652

Paluma Range National Park

Excellent upland rainforests in which several Wet Tropics endemics reach their southern limit. Rainforest birds can be seen around Paluma and en route to Paluma Dam. Don't miss the Ivy

Cottage Tea Gardens – famous for the Victoria's riflebirds and Macleay's honeyeaters that visit your table. At Jourama Falls a rainforest-lined creek carves through drier woodland, where

agile wallabies, northern brown bandicoots, goannas, freshwater turtles and a variety of birds can be seen around the picnic area and camping ground. At night listen for the 'wood-chopping' call of the large-tailed nightjar.
Mount Speculation – 80km north of Townsville,
☎ 07-4770 8526
Jourama Falls – 97km north of Townsville, ☎ 07-4777 3112

Townsville Town Common Environmental Park

Bird hides overlook wetlands where brolgas and black-necked storks feed, and at the beginning of the Wet magpie geese gather in thousands. Other waterbirds include the comb-crested jacana, cotton pygmy-goose and wandering whistling-duck, while rainbow bee-eaters and black kites are conspicuous overhead. Check out the Forest Walk for finches, honeyeaters, yellow-bellied sunbirds and bush stone-curlews. In the early morning and late afternoon look for agile wallabies, sand monitors and dingoes along the road. The Lagoon Hide often shelters tree frogs, geckoes and occasionally a Children's python.
6km north-west of Townsville via the Cape Pallarenda Rd,
☎ 07-4774 1382

Undara Volcanic National Park

The world's longest system of lava tubes, formed 190,000 years ago when molten lava

flowed along old riverbeds. Eucalypt woodland is pock-marked with collapsed tubes that create microclimates for plants and animals. Five bat species and giant millipedes, butterflies and spiders inhabit the underground tubes, but the only way to see the tubes is by guided tour (Undara Lava Lodge, ☎ 07-4097 1411). Euros, eastern grey kangaroos and common brushtail

possums are common and rufous bettongs are frequently encountered around the camping ground. Waterbirds congregate at nearby Hundred Mile Swamp.
275km south-west of Cairns,
☎ 07-4097 1485

Wooroonooran National Park – Palmerston section

Tropical rainforest in rugged coastal ranges. The track between Goolagans picnic area and Henrietta Creek camping ground is great for platypuses and freshwater turtles. Musky rat-kangaroos, spotted catbirds, double-eyed fig-parrots and Victoria's riflebirds can be seen around the camping ground. Nocturnal mammals to watch

for – with the raucous chortling of orange-footed scrubfowl in the background – include bandicoots, possums and the fawn-footed melomys.
33km west of Innisfail,
☎ 07-4064 5115

SOUTH AUSTRALIA

State faunal emblems

Southern hairy-nosed wombat The stronghold of these broad-nosed, silky-furred marsupials is the semiarid plains of the Nullarbor. To escape extreme daytime heat they rest in extensive underground burrows.

Australian magpie This striking black-and-white bird is widespread in open areas, such as farmland, and a common resident of city parks and gardens. Its morning carolling is one of the most beautiful of birdsongs.

Highlights

- At Yookamurra Sanctuary, digging is a popular pastime – for numbats by day and bilbies by night
- Being the first to spot the elongated silhouettes of honking brolgas returning in small groups to Bool Lagoon at dusk
- Witnessing Australia as it was before foxes: abundant, tiny, grey tammar wallabies feeding on the roads on Kangaroo Island
- Craning your neck back to watch squadrons of Australian pelicans soaring overhead in the Coorong
- Not knowing which part to watch of the nonstop drama in the colony of New Zealand fur-seals on Kangaroo Island
- Glimpsing the beautiful but threatened yellow-footed rock-wallaby at Brachina Gorge in the Flinders Ranges
- Looking down on whales from Nullarbor cliff tops

SOUTH Australia (SA) is the driest state. Lake Eyre, a dry salt lake in the north-east, is the most arid part of the continent, with an average yearly rainfall of only 150mm. Vegetation ranges from saltbush in arid regions, to mallee in the south-east, to river red gum floodplains along the winding Murray River. Summers are scorching, often over 40°C; winters are cooler, although temperatures well above 20°C are not uncommon inland. In the south, most rain falls in winter. Rainfall in the north is unpredictable, but rapidly brings parched regions to life.

Over one-fifth of the state, including 17 national parks, is managed for conservation by the state National Parks and Wildlife South Australia (NPWSA). Habitat clearance and exotic animals have resulted in the loss of nearly one-quarter of SA's original mammal species since European settlement, and one-quarter of the remaining 88 species are threatened. However, from the vast inland regions to the spectacular coastline, there remains a great diversity of abundant wildlife to experience – and with far fewer residents and tourists in SA than the eastern states, they are experiences you will often have to yourself.

Rare yellow-footed rock-wallabies live in the Flinders Ranges, along with red kangaroos on the plains, western grey kangaroos in woodlands and grasslands, and euros on rocky slopes.

The coastal wetland of the Coorong is one of the country's most important sites for waterbirds, particularly Australian pelicans, with at times millions of birds of dozens of species present.

Kangaroo Island has no introduced foxes or rabbits, helping to make it one of Australia's great wildlife-watching destinations. Its wealth of wildlife includes abundant tammar wallabies, almost extinct on the mainland; KI's own subspecies of the glossy black-cockatoo, Australia's most endangered cockatoo; platypuses and koalas (both introduced to the island); and colonies of Australian sea-lions and New Zealand fur-seals.

Other SA highlights include the state's faunal emblem, the rare southern hairy-nosed wombat – found mainly on the Nullarbor Plain, but also on the Eyre Peninsula and a few reserves north of Adelaide (some of their burrow systems are so extensive that they can be seen from the air); the state's diversity of reptiles, especially in mallee regions with spinifex; and the annual influx of southern right whales to their calving waters beneath the cliffs of the Nullarbor Plain. ∎

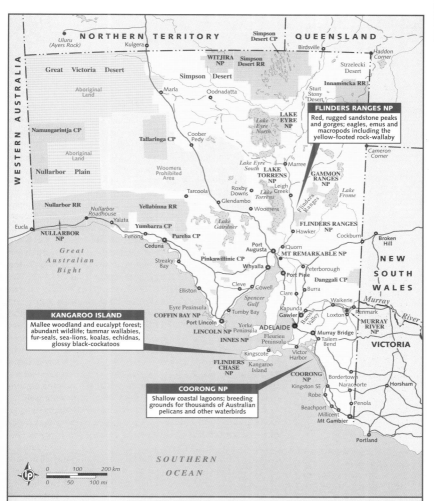

FLINDERS RANGES NP
Red, rugged sandstone peaks and gorges; eagles, emus and macropods including the yellow-footed rock-wallaby

KANGAROO ISLAND
Mallee woodland and eucalypt forest; abundant wildlife; tammar wallabies, fur-seals, sea-lions, koalas, echidnas, glossy black-cockatoos

COORONG NP
Shallow coastal lagoons; breeding grounds for thousands of Australian pelicans and other waterbirds

Suggested itineraries

One week (South – start/finish Adelaide) Spend 3 days on Kangaroo Island, taking in Flinders Chase NP, Seal Bay and Lathami CPs. Visit Coorong NP for waterbirds then end by overnighting at Warrawong Sanctuary.

One week (North – start/finish Adelaide) Take 3 days to explore Flinders Ranges NP, heading up via Mt Remarkable NP. Spend a day at Innes NP then backtrack for a night at Warrawong.

Two weeks (Start/finish Adelaide) Simply combine the two one-week itineraries; or take the northern option and spend the second week on the Strzelecki Track to Innamincka RR, or head west to Nullarbor NP. For a real taste of the arid zone take two weeks to venture into the Great Victoria Desert, or head through Brookfield and Danggali CPs to Flinders Ranges NP and then beyond into the Strzelecki Desert.

One month (Start/finish Adelaide) A longer trip gives you time to take one of the arid-zone options then either push west to look for whales in the Great Australian Bight (in winter), or enjoy the waterbird spectacle at Lake Eyre (if it's in flood). On the way back, stop at some of the parks west of Adelaide, such as Lincoln or Coffin Bay NPs; take a winter seabird trip; and there's still just time for a few days on Kangaroo Island.

ADELAIDE

The green city

ADELAIDE is a small, linear city compressed between the Mt Lofty Ranges and the Gulf St Vincent. Running along the River Torrens and surrounding the metropolitan area is a green belt of parks and gardens, in which parrots – **rainbow lorikeets**, **red-rumped parrots**, **Adelaide rosellas** (a form of the widespread crimson rosella) – **red wattlebirds** and **crested pigeons** are commonly seen. The main lake in the *Adelaide Botanic Gardens* (☎ 08-8228 2311) has a good variety of waterbirds, including **black swans**, egrets and cormorants. As in most urban centres of Australia, the **common brushtail possum** is a familiar resident of parklands and backyards; however, they are no longer common in the rest of SA.

The *Adelaide Zoo* (☎ 08-8267 3255), beside the Botanic Gardens, houses a range of marsupials, including a colony of yellow-footed rock-wallabies; a little penguin display that simulates Kangaroo Island's coastline; Australian sea-lions; and walk-through aviaries displaying native birds of the subtropical rainforest and northern coastal wetlands.

Cleland CP (☎ 08-8370 1054) has many walking tracks running through stringybark forest and along the creeks (good birdwatching areas) to Waterfall Gully and the summit of Mt Lofty, the highest peak in the Mt Lofty Ranges. It also contains *Cleland Wildlife Park* (☎ 08-8339 2444), which has emus, kangaroos, bettongs, bandicoots and potoroos living in five free-range environments; and enclosures for birds, wombats, koalas, Tasmanian devils, dingoes and yellow-footed rock-wallabies. Groups can arrange night walks during which bettongs, potoroos and bandicoots can be watched when they are active.

Black Hill and *Morialta CPs*, 12km from the city centre, are worth visiting for their waterfalls and gorges, and for the chance of seeing an **echidna** or antechinus.

The parklands flanking the River Torrens provide Adelaide's urban lorikeets, rosellas and waterbirds with a green corridor through the city. Pockets of natural vegetation in the nearby Mt Lofty Ranges support native mammals.

The beaches, muddy shores and mangroves between *Outer Harbor*, *St Kilda* and *Port Gawler* are good sites for **wading birds**. A 90-minute guided tour along the St Kilda Mangrove Trail (☎ 08-8280 8172), provides information on the ecology of this area. The extensive saltworks north of the city are renowned among birdwatchers for their **waterbirds** and migratory **waders**. At *Port Noarlunga Underwater Aquatic Reserve* (☎ 08-8323 9944) there is an 800m underwater nature swim for scuba divers and snorkellers.

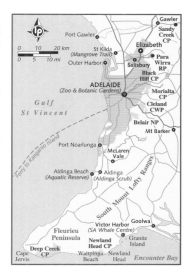

Belair NP (☎ 08-8278 5477), 13km south-east of the city centre, is SA's oldest park – and it shows: there's a golf course, adventure playground, tennis courts, ovals, exotic gardens and the old Government House. There are, however, some good areas for wildlife-watching. The creekside river red gums and yellow-gum woodlands harbour **emus**, **laughing kookaburras**, Adelaide rosellas, honeyeaters and other birds, and Playford Lake supports waterbirds. **Echidnas**, **possums** and several reptile species can also be seen.

Para Wirra Recreation Park (☎ 08-8280 7048) is 40km north-east of Adelaide. The dry, open forests are good for birdwatching – try around the southern oval – with **emus** common. The ovals also attract **western grey kangaroos** in the late afternoon. The Lizard Rock Nature Trail traverses a variety of vegetation types. Another good woodland for wildlife-watching is *Sandy Creek CP* in the Barossa Valley.

The *Aldinga Scrub* (☎ 08-8278 5477), 50km south of Adelaide, consists of dry eucalypt woodland, mallee, heath, and sand dunes with many rare plants. The birdlife is prolific, particularly in spring when the wildflowers bloom, and includes **purple-crowned** and **musk lorikeets**, **elegant parrots**, **rainbow bee-eaters**, **laughing kookaburras** and many honeyeaters. Bats and **common brushtail possums** can be seen here at night and **echidnas**, geckoes, butterflies and skinks by day. Nearby Aldinga Beach is also popular with birdwatchers and the adjacent *Aldinga Reef Aquatic Reserve*, in which lives the locally endangered **blue groper**, can be explored by snorkelling or reef walking.

Granite Island at *Victor Harbor*, 84km south of Adelaide, has a **little penguin** rookery. The penguins can be watched in the evening as they return from the sea and can be seen in their burrows near the main walking track during spring and summer. Tours can be arranged by NPWSA (☎ 08-8552 3677). Newland Head, at Victor Harbor's Waitpinga Beach, is an excellent spot to watch **seabirds**, especially during stormy winter weather. **Southern right whales** enter Encounter Bay between May and September; they are easily watched from most headlands and cliffs along this coastline and are often seen from the causeway between the mainland and Granite Island. The *South Australian Whale Centre* (☎ 08-8552 5644; Whale Information Line ☎ 1900 931 223) in Victor Harbor provides information about whales and records of sightings along the coast. *The Bluff*, at the western end of Victor Harbor, is a good dive site for **leafy sea dragons**. ∎

KANGAROO ISLAND

Rarities, endemics and pinnipeds

Wildlife highlights

A large number of rare species and KI forms of more widespread species. Tammar wallabies and western grey kangaroos (both are KI subspecies), koalas, Australian sea-lions, New Zealand fur-seals, brushtail possums and Cape Barren geese are all conspicuous. Rare birdlife includes the glossy black-cockatoo (KI subspecies), western whipbird, hooded plover, beautiful firetail and Bassian thrush. Whales, dolphins and little penguins are often encountered in the surrounding waters. Echidnas and heath monitors can be seen in the woodlands. Other animals that are widespread, but are seldom encountered, include the western pygmy-possum, southern brown bandicoot and a KI-endemic dunnart. Common birds include rosellas, lorikeets, honeyeaters, currawongs, wrens, robins and many seabirds. There are also 40 plant species found only on the island.

SKIRTED by high cliffs and sculpted dunes, the tilted plateau that is Kangaroo Island (KI), Australia's third largest island, offers some of the best wildlife-watching in the country. Over half the original native mallee, heath and woodland remains and 30% of the island is protected in 21 parks, including Flinders Chase NP. Most importantly, there are neither foxes or dingoes to prey on, nor rabbits to compete with, native wildlife. The difference this makes to the abundance of wildlife on KI compared to the mainland is striking, and it allows several rare species to thrive. KI's isolation has also seen the evolution of several distinct KI varieties of more widespread mainland species.

The tiny **tammar wallaby** is virtually extinct on the mainland, but the KI subspecies is flourishing. The open grassy area near the park headquarters in Flinders Chase NP is a sure spot to find them at dusk and they are also commonly seen grazing along roadsides at night. The KI subspecies of **western grey kangaroo**

Time to breed?

A number of features set the fur-seals and sea-lions apart from the 'true seals', such as their external ears and ability to move nimbly on land. But one characteristic of the Australian sea-lion (inset) also sets it apart from all its relatives. Females breed every 17.6 months, making it the only pinniped (ie, seal, fur-seal or sea-lion) with a non-annual breeding cycle. There is no synchrony in the timing of breeding between different colonies, so it is not seasonal changes in day length or temperature that trigger the onset of breeding. Instead, it may be tied to food supply, as KI's New Zealand fur-seals feed in richer waters than do the sea-lions, and have a typical 12-month breeding cycle.

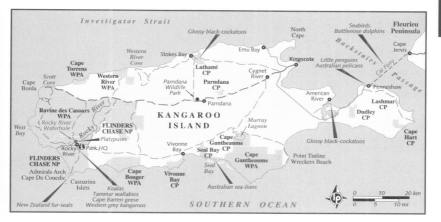

also grazes here and a few tame individuals loiter around the car park. They are slightly darker, larger and longer-furred than mainland western greys. These kangaroos are also easy to see along roads at night and in open areas adjacent to bush during the day. **Common brushtail possums** are frequently encountered at night around camping grounds.

Fur-seals, sea-lions and the sea

KI's most famous residents are its fur-seals and sea-lions. **New Zealand fur-seals** rest at Admirals Arch, one of their 'haul-out zones' to which they retire between feeding trips. There are 6000 or so living and breeding here and around Cape du Couedic. While most lie prostrate in the sunshine, scuffles break out continuously and there are always some heading into the surf to frolic, or weaving through the colony in search of a place to sprawl. **Pacific** and **silver gulls** wait around to scavenge anything they can from the colony. **Australasian gannets, crested terns, shearwaters** and other seabirds can be seen out to sea.

A viewing boardwalk and ranger-guided tour along the beach provide access to the resident colony of 600 **Australian sea-lions** at Seal Bay CP. Watch for their tracks leading into the dunes: they have been known to travel up to 1km inland to doze. This is the third-largest known colony of Australian sea-lions in the world, and Seal Bay is the only place where they can be seen at close range.

The waters around the coastline are known for their clarity, their many sunken wrecks and high diversity of temperate fish species, 80% of which are endemic to South Australia. There are also areas of gorgonian corals and sponges, and frequent encounters with fur-seals and **leafy sea dragons** – all in all, there's great diving. **Southern right whales** and their calves are regularly sighted off the island's southern coast in winter; the cliffs along the walking track to Cape Gantheaume are good vantage points. **Common** and **bottlenose dolphins** frequently accompany the ferry to the island, and are often also seen by divers.

A distinct subspecies of the wide-spread western grey kangaroo is common throughout the island.

Newer arrivals

Koalas, platypuses, common ringtail possums, Cape Barren geese, Australian brush-turkeys and emus have all been introduced to the island (KI once had its own dwarf species of emu, but it was driven to extinction in the early 1800s, only a few years after white settlement). The large, grey **Cape Barren goose** is found only along Australia's southern coast and was once in danger of extinction. They are now flourishing on KI and are easily seen at American River and around Flinders Chase NP headquarters, as are **brush-turkeys** and the single **emu** left on the island.

Location 109km south-west of Adelaide. Ferry from Cape Jervis.
Facilities Visitor centre at Kingscote. Boardwalk and viewing platform at Seal Bay.
Accommodation A full range throughout island.
Wildlife rhythms Visit in winter for southern right whales and seabirds. Winter and spring for flowering mallee plants and associated nectar-feeding birds. Summer and autumn to see young sea-lions. Late spring and early summer to more easily see glossy black-cockatoos.
Contact Visitor centre, Kingscote (☎ 08-8553 1185, 💻 www .tourkangarooisland.com.au). Rangers: Flinders Chase NP (☎ 08-8553 7235), Kingscote (☎ 08-8553 2381).
Ecotours NPWSA-led tours to see penguins at Penneshaw and Kingscote and the sea-lions at Seal Bay. Knowledgeable and enthusiastic Daniel of Daniel's Tours (☎ 08-8553 1455) has a range of walking and wildlife tours for small groups, offering all wildlife highlights, night and morning walks and much more; itineraries can be personalised and vary depending on the time of year. Penneshaw Youth Hostel (☎ 08-8553 1284) offers wildlife tours that include the major wildlife attractions, and also offers a scuba-diving course and snorkelling excursions. Sealink (☎ 08-8553 1122) offers coach tours taking in a similar range of wildlife. Parndana Wildlife Park (☎ 08-8559 6050) is home to koalas, kangaroos, parrots and other native birds.

Koalas are now widespread and are common in the manna gums in Flinders Chase (especially outside park headquarters) and around Cygnet River. They have fared so well that they are now overbrowsing some areas, killing vegetation and ultimately starving themselves. A number are being sterilised and others removed from the island to reduce their impact.

Platypuses are occasionally seen at the Rocky River Waterhole (which is also a good area for birdwatching). Platypus-spotting chances are greatest at dusk and dawn during summer.

Campside diners

Anywhere you go in Australia, you encounter furred or feathered residents willing to share your meal. KI is no exception. It begins midmorning when the cars of visitors to Flinders Chase are thoroughly inspected for edible items by an emu, the only one on the island. At lunchtime, the ritual of the Aussie barbecue is enacted in the face of an army of yellow-eyed pied currawongs, perched on every branch and fence post. In the afternoon, kangaroos poke their heads through the car window. But it is at night that the real onslaught begins: brushtail possums. This camping ground resident marches in to gas-stove dinners to steal the bread, jump into the pots and take anything that is vaguely edible. However, feeding animals harms them by creating a dependency on an artificial food supply, inciting aggression and causing diseases.
Marianne Worley

Glossy and black

Lathami CP was created to conserve the habitat of the KI sub-species of the endangered **glossy black-cockatoo**. Flocks of glossy blacks are most commonly seen here in late spring and early summer, outside the breeding season; Western River CP and near the township of American River are also good sites. Fewer than 300 of these hollow-dependent birds exist on the island and efforts are being made to increase the population through the use of nest boxes. Their main food is seeds from the cones of drooping she-oaks. As you walk through stands of this tree, cracking sounds above, and orange, woody fragments of recently chewed cones on the ground, are evidence that these birds are nearby.

Another glossy black KI inhabitant is the **black tiger snake**. They are common, their long, thick body whispering as they slide over the vegetation in rapid retreat. **Heath monitors** (Rosenberg's goanna) are often seen at roadsides, particularly in the warmer months; and **White's skinks** are common in mallee and woodland – look for a family of heads peering out from under a fallen log.

The plaintive cries of the **bush stone-curlew**, another endangered bird, are occasionally heard at night from forest edges; it is much more common on KI than on the adjacent mainland. **Wedge-tailed eagles** are also high in numbers, soaring over paddocks and roads where there are road-killed animals, especially near Flinders Chase NP. **White-bellied sea-eagles** and **ospreys** scout the coastal cliffs, and are often seen around the lighthouses at Cape Borda and North Cape.

Murray Lagoon, the island's largest inland water body, is important for waterbirds. It floods in winter and is surrounded by reeds and paperbarks which provide nesting sites for the **Australian white ibis** and several duck species, including the **blue-billed duck**. Pelican Lagoon is another important waterbird site: **Australian pelicans** are, predictably, common here and elsewhere (it isn't exactly 'wild', but there is a late afternoon pelican feeding each day at Kingscote's wharf). **Little penguins** breed along the coastline and rangers lead evening tours to view them at Kingscote and Penneshaw; and you may well see and hear them as you leave the island by ferry. ∎

> **Watching tips**
> Large flocks of yellow-tailed black-cockatoos feed in the pine plantation on Colemans Rd, in the north-west of the island. Watch for Australasian gannets, shearwaters and cormorants from the ferry. When flowering, large eucalypts at the Parndana township attract hordes of purple-crowned lorikeets, and brown-headed and New Holland honeyeaters.

Large and unmistakable, the Australian pelican is common on Kangaroo Island. At Kingscote wharf pelicans have become bold enough to accept daily handouts.

COORONG NATIONAL PARK

Waterbird and wader sanctuary

Wildlife highlights
Waterbirds feature at this wetland of international significance. Australian pelicans are most conspicuous; it is also one of the most important areas for shorebirds in Australia. Numbers of waterbird build up dramatically in the late spring and summer, when other water bodies dry up. It is the western limit of the common wombat.

THE Coorong is a landscape of lagoons, salt lakes, massive dunes and ocean beaches. At its heart is Coorong Lagoon: shallow, saline and surrounding dozens of islands, it stretches for over 100km, sheltered from the Southern Ocean by the dunes of the Younghusband Peninsula. To the north, at the mouth of the Murray River, lie the enormous water bodies of Lakes Alexandrina and Albert.

Dunes on the Younghusband Peninsula separate Coorong Lagoon from the Southern Ocean.

Access 140km to the south-east of Adelaide.
Facilities Salt Creek nature walk. Visitor centre (☎ 08-8575 7014).
Accommodation Wide range in surrounding towns and properties; camping throughout park.
Wildlife rhythms Summer sees the greatest concentration of waterbirds and waders, and the breeding of many species, including pelicans.
Contact Ranger, Meningie (☎ 08-8575 1200).
Ecotours Coorong Nature Tours (☎ 08-8574 0037) customise tours. The Ngarrindjeri people, based at Camp Coorong (☎ 08-8575 1557), run guided nature tours. Inquire at the NPWSA office in Meningie (or check the *Coorong Tattler*) for ranger-guided activities during holidays.

Pelican paradise

Birdlife is prolific and includes, in summer, up to two million waterfowl and up to almost one-quarter of a million waders. However, the bird synonymous with the Coorong is the **Australian pelican**. Their size alone makes them conspicuous and they are also abundant, often gliding in V-shaped squadrons across the sky. Most importantly, several thousand breed on the Pelican Islands (above) during spring and summer – the largest permanent breeding site in Australia. The colony can be viewed from Jacks Point. Among other breeding birds are up to 8000 **crested terns** on Stony Well Island from September to December, plus ibises, spoonbills and abundant **silver gulls**.

Good spots from which to view ducks, **black swans** and other waterbirds include around Policemans Point and along the Narrung Road. **Cape Barren geese** migrate from their breeding grounds on islands in the Spencer Gulf to spend the summer around Lakes Alexandrina and Albert. Summer is also the best time to look for migratory **waders**: the best sites are in the north of the park, especially between Pelican Point and Jacks Point.

Other good wader sites include Tea Tree Crossing and the area between Policemans Point and Magrath Flat. Nonmigratory waders include **pied oystercatchers** and **hooded plovers** probing the ocean beaches, and summer influxes of thousands of nomadic **banded stilts**. White-rumped **swamp harriers** are a common sight, quartering low over the paddocks and wetlands on upswept wings.

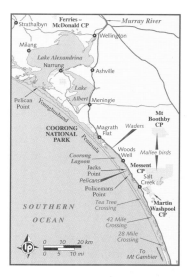

Away from the water

Common wombats and **western grey kangaroos** can be seen at night in the south of the park, along Old Melbourne Rd. The grasslands here, the result of farming and grazing, also support good numbers of **shingle-back** lizards; and **black-shouldered kites** and **nankeen kestrels** hover over the paddocks and coastal scrub. **Eastern tiger snakes** are common in wetter areas, with two colour phases occurring around Lakes Alexandrina and Albert – the typical striped form and a completely black form. Littered shellfish remains on the muddy shores of Lake Alexandrina are the work of **water-rats** – dusk and just after dark is the best time to look for the animals themselves.

Two of the more sought-after bush birds found in the park occur in the dense coastal scrub, such as that south of Salt Creek. The **beautiful firetail** is quite common in this habitat. First attempts to see them often produce little more than glimpses as they fly from vegetation alongside the road. However, with some persistence and binoculars you'll get reasonable looks at this tiny, crimson-rumped bird. The rare **rufous bristlebird** is much more difficult to see (beyond a dark shape shooting across the track ahead), but listen for its loud distinctive call – a loud, repeated squeaking followed by a whip crack.

On a grassy lawn near the petrol station at Salt Creek you can often get good looks at groups of **black-tailed native-hens** – their fluorescent pink legs are unmistakable. The Salt Creek itself is a good place to look for **long-necked turtles**. **Malleefowl** are a possibility on the nature walk at Salt Creek and along the Old Melbourne Rd, but are more likely in the nearby mallee of Messent and Mt Boothby CPs. ∎

Watching tips

Waders are notoriously difficult to identify, especially when in nonbreeding plumage: try focussing on bill length and shape. There is a malleefowl mound just off the Old Melbourne Rd just short of 4km from the petrol station at Salt Creek.

Coorong crèches

Usually regarded as a coastal bird, pelicans are actually often found on lakes and rivers, and tend to breed opportunistically on inland lakes and offshore cays. They nest close to one another, laying two or three white eggs in simple scrapes that may be lined with leaves, grass, sticks and feathers. In the first three weeks of a chick's life it grows up to six times its original size. After about 25 days in the nest after hatching, the chick wanders and joins other chicks nearby, forming a crèche which aids in protecting them from predators, and also in keeping them warm. When a sitting adult is disturbed it will temporarily abandon the nest, leaving the eggs and chicks as easy prey for predators. When watching a pelican breeding colony, keep at a distance and use binoculars.

FLINDERS RANGES NATIONAL PARK

Yellow foot, red rock

Wildlife highlights

Abundant wildlife of the Outback. This is one of the only places where yellow-footed rock-wallabies can be easily seen. Euros, red and western grey kangaroos are common. The birds include plentiful parrots, cockatoos, emus and raptors, and a recently described grasswren endemic to the area. Reptiles are diverse and conspicuous. Fossils of early marine life are also a highlight.

COVERING a vast area, the rugged, tilted mountains of the Flinders Ranges run north into increasingly arid country and thus form an important refuge for wildlife. The steep, rocky slopes of Brachina Gorge and Wilkawillina Gorge are home to the threatened **yellow-footed rock-wallaby** – the icon of the Flinders Ranges. These attractively patterned macropods have a long, thick, yellow-and-brown banded tail. During the day, they mostly shelter out of sight on cool rock ledges and in caves high on the rocky slopes; in cooler weather – and especially in the early morning – they sometimes bask on rocks in the sun. But you are much more likely to see them at night. Try scanning the large scree slope in Brachina Gorge at dusk, or wait by the waterhole at Brachina's Rawnsley Quartzite (especially in summer when water elsewhere is scarce). After dark they feed on grass on the gorge's floor; you are likely to encounter several simply by walking along the road through the gorge, although they are usually heard thumping away before they are seen.

At dusk, dawn, or with a torch at night, three other kangaroo species can easily be seen. **Red kangaroos** inhabit shrubland and woodland, especially in the north; **western grey kangaroos** inhabit open woodland and grassland on the outer slopes of the ranges; and **euros**, with a bare muzzle and shaggy coat, roam the rockier, northern areas of Brachina and Wilkawillina Gorge.

Missing mammals

The nights in the Flinders Ranges 200 years ago were filled with woylies bounding through open areas where bilbies excavated red earth in search of invertebrates; predatory kowaris and mulgaras dashing between tussocks of spinifex grass and crunching beetles with needle-sharp teeth; and the white-spotted, carnivorous chuditch stalking through woodland in search of small prey. But all of these, and another 11 species of small- to medium-sized, ground-dwelling mammal are now extinct in the Flinders Ranges. Their demise was quick – it took not more than a few decades – and complete. Not one species of this size remains. The grazing and trampling of vegetation by sheep, cattle and rabbits, and the impact of predatory cats and foxes, drove native mammal populations to extinction – a story repeated across much of the country. Since European settlement, Australia has lost more mammal species than any other country.

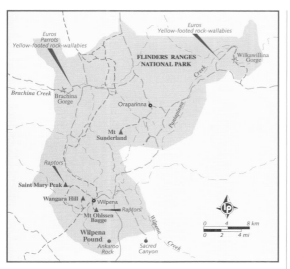

Location 460km to the north of Adelaide.

Facilities Visitor centre at Wilpena Pound; 'Corridor through time' Geological Trail in Brachina Gorge.

Accommodation Camping and motel at Wilpena Pound; several other camping grounds; wide range in surrounding towns.

Wildlife rhythms Spring best for wildflowers and nectar-feeding birds, spring and winter to see wildlife out during the day.

Contact Flinders Ranges visitor centre, Wilpena (☎ 08-8648 0048). Ranger, Hawker (☎ 08-8648 4244).

Ecotours The Bush Safari Company (☎ 08-8543 2280) runs camel treks, with a focus on scenery and wildlife, led by experienced naturalist Rex Ellis.

Raptorous heights and ancient depths

Birdlife is relatively sparse, but there is still plenty of interest to see, including a number of arid-zone specialities such as **redthroats** and the Flinders Ranges endemic **short-tailed grasswren**. The grasswren, a bird of spinifex/mallee habitat, has only recently been identified as a distinct species; a good site for it is around Oraparinna. High peaks such as Mt Ohlssen Bagge and St Mary Peak are the best spots from which to watch raptors soaring on thermals, with **wedge-tailed eagles** circling the peaks, and **brown** and **black falcons** sweeping over the plains below. Whitewash on ledges of red cliff faces mark the eyries of **peregrine falcons**. **Emus** are common on the plains.

Within Wilpena Pound (main photo), there are good areas of mallee with its characteristic birds. In wooded areas, **elegant parrots**, **Australian ringnecks**, and flocks of **galahs** and **little corellas** are common. Two forms of the widespread ringneck parrot (green with a yellow band on its nape) meet in and around the Ranges: mallee ringnecks (green head and red band above the bill) and Port Lincoln ringnecks (black hood and no red facial marking); 90% of ringnecks here are actually hybrids and show many different combinations of the features of the pure forms.

Reptiles are conspicuous: **tawny dragons** bask on rocks in high areas; **painted dragons** sprawl on red spinifex plains; and **shingle-backs** and **inland bearded dragons** – the largest of the park's dragons – are often seen crossing roads and tracks. Two species of goanna occur: **Gould's goanna** and, in the red gum woodlands along rivers, an isolated population of **lace monitors**.

Much of the ranges consist of sediments deposited over 500 million years ago in a shallow sea. The 'Corridor through time' walk in Brachina Gorge reveals the fauna that lived in this sea – some of the oldest fossils of multicelled life in the world. ∎

The extensive outcrops of the Flinders Ranges rise dramatically from the surrounding plains.

Watching tips

At night, shine a torch into the clear Rawnsley Quartzite pool to see blue yabbies and the sapphire eyeshine of spiders on the water's surface; you can also find geckoes in the debris beneath red gums. Search for short-tailed grasswrens on calm, warm days in the early morning and late afternoon – they are often located by their high-pitched calls.

OTHER SITES – SOUTH AUSTRALIA

Bool Lagoon Game Reserve

One of the best waterbird sites in southern Australia. The freshwater attracts Cape Barren geese, black swans and countless ducks. Ibis and spoonbill nesting colonies are conspicuous on the Tea Tree boardwalk. From

midsummer to late autumn, brolgas often feed in Black Rush Swamp, west of Big Hill. From December to February is best for migratory waders, the September to January breeding season best for waterbirds. There are lookouts, hides and boardwalks.
24km south of Naracoorte,
☎ 08-8764 7541

Brookfield and Swan Reach Conservation Parks

Mallee and woodland parks established to conserve the southern hairy-nosed wombat.
120km north-east of Adelaide,
☎ 08-8595 2111

Coffin Bay National Park

Dolphins and Australian sea-lions often swim in the bays; southern right whales are often seen in winter from the headlands. Rock parrots breed and the rare western whipbird can be found. Ospreys and white-bellied sea-eagles soar around cliff faces and rare hooded plovers nest on beaches. Emus and western grey kangaroos are common.
700km west of Adelaide,
☎ 08-8685 4047

Danggali Conservation Park

A large reserve of mallee, red sand and spinifex best visited in the cooler months. Emus, parrots and honeyeaters, and red and

western grey kangaroos are common. Hypurna Dam often has the only standing water; large numbers of kangaroos can be seen here at dusk.
350km north-west of Adelaide, ☎ 08-8595 2111

Gluepot Reserve

Run by Birds Australia to protect several rare birds, primarily the black-eared miner. Open to self-sufficient visitors.
64km north of Waikerie,
☎ 03-9882 2622

Innes National Park

Innes protects the habitat of the rare western whipbird. There are also malleefowl, terns, osprey breeding on the cliff faces, rock parrots in the coastal scrub and plenty of kangaroos and emus.
300km west of Adelaide,
☎ 08-8854 4040

Lake Eyre National Park

Australia's largest salt lake surrounded by desert wilderness. When the lake floods, huge

numbers of waterbirds congregate to feed. There are fossil deposits at Lake Ngapakaldi. No facilities and summers can be scorching hot; 4WD needed to reach the heart of the park.
Approximately 760km north of Adelaide, ☎ 08-8648 5300

Lincoln National Park

Coastal heathlands, woodland and mallee. Kangaroos, emus and reptiles are common; birds include the rare western whipbird, and nesting ospreys and white-bellied sea-eagles. Southern right whales and dolphins

are sometimes sighted offshore. Little penguins, shearwaters and Australian sea-lions breed on nearby islands.

653km west of Adelaide,
☎ 08-8688 3111

Mount Remarkable National Park

The smallest and most southerly park in the Flinders Ranges consists of two sections: Mt Remarkable and, to the west, Alligator Gorge and Mambray Creek; Mambray Creek is the more popular. This important park has a topography typical of the Flinders Ranges, but vegetation and wildlife that draws from both the dry Flinders Ranges and the wetter, more southerly Mount Lofty Ranges. Western grey kangaroos and euros are common around Mambray Creek and red kangaroos can be seen on the flats at the park's edges. Yellow-footed rock-wallabies also live here. Bird and reptile diversity is high.
270km north of Adelaide,
☎ 08-8634 7068

Murray River National Park

River red gum forests; huge numbers of waterbirds congregate during floods. Other birds include whistling kites and parrots. The park's Katarapko section has the Kai Kai Nature Trail, which describes floodplain ecology, and a Mallee Drive, on which kangaroos and emus can be seen.
180km east of Adelaide,
☎ 08-8595 2111

Naracoorte Caves Conservation Park

The limestone caves here are home to one of Australia's largest breeding colonies of common bentwing-bats, with a summer population that may exceed 300,000. There are tours to view the bats via an infrared camera system; to watch the bats' nightly exodus during summer; and to the Victoria Fossil Cave, which has fossils of giant marsupials.
12km south-east of Naracoorte,
☎ *08-8762 3412*

Nullarbor National Park and Regional Reserve

These large, remote, semiarid parks in SA's far south-west are dominated by vast plains of saltbush and bluebush. Southern right whales can be seen from the coastal cliffs in winter and spring. The best vantage

point is The Head of Bight, on Yalata Aboriginal Land adjoining the park's eastern boundary; for access, inquire at the Nullarbor Roadhouse (☎ 08-8625 3447). Colonies of Australian sea-lions are scattered along the coast. The Nullarbor is the stronghold of the southern hairy-nosed wombat; red and western grey kangaroos are common; and after rain, the plains bloom with wildflowers.
950km west of Adelaide,
☎ *08-8625 3144*

Great Victoria Desert

This vast stretch of land occupies SA's north-west corner and extends into WA. Much of it has restricted access, but there are accessible sections such as Unnamed CP beside the WA border. Wildlife includes many parrots, red kangaroos, euros and reptiles. During winter and spring, wildflowers often bloom.
600km (to Unnamed Conservation Park) north-west of Ceduna, ☎ *08-8625 3144*

Earth Sanctuaries

Australia has seen drastic reductions in its wildlife populations, particularly its mammals, over the last 200 years. To address this trend, in 1969 Dr John Wamsley put into action a simple concept: purchase a tract of native vegetation; surround it with a predator-proof fence; eradicate exotic mammals inside the fence, especially predatory foxes and cats; and reintroduce the native fauna that once lived in the area. The plan seems to have been a success. So far the focus has been on reintroducing mammals, especially the medium-sized species that have undergone the greatest decline. They are now abundant in the sanctuaries. Many of these species will not be seen in the wild and you certainly won't encounter such a diversity of medium-sized mammals anywhere else.

Yet Wamsley is a controversial figure. He has entered a realm traditionally left to government and has sometimes collided with local conservation groups. And his passionate crusade – including the infamous 'cat hat' – against introduced predators has not endeared him to some. There are now nine Earth Sanctuaries (🖳 *http://www.esl.com.au*) in various stages of development in Victoria, NSW and SA. Warrawong in the Adelaide Hills (the first Earth Sanctuary) and Yookamurra in the SA mallee are the two most established. The largest of the sanctuaries, Scotia, is up and running in western NSW. Buckaringa in the Flinders Ranges, SA, protects a colony of yellow-footed rockwallabies. The first coastal sanctuary, Tiparra, is planned for SA's Yorke Peninsula. The ultimate aim is to establish sanctuaries across Australia, protecting wildlife populations in all major habitats, and to have more than 1% of Australia's land area in Earth Sanctuaries by 2020.

Warrawong

The dusk walk is a must: guides discuss the ecology of local widlife, you'll look for platypuses from the viewing deck, and are sure to see kangaroos and wallabies, potoroos, bettongs, bandicoots, bats and much more. One

wall of the restaurant is glass, and while you eat you can watch potoroos, bandicoots and bettongs. Offers educational programs and overnight stays with dusk and dawn walks. Bookings essential.
25km south-east of Adelaide, ☎ *08-8370 9422*

Yookamurra

A 14km-long predator-proof fence surrounds an area of old growth mallee. On the night walk you'll encounter bilbies, burrowing and brush-tailed bettongs, and maybe southern hairy-nosed wombats. There are also morning walks (to look for numbats), educational programs and overnight stays. Bookings essential.
2km north-west of Swan Reach, ☎ *08-8562 5011*

TASMANIA

State faunal emblem

Tasmanian devil The unofficial faunal emblem of Tasmania. Black with a white band across its chest, this is Australia's largest living carnivorous marsupial. Confined to Tasmania, it is a widespread and common nocturnal hunter and scavenger.

Highlights

- Watching a platypus foraging among pebbles on the bottom of a crystal-clear stream
- Catching sight of a Tasmanian devil frozen in the glare of headlights
- Cruising slowly past rafts of shearwaters resting on the waters of the Derwent River
- Startling a 1.5m-long tiger snake sunning itself on the South Coast Track
- Hearing the screech of a flock of yellow-tailed black-cockatoos on the Mountain in Hobart
- Slurping through knee-deep mud among burrowing crayfish mounds in the south-west
- Ticking all 12 endemic Tasmanian birds in a day on Bruny Island
- Revelling in the abundance of native mammals – a sobering contrast to much of the mainland

THE island state of Tasmania sits in the Roaring Forties, a latitude renowned for high winds and rough, changeable weather. The wild south-west bears the brunt of the storms and is a rugged, mountainous landscape of forests and buttongrass moorlands that acts as a sponge for the heavy rains. The resulting rain shadow has produced a drier central plateau of grasslands and remnant woodlands, and an east coast that experiences a lower annual rainfall than most tropical resorts.

Tasmania was only isolated from the mainland by the rising waters of Bass Strait 15,000 years ago, and its flora and fauna largely overlaps that of the rest of Australia. Thus, you can expect to see kangaroos, echidnas, and possums among the eucalypts and acacias. However, the island also boasts 12 endemic birds, and distinct subspecies of numerous birds and mammals are recognised. For example, Tasmania's eastern grey kangaroos and red-necked wallabies are distinct subspecies with their own local names – forester kangaroo and Bennett's wallaby, respectively.

Much bushland remains uncleared, even close to settlements. Some 30% of the island is preserved (and managed by the Parks and Wildlife Service) in national parks and other reserves, including a World Heritage Area that covers 20% of the state. Nevertheless, the clear-felling of forests is still a major conservation issue – 29 of the state's 38 mammals rely on the forests for breeding habitat, and many require old growth with mature trees and hollow logs.

Tasmania is a stronghold for several otherwise rare birds; and is the last refuge for the Tasmanian devil. The thylacine (Tasmanian 'tiger') was also found here, until the last known one died in captivity in 1936. The Tasmanian populations of these two species were the only ones remaining at the time of European settlement, having previously become extinct on the mainland – probably at least partly because of competition from dingoes (which never reached Tasmania). Especially abundant are small- to medium-sized mammals, as the number killed by road traffic ironically demonstrates. The survival of healthy populations of eastern quolls and eastern barred bandicoots – both near extinction on the mainland – is largely because foxes were never introduced to Tasmania.

Wildlife is also prolific in the seas. There is a high incidence of whale strandings in summer and offshore islands support colonies of seals, penguins and seabirds – extra diversity is added by ring-ins from sub-Antarctic waters and beyond. ■

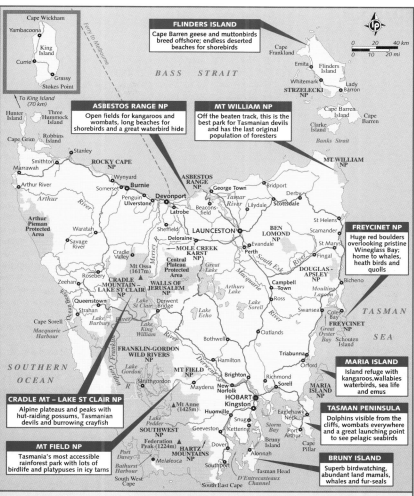

FLINDERS ISLAND
Cape Barren geese and muttonbirds breed offshore; endless deserted beaches for shorebirds

ASBESTOS RANGE NP
Open fields for kangaroos and wombats, long beaches for shorebirds and a great waterbird hide

MT WILLIAM NP
Off the beaten track, this is the best park for Tasmanian devils and has the last original population of foresters

FREYCINET NP
Huge red boulders overlooking pristine Wineglass Bay; home to whales, heath birds and quolls

CRADLE MT – LAKE ST CLAIR NP
Alpine plateaus and peaks with hut-raiding possums, Tasmanian devils and burrowing crayfish

MT FIELD NP
Tasmania's most accessible rainforest park with lots of birdlife and platypuses in icy tarns

MARIA ISLAND
Island refuge with kangaroos, wallabies waterbirds, sea life and emus

TASMAN PENINSULA
Dolphins visible from the cliffs, wombats everywhere and a great launching point to see pelagic seabirds

BRUNY ISLAND
Superb birdwatching, abundant land mamals, whales and fur-seals

Suggested itineraries

One week (start/finish Hobart) Spend a day on Bruny Island then work up the east coast, take in Maria Island and Freycinet NP, then choose between Cradle Mountain–Lake St Clair and Mt William NPs.

An alternative is to do a quick circuit through Mt Field NP (1 day) and Cradle Mountain–Lake St Clair (2 days) then head east to Freycinet NP (2 days) and Maria or Bruny Islands.

Two weeks With more time to spare, a big sweep can take in all the parks in the one-week itinerary, adding on Asbestos Range NP and time to winkle out endemic birds at, say, Mt Wellington, Tinderbox or Bruny Island.

You could also combine a one-week itinerary with a week's hiking in Cradle Mountain–Lake St Clair or Southwest NPs; or spend one week in the north and the next in the south.

One month The ultimate Tasmanian trip can comfortably take in all the state's national parks. Get to grips with wildlife on foot by walking in areas such as Cradle Mountain–Lake St Clair or Southwest NPs; take a pelagic seabird trip from Eaglehawk Neck; fly down to Melaleuca in Southwest NP to see orange-bellied parrots; or head across to Flinders Island for a different sort of wilderness experience.

HOBART

Mountain sentinel and river idyll

STREWN along the riverbanks and foothills of the dark, fluted mass of 1270m-high *Mt Wellington* – known to locals as the Mountain – lie Hobart's settled areas. From the top – a 15-minute drive from the city centre but often a quantum leap away in climate – southern Tasmania is laid at your feet like a living relief map. Occasional skinks retreat into rock crevices on the wind-blown heaths and dolerite columns of the peak, from where a maze of tracks descends through snow gum woodlands and taller eucalypt forests alive with possums and birdlife. Tree trunks are scratched orange-bare by brushtail possums, and potoroos lurk in mossy glades with huge tree ferns where secretive scrubtits sidle up trunks. Most of Tasmania's endemic birds can be seen on the Mountain; the area around *Ferntree* offers the best birding; and the Fern Glade track is particularly good for **scrubtits** and **pink robins**. Lower down are suburban gardens with **flame robins** and honeyeaters before you reach the shores of the meandering Derwent River.

When there is 'weather' on the Mountain, groups of **yellow-tailed black-cockatoos** screech down the hillsides and forage on casuarina nuts in protected waterfront gardens. Also on Mt Wellington's slopes is the *Waterworks Reserve*, where Hobart City Council runs summer spotlighting activities. If Mt Wellington is lost in cloud, head for *Mt Nelson*. This less dramatic foothill is also a panoramic lookout and the walk through *Truganini Reserve*, on the eastern slopes, down to Sandy Bay Rd is great for watching birds of dry forest, such as the inquisitive **Tasmanian scrubwren** and some of the **endemic honeyeaters**. Early morning joggers flush feeding **eastern rosellas** from the lawns of the *Domain*, at the western end of the Tasman Bridge, where **Australian magpies** (the white-backed Tasmanian race) also forage. In the city centre itself, rare

While the peak of Mt Wellington can be covered in snow, its forested slopes support many endemic bird species; and in the waters of the Derwent River fur-seals hunt and short-tailed shearwaters rest up on their annual migration.

migratory **swift parrots** can often be seen in parks such as *Franklin Square* during the summer months.

It doesn't take long to leave the city behind, and driving around Hobart's rural outskirts, **brown falcons** are seen perched on power poles, hawk-eyed for mouse prey. High in the sky are often **wedge-tailed eagles** and, close to the coast, **white-bellied sea-eagles**. On roadsides and in parks **masked lapwings** nest in the open, even on grassy traffic islands. Seeing the wildlife is often just a matter of keeping your eyes peeled and your peripheral vision alert.

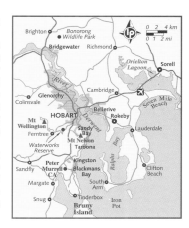

The *Peter Murrell Conservation Area*, between Huntingfield and Blackmans Bay, contains many rare heath **orchids** and the extremely rare **forty-spotted pardalote** in small numbers; even **platypuses** have been seen here occasionally. Beyond Blackmans Bay the coast road winds around the headland of Tinderbox, facing Bruny Island across the d'Entrecasteaux Channel where **bottlenose dolphins** swim below the cliffs. Human residents of these bush blocks are used to **eastern barred bandicoots** digging pointy little holes in their lawns; there's a good chance of seeing the culprits if you wait quietly at dusk. At Tinderbox you can explore a shallow, underwater snorkel trail on the sandstone reef and look for **weedy sea dragons**.

There are daily cruises on the *Derwent River* and plenty of sea kayaks for hire. Look out for **peregrine falcons** on the Alum Cliffs between Taroona and Kingston; **black-faced cormorants** resting on rocks; and **Australasian gannets** and other seabirds on your way to the Iron Pot. Dolphins are common in the Derwent and, in January and February, rafts of **short-tailed shearwaters** (or muttonbirds) rest on its protected waters before their northward migration. **Australian fur-seals** cruise the channel further south looking for salmon that have escaped from commercial fish-farms off Bruny Island. Sometimes they get greedy and jump the fence, causing fish farmers and fishermen to refer to them as 'sea wolves'.

From Glenorchy the river is dotted with the lumps of **black swans** searching out aquatic vegetation. In summer between the warmer waters of *Seven Mile Beach* and the airport, the paddocks are patrolled by **swamp harriers,** which send the resident **Tasmanian native-hens** scurrying for cover, and the air comes alive with cicada calls and the rolling screech of **musk lorikeets**. Trees lining the airport roads are popular with rosellas, lorikeets and honeyeaters. Past Lauderdale is shallow *Ralphs Bay*, good shorebird territory with resident **pied oystercatchers**, summer visitors such as stints and sandpipers, and **double-banded plovers** from New Zealand in winter.

A 25-minute drive from the city north to Brighton will take you to Bonorong Wildlife Park (☎ 03-6268 1184), where you can stroll on lawns where forester kangaroos lounge and see Tasmanian devils being fed. This is an easy introduction to the state's wildlife, but it's really only a small taste of the abundance to be found by independent exploration. ■

CRADLE MOUNTAIN –LAKE ST CLAIR NATIONAL PARK

Where familiarity breeds contentment

Wildlife highlights

One of the best places in Australia to see mammals (more than 20 species inhabit the park): Bennett's wallabies, Tasmanian pademelons, common wombats, common brushtail possums and eastern quolls are abundant; platypuses, common ringtail possums, Tasmanian devils and spotted-tailed quolls are common; and many smaller species include the dusky antechinus, long-tailed mouse and eastern pygmy-possum. Highlights among 80 recorded species of bird include the ground parrot, black currawong, southern emu-wren and yellow wattlebird. Alpine lizards live on mountain tops; native fish clamber overland between tarns; and relict invertebrates include Gondwanan crayfish and freshwater shrimps.

TASMANIA'S most famous park forms the northern tip of a great swathe of land protected in a World Heritage Area that continues through the wild south-west to the rugged coast. Visitors flock for superb scenery – pristine Dove Lake framed by Cradle Mountain (below) has become a postcard symbol of Tasmania's rugged highlands – and the 80km Overland Track is world-famous among bushwalkers. Wildlife is prolific and the park's popularity means that many mammals and birds are less shy and therefore more visible than elsewhere, but also that spotting some of the shyer wildlife needs perseverance.

Tasmanian natives

Numerous short walks around the Lake St Clair entrance to the park illustrate the diverse habitats of the area. Groups of **Bennett's wallabies** pose for photos and **black currawongs** look for handouts near the visitor centre – this is a can't-miss site for both, and birdwatchers often head straight up here to see the currawongs, especially in summer when the birds frequent higher altitudes and may be scarce near the coast. **Tasmanian**

Crustaceans in the mist

The Tasmanian mountain shrimp is a found in subalpine and alpine regions of Tasmania. It lives in open pools and tarns, and is easily spotted by walkers with a keen eye. It grows to 5cm and tolerates remarkably low water temperatures, remaining active even under a cover of snow. Its most notable feature to science, the lack of a carapace or shell, is reflected in its generic name, *Anaspides*, which means 'without a shield'. It feeds on algae and detritus from the pool bottom and occasionally catches live prey by swimming upside down at the surface. Its daylight vision seems to be poor and it navigates using tactile cues relayed by hairs on the antennae and legs. Few other creatures share the shrimp's immediate environment but tadpoles of the Tasmanian froglet are sometimes seen in the same pool.

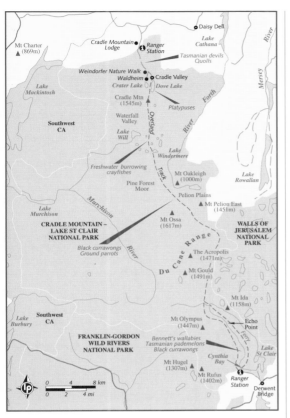

Location Cradle Mountain – 153km west of Launceston; Lake St Clair – 180km north-west of Hobart.

Facilities Visitor centres at Cradle Mountain and at Lake St Clair (disabled access); Watersmeet Nature Walk at Lake St Clair; wheelchair access rainforest walk at Cradle Mountain.

Accommodation Lake St Clair – camping, dormitory and cabins near the Lake and at Derwent Bridge. Cradle Mountain – lodge, cabins and camping just outside the park.

Wildlife rhythms Tasmanian devils are active teaching their pups to hunt from August to November; however, in winter, much birdlife retreats to the lowlands and although the mammals remain, seeing them can be hard work.

Contact Rangers: Cradle Mountain (☎ 03-6492 1133), Lake St Clair (☎ 03-6289 1172).

Ecotours Summer ranger activities include spotlighting. Many local lodges conduct night walks, including Cradle Mountain Lodge (☎ 03-6492 1303), Derwent Bridge Chalets (☎ 03-6289 1125) and Lakeside St Clair (☎ 03-6289 1137).

native-hens and **masked lapwings** are common around Cynthia Bay, and other birds of the open forest include **yellow** and **little wattlebirds**, **yellow-tailed black-cockatoos**, **green rosellas**, **common bronzewings** and, in the undergrowth, parties of **Tasmanian scrubwrens** and **thornbills**.

Tasmanian pademelons are also fairly easy to see, although they are more active at dawn and dusk and stick closer to the forest edges. Spotlighting around the camping ground should be rewarding, and regular sightings include **eastern quolls**, **common brushtail** and **ringtail possums**, and **sugar gliders**.

Part of the Overland Track follows the western shore of Lake St Clair through open woodland, cool-temperate rainforest, dense stands of tea-tree and buttongrass plains. A lack of sheltering vegetation in Lake St Clair means waterbirds are few although **Latham's snipe**, a migrant from north-east Asia, feeds along the margins in summer. However, this is one of the best places in Australia to see **platypuses** – sit quietly near Cynthia Bay or Echo Point, especially at dusk. The **Tasmanian mountain shrimp** also lives in the area, but not in the lake itself.

The park's cold alpine lakes and tarns support animals such as platypuses and native fish.

Cradle for devils and cold-loving reptiles

The park's northern entrance is dominated by Cradle Mountain. **Bennett's wallabies** and **Tasmanian pademelons** are abundant around the visitor centre and along the various tracks, and this is great country for spotlighting: **Tasmanian devils** and **common wombats** are easily seen, while **long-nosed potoroos**, **eastern quolls** (of both colour phases) and the larger **spotted-tailed quoll** all occur regularly; any of the tracks should prove rewarding. An even easier option is to visit Cradle Mountain Lodge after dark, where many of the species visit for a nightly free feed – although appearances by devils and quolls can be haphazard.

The Weindorfer Nature Walk wends through dense stands of King Billy and celery-top pines that up to forests of beech trees that change colour and drop their leaves in autumn (a rarity in Australia). Birds of wet forests are typical here, and include **pink robin**, **Bassian thrush**, **olive whistler** and **scrubtit**. In the more protected forested valleys there are enchanted places where myrtle, pandani and fragrant sassafras grow, and **Tasmanian pademelons** and **common wombats** forage on the open ground.

From the austere peaks of Cradle Mountain in the north to southern Mt Olympus and the natural amphitheatre of the Acropolis, columns of bare rock and dolerite scree harbour **metallic** and **alpine cool-skinks**. Other common reptiles in the park that are often abroad during warm weather include **blotched blue-tongued lizards** and three species of snake – the **black tiger snake**, **copperhead** and small, inoffensive **white-lipped snake**.

Damp gullies, waterways, tarns and marshy ground support several species of small frog. Most colourful is the bright-green **Tasmanian tree frog**, with a call like a goose's honk; also distinctive is the lamblike bleating of the **Tasmanian froglet**.

Wallabies, wombats and carnivorous marsupials such as quolls are common near Cradle Mountain.

Encounters on the highland tracks

Traversing the popular Overland Track between Cradle Mountain and Lake St Clair is a great way to get to grips with wildlife on an intimate basis. **Bennett's wallabies** are common around Waterfall Valley, where in the evening **common wombats** and **eastern quolls** emerge. You are also likely to meet Black Pete – a huge, black **common brushtail possum** that ransacks walkers' supplies in huts and sometimes snuggles up to them on cold nights. **Black currawongs** have also learnt that walkers represent food – they can become a nuisance at camping grounds.

So this is science?

One summer I found myself trudging up a mountain, an underwater video camera in my pack, intent on recording the private life of the Tasmanian mountain shrimp. My scientific aim was to document this critter's behavioural repertoire as background to my future studies of its nervous system. Upon finding some worthy subjects, I spent days with my backside in the chilly air and my nose in the chilly water videotaping crustacean adventures. My field assistant humoured my every whim, even when asked to leap around, arms flapping (supposedly impersonating swooping predators), so I could record the animal's responses to shadows. The news that a couple of mad scientists were in the area reached bushwalkers, who soon began arriving at our camp to check our progress. Off the mountain the hours of filming became many more hours of analysis and finally, several years later, a chapter in my thesis.

Dr Elycia Wallis, Museum Victoria

Trailing lichens and dense cushions of moss are characteristic of the park's rainforests.

Further down the track, **Tasmanian pademelons** are common around Windermere Hut. In warm weather watch out for **black tiger snakes** sunning on the track. South of Windermere, Pine Forest Moor is an expanse of buttongrass where **ground parrots** are common, although they are usually seen only when accidentally flushed from cover. More often seen are insectivorous **southern emu-wrens** and **striated fieldwrens**, calling from the tussock tops. These buttongrass moorlands are an extensive feature of south-western Tasmania and an important habitat for a variety of invertebrates. It is wet and boggy country, and very sensitive to damage – hence the long boardwalks constructed for bushwalkers. Mounds of mud spiralling upwards are the burrows of a **freshwater crayfish** that form microhabitats for invertebrates. Fish adapted to survival in the cold alpine waters include the **climbing galaxias** – found in Lakes Will and Windermere – which can spend short periods out of water and clamber over rocks with its oversized pectoral fins.

Pelion Plains features abundant **Bennett's wallabies**, **green rosellas** and **black currawongs**; and **Tasmanian devils** and **common wombats** are usually seen by spotlighting. The **long-tailed mouse** and **eastern pygmy-possum** visit huts along the track; **long-tailed mice**, **dusky antechinus** and **swamp rats** live as high as the summit of Mt Ossa. Past Du Cane Hut, the valley of the Mersey River is cloaked in rainforests, and past Windy Ridge alpine yellow gum forest is home to five species of **bat**. From Windy Ridge down to Lake St Clair tall mountain ash forest with an understorey of banksias that attract **honeyeaters** and **common ringtail possums**. **Echidnas** can be encountered on this stretch and **common wombats** can be seen towards nightfall near Hamilton Creek. ■

Watching tips
A slow drive an hour or two after sunset from Cradle Mountain Lodge, just outside the park, to the car park at Dove Lake is a recommended way to see quolls and Tasmanian devils. The swamp antechinus and a rare native rodent, the broad-toothed rat, share labyrinthine runways under the dense mats of vegetation on the buttongrass plains.

ASBESTOS RANGE NATIONAL PARK

Amphitheatre highlights natural bounty

Wildlife highlights

Conspicuous macropods include Bennett's wallabies, Tasmanian pademelons and reintroduced foresters. Other common marsupials include wombats, brushtail possums, Tasmanian devils and long-nosed potoroos, but with the exception of wombats you'll usually need to go spotlighting to see them. As well as being a good site for watching waterbirds and shorebirds, the park's coastal and dry sclerophyll habitats are home to over 80 species of bush bird.

ROUNDED bushes of boobyalla scrub line the beach dunes, concealing **yellow-throated** and **crescent honeyeaters** dancing over **long-nosed potoroo** runways at ground level. In spring the striated plumage of **New Holland honeyeaters** flashes in the sunlight as they perform their aerial courtship displays above the coastal heath. Huge, hoary banksias lining the cooler creek bed are a backdrop for the antics of **superb fairy-wrens** with their cocked tails and tiny, spiderweb-bound nest-cups which cling to the lower branches of the scrub.

Lawns of grazing kangaroos

The forested hills of the Asbestos Range form an amphitheatre facing Bass Strait, within which are beaches and headlands, tidal coastal flats, dunes, and a waterfowl lagoon nestled in tea-tree swamp. A century of farming has recreated an environment similar to that cultivated by Aboriginal communities in the past, who encouraged the growth of open grasslands through regular burning. Evidence of Aboriginal feasts of mussels and other shellfish can also be seen in shell middens among the park's dunes.

Among Tasmania's parks, this one is renowned for its accessible wildlife, and three species of macropod can be easily seen: the Springlawn area is grazed by **foresters**, **Bennett's wallabies** and **Tasmanian pademelons**. Bold **common wombats** are also abroad during the day, and their burrows can be seen along the creek bed near the camping grounds. **Masked lapwings** and **Tasmanian native-hens**, the latter with vertically flattened tails, are common in the erstwhile potato fields.

Back to nature

The grassy feeding grounds that were once swamp are now littered with scats – testimony to the abundance of the park's kangaroos and wombats. Springlawn was farmed until 1974, the swamp drained and canals dug for irrigation; and copper was mined in the early 1800s. But despite the human impact, this park has a reputation for some of the best wildlife-viewing in Tasmania. The changes wrought have created a nutrient-rich focus for grazers and high concentrations of birdlife are found along the sheltered creek beds where once there was tidal mud flat. It was also once a rich source of meat and shellfish for Aboriginal people, although when humans first arrived in Tasmania the shoreline was about 60km to the north.

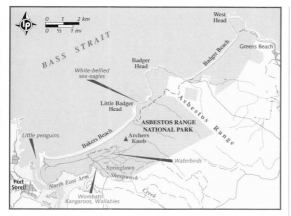

Location 37km from Devonport to Bakers Beach; 20km from Beaconsfield to Badger Head.
Facilities Basic visitor centre; good bird hide and boardwalk on Springlawn Nature Walk.
Accommodation Camping at Springlawn, Bakers Point and Griffiths Point.
Wildlife rhythms Migratory waders present September to March.
Contact Ranger (☎ 03-6428 6277).
Ecotours Devil's Playground Ecotours (☎ 03-6343 1787) can take you to Bakers Beach from Launceston.

Hide in a lake without getting wet

Crested terns rest up between feeding forays on the white, sandy beach and **kelp gulls** high-step ahead of you, fossicking for beach-washed scraps. Kelp gulls are easily confused with the larger and more common **Pacific gull** – Pacifics have a red tip to the bill, Kelps a red spot on the lower manidble only. The small islands of the Port Sorell estuary are also part of the park and are breeding sites for **little penguins**, and North East Arm is the best place to look for **shorebirds** at low tide. Red-billed **pied oystercatchers** are resident foragers along the tideline; **cormorants** and little penguins fish offshore.

A boardwalk through the meditative stillness of tea-tree thickets behind Springlawn leads to a substantial waterfowl hide that seems to sit surrounded by lake. **Black swans** glide past among other waterfowl, such as **black ducks** and **Australasian shovelers**, while **white-faced herons** patrol the marshy edges. The grey-black **musk duck** sits low in the water between dives; males have a distinctive lobe below the bill that is inflated during its spectacular summer courtship display – spraying water up with its feet while rotating slowly, paddling rapidly across the water and calling *ker-plonk* followed by a whistle and a grunt. Another duck, the **chestnut teal**, adds splashes of colour – this nomad is more common in Tasmanian wetlands than elsewhere.

The tea-tree swamp has islands of higher ground where fallen vegetation has built up to form protected nesting grounds for waterbirds. On the shady higher ground at the swamp's edge, even a midday walk will surprise dozing **Bennett's wallabies** and **Tasmanian pademelons**. The coastal heath beyond the swamp is a rare pocket, prized especially by a variety of **honeyeaters** and also home to **ground parrots**.

Take a stroll to Archers Knob through the taller eucalypts where **yellow-tailed black-cockatoos** feed; **green rosellas** pipe their metallic, two-note call; various **robins** – **dusky**, **scarlet** and **flame** – pop up from the scrub like targets in a sideshow alley; and the occasional **wedge-tailed eagle** soars higher up. ■

Oystercatchers, gulls and other shorebirds forage on Asbestos Range NP's deserted beaches.

Watching tips

Take an early morning walk from Springlawn to Badger Head and take in the Springlawn Nature Walk in the cool of the day. Look out for dozing wallabies and pademelons in shady scrub as the day heats up. White-footed dunnarts are locally common and can be spotlit along Sheepwash Creek.

BRUNY ISLAND

Whales, wallabies and wedgies

Wildlife highlights

A one-stop birdwatching destination, where all 12 Tasmanian endemics are found among 138 recorded species; highlights include the forty-spotted pardalote, ground parrot and beautiful firetail. A variety of habitats, including beach, heath and forest, supports plentiful echidnas, brushtail possums and Bennett's wallabies; whale- and seal-watching is also possible from headlands; and vagrant seals and penguins occasionally make landfall.

Location 40km south of Hobart via car ferry from Kettering.
Facilities Boardwalk and viewing platform over the penguin and shearwater nesting areas at the Neck.
Accommodation Caravan park, camping, YHA and cottages.
Wildlife rhythms Echidnas active in summer; swift parrots, shearwaters and penguins from September to March; seabirds autumn to spring.
Contact Bruny d'Entrecasteaux visitor centre (☎ 03-6267 4494). Ranger, (☎ 03-6293 1408).
Ecotours Dr Tonia Cochran of Inala tours (☎ 03-6293 1217) has accommodation and runs informative nature tours on Bruny and elsewhere in Tasmania.

BRUNY is the perfect Tasmanian wildlife sampler – easily accessible from Hobart yet wild and secluded enough for plenty of mammals and birds to survive. Birdwatchers on a mission usually head straight here to notch up all the Tasmanian endemics; anyone with a more general interest will also find plenty to see and could perhaps be rewarded with an unusual sighting.

Visitors from the subantarctic

Leopard and **southern elephant seals** occasionally haul out on the beaches of Cloudy Bay in South Bruny NP to rest after a tough breeding season in subantarctic waters. Wandering penguins from waters south of Australia – most commonly **royal penguins**, but others turn up – also make landfall at South Bruny, although like the seals their appearance is hard to predict. **Little penguins** and **Australian fur-seals** are more commonly encountered – Bruny Island has plenty of both resident, with the rocks known as the Friars off Tasman Head a good site for the fur-seals.

Tasmania's rarest bird

Perhaps no other Tasmanian endemic bird is as eagerly sought by birdwatchers, yet the forty-spotted pardalote is small, unobtrusive and rather dull. It is thought that no more than 4000 remain and the population has declined since white settlement; this pardalote is now one of Australia's rarest birds and some 50% of the population lives on Bruny Island. Habitat clearance and competition from other birds, such as the closely-related striated pardalote, appear to feature strongly in its decline. Whatever the reasons, the forty-spot is always associated with manna gum, a eucalypt with a whitish trunk that exudes sweet manna and supports the production of its other main food source, lerp – the sugary protective layer produced by small, sap-sucking insects (psyllids) that live on the leaves.

Year-round the island offers some wildlife gems. Manna gums are home to endangered **forty-spotted pardalotes**. There's a large colony at Waterview Hill, where the trees are smaller and viewing conditions better than on the other main forty-spot hotspot, Maria Island. **Dusky robins** will also be found in this area.

Along the dunes of the narrow isthmus known as the Neck, **little penguins** and **short-tailed shearwaters** (muttonbirds) can be seen at dusk between September and March returning to their nests from fishing. If you're using a torch to view them, cover it with red cellophane to reduce disturbance to the birds. **Sooty shearwaters** nest on Courts Island, off Cape Bruny, and summer seabirding from the Cape should include **muttonbirds**, **shy albatrosses** and **Australasian gannets**; onshore winter gales could bring a host of other southern **pelagic species**.

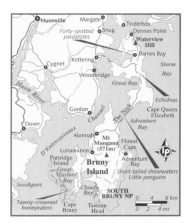

Birds common and rare

Most visitors head south, where the island is dominated by the forested slopes and wet gullies of Mt Mangana. In summer the red blooms of **Tasmanian waratahs** decorate this excellent forest habitat, where good birding includes most of the endemic species (**strong-billed honeyeaters** and **green rosellas** are common), plus **eastern spinebills**, **pink robins** (especially in gullies) and marauding white-phase **grey goshawks**.

Another Tasmanian speciality, the migratory **swift parrot**, feeds in these forests during the summer months, although they move around according to what's in flower. **Black currawongs** are also seasonal, being far more common in winter when they migrate from higher altitudes to the coast. **Wedge-tailed eagles** also occur on Bruny, although they are not common.

Echidnas are commonly seen in the daytime along the scrub-lined dirt roads in summer. **Tasmanian pademelons** and **Bennett's wallabies** are common throughout the island – an unusual white form of the latter can be seen near the Fluted Cape entrance to the national park. The island also supports a healthy population of **eastern quolls** (both dark and light colour varieties) and among the many **common brushtail possums** are those of a 'golden' form with cream-coloured fur. In the heaths of the camping grounds in Great Taylors Bay, or near Cape Bruny lighthouse, you may hear the sneezing call of **tawny-crowned honeyeaters** while **white-bellied sea-eagles** soar overhead. **Ground parrots** also inhabit these heaths – listen for their high-pitched tinkling at dawn and dusk.

Spectacular Fluted Cape, a short walk from the southern end of Adventure Bay, was once a lookout for whalers. **Southern right whales** on their northward migration pass the island from June to September, heading south again from September to late October. It is still a good lookout, but these days you might have to wait a little longer to see the whales – you can pass the time looking for **beautiful firetails** along the track from the caravan park. ∎

Short-tailed shearwaters ('muttonbirds') hurtle over the Neck at dusk during summer.

Watching tips

Visit the Neck after sunset in summer for a ranger-guided look at little penguins and short-tailed shearwaters. More good spots for forty-spots are among the manna gums near the bridge at Mc-Crackens Gully, near Barnes Bay, and at Inala.

FREYCINET NATIONAL PARK

Surfing dolphins and circling eagles

Wildlife highlights
Several large marsupials are common, eg, Bennett's wallaby, Tasmanian pademelon and common wombat; and most of Tasmania's marine mammals have been sighted here. At least 146 species of bird have been recorded, including Tasmanian endemics such as the yellow wattlebird, Tasmanian thornbill, dusky robin and yellow-throated honeyeater. Offshore islands are important seabird breeding grounds.

Location 208km north of Hobart.
Facilities Interpretation trail to Wineglass Bay lookout.
Accommodation Full range in and around Coles Bay township; camping grounds in park.
Wildlife rhythms Spring/summer for birds; May to July for humpback whales or June to September for southern right whales.
Contact Ranger (☎ 03-6257 0107).
Ecotours Freycinet Experience (☎ 03-6223 7565) does a great four-day walk with naturalist guides, luxury camping and boat connections. Freycinet Sea Charters (☎ 03-6375 1461) and Keno Sea Fisheries (☎ 03-6257 0344) will both take you out to watch marine mammals and seabirds.

BOTH **white-bellied sea-eagles** and **wedge-tailed eagles** circle above visitors who climb the Wineglass Bay Track to the saddle between the boulder-strewn peaks of Mts Amos and Mayson. Semi-tame **Bennett's wallabies** greet walkers who continue down to the beach (below), where **bottlenose dolphins** can easily be seen surfing through the white sandy shallows; **silver** and **kelp gulls**, **crested terns** and **plovers** rest on the sand; and **Australasian gannets** feed further out in the bay. The loop west back to the car park (more Bennett's wallabies!) takes in the shore of Great Oyster Bay, where **beautiful firetails** are common in heath that puts on a display of **wildflowers** in spring and early summer.

Abundant marsupials and returning great whales

Campers overnighting on the peninsula can expect to see abundant **Tasmanian pademelons** as well as Bennett's wallabies. Spotlighting offers the possibility of **eastern quolls** (spotted-tailed quolls are also present but rarely seen), **common wombats**, and (if you are patient) **long-nosed potoroos**; **common brushtail possums** will come looking for you – keep food inside the tent. Look for the eyeshine of **sugar gliders** and **common ringtail possums** in the canopy of the tall blue gum forests behind Cooks Beach. **Tasmanian devils** are also common in the park. There's as good a chance of seeing many of these species along roads at night as anywhere – even the sealed road from the park entrance is good.

Other areas of the park have more coastal heath and dry sclerophyll forests – habitat where **echidnas** enjoy the abundance of ants, and den among rocks and fallen timber. Birdwatchers can expect parrots such as **yellow-tailed black-cockatoos**, **green**

Sleepy Bay, Freycinet NP.

rosellas and **swift parrots** (summer only); and various **robins** and honeyeaters, such as **yellow-throated honeyeaters** and **yellow wattlebirds**.

In 1824 a whaling station was set up in Great Oyster Bay, but in just two decades whales became too scarce to hunt near shore. After a long absence they are now beginning to return during winter, with **humpback** and **southern right whales** hoving to in Great Oyster Bay during their migration along the coast. Boaters now see **common** and **bottlenose dolphins** or **Australian fur-seals** more often than for many years. It's worth getting out on a boat to view the offshore islands on which the fur-seals and **seabirds** breed.

Friendly beaches...for some

Most visitors explore south along the peninsula, but the park actually extends north of Cape Tourville lighthouse along the coastline of the Friendly Beaches to Binghams Bay. Cape Tourville itself is a good seawatching post to look for **marine mammals** and **seabirds**; sightings of **shy albatrosses** and **Australasian gannets** are virtually guaranteed, while onshore gales can bring in several other albatross species plus various **petrels**. About 1km north-east of Cape Tourville are the Nuggets, a breeding site for **little penguins**, **fairy prions**, **white-faced storm-petrels** and **black-faced cormorants**, among others; with binoculars or a spotting scope you should be able to make out a few species.

The beaches north of the lighthouse, often deserted in summer, are home to pairs or families of the rare **hooded plover**. During summer, carcasses of storm-battered **short-tailed shearwaters** and the occasional **little penguin** are sometimes found beach cast. Heath and woodland backing the dunes are good for birdwatching and night walks.

Freycinet's boulders and dry coastal scrub are ideal habitat for a variety of reptiles. Tasmania's largest lizard, the **blotched blue-tongued lizard**, is common and others seen here include **White's skink** – grey with spotted flanks and often seen disappearing under weathered flakes of exfoliating granite; and the **mountain dragon**, a miniature, rough-scaled cousin of the frill-necked lizard. **Black tiger snakes** will be out in warm weather and should be given a wide berth. ∎

Blue tongues and escargots

In Tasmania bluetongue lizards (strictly, blotched blue-tongued lizards) are known to many as goannas, though they are actually large skinks. Their low-slung bodies are ill-adapted for dashing across highways and their reckless summer courtship wanderings often result in unfortunate encounters with vehicles. Bluetongues are abundant even in suburban gardens, where they hide among thick vegetation, rock walls or piled-up debris. Many know the satisfying crunch of feeding garden snails to their semitame bluey. But they also have a darker reputation in Tassie, with many still believing the folklore that they are poisonous. Not so – indeed, their taste for snails should make them a gardener's best friend.

MARIA ISLAND

Convict prison, wildlife haven

🦘 **Wildlife highlights**
One of the best places to see forester kangaroos, Bennett's wallaby and Tasmanian pademelon, Maria also supports good populations of eastern barred bandicoots, wombats and brushtails. Excellent birdwatching, especially for those seeking Tasmanian endemic species, of which all but one (the scrubtit) occur. It is one of two main sites to see the rare forty-spotted pardalote; other highlights among the 129 bird species recorded include the world's largest colony of Cape Barren geese, swift parrots (summer only), introduced emus and seabirds in season.

Location Ferry ride from Louisville (30 minutes), 89km north of Hobart.
Facilities Information centre at the Commissariat.
Accommodation Dormitory or camping on island; other accommodation at Louisville or at Orford on the mainland.
Wildlife rhythms Spring for goslings and joeys; migratory birds from December to March; seal pups in summer.
Contact Ranger (☎ 03-6257 1420).
Ecotours Summer ranger activities December to February. Dive trips organised by Bicheno Dive Centre (☎ 03-6375 1138).

WHEN Europeans arrived, Maria's largest land animals were the **common wombat**, **Tasmanian pademelon** and **long-nosed potoroo**. There were no bandicoots or brushtail possums, devils or quolls, foresters or wallabies – the island's size meant numbers could never be large and the indigenous Tyreddeme people probably took a heavy toll. But **common brushtails**, **foresters**, **Bennett's wallabies**, **Tasmanian bettongs**, and **eastern barred** and **southern brown bandicoots** have all been reintroduced, and thriving populations make Maria a great spot for up-close viewing. This is also one of the few places in Tasmania with **emus**, although they have been introduced from mainland Australia – the endemic Tasmanian emu is extinct.

Stronghold for endemic birds

Tasmanian native-hens virtually greet visitors as they alight at Darlington, where the rolling, grassy paddocks fronting the penitentiary are trimmed by waddling flocks of **Cape Barren geese** and ranks of **forester kangaroos**. In overcast weather, the roos and wallabies confidently graze all day, far from forest cover. **Tasmanian pademelons** are also easily seen here, and distinguished from the larger **Bennett's wallabies** by their timid, hunched-over stance. Overnight campers should have no trouble seeing **eastern barred bandicoots**. Ponds around the old settlement reverberate with the *plunk* of **eastern banjo frogs** and the *ree-ree-ree-ree* of **brown tree frogs**.

Maria hosts the second largest population of the **forty-spotted pardalote**, although you'll need binoculars – or to learn their calls – to distinguish them from **spotted** and **striated pardalotes**. Probably the best place to look is in the trees around Convict Reservoir, where migratory **swift parrots** also show up; another good spot is on the track to Mt Maria along Counsel Creek.

In the swamps near Chinamans Bay, 11km south of Darlington, **white-faced herons** stalk among the reeds as **chestnut teal** glide on the water. The migratory **Latham's snipe** frequents vegetated verges, along with the plaintive-voiced **little grassbird**, while **Tasmanian native-hens** scurry along the shore. The swamps near the isthmus are good for **waterbirds** and migrant **shorebirds**, while **little pied cormorants** fish offshore and **pied oyster-catchers** forage along the shore of the bay. The beach at Darlington Bay is a regular haunt of **hooded plovers**.

In the dry forests that clothe the slopes between Darlington and Bishop and Clerk, noisy groups of **green rosellas** feed on the open ground and **Tasmanian scrubwrens** make forays from the understorey. Other endemic birds visible on this walk include the large **yellow wattlebird**, and flocks of **strong-billed** and **black-headed honeyeaters**. Climbing B & C will turn up wet gullies worth exploring.

Watery playground

Local water currents contribute to a nutrient-rich and diverse marine community, attracting seals and feeding pelagic seabirds. This marine abundance has warranted protection of Maria Island's northern coast as a marine reserve. **Kelp beds** decorate the underwater landscape and this area, north to Bicheno on the East Coast, is famous for spectacular cold-water diving. North of Maria, about halfway to Freycinet, is a little rock called Ile des Phoques (Island of Seals) – a breeding colony for **Australian fur-seals** which feed in this rich marine patch. Keep an eye out for fur-seals in the waters of the Mercury Passage during the ferry crossing.

From a coastal lookout such as Fossil Cliffs, scan for **black-browed** and **shy albatrosses**, usually visible year-round. It's easy to pick the **Australasian gannet's** fishing technique – a deadly, vertical dive – imitated with marginally less bravado by **crested terns**. **Giant-petrels** follow fishing vessels, sometimes close enough to shore to distinguish between the northern and southern species (and it has to be a close look – they are almost identical except for the colour of their bill tips: reddish brown and pale green respectively); and watch for smaller seabirds, such as **common diving-petrels** and **fairy prions**, skimming the waves. ■

Watching tips

Look for forty-spots at the top of manna gums, preferably on a windless day. The lagoon behind Chinamans Bay is good for water-birds, and at Riedle Bay look for little penguins and shore-birds. Many of the Tasmanian native-hens have coloured bands on their legs – identification tags from a former long-term study into their behaviour and ecology. Bring a mountain bike to access the further reaches of the island more easily.

No room on the island ark

Until the 1970s, concern for the future of native wildlife led to the introduction of mammals and birds to Maria Island where, it was hoped, they would proliferate and secure the survival of their species on an island 'ark'. The list included echidnas, wombats, potoroos and bandicoots, as well as foresters, wallabies, emus, Cape Barren geese and even Tasmanian native-hens. But in the absence of predators some species have proliferated to the point where it is doubtful whether the island can support them. Foresters, for example, have put immense grazing pressure on pasture and strategic culling has been periodically implemented. Maria is a lesson in how meddling with nature is not to be taken lightly, however commendable the intention.

FLINDERS ISLAND

Islands in the storm

Location By air from Launceston or from Melbourne or Moorabbin (Victoria); by barge from Bridport.

Facilities Self-guiding Flinders Island Ecology Trail.

Accommodation Camping at Trousers Point; hotels and B&Bs at Whitemark and Lady Barron.

Wildlife rhythms Shearwaters and waders present September to March; geese best in late spring to summer.

Contact Flinders Island Tourism Association (☎ 03-6359 6526). Ranger, Strzelecki NP (☎ 03-6359 2217).

Ecotours Flinders Island Adventures (☎ 03-6359 4507) – wildlife, diving and boating trips.

Watching tips

Explore some of the offshore islands by boat to see shearwaters flying in at dusk, seabirds and seals. Be very careful when driving at dusk – the wallabies seem suicidal.

ONCE part of a land-bridge between Tasmania and mainland Australia, Flinders Island is the largest in the remaining string of 80 islands and rocks that spans Bass Strait. Warm ocean currents bring mild weather to the east coast, where **sooty** and **pied oystercatchers**, **hooded plovers** and **white-bellied sea-eagles** patrol deserted sandy beaches backed by large lagoons teeming with **waterbirds**.

Logan Lagoon Wildlife Sanctuary is a breeding site for **black swans** and an important summer feeding ground for migratory **waders**; its western shore is good for bush birds, including **honeyeaters**, **whistlers** and **pardalotes**. Waders also flock to Adelaide Bay at low tide.

Grey geese grazing

Flocks of honking **Cape Barren geese**, with a distinctive yellow-green bill, can be seen in paddocks over much of the island. This is the second rarest goose in the world, but ironically farmers regard them as a nuisance because they eat pasture and foul dams. The geese breed on the islands around Flinders and fly in to feed on the lush, fertilised farming lands of the big island in summer, especially after good rains. Patriarchs Wildlife Sanctuary on the east coast and Lackrana Wildlife Sanctuary at Cameron Inlet both protect habitat for Cape Barren geese.

Strzelecki NP protects eucalyptus forests, ferny gullies and boulder-strewn casuarina coast in the mountainous south. The island's only large land animals – **common wombats**, **Bennett's wallabies** and **Tasmanian pademelons** – can be readily seen here. Bird attractions include **brush bronzewing** pigeons and **beautiful firetails**.

Most of the surrounding islands are used as breeding sites by **short-tailed shearwaters**; their wailing, sobbing calls led to an island off the eastern coast being named

Babel Island. The fat chicks are still hunted by Tasmanian aboriginals as well as by **black tiger snakes**; on nearby Chappell Island tiger snakes have evolved into the largest and most venomous members of their species. Other seabirds include **little penguins**, **white-faced storm-petrels**, **fairy prions** and **white-fronted terns** (Battery Island and Adelaide Bay). ■

MT FIELD NATIONAL PARK

Tigers' stamping ground

MT Field became Tasmania's first national park in 1916 – it's an oldie but a goodie, and the park's Gondwanan relics indicate just how old. Deciduous beech, myrtle, sassafras and celery-top pine belong to an earlier Australia; under the leaf litter is another ancient relic, the **peripatus**, or velvet worm; and the **Tasmanian mountain shrimp** is a 'living fossil' that has inhabited Mt Field's glacial tarns for the last 200 million years. The last **thylacine** (or Tasmanian tiger) was captured alive in the adjacent Florentine Valley in 1933 and 100m-high swamp gums – the world's tallest hardwoods, known on the mainland as mountain ash – still grow near the park entrance.

Platypus nirvana

Look no further than the picnic ground for grazing **Bennett's wallabies** and **Tasmanian pademelons**, the latter sticking closer to the forest edge. **Common brushtails** forage round here at night and campers should also have no trouble seeing **eastern barred bandicoots**. Other possible mammals include **echidnas**, **wombats** and, by spotlighting, **ringtail possums, Tasmanian devils, long-nosed potoroos**, and both species of **quoll**.

Streams and waterfalls in the lower gullies are fringed by accessible rainforest, with tall stands of tree ferns ('manferns'). Many of the park's common birds can be seen along the track that takes in Russell and Lady Barron Falls – look here for **scrubtits, brush bronzewings** and **beautiful firetails**. Pink robins may also be found here (if unsuccessful try the Tall Trees Circuit). Introduced **superb lyrebirds** are sometimes seen along Lyrebird Nature Walk, where they mimic common songsters like **grey shrike-thrushes** and **olive whistlers**, the metallic piping of **green rosellas** and stifled screams of **yellow-tailed black-cockatoos**.

Higher up, glacial tarns are home to **platypuses**. On a windless, overcast day, if you sit quietly for half an hour or so by Lake Dobson, Eagle Tarn (just north of Lake Dobson) or even the Tyenna River near the town of National Park, you may be rewarded with a sighting of a **platypus** or even a **water-rat**. Birds are fewer in these alpine regions, but include **black currawongs, forest ravens** and **flame robins**. ■

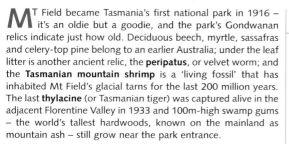

Wildlife highlights
Easily accessible park for common macropods, including Tasmanian pademelons and Bennett's wallabies; and overnight campers are likely to see shyer nocturnal mammals, such as long-nosed potoroos and eastern barred bandicoots. Home to 59 species of bird, including nine Tasmanian endemics and introduced superb lyrebirds.

Location 78km west of Hobart.
Facilities Nature walks on the Russell Falls, Lyrebird and Pandani Grove tracks illustrate the park's different habitats; ranger-led talks and walks in summer.
Accommodation YHA and hotel opposite park entrance.
Wildlife rhythms Animals court and are more active during spring and summer; currawongs and flame robins migrate from peaks in winter.
Contact Ranger (☎ 03-6288 1170).
Ecotours Close to Nature Tours (☎ 03-6288 1477) runs day tours and spotlighting tours, including slide shows and glow-worm spotting.

Watching tips
Take a night stroll down the Russell Falls track with a torch. This is when the possums, bandicoots and quolls will be around and you may see devils and Tasmanian bettongs.

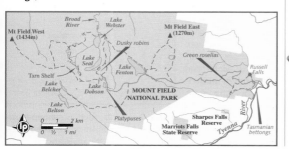

MT WILLIAM NATIONAL PARK

Follow the devils' footprints

Location 128km east of Launceston.
Facilities Walking tracks; signboards with basic wildlife information.
Accommodation Camping; good range in Launceston.
Wildlife rhythms Whales travel north between May and July (humpbacks) or June to September (southern right whales).
Contact Ranger (☎ 03-6357 2108).
Ecotours Mt William is best experienced with camping equipment and a car.

IN addition to uncrowded and secluded beaches, Mt William has the mildest climate on the island and is well known to Tasmanians as the state's best park for wildlife. A morning stroll on the beach is likely to find it littered with tracks of **Tasmanian devils** and there's a good chance of seeing devils on a night drive; both species of **quoll** living in Tasmania (spotted-tailed and eastern quoll) also inhabit the park.

Spotlighting through the black peppermints you're likely to see **common brushtail possums**, **Tasmanian pademelons**, **Tasmanian bettongs** and **common wombats**. **Echidnas** are commonly encountered ambling through open forest, and coastal heaths sheltered by sand dunes support **beautiful firetails** and **superb fairy-wrens**. Heath flowering in spring and early summer attracts a variety of **honeyeaters**, such as **tawny-crowned** and **crescent**, and grass trees are another common plant of the park.

Refuge for rare kangaroos

During the 19th century, European settlers took a toll of native animals as they cleared the land for pasture. Large targets went first, including significant numbers of **foresters** (the Tasmanian race of the eastern grey kangaroo), and Mt William now protects the largest surviving original population. Dozens can be seen along Forester Kangaroo Drive, along with **Bennett's wallabies**, and many injured animals have been rehabilitated into the park – don't be surprised at their boldness. Females usually carry joeys from late summer until October. Two of the noisiest bird inhabitants are **yellow-tailed black-cockatoos** and introduced **kookaburras**; both can be easily seen.

Eddystone Point lighthouse, isolated at the southern end of the park, is an ideal eyrie from which to watch for soaring **white-bellied sea-eagles**, snow-white **Australasian gannets** plunging into the sea, and the effortless gliding of occasional **shy albatrosses**. But the point is at its best when wildlife passes by on migration: **humpback whales** and **southern right whales** in autumn and winter, and thousands of **mutton-birds** heading north in March (they return

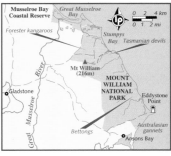

in September). For other migrating birds, such as **swamp harriers**, **grey fantails** and **silvereyes**, Mt William marks the departure point on their autumn migration to the mainland. ■

TASMAN PENINSULA

Cetaceans, seals and outstanding seabirds

THE vertiginous cliffs of the rugged Tasman Peninsula offer superb vantage points for watching wildlife of the Southern Ocean. **Bottlenose dolphins**, sometimes in their hundreds, are an everyday sight streaming past Cape Pillar; **Australian fur-seals** haul out at the foot of Capes Raoul (on its eastern side), Pillar and Hauy, and on Hippolyte Rocks (visible from Cape Hauy); and vagrant **leopard** and **elephant seals** sporadically appear virtually anywhere. Other cetaceans include **common dolphins**, **humpbacks** and **southern right whales** (especially on migration).

Thousands of **fairy prions** and **short-tailed shearwaters**, plus a few **sooty shearwaters**, nest in summer on Hippolyte Rocks, where **Australasian gannets**, **black-faced cormorants** and **peregrine falcons** can be seen perched at any time of the year.

The Blowhole, at the park's north end, is the departure point for pelagic trips that almost guarantee brilliant seabird-watching year-round. If you are prepared to brave the ocean, expect to see up to eight species of albatross – **wandering** and **royal** included – plus **common diving-petrels** and specialities in the winter such as **southern fulmars**.

Rare butterflies

Eucalypt forests and heaths are home to **Bennett's wallabies** and **Tasmanian pademelons**. Driving slowly along the road to Fortescue Bay at night gives a good chance of seeing them, plus **common wombats, eastern barred bandicoots** and, with luck, a **masked owl**; **Tasmanian devils** and **eastern quolls** also occur but are scarce. **Little penguins** nest in colonies in coves and beaches, such as Fortescue Bay, where **hooded plovers** pick over the tideline. Both **wedge-tailed eagles** and **white-bellied sea-eagles** are regularly seen over the peninsula; **yellow-tailed black-cockatoos** can be seen on the way to Cape Raoul; and heathland between Tasmans Arch and Waterfall Bay attracts many **honeyeaters**. Look for **swift parrots** near Mt Spaulding in summer.

Lime Bay is one of the best places to see **Bennett's wallabies**; lepidopterists know the site for the rare **hairstreak butterfly**. ∎

Wildlife highlights
Bounty of the Southern Ocean, including dolphins, seals, whales, and seabirding that varies from very good to excellent. Marsupials include Bennett's wallabies, Tasmanian pademelons and common wombats. Lime Bay NR protects rare hairstreak butterflies.

Location 62km east of Hobart.
Facilities Still being developed.
Accommodation Full range on the Tasman Peninsula; camping ground at Fortescue Bay in park.
Wildlife rhythms Pelagic birds are best seen from shore when blown in on wild weather in spring; butterflies commonest September to October.
Contact Ranger (☎ 03-6250 3497).
Ecotours Summer ranger program. Tasman Nature Guiding (☎ 03-6250 3268) takes short walks. Pawletta Charters (☎ 03-6248 9432) runs infrequent boat trips to look for pelagic birds and seals. Dive with seals at Hippolyte Rock with Eaglehawk Dive Centre (☎ 03-6250 3566).

Watching tips
The wildlife is plentiful but dispersed so plan some walks, eg, to Cape Hauy or Cape Raoul. Ask around to see if a fishing boat can take you out on the water.

OTHER SITES – TASMANIA

Arthur-Pieman Protected Area

This huge expanse of the west coast is not easy to get to and the only time the small town of Marrawah, in the north, gets busy is when there's a whale stranding. The dunes, heath and scrub give way to buttongrass and sedge in an open mosaic ideal for wombats, quolls, blue-winged parrots, grey goshawks and striated pardalotes. Rare ground parrots are resident on the plateau and orange-bellied

parrots pass through on migration. The higher ground is rainforest which connects with an area sometimes referred to as the Tarkine Wilderness; it's currently unprotected but is the subject of local conservation campaigns. Personalised tours in the area are run by Jeff (Jo) King (☎ 03-6457 1191) at Glendonald Cottages near Arthur River.
287km west of Launceston,
☎ *03-6457 1225*

Douglas-Apsley National Park

The only park in Tasmania set aside to protect dry forest, 14 eucalyptus species grow in Douglas-Apsley and the grassy understorey is prime habitat for Tasmanian bettongs. Other mammals include Bennett's wallabies, Tasmanian pademelons and long-nosed potoroos. Endemic green rosellas and endangered swift parrots (summer only) frequent the forests; South Esk and Oyster Bay pines, both endemic to Tasmania, grow here; and a rare freshwater fish, the southern grayling, is also found in the park's streams.
195km north of Hobart,
☎ *03-6375 1236*

Forest Glen Tea Gardens

From October to March there are few better places anywhere to see rare swift parrots, which flock to the gardens and surrounding plantations. The parrots are tame, confiding and easily photographed, and several endemic birds can also be seen here, including dusky robin, yellow wattlebird, and yellow-throated, strong-billed and black-headed honeyeaters.
3km south of Spreyton (south of Devonport)

Governor Island

Water temperatures of 11°C in winter and 20°C in summer bring clear visibility, at times more than 30m, which makes the sheer walls and overhangs of this diverse area popular with divers. There are myriad brightly coloured invertebrates, sea whips, basket stars, sea fans, feather stars, ascidians and hydroids. Huge sponges grow in the sandy trenches and fish abound, including bullseyes, boarfish, zebrafish and schools of jack mackerel. The island itself is a rookery for Tasmania's largest breeding population of crested terns.
Off Bicheno, 178km north of Hobart, ☎ *03-6257 0107*

Melaleuca, Southwest National Park

Birdwatchers seeking the endangered orange-bellied parrot can fly to the parrots' breeding ground in this remote corner of the south-west. The parrots return from their wintering grounds on the mainland in October and usually stay at Melaleuca until the end of March before heading back across Bass Strait. Both wild birds and some that have been reared in a captive-breeding program visit a feeding station near a hide. Beautiful firetails are another attraction at the feeding station and ground parrots can be found in nearby buttongrass. Elsewhere in the

park, the spectacular landscapes (above: Mt Anne) and wilderness attract numerous bushwalkers.
115km south-west of Hobart (accessible only by air)

Mole Creek Karst National Park

This small national park protects a system of more than 200 caves and sinkholes, some containing underground streams and springs. Unique invertebrates supported by organic matter washed into the system include the Tasmanian cave spider, cave crickets and a mountain shrimp, but the main wildlife attraction is a spectacular glow-worm display at Marapooka Cave.
73km west of Launceston,
☎ *03-6363 5182*

Moulting Lagoon

One of Australia's most important sites for black swans; some are present year-round and thousands may congregate during the breeding season. Other waterbirds usually present include Australian pelicans, cormorants, and waterfowl such as Australian shelduck, black duck, teal and musk duck. Public access is limited.
165km north-east of Hobart

Ninepin Point

This small reserve is a unique spot in which the dark, tea-coloured waters of the Huon River overlay the nutrient-rich waters of the cold Southern Ocean. The reduction in light, which results from the tannin staining, means that there are many species of invertebrate, fish and seaweed here that normally live at greater depths. Delicately branched red sea-weeds and red coralline algae occur on the reef, as well as lacy bryozoans and colourful biscuit and firebrick sea stars.
Off Verona Sands, 55km south of Hobart, ☎ 03-6233 6560

Ocean Beach and Henty Dunes

North of Strahan on the west coast is a remote stretch of beach where huge numbers of short-tailed shearwaters (muttonbirds) nest between September and April. The Henty Dune system is

an active, wind-blown dune system where Aboriginal shell middens and stone-tool sites are uncovered as the dunes shift.
300km west of Hobart, ☎ 03-6471 7122

Orielton Lagoon

This saltwater inlet bisected by a causeway is famed among bird-watchers for common and rare migratory shorebirds; and the nearby Waterview Sanctuary at Sorell provides good viewing opportunities, especially at high tide. The lagoon itself supports waterfowl, cormorants, pelicans and grebes; and in summer attracts sandpipers, godwits and stints – plus the odd rarity. Tasmanian native-hens can't be missed at Waterview and the saltmarsh on Orielton's western shore is a good spot for blue-winged parrots.
25km north-east of Hobart

St Helens Recreation Areas

Around the east coast town of St Helens there's a number of small but excellent coastal reserves for birdwatchers. Beerbarrel Beach often has a flock of ruddy turn-stones in summer. Humbug Point State Recreation Area has coastal heath which attracts wattlebirds, the yellow-tailed black-cockatoo and various honeyeaters (tawny-crowned honeyeaters are usually in the heath along the road to The Gardens). The swamps and lagoons south beyond Scamander at Four Mile, Little Beach and Lagoons Beach Coastal Reserves, are stopping points for migra-tory red-necked stints commut-ing from Siberia. Pelicans, ducks, herons and other waders also frequent these lagoons.
163km east of Launceston, ☎ 03-6376 1550

Tinderbox

Apart from its terrestrial attrac-tions (see the Hobart section), this area was at one time a popular fishing spot. There are few large fish to be seen, but there is instead lots of fish food, such as urchins and sea snails. Weedy sea dragons and related sea horses and pipefish can be found here, as well as anem-ones, hydroids, sponges and as-cidians. In the shallow water, there is an excellent underwater snorkel trail, and most of the reef (which extends 100m off-shore) is easily accessible by snorkelling.
Off Tinderbox Bay, 24km south of Hobart, ☎ 03-6233 6560

Waterbird Lagoons

Just upriver from Hobart, check out the reedy Goulds Lagoon Wildlife Sanctuary; when the water level drops it's an ideal spot for crakes, rails and waders (including an occasional va-grant). Lake Dulverton, up the Midlands Hwy, is currently being restored after drought depleted both the water level and birdlife, but it was once the only known nesting site in Tas-mania for great crested grebes – it is hoped reflooding will attract nesting grebes again. Rostrevor Lagoon, north of Tri-abunna, often has species diffi-cult to see elsewhere in the state, such as blue-billed duck. North of Launceston in the Tamar River there is a bird hide at Tamar Island, where intro-duced rice grass has silted the river, slowing its passage of nu-trients and making it attractive to waterbirds.
Goulds Lagoon – 19km north of Hobart
Lake Dulverton – 85km north of Hobart
Tamar Island – just north of Launceston

Wildlife Parks

Trowunna Wildlife Park at Mole Creek is the main wildlife park in the state's north; its exhibits include a nocturnal house, snakes and kangaroos. In the south-east, the best is Bonorong Wildlife Park at Brighton, which has well-kept displays of Tasmanian devils and quolls, among others. The East Coast Birdlife and Animal Park at Bicheno is also worth a visit.
Trowunna – 70km west of Launceston (☎ 03-6363 6162)
Bonorong – 27km north of Hobart (☎ 03-6268 1184)
East Coast Birdlife and Animal Park – 178km north of Hobart (☎ 03-6375 1311)

VICTORIA

State faunal emblems

Leadbeater's possum Once presumed extinct, this small, nocturnal possum was rediscovered in 1961. Endemic to Victoria, its last stronghold is the eucalypt forests of the Central Highlands.

Helmeted honeyeater This endangered honeyeater, a subspecies of the more widespread yellow-tufted honeyeater, only occurs at Yellingbo Nature Conservation Reserve, 50km east of Melbourne.

Highlights

- Southern right whales cavorting at Warrnambool – a stone's throw from shore
- Trying to choose between the sea life attractions of Phillip Island – penguins, seals and muttonbirds – and then doing them all
- Stumbling over wombats between camp sites at Wilsons Promontory
- Picnicking by moonlight to the gurgling shrieks of overhead yellow-bellied gliders in the Angahook-Lorne SP
- Rounding a corner in the Dandenongs to find a superb lyrebird displaying nonchalantly metres away
- Walking among grazing eastern grey kangaroos, with joeys peering from pouches, in the Grampians
- Spotting koalas dozing in the branches of trackside manna gums in the Brisbane Ranges
- Finding rare honeyeaters, parrots and gliders in Chiltern Box-Ironbark NP

VICTORIA comprises only 3% of Australia's total land area, yet encompasses an enormous variety of habitats and wildlife. The southern reaches of the Great Dividing Range, which runs east to west through Victoria, buffer the north of the state from rain and cold southerly winds; inland regions are thus much drier and warmer than the coast. Sixteen landform and vegetation regions are recognised, ranging from semiarid mallee in the north-west, to grassy woodlands on the western plains, to tall, wet forests with pockets of temperate rainforest in the highlands and eastern coastal areas. Around 16% of Victoria is protected in reserves, including 31 national parks, managed by Parks Victoria. (Parks Victoria's hotline gives information for all Victorian parks.)

The wetter forests of the south contain the tallest hardwoods in the world. In them live superb lyrebirds and several possum and glider species. In the state's north-west lies Australia's largest tracts of mallee. Mallee supports wildlife from both the Outback and the forests and woodlands of the south (it is the only area in Victoria with red kangaroos), as well as a high number of species restricted to the mallee itself, including malleefowl. Koalas are common in some of the heavily wooded areas of the south, with large populations close to Melbourne. Platypuses and wombats are widespread throughout the state. Easy-to-see wildlife is not restricted to reserves; for example, two possum species are abundant in the heart of Melbourne, and grey kangaroos and emus are common in farmland adjacent to bushland.

The coasts also offer fantastic wildlife-watching. Victoria's most famous wildlife attraction is the little penguins of Phillip Island; however, dolphins, seal colonies, southern right whales, muttonbirds and stunning temperate-water diving are all on offer. In the west, there is spectacular coastal scenery along the Great Ocean Road – one of the world's great coastal drives – and in the east the mildest weather in the state keeps the prolific wildlife in the extensive coastal parks of the region accessible year-round.

As recently as the 1960s and 1970s new mammals were discovered in Victoria, including the New Holland mouse, long-footed potoroo and mountain pygmy-possum. However, 19 mammals have disappeared from Victoria since European settlement, and a further 29 are threatened; the two faunal emblems of Victoria, endemic to the state, are both endangered. ■

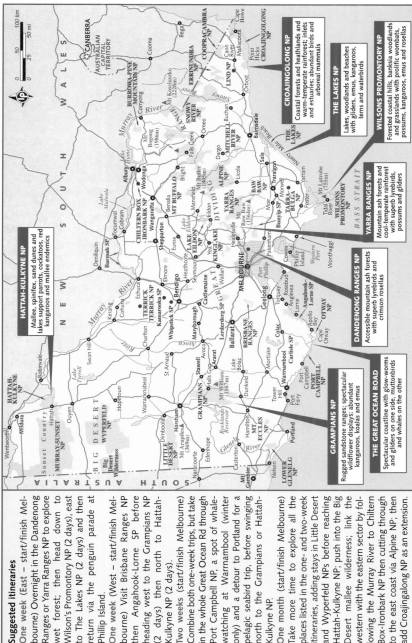

HATTAH-KULKYNE NP

Mallee, spinifex, sand dunes and lakes support parrots, cockatoos, red kangaroos and mallee endemics

CROAJINGOLONG NP

Coastal forests and heathlands and warm-temperate rainforest; inlets and estuaries; abundant birds and arboreal mammals

THE LAKES NP

Lakes, woodlands and beaches with gliders, emus, kangaroos, terns and waterbirds

WILSONS PROMONTORY NP

Forested coastal hills, banksia woodlands and grasslands with prolific wombats, possums, kangaroos, emus and rosellas

YARRA RANGES NP

Mountain ash forests and cool-temperate rainforest with superb lyrebirds, possums and gliders

DANDENONG RANGES NP

Accessible mountain ash forests with superb lyrebirds and crimson rosellas

THE GREAT OCEAN ROAD

Spectacular coastline with glow-worms and gliders on one side, muttonbirds and whales on the other

GRAMPIANS NP

Rugged sandstone ranges: spectacular wildflower displays; abundant kangaroos, koalas and emus

Suggested itineraries

One week (East – start/finish Melbourne). Overnight in the Dandenong Ranges or Yarra Ranges NP to explore wet forest; then head down to Wilson's Promontory NP (2 days), east to The Lakes NP (2 days) and then return via the penguin parade at Phillip Island.

One week (West – start/finish Melbourne) Visit Brisbane Ranges NP then Angahook-Lorne SP before heading west to the Grampians NP (2 days) then north to Hattah-Kulkyne NP (2 days).

Two weeks (start/finish Melbourne). Combine both one-week trips, but take in the whole Great Ocean Rd through Port Campbell NP, a spot of whale-watching at Warrnambool (winter only) and a detour to Portland for a pelagic seabird trip, before swinging north to the Grampians or Hattah-Kulkyne NP.

One month (start/finish Melbourne) Take more time to explore all the places listed in the one- and two-week itineraries, adding stays in Little Desert and Wyperfeld NPs before reaching Hattah-Kulkyne NP; push into the Big Desert mallee wilderness; link the western with the eastern sector by following the Murray River to Chiltern Box-Ironbark NP then cutting through to the east coast via Alpine NP; then add Croajingolong NP as an extension.

MELBOURNE

AS the capital of the Garden State, and being bordered by diverse habitats – the towering and fern-filled forests of the Dandenong Ranges to the east; the drier slopes of Kinglake NP to the north; the unusual, semiarid Brisbane Ranges to the west; and the massive Port Phillip and WesternPort bays to the south – it is not surprising that Melbourne has a great deal of wildlife both within and near the city.

In the *Royal Botanic Gardens* (☎ 03-9252 2300) waterbirds, including **black swans**, frequent the lakes and eels can be seen at the water's edge. In the Fern Gully is a colony of hundreds of **grey-headed flying-foxes** – the most southerly colony of fruit bats in the world (but there are plans to reduce the colony because the bats damage the Gardens). The *Cranbourne Annexe* of the Gardens (☎ 03-5996 3782) is a natural heathland and woodland; its picnic area offers a rare opportunity to see **southern brown bandicoots** by day.

At night, **common brushtail possums** forage in the parks fringing the city centre – you're sure to see them in the *Fitzroy* and *Treasury Gardens*, where they are a tourist attraction. There is a small colony of **little penguins** on the breakwater at *St Kilda Pier*, which can only be seen on guided tours (☎ 03-9531 5036). **Water-rats**, Australia's largest rodents, can also be seen here.

On *Port Phillip*, **common** and **bottlenose dolphins** are frequently sighted, and **Australian fur-seals** often haul-out on channel markers. Dolphin-watching cruises include Looking Good (☎ 03-9621 1450), Moonraker (☎ 03-5984 4211), Polperro (☎ 03-5988 8437), Sea-all (☎ 03-5258 3889) and Wild Dolphin (☎ 03-5984 3664). Diving (and snorkelling, especially under piers) is excellent in the south of Port Phillip; Portsea and Queenscliff are the main access centres. Off Queenscliff there are small colonies of **Australasian gannets** at Pope's Eye (which offers some of the best diving and snorkelling) and nearby Wedge Light. Gannet numbers are highest in the spring-summer breeding season. Mud Islands MR is a breeding site for **terns** and other **seabirds**.

Parks bordering Melbourne's CBD support rosellas, honeyeaters and occasionally itinerant owls. At dusk you may see a grey-headed flying-fox dip down to the Yarra River for a drink as it leaves the Royal Botanic Gardens.

The *Melbourne Zoo* (☎ 03-9285 9300) and *Open Range Zoo* (☎ 03-9731 9600) display many native animals along with exotic fauna. *Healesville Sanctuary* (☎ 03-5962 4022), 65km east of Melbourne, displays only native fauna; highlights include the platypus centre, nocturnal house and raptor flight displays.

Phillip Island is famous for the *Penguin Parade* (☎ 03-5956 8300). Each evening at dusk crowds gather to watch **little penguins** march from the sea to their burrows. Sit tight, as most people lose interest

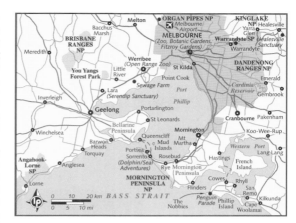

quickly and you can then enjoy the penguins in peace. **Koalas** are easily seen from the boardwalk at the *Koala Conservation Centre* (☎ 03-5952 1307). At Seal Rocks, off the western tip of the island, there's a colony of thousands of **Australian fur-seals**. *Seal Rocks Sea Life Centre* (☎ 1300 367 325) overlooking the colony has educational displays and telescopes for viewing the seals. **Short-tailed shearwaters** nest on the cliff tops of Cape Woolamai: huge flocks can be seen wheeling in at dusk between October and early May from a viewing platform.

The coast between Melbourne and Geelong is one of Australia's best areas for migratory **waders**, and also supports large numbers of **waterbirds**. The prime site is *Werribee Sewage Farm*: contact Melbourne Water (☎ 03-9235 7100) about access to the farm and to adjacent *Laverton Saltworks*. A similar range of bird-watching is on offer at *Point Cook Coastal Park* and nearby *Cheetham Wetlands*, and both are open to the public.

You Yangs Regional Park offers excellent birdwatching in its dry forests. **Koalas** and **eastern grey kangaroos** are common. At dusk sit on Flinders Peak and listen to **southern boobooks** start up and the grunts of male koalas. Nearby, the *Serendip Sanctuary at Lara* (☎ 03-5282 1584) has many waterbirds, along with brolgas, Australian bustards and eastern grey kangaroos.

Possums are ubiquitous in suburban Melbourne, but you'll need to go to the city's outskirts to see many other marsupials. *Cardinia Reservoir Park* has plenty of **eastern grey kangaroos** in its open grassy areas at dusk and dawn. In the forests of *Bunyip SP* near Gembrook, **common wombats** are often seen on the tracks at night; **swamp wallabies** are not uncommon; and Dyers Picnic Ground is a good place to spotlight for **possums** and **gliders**. Other nocturnal wildlife includes **tawny frogmouths**, **nightjars** and **owls**. *Warrandyte SP*, along the Yarra River, is also good for **possums**, **wombats**, **wallabies** and **kangaroos**, but **koalas** are its star attraction – the largest population in the suburbs, they should be seen along the track by the river in the park's Pound Creek section. ■

GRAMPIANS NATIONAL PARK

Wildlife island in the western plains

Wildlife highlights

Expect to see kangaroos, swamp wallabies and red-necked wallabies during any visit to the park. You'd be unlucky not to also see koalas and possums, but platypuses are less visible. There is an abundance of several species of cockatoo and parrot, including galahs, long-billed corellas, crimson and eastern rosellas, and sulphur-crested and gang-gang cockatoos. Emus are common in the lowlands. Victoria's greatest wildflower display in spring.

THE craggy sandstone escarpments and sweeping north-west-facing slopes of the Grampians rise from surrounding plains to form the western extremity of the Great Dividing Range. As well as traces of a long Aboriginal occupation, the folded ridges, forests, swamps and heathy woodlands are home to much wildlife and support a particularly diverse flora, which puts on a spectacular wildflower display in spring.

Island of flowers

The Grampians is renowned for its flora. At least 800 native plant species – over one-third of Victoria's entire indigenous flora – grow here, while about 20 plant species, including orchids, peas and the Grampians gum, occur nowhere else. The folded, sedimentary sandstone peaks of the Grampians are effectively an island, distinct from the younger, volcanic basalt plains that surround them. Infertile, sandy soils produced by the weathered sandstone create harsh growing conditions that prevent any single plant species from dominating. The diversity of vegetation means a great array of habitats, ranging from wet heathlands, to woodlands on rocky outcrops, and a corresponding range of animal communities.

East meets west

Mammals are very easy to see in the Grampians. The most obvious are **eastern grey kangaroos**; you can see them throughout the park, especially in areas with a grassy understorey, but the best site is Zumstein, where they are especially abundant and unusually tame. They are also easy to see at dusk as they graze in the grassy valley of Halls Gap – try the lawns of the Grampians Motel. **Western grey kangaroos** can be found in heathy woodland. This is one of the few areas where the two species of grey kangaroo overlap. They have a similar build, but western greys are distinctly brown in colour. **Red-necked wallabies** are often seen grazing around picnic and camping areas – there are always one or two at Troopers Creek picnic area.

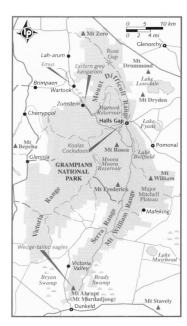

Swamp wallabies are also common, especially in the north and along the Grampians Rd towards Dunkeld. Sadly, old, dried scats on ledges in sections of the northern ranges are reminders that the **brush-tailed rock-wallaby** was once also widespread. Now endangered in Victoria, it is estimated that only a handful of rock-wallabies hold on in the park – one of only two Victorian sites where they remain.

At Halls Gap and in the surrounding tall forest in the Wonderland Range, **koalas** may be seen in the forks of manna gums; their grunting is often heard at the Rosea camping ground at night. Koalas are also sometimes found at Zumstein, where nocturnal encounters with **common brushtail possums** and smaller **common ringtail possums** are also likely. In the Mackenzie River, **water-rats** are common and **platypuses** frequent the river's lower reaches outside the park around Wartook. Water-rats are not entirely nocturnal and sometimes forage in daylight, although they are most active around sunset. **Echidnas** are often seen in heathy woodlands throughout the park during the day.

Emus, corellas and brolgas

Emus are easily observed in open areas and woodlands, and males are sometimes seen running along roads with their chicks. Good places to look are in the paddocks around Wartook and among the plentiful olive groves adjacent to the park.

Just out of the park, **brolgas** are regularly seen in the Victoria Valley around Bryan Swamp and nearby Freshwater Lake. These and some other wetlands in and around the park attract large numbers of waterbirds. The wetland at Cherrypool (Djarabul) has several hides.

Large numbers of parrots and cockatoos feed and roost around Halls Gap. **Long-billed corellas** are a constant presence here, feeding in huge flocks on the lawn outside the shops at the north end of town; from Lake Bellfield at dusk you can see small groups winging their way to roosts. **Crimson rosellas**, **sulphur-crested cockatoos** and **gang-gang cockatoos** are also common in the valley of Halls Gap. The track winding along the

Location 260km to the west of Melbourne.

Facilities Brambuk Aboriginal Cultural Centre (☎ 03-5356 4452) has excellent information on the Aboriginal history of the area. The Grampians NP visitor centre has very good displays and information on the park's natural history.

Accommodation Many camping grounds throughout the park; wide range at Halls Gap and surrounding towns.

Wildlife rhythms Spring for wildflowers and birdlife; spring and summer for reptiles.

Contact Grampians NP visitor centre, located at Halls Gap (☎ 03-5356 4381).

Ecotours Guided spotlighting walks for koalas, possums, gliders, owls and bats run by the Grampians Bushwalking Company (☎ 03-5356 4654) and Grampians Adventure Services (☎ 03-5356 4556).

Mackenzie River east from Zumstein is also a good place to see crimson rosellas and gang-gang cockatoos. **Yellow-tailed black-cockatoos** are often seen throughout the region, but especially in pine plantations on the edges of the park.

Pied currawongs and families of **laughing kookaburras** are also common around Halls Gap. Kookaburras watch lunching holiday-makers carefully and occasionally swoop to steal food directly from your hands. As night falls, the *mo-poke* calls of the **southern boobook** and the deep *hoo hoo* of **powerful owls** can be heard throughout the forest.

Other birdlife is also abundant. Yellow-and-black **New Holland honeyeaters** and **crescent honeyeaters** dart between the grass trees and desert banksias that grow in fire-scarred soil at the base of Mt Zero. In spring and summer, the green-and-blue shimmer of **sacred kingfishers** is regularly seen above streams and rivers, and **fan-tailed cuckoos** trill from prominent perches. Groups of aerobatic **dusky woodswallows** are present year-round in woodlands. On the walk to the Pinnacles, watch for **eastern spinebills** among Oyster Bay pines encrusted with orange lichen. Raptors are common throughout the park and its surrounds: **wedge-tailed eagles** and **peregrine falcons** circle over the rocky escarpments and cliff faces (a pair of wedgies is frequently seen over Mt Abrupt, near Dunkeld); **whistling kites** and **swamp harriers** are common in the Victoria Valley; and on the plains between Stawell and Halls Gap, **brown falcons**, **nankeen kestrels** and **black-shouldered kites** hover in search of small quarry.

McKenzie Falls tumble over the rugged boulder country in the Grampians NP.

Blue tongues, orange throats

There are many different species of skink in the park and it doesn't take much effort to find and identify some of them. Large **shingle-back** lizards – like an elongated pine cone with legs – bask on tracks in sandy heathlands and woodlands. You are sure to see several on a warm day along the road between Mt Zero and Rose Gap. When alarmed, they gape in a threat display showing orange throat and blue tongue. Black-flecked,

The Grampians puma – fact or fiction?

Big cats do not occur naturally in Australia, but the phenomenon of big-cat sightings is widespread and persistent, with more than 1000 reports from all states since the turn of the century. The Grampians is one of the hotspots for sightings of puma and pantherlike creatures – one researcher has a file on Grampians sightings the size of the Sydney phone book.

Greg Knight, a Grampians landowner, and some friends had a close encounter one night. Out shooting rabbits, the others were approaching Greg for a rendezvous around midnight when, in front of them, a large eucalypt suddenly began shaking violently, as though something very large were descending it branch by branch. In the beams of their spotlights they saw a creature leap down from the tree and bound, catlike, over the bracken on the ground. The animal was so black that it was hard to make out its shape, but they all saw that it was big – much larger than a feral cat.

Sightings in the Grampians go back to the 1940s, although in the late 1960s their frequency increased markedly. In addition to sightings there are casts of tracks, photographs, and reports of livestock killings – but nothing definitive. In 1996 the Victorian government took the reports seriously enough to send an ecologist to the USA to spend time with puma researchers. There is even a theory to explain the origin of the creatures – US regimental mascots from WWII released in the area in the 1940s.

olive-brown **cool-temperate water-skinks** bask on sandstone, dashing for cover when disturbed. In high rocky areas, crevices in the lichen-covered sandstone harbour families of chunky, slate-coloured **black rock skinks** (at the western and southern edge of their range here); and in many places, such as up the steep road to Mt William, innumerable tinier skinks scuttle from view. On warm days, **eastern brown snakes** can be seen in the rocky ranges and **eastern tiger snakes** can be found in wetter areas, such as along the McKenzie River.

Mt William peak supports a variety of uncommon plants and animals, including populations of the little-known and rarely seen **smoky mouse**. Also noteworthy is the **southern brown bandicoot**: usually inhabiting low-lying coastal areas, a population of these fungus-eaters occurs at up to 1000m in altitude on the slopes of Mt William – unfortunately you have almost no chance of seeing one. ■

Watching tips
When birders identify a bird with barely a glance or from an impossible distance, they are doing so from its 'jizz' – a combination of subtle features such as its shape, how it moves and how it behaves. Raptors are ideal for learning this art. Whistling kites and swamp harriers are common in the Grampians, but from afar or when zooming past, telling one from the other may seem impossible. At first, look for distinctive features, such as the clearly bowed wings of the kite in flight and the prominent white rump of the harrier. Before you know it, the jizz will have sunk in unconsciously and you'll be nonchalantly identifying raptors that appear as little more than a dot in the sky.

CROAJINGOLONG NATIONAL PARK

Diversity in the far east

> **Wildlife highlights**
> Croajingolong is one of the best areas for birdwatching in Victoria, with over 300 species recorded. Possums, gliders, wombats, wallabies and bandicoots all frequent the forests, with eastern grey kangaroos abundant in open areas. Reptiles include diamond pythons, lace monitors and eastern water dragons. The diversity of frogs in East Gippsland is the highest in Victoria.

Location 450km to the east of Melbourne.

Facilities The Orbost Rainforest Centre (☎ 03-5161 1375) has an excellent audiovisual display on East Gippsland's forests.

Accommodation Wide range in surrounding towns; camping grounds in and around park.

Wildlife rhythms Summer for frogs, reptiles and migratory birds.

Contact Ranger, Cann River (☎ 03-5158 6351).

Ecotours Eco Explorer (☎ 03-5157 5751) runs wildlife research tours. Gipsy Point Lodge (☎ 03-5158 8205) holds a 'bird week' each September. Natural Adventures Mallacoota (☎ 03-5158 0166).

HUGGING the coastline of far East Gippsland for almost 100km, Croajingolong is where vegetation associations from further north and west converge. The extensive eucalypt forests and coastal heathlands, pockets of warm-temperate rainforest, and estuarine inlets and ocean beaches support a number of species at the southern limit of their distribution.

Peak wildlife

From Genoa Peak you can see the region's layout. The walk to the top passes through dry forests, where **superb lyrebirds** are often heard and there is a chance of seeing the threatened **glossy black-cockatoo**. **Eastern small-eyed snakes** shelter under sheets of granite, and along the edge of the track in summer are dozens of **eastern water-skinks** (flecked gold and black) and **White's skinks** (pale eye-ring and pale spots on their back). At nearby Genoa Falls you'll see **eastern water dragons**, which are right at the limit of their range. These large, striking lizards often sit on branches or rocks above running water, dropping into it when disturbed. **Lace monitors** and spectacular **red-bellied black snakes** are common throughout heathlands and forests.

Waterbirds are conspicuous around Genoa and Mallacoota. **Black swans** are often abundant on the wetlands around Genoa while Mallacoota Inlet is a good site to see fish-eating birds, including **Australian pelicans** (especially at Mallacoota's main wharf), **Caspian terns** and **white-bellied sea-eagles**. Waders

Forests, fungi and potoroos

The long-footed potoroo was only discovered in the forests of East Gippsland in 1980. Even more recently we have begun to understand the important role that potoroos and bettongs play in forest ecosystems. At night they search for underground fungi ('truffles') which grow on tree roots and assist the trees in the uptake of soil nutrients – a vital role, given the paucity of nutrients in Australian soils. Truffles look like small pebbles and are a bit larger than button mushrooms, with a thin outer crust and a pale, nougat-soft interior. After eating the fungi, the potoroos and bettongs unwittingly spread fungal spores throughout the forest in their droppings. With such tightly woven relationships, the loss of any of these marsupials could have serious consequences for the health of the forests.

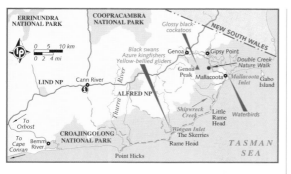

often roost on sand bars in the inlet. **Eastern grey kangaroos** are common on the lawns before the Gipsy Point jetty and on the Mallacoota golf course. At night, bush tracks between Cape Conran and Marlo are good for **common wombats**.

From Mallacoota, Betka Rd passes through heathlands that offer excellent birdwatching, particularly in spring when the wildflowers bloom. Between Shipwreck Creek and Little Rame Head is a good place to listen at dawn and dusk for the rare **ground parrot's** thin, ascending, bell-like call. Another hotspot is just out of the park in the heathlands around Cape Conran, including the heathland beside the camping ground. Just out of Mallacoota, the Shady Gully and Double Creek nature walks are easily accessible places to see birds of the wetter forests.

Wingan it

Satin bowerbirds and **wonga pigeons** can be seen in the camping ground at Wingan Inlet. **Long-nosed bandicoots** inhabit the area: your chances of seeing one are much less than in the past, but you may find their small, conical diggings. The nature walk here passes banksias which, when flowering, attract **rainbow lorikeets** and honeyeaters by day, and **sugar gliders** and **eastern pygmy-possums** by night. Vibrant blue-and-orange **azure kingfishers** are commonly seen perched in waterside trees. **Australian pelicans** and **black swans** are numerous on the inlet, especially in late summer. The walk ends at the ocean beach, where dingo tracks are often found in the sand but dingoes themselves are seldom seen. Through binoculars you can just see **Australian fur-seals** on The Skerries 100m offshore; this group of rocky islets also has a colony of **little penguins**.

At night, tiny bats flutter through forest clearings; **common ringtail possums** feed in the understorey; **grey-headed flying-foxes** squabble in flowering eucalypts; and **common brushtail possums** roam the camp sites. The gurgling shrieks of **yellow-bellied gliders** ring out in succession as the members of a colony communicate – camping grounds can resound with their calls one night but be silent the next because the gliders move around large territories. The trunks of some eucalypts display deep, V-shaped incisions made by yellow-bellies to induce sap flows. The oozing sap also attracts feathertail and sugar gliders. ■

Croajingolong's tidal inlets attract herons and waterfowl.

Watching tips

On humid, stormy summer nights, the bitumen roads come to life with frogs. Drive slowly and look carefully because many are small. The Bonang Hwy north of Orbost and the road between Marlo and Orbost are good places to start. If you are hoping to see a rare masked owl, around Cape Conran is one of your best bets. In the centre of Mallacoota there is a large Mallacoota gum (conveniently signposted) – only about 40 of these trees are known. Nearby Lind, Alfred and Errinundra NPs are also worth visiting.

THE GREAT OCEAN ROAD

Gliders and glow-worms, seals and shearwaters

Wildlife highlights
Yellow-bellied and sugar gliders can be easily seen. Southern right whales, fur-seals and glow-worms are major attractions. A high diversity of birdlife includes rufous bristlebirds, grey goshawks, sulphur-crested cockatoos, little penguins and short-tailed shearwaters.

THE Great Ocean Road, winding along Victoria's south-west coastline for almost 250km, is one of the great coastal drives of the world. On one side rise the forested gullies of the biologically intriguing Otway Ranges; on the other, sheer cliffs overlook the Southern Ocean and its abundant marine life.

Several species common in the forests further east do not occur in the Otways, including superb lyrebirds and greater gliders, but the Otways have some wildlife that is more common or more accessible than elsewhere in Victoria. **Grey goshawks** come in two colours, grey and white; in contrast to most of the east coast of Australia, the spectacular white form is the more common in the Otways. Most white birds will be **sulphur-crested cockatoos**, which are abundant, but check solitary birds or those in pairs – goshawks lack a crest and have telltale long, yellow legs.

The Sheoak Creek picnic ground in Angahook-Lorne SP is almost a sure bet for **yellow-bellied gliders**. You can hear their gurgling shrieks at night, as well as the *yap-yap* of **sugar gliders** and the *mo-poke* of **southern boobooks**. Spotlight the picnic ground for a chance to see them all: the best time for southern boobooks is around dusk, and for gliders after dark.

Rufous rarity

The vigorous call of the rare rufous bristlebird was described by the first European settlers as 'the squeaking of the wheels of an ox cart, followed by a whip crack'. It is commonly heard coming from dense coastal vegetation at many places along the Great Ocean Road, but the birds themselves are extremely wary and not often seen. Bristlebirds almost never fly: they mostly run swiftly on the ground, often along 'runways' beneath dense shrubs; if approached, they usually dash for cover, running with the tail fanned and cocked slightly, exposing dark, delicate barring on the otherwise rich-rufous tail feathers. At the Twelve Apostles car park, bristlebirds have apparently lost their wariness and often feed in the open, seemingly oblivious to the constant throng of passersby. Around the Aireys Inlet lighthouse is another bristlebird hotspot, but nowhere is the search as easy as at the Twelve Apostles.

John Peter, ornithologist

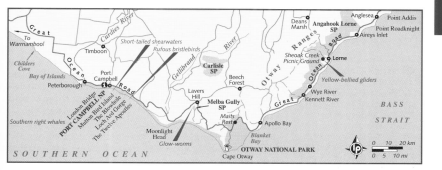

The cool-temperate rainforest along Marsdens Track in Melba Gully SP is a terrific place to see **glow-worms** at night (they are actually insect larvae, not worms). Switch off your torch and wait – one by one tiny, green lights will appear along embankments. The walk at Maits Rest also offers easy access to the rainforest.

The right stuff

The most famous of Port Campbell NP's coastal formations are the Twelve Apostles (opposite page). But its viewing area is also famous among birdwatchers for the **rufous bristlebird**. There is also a **little penguin** colony below the Twelve Apostles viewing area, the penguins coming ashore at dusk. Dusk in the car parks may also see small mammals such as **southern brown bandicoots** emerging from the windswept vegetation.

A little further west, the steep cliffs over Loch Ard Gorge provide a view of Mutton Bird Island, home to a colony of 50,000 **short-tailed shearwaters**. They can be seen at dusk during summer amassing in the skies around the island. Just beyond Port Campbell NP, the lookout over the Bay of Islands also offers great views of a colony of **black-faced cormorants** on one of the nearby stacks. There are only a few dozen colonies of this Australian marine cormorant, and only a handful of them in Victoria.

West of the Great Ocean Rd, Logans Beach at Warrnambool is one of Australia's prime whale-watching sites. From May to October, **southern right whales** and their calves are often seen just offshore from the viewing platforms. At Port Fairy, there is another **short-tailed shearwater** colony on Griffiths Island, where boardwalks take you among the wheeling and crash-landing birds. The only onshore colony of **Australasian gannets** in Australia at Point Danger in Portland (all other colonies, except for three in New Zealand, are on islands, including Lawrence Rocks off Portland). Beyond Portland at Cape Bridge-water, there is a colony of **Australian fur-seals** with viewing platforms directly above it. Cape Bridgewater is also a prime land-based seabird-viewing site. Winter, particularly during stormy weather, sees the greatest numbers of **albatrosses**, **petrels**, **skuas** and the like coming close to shore. ∎

Location Starts 120km south-west of Melbourne.
Facilities Maits Rest rainforest walk. Viewing platforms for whales and fur-seals. Boardwalk in shearwater colony.
Accommodation Wide range along Great Ocean Rd.
Wildlife rhythms Spring and summer for shearwaters; winter for whales.
Contact Great Ocean Road visitor centre, Apollo Bay (☎ 03-5237 6529). Port Campbell NP information centre (☎ 03-5598 6369). Whale sighting information (☎ 03-5564 7837; 🖥 www .whales,warrnambool.com).
Ecotours Last Chance Tours (☎ 03-5237 7413). Otway Eco-guides (☎ 03-5237 7240). Glow-worms (☎ 03-5237 6791). Seals by Sea (☎ 03-5526 7247) for boat tours to the fur-seals at Cape Bridgewater.

Watching tips

A significant invertebrate at Maits Rest is the black-shelled snail: found only in the Otways; there is a good chance of seeing one on the track after rain. Around February to March, keep an eye out on beaches for any penguin larger than the resident little penguins; nearly every year at least one or two individuals of species from New Zealand and beyond come ashore along this coastline to moult.

HATTAH-KULKYNE NATIONAL PARK

Red roos and pink cockatoos

Wildlife highlights

Wildlife includes mallee endemics and species found more widely in the Outback. There is an astounding diversity and abundance of parrots, wrens, waterbirds, raptors and honeyeaters, with malleefowl, emus and other mallee and arid-country birds. To top it off, western grey, eastern grey and red kangaroos are prolific, as are reptiles.

Location 580km north-west of Melbourne.
Facilities Excellent visitor centre; Hattah Nature Drive; Mallee Nature Walk.
Accommodation Full range at Ouyen and Mildura; camping grounds at Lake Hattah and Lake Mournpoul.
Wildlife rhythms Spring and autumn (when the lakes are full) for waterbirds; wildlife, especially birds, is much less active in summer.
Contact Hattah-Kulkyne visitor centre (☎ 03-5029 3253).
Ecotours Check with state- and national-based operators.

COASTAL Victoria is green and lush, but inland of the Great Dividing Range the country dries out rapidly. Hattah-Kulkyne lies in the semiarid transition zone between the arid centre and the moister regions. It showcases prime examples of unique mallee vegetation; spinifex and sand dunes typical of the centre; and lakes and woodlands associated with the adjacent Murray River. It is the lakes that attract much of the wildlife: although not all of them are always full, usually at least some have water.

The chattering masses

Cockatoos and parrots are prominent. Flocks of **sulphur-crested cockatoos**, **galahs**, **little corellas**, bright-yellow **regent parrots** and pink **Major Mitchell's cockatoos** can all be seen (in Victoria, the last two species occur only in the north-west); flocks of **budgerigars** and **cockatiels** also sometimes arrive from further inland. In the evening many come to drink from the lakes and to roost in the surrounding river red gums. Sulphur-crested cockatoos and galahs are also common around the lakes during the day, and can nearly always be seen at the Lake Hattah camping ground, as can pairs of **yellow rosellas** (a distinct form of the crimson rosella). Other less gregarious but nonetheless abundant parrots include **mulga** and **red-rumped parrots**, **blue bonnets** and the mallee form of the **Australian ringneck**. **Grey butcherbirds**, **noisy miners** and groups of **white-winged choughs** are a

Composter extraordinaire

Rather than use body heat to incubate their eggs, malleefowl rely on heat produced by decaying vegetation. Males first build a mound of leaf litter and sand – which may reach 1m in height and 5m across – then excavate an egg chamber within. They wait for rain to saturate the organic material inside the mound before closing it up. Because its temperature must be kept around 33°C the male inspects his natural incubator daily, for up to 11 months of the year, and makes continual adjustments in response to temperature variations – opening it to cool it down or, as the rate of decomposition decreases over time, to expose it to heat from the sun. Of 19 mound-building birds worldwide, the malleefowl is the only one that lives outside the tropics or subtropics.

constant presence at camping grounds. The lakes attract **waterbirds** – at times in very large numbers – with the track alongside Lake Hattah affording excellent views.

Wrens, raptors, reptiles and roos

The nature walk near the park entrance is a great introduction to mallee wildlife. **Mallee emu-wrens** and rufous **striated grasswrens** are intimately connected with spinifex; both are worth searching for: the emu-wren is endemic to the area; and though the grasswren is widespread, most of its range is less accessible than here. Emu-wrens have been seen on the nature walk, but both species are more regularly seen on the Lendrook Plain (south of the main entrance road) and along Nowingi Track. At times, bush bird activity in the mallee is frenetic, with **honeyeaters** especially conspicuous and diverse. **Malleefowl** mounds are relatively common but the birds are harder to find.

Raptors are everywhere and a walk around the lakes adjacent to Hattah Lake could encounter up to ten species, including three eagles – **white-bellied sea-eagle**, **wedge-tailed eagle** and **little eagle**. The bulky stick nests adorning tall eucalypts belong to **whistling kites**. The lakes walk is also good for **pied butcherbirds**, their morning carolling arguably the most beautiful of Australian birdsongs.

Small, orange **mallee dragons** are easily seen in summer. They dash for spinifex tussocks when disturbed, so approach quietly and view them with binoculars. With some luck, **Burton's snakelizards** can also be seen. Like a snake in appearance but with a long, pointed snout, these harmless lizards lie among fallen bark beneath eucalypts. Other common lizards include ruggedly scaled **shingle-backs**, **eastern blue-tongued** lizards (larger than the blotched blue-tongue of southern Victoria), **lace monitors**, **bearded dragons** – often seen sunning themselves on tree stumps – and a multitude of skinks and geckoes. You should also be able to see reptiles on warm nights on the entrance road.

You will have no trouble finding the largest animals in the park. **Western grey kangaroos** rest by day in the shade under native pines and eucalypts; **red kangaroos** (at the very eastern edge of their geographic range) can be seen in grassy clearings or open woodland; and **emus** are ubiquitous. They all also drink at the lakes at dawn and dusk, emus sometimes wading out to do so. Drive the tracks at night to see the roos in action (the Mournpoul track also offers **common brushtail possums**). ∎

Watching tips
Spotlight the trunks of river red gums for marbled geckoes and the brilliant-blue eyeshine of spiders. Spotlighting in the mallee could turn up Mitchell's hopping-mouse, southern ningaui and other small native mammals – they are common but very cryptic. The embankment by the railway along the western side of the Calder Hwy is a favoured spring–summer site for three tunnel-nesting birds: rainbow bee-eaters, white-backed swallows and red-backed kingfishers.

WILSONS PROMONTORY NATIONAL PARK

Tasmanian connections

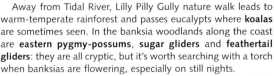

Wildlife highlights

Eastern grey kangaroos and swamp wallabies are conspicuous and it is probably the best place in Victoria to see common wombats. Common ringtail possums are abundant and echidnas are not uncommon. Birdwatching is excellent: you'll be inundated with crimson rosellas; emus are easily seen; and there is a high diversity of parrots, bush birds, seabirds and waders, including several rare species.

Location 200km south-east of Melbourne.

Facilities The Tidal River visitor centre has excellent displays and information. Four different nature walks.

Accommodation Lodges, huts and 480 camp sites at Tidal River; 11 bush camping areas.

Wildlife rhythms The warmer months for most migratory waders; winter for most seabirds and whales.

Contact Tidal River visitor centre (☎ 03-5680 9555; accommodation booking ☎ 1800 350 552).

Ecotours Ranger-guided activities, walks and spotlighting from Tidal River. Surefoot Explorations (☎ 03-5952 1533) conducts full-day wildlife tours.

Tree ferns along Sealers Creek.

IN Victoria's favourite park, dry eucalypt forests and coastal heathlands surround gullies of warm-temperate rainforest. And patches of cool-temperate rainforest have persisted for 15,000 years from before a time when Tasmania was isolated by rising seas. The Tasmanian connection is reflected in the wildlife, with several of the Prom's species most common in Tasmania.

Abundant marsupials and birds

There are two big attractions at Tidal River: large numbers of **crimson rosellas** are always present during the day, and **common wombats** are easily seen at night grazing the lawns – both species are very approachable. Flocks of **rainbow lorikeets** arrive when the trees flower. **Forest ravens** (one of the 'Tasmanian' species) strut about in small groups – their tails shorter and voices more gravelly than the widespread Australian raven. It is not uncommon to find **echidnas**, particularly in the surrounding open vegetation. From dusk, **common ringtail possums** abound in the shrubs and trees. All along the main road **eastern grey kangaroos, wombats, echidnas, emus** and occasional **swamp wallabies** can be seen at any time, especially in the grassy area around the airstrip – at night the road is thick with wildlife.

Away from Tidal River, Lilly Pilly Gully nature walk leads to warm-temperate rainforest and passes eucalypts where **koalas** are sometimes seen. In the banksia woodlands along the coast are **eastern pygmy-possums, sugar gliders** and **feathertail gliders**: they are all cryptic, but it's worth searching with a torch when banksias are flowering, especially on still nights.

Birdwatching is excellent anywhere (Lilly Pilly Gully and the track from the Darby River car park to the beach are two hotspots), but many of the highlights of the Prom's more than 250 bird species are found in the north. On the grasslands of the Yanakie Isthmus, **emus** are often seen from the main road, and flocks of stocky, grey **Cape Barren geese** visit in summer to graze in grassy areas – try around Shallow Inlet and around the road to Sandy Point on the north-east shore of Waratah Bay. The unusual, grass-green **ground parrot** is rare in Victoria, but in the northern heathlands at dusk and dawn you can hear them call, and possibly see their short display flights – around the road to Millers Landing is a good site.

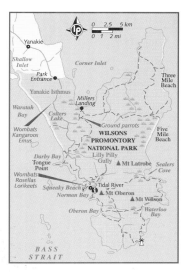

Mudflats and mangroves, seabirds and sea caves

Tens of thousands of migratory waders of over 20 species congregate at Corner and Shallow Inlets in summer (Shallow is more accessible than Corner). The inlets are one of the two most important areas for **eastern curlews** in Australia. When the tide is in, **black swans**, ducks and cormorants dominate the scene, gradually giving way to waders and **soldier crabs** as the tide recedes. The southernmost mangroves in the world grow in Corner Inlet.

The shores and waters elsewhere are also rich in wildlife. **Pacific gulls** and red-legged **pied oystercatchers** frequent the beaches, such as Squeaky Beach and Whisky Bay. **Australasian gannets** regularly dive offshore and **white-bellied sea-eagles** sometime pass overhead. Rare **hooded plovers** feed and breed on the beaches: walk north along Darby Beach, especially in the warmer months, and you should see them. There are usually **sooty oystercatchers** – another species for which the Prom is a stronghold – at the southern end of Norman Bay. **Bottlenose dolphins** and **little penguins** are sometimes spotted off the beaches and headlands. Colonies of **Australian fur-seals** frequent offshore islands and individuals occasionally enter Sealers Cove (if you have a telescope, you can view some on the islands off the beach at Tidal River). In winter, **southern right whales** are sometimes sighted offshore: Kersop Peak, Tidal Overlook (above Tidal River) and the top of Mt Oberon are great vantage points.

The Prom also has great diving, with extensive seagrass meadows in Corner Inlet, and, around offshore islands, enormous caves and kelp forests harbouring many fish species, sea whips and giant sea fans. ■

Watching tips
Take time to watch the change of wildlife in Corner Inlet as the tide ebbs and flows. The world's southernmost warm-temperate rainforest is at Little Waterloo Bay's camping ground. From Tongue Point, look for flocks of short-tailed shearwaters offshore in summer and other seabirds, such as albatrosses, during winter (best when strong winds are blowing from the south-west).

Minuscule mammalian pollinators

Large banksia inflorescences, dripping with nectar, lure honeyeaters, rainbow lorikeets and insects. While feeding, these 'pollination vectors' become covered in pollen which they inadvertently courier to other flowers. However, at the Prom there is more to pollination than the birds and the bees. At night eastern pygmy-possums (inset) emerge to lap nectar with their brush-tipped tongue, drawn to the strong, sweet odour of the bright yellow flowers – a colour more easily detected at night than red or purple. Unlike most flowering plants, banksias continue to produce nectar throughout the night. The possums also transport pollen, but they exact a toll additional to the nectar feed – they also eat the pollen. Unlike honeyeaters, but in common with lorikeets, the pygmy-possums can digest this high-protein food.

YARRA RANGES NATIONAL PARK

Reaching for the sky

ONLY 70km north-east of Melbourne stand the world's tallest hardwood forests. Mountain ash, the world's tallest flowering plant (up to 95m high), towers over a dense understorey and sheltered gullies of cool-temperate rainforest. Take the Cumberland walking track, just before Cambarville, to see the tallest living tree (83m high) known in Victoria. On Mt Donna Buang and Lake Mountain, the ash gives way to sprawling snow gum subalpine woodland.

With so many levels to the vegetation in tall forests, there is a diverse community of birds. On warm spring days there are birds calling everywhere, with **rose robins**, **golden whistlers**, **eastern whipbirds**, **white-throated treecreepers** and **eastern yellow robins** all abundant. Among the most distinctive calls are the rusty-gate wailing of **yellow-tailed black-cockatoos** and the *egypt* of **crescent honeyeaters**. Damp, autumn and winter days can be still and quiet, but it is in such conditions that **superb lyrebirds**, one of the area's specialities, are most easily seen – often running across roads – and it is at this time of year that they most often display. Badger Weir Park is a good site to see lyrebirds, and **crimson rosellas** and **laughing kookaburras** are also common.

A hollow outcome

Tree hollows are homes for a variety of Australian wildlife – parrots, cockatoos, treecreepers, owls, bats, possums and gliders. It takes a mountain ash eucalypt 120 years to start developing hollows – and typically 200 years before it becomes suitable for a colony of endangered Leadbeater's possums. Most of the mountain ash forest (inset) in the Victorian Central Highlands is 60-year-old regeneration from the devastating 1939 'Black Friday' bushfires, and thus it will be another 60 years before its trees start to develop hollows. For Leadbeater's possum, hollows will be in short supply for the next 140 years. Considering the risk of another large fire, and extensive logging (which clear-fells areas on a 50- to 80-year cycle), the outlook is bleak for the animals of Victoria's Central Highlands which depend on hollows – an all too common story in Victoria's forests.

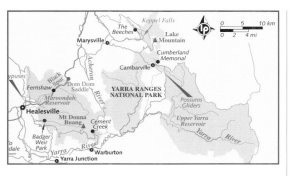

Arboreal antics

Few mammals are visible by day (except for occasional **swamp wallabies**), but at night the forests are literally jumping with them. Mouse-sized **dusky antechinuses** are the first to emerge, often doing so in the late afternoon, especially in winter – watch for them hunting invertebrates beside tracks. **Common wombats** bash through the understorey while native **bush rats** rustle more quietly. **Platypuses** live in many of the park's creeks; sections of Badger Creek and the Watts River near Healesville are good places to watch for them at dusk.

Possums and gliders are the mammalian highlight of this area. You are likely to see at least a couple of **greater gliders** without much effort, but you'll need a spotlight to pick up their diagnostic bright-yellow eyeshine as they feed quietly high in the canopy – they do not call and are not particularly active. If you do hear calls and crashing around, it's likely to be a **mountain brushtail possum**. You can find these in the trees, in the shrubs and on the ground, but they are a bit more hit and miss – you might come across a hotspot and see a dozen, or not see one at all.

The overlapping branches of wattles provide runways for the endangered **Leadbeater's possum**, which are virtually confined to these forests because of their reliance on tree hollows near a dense wattle understorey. Keep your eyes open, as you might chance a sighting anywhere, but your best bet for seeing one is to 'stag watch': sit near a large eucalypt (living or dead) with conspicuous hollows just before dusk, so that the hollows are silhouetted against the sky; wait for an hour or so to see if any Leadbeater's, or other possums and gliders, emerge. Good places to spotlight for arboreal mammals are the Cumberland Rd near Cambarville and, closer to Healesville, Myers Creek Reserve. Warm, still summer nights are often the best for spotlighting.

There are also several species of owl in the park, including Australia's largest, the **powerful owl**. Seeing owls is largely a matter of luck and spending time in the bush, but hearing them call is almost as good, and much easier: powerfuls have a deep *whoo-hoo*; the **southern boobook's** repeated *boo-book* is readily heard throughout the forests; and the call of the rare **sooty owl** of wet, forested gullies – a haunting, falling-bomb scream – is an aural highlight of Australian birding. ■

Location 70km to the east of Melbourne.

Facilities Many walking tracks; Rainforest Gallery with observation platform and rainforest walkway at Cement Creek near Warbuton.

Accommodation Wide range in the towns of Healesville, Warburton and Marysville; no camping within the park.

Wildlife rhythms Winter is best for superb lyrebirds.

Contact Parks Victoria Information Line ☎ 131 963.

Ecotours Eco-Adventure Tours (☎ 03-5962 5115) conducts night-walks in the Yarra Ranges, a 'backpackers' tour' (including Healesville Sanctuary), and educational special-interest tours on environmental topics.

> **Watching tips**
> Mountain brushtail possums have shorter, more rounded ears, darker fur and are more thickset than the common brushtails you see around Melbourne. Lace monitors visit Badger Weir Park during summer (often seen between the toilet blocks). The constant (except during winter) nocturnal *waaaark pip-pip-pip-pip* in the forests is from the Victorian subspecies of the eastern smooth frog.

DANDENONG RANGES NATIONAL PARK

Lyrebirds, wallabies and rosellas

Wildlife highlights
Very accessible, spectacular mountain ash forest and conspicuous wildlife. Good birdwatching, with superb lyrebirds and plentiful parrots (especially crimson rosellas) and cockatoos. Swamp wallabies are readily encountered during the day.

Location 40km to the east of Melbourne.
Facilities Information boards at picnic grounds; wheelchair access track at Grants picnic ground.
Accommodation B&Bs throughout the Dandenongs; caravan park at Monbulk; no camping within the park.
Wildlife rhythms Autumn and winter for superb lyrebird displays; spring and summer for smaller bush birds.
Contact Fern Tree Gully NP information centre (☎ 03-9758 1342).
Ecotours Ranger-guided walks and spotlighting.

Watching tips
The call of the male eastern whipbird is an echoing whip crack, to which his mate instantly replies (most of the time) with a ringing *tiew tiew* – it can sound like only a single bird is calling. Keep an eye out for the bodies of male antechinuses after their mass die-off immediately after the early, summer mating season.

THERE are five sections to this park east of Melbourne, but it is in the wettest and most southerly – Sherbrooke Forest, where mountain ash eucalypts tower over a ferny understorey – that wildlife is most conspicuous. Nearly all inhabitants of the park can be seen along walks from Grants and Sherbrooke picnic grounds.

Superb lyrebirds are the main wildlife drawcard. Along the Neumann Track, and tracks around and downhill from Sherbrooke Falls, are good places to look for them – especially early and late in the day when it is quieter and the birds are more active. It is not uncommon for them to display alongside the tracks and they can sometimes be approached closely.

The red and the blue
At Grants picnic ground large numbers of **crimson rosellas** congregate to feed on handouts (it is best not to feed them); **sulphur-crested cockatoos** and **galahs** often show up in smaller numbers. Sherbrooke picnic ground is quieter than Grants and still has plenty of rosellas.

Other large birds include **laughing kookaburras**, which are common around picnic grounds and other open areas, and small but noisy flocks of **yellow-tailed black-cockatoos**. **Eastern yellow robins** can be confiding in picnic areas; other small bush birds include **white-browed scrubwrens**, **white-throated treecreepers** and the noisy but cryptic, green **bell miner** ('bell bird').

Swamp wallabies are widespread, but are most often heard as they thump away through the forest. But they also come out to graze – try early and late in the

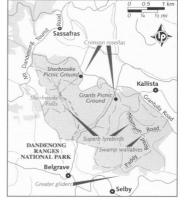

day in open, grassy areas along the Neumann Track. Some individuals are very wary, but others will tolerate a close approach.

After dusk, **common ringtail** and **brushtail possums** and **sugar gliders** are common enough; **greater gliders** less so and localised (Minak Reserve, at the edge of the park in Selby, is a good bet); and **yellow-bellied gliders** are present but rare and mobile. **Dusky** and **agile antechinuses** are also nocturnal; however, you might see them along the edge of tracks in the late afternoon. **Echidnas** are quite common and can be seen by day in the drier northern sections of the park. ∎

THE LAKES NATIONAL PARK

Birds and banksias

THE coastal bushland between Lakes Victoria and Reeve supports a large number of nectar-feeding animals, and the lakes themselves are breeding sites for many **waterbirds**. **Emus** and **eastern grey kangaroos** feed in camping grounds adjacent to the woodland at Emu Bight. **Australian magpies** fossick between picnic tables and flocks of **rainbow lorikeets** screech through. **Koalas** can be spotted in the nearby woodland; **echidnas**, **blotched blue-tongued lizards** and **lace monitors** can also be seen here and on sandy tracks. **Swamp wallabies** are easily seen on Rotamah Island (as are most species found in the Lakes).

Rope dancers

Dawn at Emu Bight brings wattlebirds – the largest of honeyeaters – to feed on the saw banksias surrounding the camping ground. **Little wattlebirds** lack the obvious scarlet wattles of the larger **red wattlebirds**. By night, **sugar gliders** (their scientific name means 'rope dancer') run quietly along branches and leap between the trees, landing with a soft thud – they are unusually easy to see at night with a torch, especially in peaceful, off-peak times of the year. **Common ringtail possums** and **eastern pygmy-possums** are also present; the latter are notoriously hard to find, but searching flowering banksias gives you a chance.

At Point Wilson **white-bellied sea-eagles** glide over the lake, tame **eastern grey kangaroos** graze the lawns and **common wombats** are sometimes seen at night. **Laughing kookaburras** are common around the picnic area and the heathy woodland supports the rare **New Holland mouse**. **Bottlenose dolphins** often swim near the jetty. On the spit beyond, waterbirds congregate – **Australian pelicans**, **black swans** and the endangered **little tern**. The little terns often also perch on the jetty: smallest of the terns, their black legs and bill turn yellow when breeding, whereas the bill and legs of the slightly larger and more common **fairy tern** are always orange. The hides at Lake Killarney and Cygnet Swamp Good also offer good views of **waterbirds**. ∎

Location 320km to the east of Melbourne.
Facilities Bird hides, lookout tower; Rotamah Island Bird Observatory (☎ 03-5156 6398).
Accommodation Rotamah Island Bird Observatory; camping; wide range in nearby towns.
Wildlife rhythms Spring and summer for waders; banksias flower autumn to winter.
Contact The Lakes NP visitor centre (☎ 03-5146 0278).
Ecotours Rotamah Island Bird Observatory (☎ 03-5156 6398). Early Bird Tours (☎ 03-9882 6935).

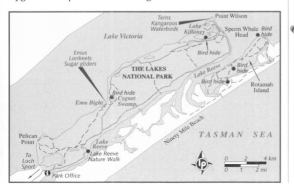

Map showing THE LAKES NATIONAL PARK, Lake Victoria, Lake Reeve, Rotamah Island, Point Wilson, Emu Bight, Cygnet Swamp, Bird hides, Pelican Point, Lake Reeve Nature Walk, Park Office, Ninety Mile Beach, TASMAN SEA, To Loch Sport. Scale 0–4 km / 0–2 mi.

OTHER SITES – VICTORIA

Barmah State Park

This river red gum forest along the Murray River is the largest of its kind, and Barmah's wetlands are important for breeding waterbirds. It is the best site in Victoria for superb parrots. Eastern grey kangaroos are common. Dharnya Centre offers environmental and Aboriginal cultural education.
250km north of Melbourne,
☎ 03-5869 3302

Big Desert Wilderness and Wyperfeld National Park

Wyperfeld is the best place to find malleefowl in Victoria; they can be seen in scrub near Eastern Lookout. Other birdlife is prolific, especially parrots and cockatoos including Major Mitchell's cockatoos and regent parrots. Brushtail possums and bats use hollows in river red gums along Outlet Creek; emus and western grey kangaroos congregate on black box flats. Big Desert, an expanse of mallee wilderness, lies 60km to the west of Wyperfeld – more superb mallee birding and the best area for reptiles in Victoria with over 50 species.
450km north-west of
Melbourne, ☎ 03-5395 7221

Brisbane Ranges National Park

The best site near Melbourne for dry-country birds – and the birdwatching is excellent. Koalas are very common: try the walk from Anakie Gorge to Stony Creek picnic ground. Swamp wallabies are common at the Stony Creek end of the walk – also a good area to spotlight for possums and gliders. Tawny frogmouths are often seen, and southern boobooks and owlet-nightjars are frequently heard. Rarer nocturnal fauna includes brush-tailed phascogales, white-throated nightjars and powerful owls – the latter often roost along Stony Creek.
80km west of Melbourne,
☎ 03-5284 1230

Chiltern Box-Ironbark National Park

One of the best stands of box-ironbark forest remaining in Victoria, this park is renowned among birdwatchers. In winter and spring honeyeaters and lorikeets – including the threatened regent honeyeater and swift parrot – flock to flowering ironbarks. It is of the best Victorian sites for turquoise parrots and painted button-quail. At dusk, eastern grey kangaroos graze around the park. It is a stronghold for the rare squirrel glider and brush-tailed phascogale. Sugar gliders and yellow-footed antechinuses are also common – try along Donkey Hill Road.
275km north-east of
Melbourne, ☎ 03-5726 1234

Errinundra National Park

Tall, wet mountain forests dominate this East Gippsland park. It

contains the largest patch of cool-temperate rainforest in Victoria; a number of frog species; birds typical of wet eucalypt forest, including powerful and sooty owls; mountain brushtail possums; and greater, sugar and yellow-bellied gliders. Waratahs flower spectacularly in December.
Approximately 465km east of Melbourne, ☎ 03-5161 1222

Kinglake National Park

An excellent place for superb lyrebirds, especially at Masons Falls and Jehosaphat Gully picnic areas. Eastern grey kangaroos graze open areas and swamp wallabies inhabit wet forest. Platypuses and water-rats are widespread in creeks;

koalas are often seen along the Cicada Circuit Track. Crimson rosellas, gang-gang cockatoos, laughing kookaburras and pied currawongs are common.
65km north of Melbourne,
☎ 03-5786 5351

Lerderderg and Werribee Gorge State Parks

Rugged gorges and rivers dissect the forested slopes of these two parks. Peregrine falcons nest on cliff ledges, wedge-tailed eagles are common and other wildlife includes echidnas, koalas, wallabies, kangaroos and platypuses.
65km west of Melbourne,
☎ 03-5367 2922

Lind National Park

Euchre Valley Nature Drive – a short detour off the Princes Highway – passes through tall, wet eucalypt forest, with warm-temperate rainforest lining the creek. Superb lyrebirds are common, and at night yellow-bellied gliders call in the forest canopy and leaf-green tree frogs call in the creeks.
430km west of Melbourne,
☎ 03-5158 6351

Little Desert National Park

Neither little nor a desert, the area includes mallee, heathland and woodland. Wildflowers bloom en masse in spring; and western grey kangaroos, emus, parrots and cockatoos are abundant. Visit Whimpey's Little Desert Lodge (☎ 03-5391 5232) to see malleefowl.
375km north-west of
Melbourne, ☎ 03-5391 1275

Lower Glenelg National Park

Eucalypt woodland supports many mammals including possums, gliders, koalas, echidnas, red-necked wallabies and both the western and eastern grey kangaroos. The limestone caves shelter bats. Yellow-tailed black-cockatoos feed in pine plantations in the area. On the Glenelg

River, keep an eye out for platy-puses, water-rats and waterbirds.
400km west of Melbourne,
☎ *03-8738 4051*

Mornington Peninsula National Park

This park encompasses the rocky coastline along Bass Strait, and Greens Bush, a tract of tall, open eucalypt forest. Cape Schanck is a well-known place from which to spot seabirds. Short-tailed shearwaters feed over Bass Strait between September and May. Dolphins and the rare Arctic jaeger are possibilities from the Sorrento-Queenscliff ferry. Australian fur-seals sometimes rest on rocky areas; there are many rock pools to explore; and cliff faces are home to peregrine falcons and nankeen kestrels.
95km south of Melbourne,
☎ *03-5987 3078*

Mt Buffalo National Park

Outside snow season, superb lyrebirds can be seen on the road to Mt Buffalo Chalet, where crimson rosellas are common. Wombats emerge at dusk around Dicksons Falls. Common ringtail possums can be spotlit at Lake Catani camping ground.

Tracks lead through snow gum, alpine ash and sphagnum bogs

where many birds, insects (including Bogong moths massed in rock crevices) and reptiles can be seen during summer.
320km north-east of Melbourne, ☎ *03-5755 1466*

Murray-Sunset National Park

A large semiarid area – one of the few in the world that remain relatively pristine – of mallee, spinifex, woodlands, saltbush and a system of wetlands fed by the Murray River. Both red and western grey kangaroos are common, as well as a variety of reptiles. Birds include Major Mitchell's cockatoos, emus and malleefowl. Waterbirds flock in thousands over floodplains. In late summer, the saline Pink Lakes take on the hue of their name from algal secretions.
480km north-west of Melbourne, ☎ *03-5092 1322*

Snowy River National Park

This park supports a diverse array of vegetation communities including tall, wet eucalypt forests

and pockets of both warm-temperate and cool-temperate rainforest. Severely endangered in Victoria, the brush-tailed rock-wallaby just hangs on in the park; it is also one of the last Victorian strongholds of the spotted-tailed quoll. Platypuses inhabit the Deddick River.
450km east of Melbourne,
Deddick – ☎ *03-6458 0290,*
Buchan – ☎ *03-5155 9264,*
Orbost – ☎ *03-5161 1222*

Terrick Terrick National Park

One of the largest grasslands left in Victoria, as well as box and native pine woodlands. Eastern

grey kangaroos are common; swamp wallabies, echidnas and common brushtail possums less so. Fat-tailed dunnarts are not difficult to find on the grasslands at night with a torch. The birding is good around large granite outcrops such as Mt Terrick, and the endangered plains-wanderer is the park's most famous denizen. Brolgas and bush stone-curlews are sometimes seen by the river close to nearby Mitiamo.
225km north-west of Melbourne, ☎ *03-5450 3951*

Tower Hill State Game Reserve

An extinct volcano great for waterbirds and raptors. Magpie

geese and Cape Barren geese have been reintroduced; you are almost guaranteed to see emus; and other common animals include koalas, echidnas and eastern grey kangaroos. Visit the excellent natural history centre.
270km west of Melbourne,
☎ *03-5565 9202*

Whipstick and Kamarooka State Parks

Wattles dominate the spring wildflower show of these parks – Old Toms Mine Circuit in Whipstick is spectacular. The whipstick and Kamarooka mallees are interspersed with box and ironbark forests. This association of two of the most bird-rich of habitats results in a birdwatcher's dream: huge numbers (it is said to have the greatest concentration of songbirds in Australia) and diversity of highly visible and vocal species. Echidnas, swamp wallabies and, especially, eastern grey kangaroos are common.
168km and 183 north-west of Melbourne, ☎ *03-5430 4444*

WESTERN AUSTRALIA

State faunal emblems

Black swan Jet-black waterbird with a scarlet beak and white flight quills. One of WA's most conspicuous birds, found in all freshwater habitats including inner-city wetlands.

Numbat A slender, amber-striped marsupial, endangered and confined to WA's south-west. Active only during daylight, it is sometimes seen foraging for termites around logs in open woodlands at Dryandra and Perup.

WESTERN Australia (WA) covers almost one-third of the continent and boasts a huge range of climates, landscapes, habitats and wildlife. The temperate south-west has one of the world's richest floras, including extensive heathlands that attract diverse birdlife during Australia's most spectacular wildflower season. Tall eucalypt forests and woodlands support WA's highest diversity of marsupials, many of which are endemic subspecies with distinct common names – you will probably hear about boodies, woylies and quenda rather than burrowing and brush-tailed bettongs and southern brown bandicoots. The state conservation authority, CALM (Conservation and Land Management), is reintroducing endangered mammals to many areas.

Reptiles, raptors and desert birds are prolific in the rangelands (the Outback) and central deserts that cover 85% of the state. Mammals, including rock-wallabies, shelter in gorges and ranges such as Cape Range; and kangaroos and dingoes roam spinifex grasslands. Occasional rains in the 'red heart' fill dry river courses, attract myriad animals and bring vegetation into brilliant bloom.

The greatest seasonal contrasts are experienced in the tropical wilderness known as the Kimberley. The annual wet season (October to May) creates extensive wetlands which recede during the Dry to leave lagoons crowded with reptiles and birds. Expansive tidal flats near Broome attract one of the world's great shorebird spectacles, supporting up to a million birds in summer.

WA's most famed wildlife experiences are its accessible marine encounters. The 12,500km coastline includes tropical Ningaloo Reef – Australia's second-largest system of coral gardens – which offers the chance to swim (safely) with the world's largest sharks. Monkey Mia on Shark Bay is famous for its bottlenose dolphins, and dugongs and sea turtles are also abundant. Islands and limestone reefs around Perth provide excellent diving; and there are tours to see dolphins, penguins and other seabirds, sea-lions and humpback whales just off Perth's beaches.

Some wildlife has peak viewing seasons: spring for humpback whales; winter for southern right whales; autumn for whale sharks; and summer for waders. Much of the north's wildlife avoids extremes of heat and floods by being most active between May and October. Don't be deterred by long distances: many remote parks offer sensational wildlife-watching – and with around 70 parks and 1100 reserves, there is plenty of choice. ∎

Highlights

- Wading into coral gardens and swimming with giant whale sharks and rays at Ningaloo Reef on the Coral Coast
- Sailing from Monkey Mia on a glass-calm day to find dugongs, turtles and bottlenose dolphins
- Flocks of thousands of shorebirds wheeling en masse above the tidal flats around Broome
- Spotlighting in the jarrah forests of the south-west for endangered marsupials
- Humpback whales erupting from the water beside your tour boat, or approaching to eyeball you
- The proliferation of wildflowers and feeding birds in coastal parks and the south-west forests after winter rains
- Searching crevices for hidden corellas and bats while dodging freshwater crocodiles in Windjana Gorge in the Kimberley

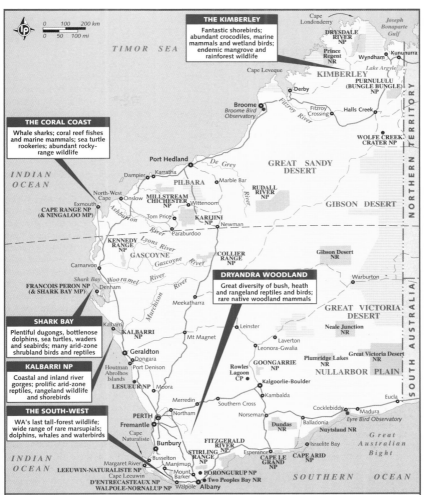

THE KIMBERLEY
Fantastic shorebirds; abundant crocodiles, marine mammals and wetland birds; endemic mangrove and rainforest wildlife

THE CORAL COAST
Whale sharks; coral reef fishes and marine mammals; sea turtle rookeries; abundant rocky-range wildlife

DRYANDRA WOODLAND
Great diversity of bush, heath and rangeland reptiles and birds; rare native woodland mammals

SHARK BAY
Plentiful dugongs, bottlenose dolphins, sea turtles, waders and seabirds; many arid-zone shrubland birds and reptiles

KALBARRI NP
Coastal and inland river gorges; prolific arid-zone reptiles, rangeland wildlife and shorebirds

THE SOUTH-WEST
WA's last tall-forest wildlife; wide range of rare marsupials; dolphins, whales and waterbirds

Suggested itineraries

One week (The Kimberley) Start at Broome or Kununurra and spend a week on the Gibb River Rd. Essentials include Roebuck Bay (1 day), Tunnel Creek and King Leopold Range NPs, and a cruise on Lake Argyle.

One week (South-west – start/finish Perth) A day on Rottnest Island then head down to Walpole-Nornalup NP (2 days), Stirling Range NP (2 days) and back via Dryandra Woodland.

Two weeks (North – start Kununurra/finish Perth) Follow the one-week Kimberley trip (with a detour to the Mitchell Plateau) to Roebuck Bay then spend a week taking in Shark Bay via Karijini NP en route to Perth.

Two weeks (South – start/finish Perth) Follow the one-week south-west itinerary, adding Porongurup NP or Two People's Bay NR, then spend the second week exploring Kalbarri NP and Shark Bay.

One month (start at Kununurra/finish Perth) A longer trip could take in most of the state's major sites at a comfortable pace, including the Gibb River Rd, Roebuck Bay, Karijini NP, Shark Bay and Kalbarri NP. After Rottnest Island you could extend the south-west loop by following the coast south to Leeuwin-Naturaliste NP; head east for places covered in the one-week trip; and take in Fitzgerald River NP as an eastern extension.

PERTH

On the rivers of the Dreamtime serpent

BACK in the Dreamtime, the giant *Waugal* – the Nyoongar people's Rainbow Serpent – carved Perth's Swan and Canning rivers out of the coastal plain. Today, **bottlenose dolphins** chase speedboats on the rivers, and **Australian pelicans** and **black swans** sail in the reflections of skyscrapers. Australia's 'sunniest city' sprawls around the estuaries; from the marsupial-filled bushlands of the Darling Range, down past inner-city wetlands teeming with birds, to the Indian Ocean – where **Australian magpies** begin carolling as the sun sets over the islands, and beachside bars and cafes have views of breaching **humpback whales**.

South of Perth, *Shoalwater Islands MP* protects a chain of limestone islands accessible by ferry, where **wedge-tailed shearwaters**, terns and many other seabirds rest and breed on the weathered cliffs. As night settles on *Penguin Island*, hundreds of **little penguins** toddle ashore to shelter in the vegetated sand dunes. Penguins rehabilitated after injury or illness are displayed at the Discovery Centre (☎ 08-9592 2636). The island is closed from June to October when the colony breeds. Male **Australian sea-lions** haul out on *Seal Island*, lounging on the sand between fishing trips. Underwater, a colourful diversity of tropical and temperate marine life includes schools of large bream, various pastel-coloured wrasse and **leafy sea-dragons** among fringing reefs, as well as stingrays 'flying' over shallow seagrass beds.

West of Perth, *Rottnest Island* is one of the last refuges for **quokkas** – small wallabies endemic to WA – which often hop right up to startled visitors around the island's salt lakes. Excellent birdwatching opportunities on Rottnest include olive-green **rock parrots** scavenging for seeds at Parakeet Bay; an isolated colony of **red-capped robins** in the woodlands; **ospreys** patrolling the southern coast; and a wide variety of **waders** on the lakes, swamps and secluded beaches.

Throughout spring, **humpback whales** migrate south past Perth's beaches, 'spy-hopping' – lifting their huge, gnarled

Waterbirds including ducks and cormorants, but especially black swans, glide past the skyline of downtown Perth on the Swan Estuary. Ospreys are commonly seen patrolling the reaches.

heads above water – to examine boat passengers. *Mills Charters* (☎ 08-9401 0833) runs one of the most informative whale-watching cruises. *Underwater World* (☎ 08-9447 7500) features underwater viewing of **fur-seals**, and a huge tunnel aquarium where sharks cruise among 200 other local marine species – fearless visitors may even dive with them.

The *Swan-Canning estuary* meanders through the city, with wetland habitats such as Point Walter and Alfred Cove supporting one of WA's widest ranges of **waterbirds** and **waders**. At low tide they raid the river flats – solitary, white **great egrets**, metallic-black **straw-necked ibis** and, in summer, waders in their hundreds. In deeper water, flocks of **little black cormorants** duck-dive and bob to the surface, tossing wriggling fish to swallow them headfirst. Perth's golf courses are also suburban wildlife havens – **western grey kangaroos** often take over the fairways at dusk.

Hills Forest in the Darling Range encompasses five national parks, with CALM's Activity Centre (☎ 08-9295 2244) running wildlife activities that include spotlighting for marsupials, bats, frogs, and **southern boobooks** and other owls in tall jarrah forest. **Shingle-backs** (or bobtail skinks) and other reptiles bask among granite outcrops on warm days. Bird activity peaks during wildflower season (late winter) when slow-flying, screaming flocks of **short-billed black-cockatoos**, restless bands of honeyeaters and other small birds descend to feed on cascades of flowers. After dark, **western grey kangaroos** and **western brush wallabies** graze open areas such as Fred Jacoby Park, and **quenda** frequent creek-side thickets. *Karakamia Sanctuary* (☎ 08-9572 3169, bookings essential) holds interpretive night-walks with chances to see **common brushtail** and **western ringtail possums** munching in the canopies, or rabbit-sized **woylies** digging for buried bulbs and fungi.

On the coastal plains 50km north of Perth, *Yanchep NP* (☎ 08-9561 1004) has pristine wetlands and banksia woodlands, where **oblong turtles** and scarlet-beaked **purple swamphens** rummage among the rushes; **Australian ringnecks** – brilliant green birds with red foreheads – and other parrots whistle loudly in the eucalypts; and **kangaroos, Australian wood ducks** and black-and-white **willie wagtails** harvest grasses and insects from lakeside lawns.

Perth Zoo (☎ 08-9474 3551) is great for familiarising yourself with local wildlife: it features a huge, walk-in wetland with thriving birds and turtles, an 'Australian bushwalk' including arid-zone fauna, and reptile and nocturnal houses displaying many endangered species. *Armadale Reptile & Wildlife Centre* (☎ 08-9399 6927) offers visitors well-supervised interactions with pythons, large lizards such as Gould's goannas and rehabilitated WA animals. *Parrots of Bellawood* park near Mandurah (☎ 08-9535 6732) runs educational tours and exhibits an excellent range of Australian parrots. ∎

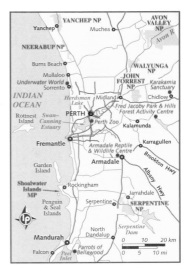

THE KIMBERLEY

Encounters in the tropical Outback

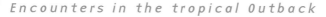

> ### Wildlife highlights
> The Kimberley is one of Australia's prime birdwatching destinations. It has 300 bird species – one-third of all Australian species of bird – including one-quarter of the world's wader species; tropical endemics such as the comb-crested jacana; most grass-finches; several parrots and cockatoos; WA's greatest diversity of birds of prey; and a multitude of highly sought-after species. Red kangaroos and agile wallabies are the most visible mammals in grasslands, with euros and short-eared and brush-tailed rock-wallabies on escarpments, and black flying-foxes in mangroves. The coast has humpback whales, dugongs and significant green turtle rookeries. Reptiles are also diverse, with freshwater and saltwater crocs conspicuous.

WESTERN Australia's far north is the Kimberley – a huge, isolated, largely semiarid region where most national parks are remote and infrequently visited. Kimberley wildlife contends with extreme contrasts of habitats and seasons: dense, coastal mangroves give way to plains and plateaus of tropical savanna and eucalypt woodlands with rainforested gorges; and a summer wet season of monsoonal storms and floods is followed by a winter dry season when entire rivers disappear and wildlife gathers around the remaining waterholes. **Red kangaroos** (in the southern Kimberley), **emus** and cattle are ever-present dangers to traffic on deserted roads.

Back from beyond

North-west WA is Australia's most important **shorebird** viewing site, best experienced from Broome Bird Observatory (☎ 08-9193 5600) on Roebuck Bay. In September, migratory waders return from their northern hemisphere breeding grounds to join resident shorebirds on the intertidal flats until up to a million inhabit the area. The spectacle is most impressive as the tide comes in, covering feeding grounds and sending colourful crowds of thousands streaming off the mudflats to roost on higher beaches. In April, huge migratory flocks depart daily, many in breeding plumage. The point beside the Observatory

Journey to the ends of the Earth

Every spring, nearly one million waders descend on Australia's north-west coast. They arrive exhausted and hungry, having just travelled up to 15,000km, flying continuously at 70kmph for 18 days. Many are barely more than chicks, born during June and July in high latitudes as far away as Arctic Canada and western Siberia. The young birds travel to Australia separately from their parents – those that survive their first trans-equatorial journey will have established a migratory path that they will continue to take for up to three decades. Their efforts are rewarded at Roebuck Bay (inset) – one of the very few intertidal sites in the world that offers shelter, a warm climate and abundant food. The visitors exploit the mudflats' smorgasbord of worms and crustaceans to recover quickly, building up energy reserves for their return journey north.

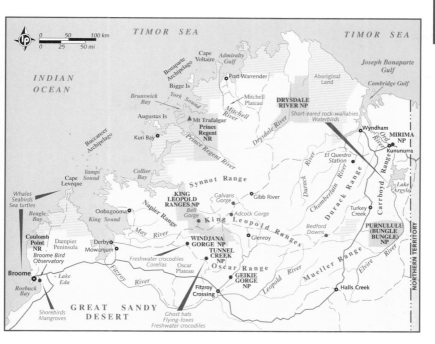

is an excellent place to start your wader-watching and you'll also see egrets and terns in abundance. Other exceptional shorebird sites outside Roebuck Bay include the mouths of the Fitzroy and Ord Rivers.

The mangroves along Roebuck Bay's Crab Creek bustle with mangrove specialists such as **mangrove golden whistlers** and **mangrove grey fantails**; and ring with the insistent *ki-ki* notes of **sacred kingfishers** and rarer **collared kingfishers** – both blue-green, but with buff and white underparts, respectively. The Observatory's birdbaths attract **peaceful doves**, finches, honeyeaters and **agile wallabies**.

Beasts of Broome

Broome's freshwater wetlands are excellent for birds. The 80 or so species at Lake Eda include **magpie geese** and Australia's smallest waterfowl – **green pygmy-geese**. In spring, look for irregular visitors such as **yellow** and **orange chats**. Barred Creek, 25km north of Broome, harbours **green turtles** (look around the creek's mouth), more mangroves and waders, and fork-tailed **lesser frigatebirds**, which skim fish from the waves or harass other seabirds until they disgorge before swooping to steal the ejected meal.

Within Broome, **agile wallabies** roam golf-course fairways; **ospreys** nest on every tall tower; and on moonless nights **yellow-bellied sheathtail-bats**, and others, chase moths around street lights. Kimberley Natural Eco Centre (run by

Location Broome – 2400km north of Perth; Kununurra – 700km north-east of Broome.
Facilities Walking tracks, cruises and/or hides at Geikie Gorge, Mirima, Lakes Kununurra and Argyle, and several other sites.
Accommodation Full range at Broome, Kununurra and other towns; camping at several parks including Windjana Gorge and Mirima.
Wildlife rhythms Early- to mid-October for birds. Reptiles and mammals active throughout the Dry. Can be inaccessible during the Wet.
Contact CALM: Broome district office (☎ 08-9191 1036); Kimberley regional office, Kununurra (☎ 08-9168 0200).
Ecotours Kimberley Birdwatching, Broome (☎ 08-9192 1246). Broome CALM runs spotlighting trips. R and B Kimberley Ecotours (☎ 08-9168 2083) tours the Kununurra wetlands. Lake Argyle Cruises (☎ 08-9168 7361).

Broome CALM ☎ 08-9191 1036) has wildlife displays, including a free-range bilby enclosure.

Whale-watching tours depart Broome and Cape Leveque during winter when **humpback whales** arrive to breed; other marine animals that may be sighted include **dugongs**, **green turtles**, **bottlenose** and **Indo-Pacific hump-backed dolphins**, and **saltwater crocodiles**. Salties are hazards near any saltwater, but also inhabit freshwaters inland, which they reach during floods.

Tunnel of ghosts

Much of the Kimberley is an ancient sea bed. Two fossil limestone reefs still weave across the inland plains, forming the Napier and Oscar Ranges. At Tunnel Creek NP you can walk for 750m through a water-worn tunnel beneath the Napier Range (take a torch). The tunnel is home to **freshwater crocodiles**, and among the stalactites and Aboriginal paintings roost several bat species, including pale **ghost bats**. Ghost bats are Australia's only predatory bats, and prey on small mammals, birds and other bats.

The Aboriginal word pindan *refers to both the orange soil at Roebuck Bay and a local wattle species.*

Similar encounters are available above ground at Geikie Gorge in the Oscar Range. Here freshies bask along river banks fringed with eucalypts and mangroves, where colonies of **black flying-foxes** – readily located by their pungent smell – hang high in the canopies like thousands of crumbled paper lanterns. Boat cruises up Geikie Gorge provide views of **darters**, **great bowerbirds** foraging on river banks, and **fairy martins** nesting in eroded, 30m-high rock walls. Tunnel Creek and Geikie Gorge are day-access-only parks; however, Windjana Gorge in the Napier Range offers camping. Here you can witness a daily exodus of clouds of bats that at dusk unfold a wingspan of up to 1m and head for their feeding grounds – **freshwater crocodiles** sometimes lunging from the water to grab them as they pass; and be awoken at dawn by hundreds of screeching **little corellas**. From April to October the Lennard River 'runs dry', allowing access through Windjana Gorge between walls rising 100m above the floodplains. **Common sheathtail-bats** and **little corellas** are visible in crevices at the gorge's entrance, and freshies are conspicuous in pools. In the nearby King Leopold Ranges, **northern snake-necked turtles** and paddle-tailed **Mertens' water monitors** often float among lilies in waterfall pools at Bell Gorge. Watch for sandy-coloured **northern nailtail wallabies** on the track out.

Up to 24 species of migratory wader – and many resident birds – feed and roost at Roebuck Bay.

Clash of the Titans

While in the north I camped at El Questro station on the Gibb River Rd – the original stock route across the Kimberley. El Questro is a working cattle station that offers accommodation to travellers, along with tourist activities including scenic helicopter tours. Akubra-hatted stockmen and jackaroos entertained us with local stories around the campfire. One recounted an incident from a recent helicopter flight along the Chamberlain River, where a 5m saltie was spotted lying in the shallows. Further up the bank a fully grown steer was approaching to drink, its eyes fixed on the crocodile, which remained motionless. As the pilot descended for a better look the chopper distracted the steer, which looked up – and the croc struck. Thrashing its tail for power it lunged forward, seized the 700kg steer and dragged it, kicking and bellowing, into the water. It is sobering to remember that at many places in the Top End, that steer could be you.

Bec Donaldson

Along the coast from Broome to Wyndham, pockets of monsoon forest and vine thickets survive; their wild grapes and berries attract rainforest birds, including **silver-crowned friarbirds** and pure-white **pied imperial-pigeons**. Inland patches of semirainforest include that at El Questro Gorge.

Shooting fish and dancing birds

East Kimberley's wetlands have stunning concentrations of birds. They are best seen at the Grotto and Marglu Billabong near Wyndham, and from cruises on Lakes Kununurra (just out of Kununurra town) and Argyle (Argyle has up to a million waterbirds) – specialised bird tours reveal 70 to 100 species. Flocks of **brolgas** dance on the banks and **archerfish** take aim below, shooting mouthfuls of water to knock insects from overhanging foliage. Other common sightings on cruises include **comb-crested jacanas**, and **short-eared rock-wallabies** emerging at dusk from crevices around Lake Argyle. On the lake's islands, **euros** feed on shore-strewn aquatic vegetation near lounging **freshwater crocodiles**.

One of the highlights of the Kimberley is the rare and stunning **Gouldian finch**. There's a good chance of seeing them in the Kununurra and Wyndham area, either fossicking for grass seeds in the woodlands or, especially, at waterholes and creeks, such as the Grotto, where they come to drink. An even easier hotspot is during the Dry around the pool at the Lake Argyle Tourist Village.

Mirima NP near Kununurra has the surreal 'beehive dome' geological formations typical of the Purnululu (Bungle Bungle) Ranges 200km further south, but its wildlife is more readily observed than that of its famous 'neighbour'. **Black kites** (slightly fork-tailed) and many other raptors wheel over Didbagirring Track; boab trees cling to the cliffs where **white-quilled rock-pigeons** and **rock-wallabies** have scattered seeds; and **dingoes** howl at night around Lily Pool. **Frilled lizards** and other reptiles may be discovered along Lily Creek – look for 'ta-ta lizards' (**Gilbert's lashtails**) waving 'goodbye'. ■

Watching tips

Sneaking through knee-deep mud towards waders on a Broome Bird Observatory tour is the most informative and entertaining way to experience wildlife at Roebuck Bay. Dawn visits to any freshwater wetlands are always rewarding – concentrations of birds and turtles increase towards the end of the Dry. Less rewarding, however, are the Kimberley's famous Purnululu (Bungle Bungle) Ranges: while spectacular in other ways, they are singularly lacking in visible wildlife.

THE CORAL COAST

Giant sharks and coral lagoons

Wildlife highlights

The whale sharks are the big attraction, but Ningaloo Reef's sea turtles, dolphins, dugongs, 220 species of coral and 500 of fish are equally stunning. Coupled with Cape Range's attractions – black-footed rock-wallabies, red kangaroos, euros and diverse birdlife – the region has an enormous amount to offer.

Location 1200km north of Perth.
Facilities Visitor centre (Milyering); observation hides at Mangrove Bay.
Accommodation Full range at Exmouth, Coral Bay; camping grounds within the park.
Wildlife rhythms Winter to early spring for humpback whales. Sea turtles nest October to February. Migratory waders from mid-spring until mid-autumn. Coral spawning and whale shark arrivals (contact CALM for predicted timings) in autumn.
Contact Ningaloo MP – CALM office for Exmouth district (☎ 08-9949 1676). Cape Range NP – visitor centre at Milyering (☎ 08-9949 2808).
Ecotours Ningaloo Deep (☎ 08-9949 1663) has whale shark and other marine tours; Coates Wildlife Tours (☎ 08-9455 6611) has turtle-tagging tours and wildlife bushwalks.

The arid Cape Range NP.

JUST offshore from a remote coast in WA's arid north-west, Ningaloo MP protects Australia's largest fringing coral reef (barrier reefs form further out to sea) – brilliant displays of coral and fish rivalled only by the Great Barrier Reef, yet so accessible you can fin to them from shore. Coastal wildlife is plentiful in mangrove and lagoon communities; sea turtles breed on the beaches; and on adjacent Cape Range Peninsula, desert animals thrive among 300m-high plateaus and rocky gorges.

Ningaloo Reef ribbons down the coast for 260km. At Coral Bay on calm days the seas are crystal-clear and you can swim out to the coral gardens. Over beds of **lavender coral** and forests of **blue staghorn** meander schools of iridescent reef fish, including **blue-barred parrotfish** and leaf-thin, **long-nosed butterflyfish** hovering (sometimes upside down) around each colony, nibbling polyps. Clusters of **sea anemones** shelter flame-coloured, white-striped **false clown anemonefish** among their stinging tentacles, and **blue-spotted fantail stingrays** flap over sandy areas. The corals at Paradise Beach, a half-hour walk south of Coral Bay, are possibly even more spectacular. Here **common reef octopuses** peer from crevices or jiggle puppetlike through the water; inquisitive **golden seasnakes** follow you; and vividly painted wrasse dance around larger fish. Many tropical fishes have flowing fins for camouflage or display; these include the boomerang-shaped **batfish**, juveniles of which often flutter on their sides.

Excellent dives around the Oyster Stacks reveal ancient domes of massive corals and petal-like **plate corals**, jewelled with sea urchins and **nudibranchs**. Turquoise Bay is known for its fish diversity; the best snorkelling here is just around the point at the southern end of the bay, where there are many large coral **bommies** and large numbers of fish – just snorkel out and let the current carry you north over the bommies.

The real 'Jaws'

Beyond the reef the continental shelf plunges. In late winter and spring **humpback whales** are often visible from headlands as they migrate south. From mid-March to June, **whale sharks** aggregate off the coast. These, the largest sharks – up to 12m long – move slowly at the surface filtering plankton and allow visitors to swim beside them. Boat cruises offer close encounters with whale sharks, **bottlenose** and pale **Indo-Pacific hump-backed dolphins**, occasional **dugongs** and predatory sharks – including one **tiger shark** so large that it was mistaken for a whale shark and divers leapt in beside it!

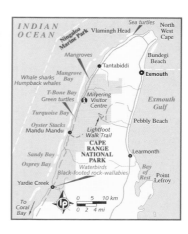

North-West Cape is a rookery for sea turtles, particularly **green** and **loggerhead turtles**, which come ashore to lay at night around high tide from October to February. You should see them by waiting at Turquoise Bay or Vlamingh Head and the beaches just south of it, such as Mauritius Beach. At Mangrove Lagoon, one hide overlooks **Australian pelicans** and **shorebirds** roosting at high tide beside mangrove-endemic **white-breasted whistlers** and **collared kingfishers**. A second hide overlooks a watering spot for **red kangaroos**, and **emus**, **galahs** and other birds – dawn and dusk are the best viewing times.

Off-road traction

At Cape Range NP mobs of **red kangaroos** roam the flats; watch for them at dusk on the park's roads. **Euros** and **black-footed rock-wallabies** inhabit steeper gorges such as Yardie Creek, along which there are walking tracks. Boat cruises along Yardie Creek reveal waterbirds, with cliff-face audiences of rock-wallabies. The rock-wallabies shelter in caves, emerging with the **yellow-bellied** and other **sheathtail-bats** at sunset. The creek's walking tracks may reveal **painted dragons** around rocky outcrops, and **wedge-tailed eagles** circling overhead. Shrubland birds around Mandu Mandu Gorge include 1m-high **Australian bustards**, **zebra finches** – often found huddled together preening – and **pied butcherbirds**, which have perhaps the most beautiful of Australian birdsongs, and mix mimicry of other bird calls with their own chime-like carolling. ■

Watching tips

Euros are often found at Osprey Bay (at dusk), and seeking shade around Milyering visitor centre. When visiting the sea turtle rookeries on North-West Cape's western tip, rely on natural light and keep still – bright lights and movement disturb the turtles' nesting.

The night the ocean turns pink

Every autumn, on only one or two nights just after a full moon, a phenomenon occurs on Ningaloo Reef which fills the ocean with a pink, slowly swirling mist. For the first hour after sunset, the entire reef – usually stirring with feeding coral polyps – is closed and still. Then, within moments, billions of polyps blossom open (inset), flooding the ocean with tiny pale 'birth bundles' of eggs and sperm. The mass spawning lasts several hours, the bundles rising in a colourful haze through the water. Fertilised eggs become coral larvae which drift on currents and settle in shallow seas. The synchronised release attracts swarms of zooplankton and bait fish to feed on the spawn. Soon afterwards whale sharks appear offshore, coinciding with huge aggregations of jellyfish and manta rays – all probably arriving to devour the smaller creatures feasting on the larvae.

SHARK BAY WORLD HERITAGE AREA

Devils and dolphins

> **Wildlife highlights**
> Shark Bay is famous for its tropical and temperate marine animals. It is one of the best places in Australia for bottlenose dolphins, dugongs, and green and endangered loggerhead turtles. The bay is a transition zone between south-west vegetation and arid shrublands, and provides habitats for a great diversity – 230 species – of south-western and 'Outback' birds, including thick-billed grasswrens, ospreys and many waders. The dozens of conspicuous reptiles include thorny devils.

Location 800km north of Perth. Many roads 4WD only (sealed road to Monkey Mia).

Facilities Walking tracks, bird hide, wheelchair with sand tyres (access to dolphins) at Monkey Mia; interpretation centre at Peron Homestead.

Accommodation Full range at Denham and Monkey Mia; basic camping at various beaches.

Wildlife rhythms April to October for terrestrial wildlife; sea turtles and dugongs from September; migratory wading birds throughout summer.

Contact CALM: Gascoyne district office, Denham (☎ 08-9948 1208); ranger centre at Monkey Mia (☎ 08-9948 1366).

Ecotours Shark Bay Under Sail (☎ 08-9948 1616, 0418 966 210); Monkey Mia Wildlife Sailing (☎ 08-9948 1482); Monkey Mia ranger centre (☎ 08-9948 1366) runs short, guided bird walks (except midsummer).

SHARK Bay's peninsulas and islands stretch into the Indian Ocean on the edge of the Gascoyne region – WA's 'Outback Coast' – and possess natural features so significant that the bay is listed as a World Heritage Area. Shorelines of ochre-red dunes, cliffs and inlets fringed with sweeping beaches meander for 1,500km beside a vast marine park of seagrass meadows and reefs, and provide exceptional opportunities to watch some of north-west Australia's most threatened and sought-after wildlife.

From dinosaurs to mermaids

Many reptiles sunbake along the road to Monkey Mia on sunny days. Most frequently seen are **thorny devils** – slow-moving, ant-eating lizards resembling miniature stegosaurs. Snakes, including **king brown snakes** – with thick, variously coloured bodies and flat heads – are also drawn to the warm roads. Bushwalks around Peron Homestead occasionally reveal large goannas, including yellow-dappled **Gould's goannas**.

On calm days, locals joke 'welcome to the Shark Bay Aquarium' – a sheet of turquoise glass hundreds of kilometres square. The most popular attraction is Monkey Mia beach, where wild **bottlenose dolphins** visit shore to grab a fast feed and interact with people. Rangers control the interactions, selecting people to handfeed the dolphins.

There is plenty more to see out on the bay. Beneath the transparent surface, **manta rays** flap slowly, shoals of fish twist in unison, vividly striped **olive-headed seasnakes** ripple to the surface, and **green** and **loggerhead turtles** – some the size of beach umbrellas – poke noses out to breathe. Sailing cruises guarantee dolphins, leap-feeding or resting in small groups while their calves socialise nearby (a more natural experience than the handouts at Monkey Mia). The namesakes of the bay are abundant, particularly **tiger sharks** – they usually avoid boats, but by taking a scenic flight on a still day you should see dozens of dark forms patrolling the waters. Shark Bay is inhabited by one-tenth of the world's remaining **dugongs** – one of the 'sea cows' once reputedly mistaken for mythological mermaids. There is always a chance of seeing dugongs on longer boat trips, but from September they return inshore to graze seagrass beds and are then almost a certainty; they are also often visible, especially on very calm days, from cliffs such as Eagle Bluff and Cape Peron.

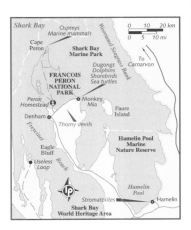

Mysterious voices

Francois Peron NP encompasses undulating, red sand plains carpeted with arid shrublands. There is abundant birdlife, including **blue-breasted fairy-wrens** skipping between bushes and **little button-quail** scurrying between spinifex clumps. The birding highlight is the threatened **thick-billed grasswren** – chestnut-brown streaked with white; it is common in the scrub along the road to Monkey Mia, but possibly the best place to see it is around Monkey Mia caravan park. On calm, sunny days the males perch in low shrubbery and pour out clear melodious songs, often accompanied by the 'ringing bells' of **chiming wedgebills** and the deceptive, ventriloquial *pan-pan-panella* of the chestnut-coloured **crested bellbird**.

Many of the park's birds have musical territorial calls, contributing to an outstanding dawn chorus. You can best experience this along the Monkey Mia road, particularly in spring when swathes of wattles and other flowering shrubs attract **singing honeyeaters** and other spiritedly voiced honeyeaters.

You should also have no trouble seeing **emus**; and **ospreys** are often seen from Cape Peron. Between October and April, migratory **waders** paddle in the intertidal flats and crowd Monkey Mia's sand bars, alongside **Australian pelicans** and masses of **pied cormorants** drying their outstretched wings. The park's mammals are less visible, but a twilight wait by the dam near Monkey Mia may reveal **euros** and, if you are lucky, endangered **woylies**. ∎

Recreating Eden

For decades, visitors to Shark Bay have seen more foxes and feral cats than small Australian mammals. These predators have hunted several native species to local extinction. 'Project Eden', a CALM initiative, entails trapping and baiting cats and foxes as part of the state-wide Western Shield campaign against introduced predators; and a barrier fence has been built at Peron to prevent another feral invasion. As feral numbers fall, rare and endangered wildlife is being returned to Peron: western barred bandicoots, banded hare-wallabies, and boodies – so rare that they survive only on a few small islands – are being bred in captivity to be released on the peninsula. Shark Bay may soon be as renowned for its unique opportunities to see marsupials as it is now for its marine mammals, but this will depend on keeping the numbers of feral predators in check.

Watching tips

Try Monkey Mia early in the morning for dolphins. Boat trips are best taken in very calm conditions, when good below-surface visibility offers outstanding wildlife-viewing. As an alternative to a boat tour, you could paddle out on a kayak for an up-close, personalised encounter. Nearby Hamelin Pool has some of the world's best examples of stromatolites – structures formed by some of the most ancient life forms.

THE SOUTH-WEST

Last strongholds for forest species

Wildlife highlights
The greatest drawcards of the Walpole district are species confined to the south-west, including red-capped parrots, western rosellas and red-eared firetails. Other attractions include stingrays, white-tailed black-cockatoos, western grey kangaroos and southern right whales in season. The Manjimup district is WA's best site for marsupials, including western ringtail possums, tammar wallabies and woylies.

WALPOLE-NORNALUP NP and the area around Manjimup hold some of the last of the forests that once dominated WA's southern corner. The nearest 'neighbouring' forests are 2000km east across the Nullarbor. Walpole has an extraordinary diversity of habitats: 90m-high tingle and karri wildernesses, bird-filled wetlands, quiet rivers and coastal heath, dunes and the rocky southern coast. Inland near Manjimup, the jarrah bushlands have an exceptional range of highly visible marsupials.

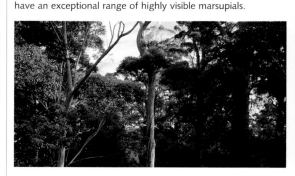

Valley of the giants

The colossal karri and tingle trees of Walpole-Nornalup, both unique to the south-west, form lichen-draped forests such as Valley of the Giants. On cool mornings the dawn chorus echoes through the valley as myriad songbirds redefine their territories; they are easily seen from the valley's road, and from the roads alongside Deep River. Birdlife becomes even more prolific in spring when deafening **purple-crowned lorikeets**, **New Holland honeyeaters** – black-and-white with gold-threaded wings – and other blossom feeders flock to the flowering canopies. The valley's elevated Tree Top Walk takes you high into the crowns of tingles to meet birds eye to eye. Below, on the Ancient Empire Trail, **common brushtail possums** are easily seen and there is a chance of seeing, or at least hearing, the rare **masked owl**; **barn** and **barking owls**, **southern boobooks** and **tawny frogmouths** are all far more frequently seen and heard.

Sweet addictions

After winter rains, the 'wildflower state' splashes into bloom almost overnight. WA has one of the richest floras known, with over 10,000 flowering species. In spring, nomadic lorikeets and other birds follow the flowers, arriving en masse to feast in any blossoming forest. Nectar specialists fill the heathlands – white-naped honeyeaters dip into crimson grevillea and dryandra blooms, and western spinebills probe kangaroo paws while balancing on their stems. Some animals alter their diet to exploit the nectar: seed-eating king-parrots banquet on golden banksia candles, and western ringtail possums mix their staple diet of leaves with a selection of blossoms. After dark, western pygmy-possums and honey possums feed in the heathlands, dwarfed by the flower clusters to which they cling.

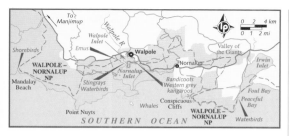

Location Walpole – 430km south of Perth; Manjimup – 300km south of Perth.
Facilities Walpole – Tree Top Walk (wheelchair access); Manjimup – Perup Ecology Centre (bookings essential).
Accommodation Walpole – full range (except backpackers) at Walpole and Peaceful Bay; Manjimup – full range.
Wildlife rhythms April to November for mammals; spring for whales, wildflowers and birds.
Contact Walpole – CALM district office (☎ 08-9840 1027); Manjimup – CALM regional office (☎ 08-9771 7988).
Ecotours Walpole – Coate's Wildlife Tours (☎ 08-9455 6611); WOW Wilderness Cruises, Nornalup Inlet (☎ 08-9840 1036). Manjimup – Pemberton Hiking Company (☎ 08-9776 1559); Design A Tour (☎ 08-9841 7778, Albany). For activities at Perup Ecology Centre, contact Manjimup CALM.

Place of the tiger snakes

Towards the ocean, karri/tingle forest is replaced by a mosaic of coastal vegetation. To the Minang people, Nornalup means 'place of the **tiger snakes**', which sunbake on the Bibbulmun Track; however, you are more likely to encounter **western grey kangaroos**, **emus** and **quokkas**. **Quenda** are sometimes seen at dusk on Coalmine Beach Heritage Trail (on the north-east shores of Nornalup Inlet). The Knoll track around the inlets brims with birds, including crimson-and-green **western rosellas**, and both red- and **'white-tailed' black-cockatoos**.(there are two species of the latter: short-billed and long-billed) **Black swans, Australian pelicans**, egrets and other waterbirds are easily seen on Peaceful Bay, while **Caspian terns** and shorebirds assemble on Mandalay Beach. At Coalmine Beach, **white-bellied sea-eagles** and **ospreys** (smaller, with brown tails) spiral in thermals or wing back to fledglings on nearby cliffs, fish twisting in their talons.

Nuyts Wilderness (south-west of the inlets) offers remote walking tracks into wooded gorges, and forest and heathland birds, including **red-eared firetails** – one of Australia's rarest finches. **Stingrays** (including an old, tail-less individual known as 'Stumpy') scavenge around the Rest Point jetty. In spring, **southern right whales** and **humpback whales** are often seen from Conspicuous Cliffs, and **bottlenose dolphins** can be seen year-round.

Marsupials in the spotlight

The drier jarrah forests around Manjimup (105km north-west of Walpole) are a marsupial mecca. A spotlighting pilgrimage to Perup NR provides an excellent chance of glimpsing some of WA's rarest marsupials. Watch for **woylies** around the veranda of the Perup Ecology Centre, and listen for **quenda** ferreting through leaf litter beside the Bandicoot Scoot wetland track. **Numbats** sometimes scamper around termite-riddled logs along the Numbat Path on sunny days. When spotlighting along Ringtail Trail, scan branches for red-eyed families of **western ringtail possums**; look for reddish-flanked **tammar wallabies** in melaleuca thickets; and **common brushtail possums** hissing and coughing loudly over territorial disputes.

Arguably Perup's most sought-after prize is the cat-sized **chuditch** (western quoll), WA's largest marsupial predator. They are seldom seen, but one trick is to pan your torch over the ground – their eyes glow a distinctive bright gold. Perup also offers good birdwatching, as do the nearby Lake Unicup Wetlands. ∎

Giant karri trees are a feature of Walpole-Nornalup NP.

👀 Watching tips
The summit of nearby Mt Frankland, in Mt Frankland NP, offers superb birdwatching. Kingston Forest around Manjimup is a good alternative to Perup for marsupials, and the dam at Karri Valley Lodge is great for birds.

DRYANDRA WOODLAND

Best chance for WA's most wanted

Location 160km south-east of Perth.
Facilities Good walking tracks, some suitable for wheelchairs.
Accommodation Huts at Dryandra Village; camping ground at nearby Congelin.
Wildlife rhythms July to October for breeding birds; numbat young active from September to November.
Contact CALM Narrogin district office (☎ 08-9881 1113).
Ecotours CALM Narrogin seasonally run spotlighting and other wildlife activities.

DRYANDRA'S open woodlands offer the best chance to observe some of WA's rarest and most endangered marsupials. These few remaining pockets of native forest and heath have become ecological islands within the extensive wheat-farming areas.

Exploring Dryandra after dark is easy. Around Dryandra Village you can't miss the **woylies**, and **western grey kangaroos** are common in paddocks at twilight. Several walking tracks lead through jarrah and wandoo woodland where common animals include black-gloved **western brush wallabies** in the understorey, and **common brushtail possums** and **tawny frogmouths** in the trees. Endangered russet-and-grey **tammar wallabies** are less common, more wary and keep near thicker vegetation. Kawana Rd Walk is one of the best on which to see kangaroos and brush wallabies.

Endangered emblems

Dryandra is one of the last sanctuaries for **numbats** (one of WA's faunal emblems). They are best glimpsed in open, sunlit woodlands among fallen logs – try mid-morning on sunny days when termites are active; and if you are staying at the Village, ask the caretaker for the latest sighting locations. Check also for **echidna** diggings around logs. Rare **red-tailed phascogales** are also present at Dryandra; you are not likely to see one, even with a lot of effort, but spotlighting in areas with rock she-oak thickets – one of the best stands is on Lol Gray Trail – offers the best chance (this is also a favoured habitat of the tammar wallaby). If you're keen on lo-

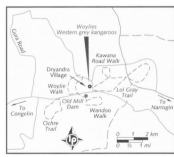

cating elusive mammals, you could also try the heathland near Lol Gray Trail for **honey possums** and **western pygmy-possums**.

The best areas for birdwatching – parrots and honeyeaters are abundant – are the woodlands along the Wandoo Walk and around Old Mill Dam, and the heathland near Lol Gray Trail. Along the Ochre Trail you can see abandoned **malleefowl** mounds; the birds themselves are occasionally sighted in deeper groves off Gura Rd.

Reptiles are a common feature at Dryandra. On warm sunny days you'll almost certainly see numerous **shingle-backs** and probably **goannas**. There is a reasonable chance of finding the WA subspecies of **carpet python** – one lives in and around the Village huts. ∎

KALBARRI NATIONAL PARK

Soaring cliffs and burning gorges

ALONG the Murchison River spectacular gorges and blazing wildflowers provide a dramatic showcase for desert wildlife. At first light in the Loop and other gorges, **red-tailed black-cockatoos**, brilliant-green **mulga parrots** and other chorusing birds approach the river to drink. They are best observed from lookouts such as Nature's Window, or by scrambling to the chasm floor for a closer experience. **Euros** and both **red** and **western grey kangaroos** may arrive, filtering their water by digging depressions beside the river and lapping (euros are also often seen at twilight on Mushroom Rock walking track). Sunrise over the canyons reveals bands of rose-coloured rock where slim-winged **fairy martins** and their flask-shaped mud nests are conspicuous. **Nankeen kestrels** soar along the labyrinthine waterways – Hawk's Head offers secluded vantage points and is a good site for **peregrine falcons**.

As the day heats up, the gorges become ovens and most animals take shelter. When leaving the gorges, drive slowly: **thorny devils** shimmer out of heat mirages on the roads, and in summer kangaroos recline under roadside shrubbery. **Emus** are likely to be seen, especially early in the morning, on Emu Flats (unsignposted sand plains 10km into the park). **Malleefowl** are sometimes seen in the mallee scrub around Meanarra Hill.

Rooms with a view

Where the Murchison River nears the ocean, **black swans**, **Australian pelicans** and other waterbirds can be seen. Waders, gulls and terns congregate on Oyster Reef at the river's mouth, and on adjacent Chinamans Beach. The woodland areas around the river mouth are more accessible than those further up the river, and make a good spot for searching for bush birds. Colonies of seabirds make high-rise homes in Red Bluff and adjacent headlands, where panoramic views take in **bottlenose dolphins**

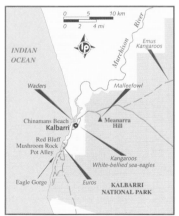

surfing, and, in spring, **humpback whales** migrating south. In Kalbarri town, **white-bellied sea-eagles** nest on radio towers, **western grey kangaroos** abound on the golf course at dusk, and Rainbow Jungle's (☎ 08-9937 1248) huge walk-through aviary highlights parrots and other arid-zone birds. ∎

Wildlife highlights

A relatively easy area in which to experience arid-country wildlife. There are abundant euros and western grey kangaroos; 70 species of reptile, including plenty of thorny devils; and a good variety of birds including sea-eagles, red-tailed black-cockatoos and a multitude of honeyeaters and wrens.

Location 590km north of Perth.
Facilities Walking track, interpretive signs; Kalbarri tourist centre.
Accommodation Full range at Kalbarri; no camping in park.
Wildlife rhythms June to November animals become active. Wildlife gathers around pools in autumn, attracting predatory birds. Reptiles visible throughout winter. Birdwatching is best in the spring wildflower season.
Contact Kalbarri NP (☎ 08-9937 1140).
Ecotours Coate's Wildlife Tours (☎ 08-9455 6611). Kalbarri Coach Tours (☎ 08-9937 1555) runs overnight canoe trips through the gorges.

Watching tips

Visit gorges at dawn to optimise wildlife sightings and avoid tourist buses. White-winged fairy-wrens can usually be seen at the caravan park at Red Bluff.

OTHER SITES – WESTERN AUSTRALIA

Cape Arid National Park

Coastal walking tracks regularly reveal fur-seals, southern right whales (in winter), Cape Barren geese and many other birds. However, birdlife is most prolific on the inland bushwalks such as Boolenup Walk through woodland, swamp and heath to Lake Boolenup. Watch for skinks, other reptiles, quenda and western brush wallabies.
120km east of Esperance,
☎ *08-9075 0055*

Cape Le Grand National Park

Granite peaks, undulating heaths and sand plains beside sandy bays provide good opportunities to observe quendas, and many bush and waterbirds around banksia-fringed wetlands. Rock parrots, Cape Barren geese, seabirds and abundant shorebirds inhabit the coast, and cruises from Esperance to nearby islands provide sightings of fur-seals and southern right whales.
40km east of Esperance,
☎ *08-9075 9022*

Eyre Bird Observatory

About 230 different bird species inhabit the Nuytsland Nature Reserve's mallee woodlands and sand dunes on the Great Australian Bight, including plentiful Major Mitchell's cockatoos, brush bronzewings and blue-breasted fairy-wrens, occasionally glimpsed malleefowl, and thousands of migratory waders. Nullarbor travellers may call the observatory to be collected from Cocklebiddy.
50km south-east of Cocklebiddy, ☎ *08-9039 3450*

Fitzgerald River National Park

An internationally recognised Biosphere Reserve, rich in flora and birdlife with sightings of humpback and southern right whales in spring and winter respectively (southern rights calve in protected waters at Point Ann). New Zealand fur-seals, Australian sea-lions, dolphins and many seabirds are present year-round, with ospreys nesting at Quoin Head camping ground. Malleefowl are observed regularly along Fitzgerald River where it crosses the South Coast Hwy; quenda are sometimes seen around wetland vegetation; western grey kangaroos graze the Quaalup Homestead lawns; and mountain bushwalks are good for raptors and reptiles.
200km north-east of Albany,
☎ *08-9835 5043*

Houtman Abrolhos Islands

An archipelago of coral islands off Geraldton's coast, largely uninhabited except by wildlife that includes nearly 100 bird species, many reptiles, and an excellent range of reef species. Birdwatching and dive tours are available.
60km west of Geraldton,
☎ *08-9921 5955*

Karijini National Park

Inland Pilbara park with steep red gorges, waterfalls and 'sunken gardens' – deep pools decorated with ferns, waterlilies and palms – which are some of WA's most renowned scenic attractions. The park encompasses the Hamersley Range, where dragon

lizards, euros and wedge-tailed eagles abound on rocky slopes, and goannas, mobs of red kangaroos and howling dingo packs rove the flats. Look on hillsides (rangers can give you directions) for the mounds of pebbles constructed by rare ngadji (western pebble-mound mice) above their underground nesting chambers. Four gorges converge at Oxers Lookout – birds plentiful here and at other waterholes include spinifex pigeons, bush birds and sought-after, pastel-coloured Bourke's parrots.
285km south of Port Hedland, unsealed roads impassable after heavy rains, ☎ *08-9189 8157*

Leeuwin-Naturaliste National Park

The green coastal hills, beaches and cliffs between Cape Naturaliste and Cape Leeuwin are the south-west's best sea-watching sites. Humpback whales (spring) bottlenose dolphins and myriad seabirds can be seen from either

of the capes, particularly from Cape Leeuwin's lighthouse. Near Cape Naturaliste, Sugarloaf Rock lookout is the only Australian mainland site where red-tailed tropicbirds are observed reliably (try after midday, September to May). Seabirds, including Cape petrels, shelter in Bunker Bay during strong westerlies, and the coast offers excellent dives for underwater wildlife, including off Busselton's 1.8km-long wooden jetty. Boat tours such as Naturaliste Charters (☎ 08-9755 2276) may provide close encounters with whales, seabirds, Australian sea-lions or New Zealand fur-seals. The Vasse-Wonnerup wetlands support many thousands of waterbirds including breeding ibis. Western ringtail possums build dreys (stick nests) in peppermint woodlands, and many birds, possums and quendas are

visible around Boronup Forest's camping grounds.
280km south of Perth,
☎ *08-9752 1677*

Lesueur National Park

An exceptionally diverse sand-plain flora of coastal heaths, shrublands and mallee woodlands supports a large diversity of reptiles and birds. Migratory waders and bush birds gather around salt lakes and freshwater springs, and honeyeaters and

parrots feed on profuse blossoms. Several small islands just offshore are breeding refuges for Australian sea-lions and seabirds, which prey on tropical and temperate fishes around the limestone reef (sea-lion cruises run outside the breeding season, which varies from year to year). Old trees provide some of the last nesting sites for endangered short-billed black-cockatoos.
200km north of Perth,
☎ *08-9651 1424*

Millstream-Chichester National Park

The Chichester Range stretches through the arid Pilbara beside the Fortescue River, the tree-lined watercourses of which include Millstream 'oasis' – a chain of springs and pools laced with lilies, paperbarks and palm groves. At the main camping ground every evening, rainbow bee-eaters chase insects over the river, replaced after dark by hundreds of flickering bats. Reptiles and mammals shelter during hotter periods; however, on milder days many reptiles are visible, including Stimson's pythons and goannas – often scavenging beside roads. Near the visitor centre, Chinderwarriner

Pool attracts flocks of budgerigars and cockatiels. Hand-raised kangaroos and euros may solicit food.

160km south-west of Port Hedland, ☎ *08-9184 5144*

Porongurup National Park

The Porongurups have different vegetation and habitats from the nearby Stirling Range. Its moss-cloaked granite spires are surrounded by heaths, fern gullies, marri–jarrah forest and one of the last remaining pockets of luxuriant karri. The most commonly seen reptiles and mammals of the Stirling Range are also seen here. Karri forest is good for bush birds – easily observed around picnic grounds – and when the heathlands are flowering, they brim with honeyeaters.
45km north-east of Albany,
☎ *08-9853 1095*

Rowles Lagoon Conservation Park

After rain Rowles Lagoon and adjacent lakes transform into one of the state's best bird spectacles, with nomadic waterfowl and bush birds arriving to join the residents. Contact Kalgoorlie CALM about birdwatching.
80km north-west of Kalgoorlie,
☎ *08-9021 2677*

Stirling Range National Park

The south-west's highest mountain range includes rocky peaks, heath-covered slopes, deep gullies, wetlands and woodlands. There are 170 bird species. Toolbrunup Peak's walking track usually reveals several wet-gully birds including red-eared firetails. Peregrine falcons are a chance among commoner raptors on higher peaks; shingle-backs and

dragon lizards often bask along tracks on warm days. Moingup Springs camping ground is good for woodland birds, particularly among the abundant spring wildflowers. The Stirling Range caravan park has mud maps of bird-rich walks. Western grey kangaroos graze open areas at dusk; western brush wallabies and tawny frogmouths live in denser woodlands.
85km north-east of Albany,
☎ *08-9827 9230*

Two People's Bay Nature Reserve

These coastal heathlands and swamp area protect the noisy scrub-bird and the Gilbert's potoroo, both recently rediscovered here long after their

presumed extinction. Western grey kangaroos are seen on tracks around Little Beach and quokkas inhabit denser vegetation around swamps. Rich and conspicuous birdlife includes waders, seabirds, resident bush birds, and nomads including lorikeets that arrive when the bush is blossoming. Visitors may spot endangered noisy scrub-birds, western whipbirds and western bristlebirds; the latter sometimes run across the road from Little Beach car park just after dawn, with the other two species are often heard (and occasionally glimpsed) nearby. Other hotspots around Albany include Kalgan River mudflats (waders) and the Gap (seabirds, Australian sea-lions). Winter whale-watching charters offer opportunities to see southern right whales and bottlenose dolphins.
20km east of Albany,
☎ *08-9846 4276*

WILDLIFE GALLERY

*Recognising, understanding and
finding Australia's key wildlife*

AUSTRALIAN MAMMALS

EVER since the first captive kangaroo caused a sensation in late-18th-century London, Australia has been renowned as a treasure-trove of 'bizarre' mammals. But long before the continent was traversed by explorers its animals were part of the myth of *Terra Australis* – the fabled Great Southern Land. And they have always been part of Aboriginal peoples' Dreamtimes.

Some mammals, such as the many species of native bat and rodent, and a wealth of marine mammals, are familiar to visitors from overseas. Thus it is the unusual 'old mammals' – marsupials and monotremes – that steal the limelight. Eons ago when mammals began evolving from reptiles, the marsupials and monotremes evolved along separate ancestral lines from the rest of the world's mammals (eutherians, also known as placentals). When Australia separated from the rest of Gondwana and began drifting north, marsupials and monotremes were the continent's only mammals. Only when Australia neared South-East Asia did some eutherians – rodents, bats, humans and the dingo – reach the new shores. Eutherians and the old mammals share defining mammalian features – they have hair and nurse infants on milk – but they also have striking differences. Marsupials are born at an embryonic stage and partly formed newborns must crawl up their mother's belly to attach to teats, often inside a pouch. Monotremes are even more extraordinary – they lay eggs, an inheritance from their reptilian past.

Although marsupials also inhabit the Americas and there is one species of monotreme in New Guinea, only in Australia can all three subclasses of mammal be readily seen. And the staggering diversity of shape, size and colour of Australia's marsupials are just a few reasons why it's an exceptional wildlife destination.

Well-kept secrets

On their giant island, early mammals radiated into the variety of forms they show today. A hidden wonder of Australia is that so few of its native mammals are well known to the outside world. Visitors wanting the popular icons (kangaroos, koalas, Tasmanian devil) are bombarded with surprise bonuses. Echidnas and platypuses are pinnacles of the unusual, but there are many intriguing species, each novelly adapted to exploit a niche in the vast range of often-harsh environments.

Specialised feeders, including leaf-munching tree-kangaroos, nectar-lapping gliders and truffle-eating bettongs, inhabit wooded areas and grasslands. Marsupial carnivores – from quolls to the world's tiniest marsupials, spectacularly aggressive planigales – sometimes survive even deep in the heart of the Red Centre. And many of Australia's mammals are so well adapted to a dry climate that they never need to drink. Yet much remains unknown about the biology and behaviour of Australian mammals – keep your eyes open, and you might just see something that you won't find in a book. ■

PLATYPUS

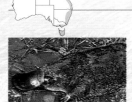

Recognition Dark fur, and a somewhat otter-shaped body (40–60cm long) with large leathery bill, large paddle-shaped tail and short limbs with webbed feet.

Habitat Freshwater streams in a variety of highland and low-altitude habitats, preferring still or slowly flowing water.

Behaviour Solitary, sheltering during the day in a burrow. Most active (and most clearly seen) around dusk and dawn, floating near the water's edge. Prey is stored in cheek pouches and chewed while floating on the surface.

Breeding 1–3 eggs laid a fortnight after mating (usually August–October) are incubated 10–12 days.

Feeding A wide range of freshwater invertebrates, such as yabbies, insects and snails, plus occasionally small amphibians and fish.

Voice Usually silent, although a soft growling may be uttered when disturbed.

Hotspots
Carnarvon NP, Cradle Mountain–Lake St Clair NP, Eungella NP

Baby bunyips

Australian folklore tells of bunyips – billabong-haunting monsters dressed in a bizarre combination of fur, webbed feet and bills. The origins of such descriptions become clear after meeting your first platypus – it resembles a miniature version of the fabled bunyip. Convinced the platypus was a hoax, scientists examined the first stuffed specimens for evidence that they were stitched together from parts of other animals. Platypus habitat also fits the bunyip legend; the first sign of its presence is usually a glinting bow wave on the surface of a pool or quiet river at twilight, as it swims with a distinctive smooth motion and low profile (if it's dog paddling and has pointed ears, you're watching a water-rat).

A subtle touch

Platypuses usually forage from dusk to dawn, submerging with characteristic rolling dives for half a minute before surfacing for a 10-second break, during which they may groom their waterproof underfur. Occasionally they are seen scurrying near their burrow – look for a horizontally oval entrance among vegetation just above the water. Underwater, the webbed forefeet become powerful oars, while hind webs act as steering and brakes. During diving the eyes, ears and nose are all tightly closed and platypuses rely on unique secret weapons to locate prey: a rubbery, ultrasensitive bill used to nose through sediments to find small prey by touch and by detecting the faint electric currents that radiate from living organisms. Males also have a pair of poison spurs capable of injecting painful venom, but this is used against rivals, not prey.

Platypus females have an even more extraordinary feature – they lay eggs, which they incubate between their belly and curled tail in a chamber at the end of a nursery burrow up to 20m long. Females lack teats and infants suck milk directly from ducts on their mother's abdomen. Young first emerge from their burrows at six weeks, and the natural water-babies soon begin paddling in the shallows. ■

SHORT-BEAKED ECHIDNA

Led by the nose

One Dreamtime story about how the echidna got its spines tells of a Nyoongar man who took too many wives: as payback, his tribe stuck all their spears into him and he became the first echidna. In reality, the opposite occurs – during breeding season, a single female may be seen trundling along with many males, seduced by her perfume of pheromones, trailing behind in devoted single file. During mating the female lies flat while several males shamble in a circle around her, digging a surrounding trench. Spectators may then witness a shoving contest – the males bulldoze each other out of the trench until the only one remaining earns a single mating session.

Recognition Football-sized, tailless pincushion with long, tubular 'beak', stumpy legs and powerful claws. Dark to light brown with stout, cream-coloured spines.

Habitat Widespread from alpine slopes to arid plains, wherever termites and ants are abundant.

Behaviour Solitary. Forages day or night depending on temperature (around 18°C is optimal). Shelters during extreme temperatures in logs or other animals' burrows, but digs own nursery burrow. Juveniles first become visible and range widely in spring.

Puggles and pink milk

Along with platypuses, echidnas are the world's last surviving monotremes – an early branch of mammals which retain their reptilian ancestors' ability to lay eggs. Monotremes also lack teats, instead oozing milk from abdominal pores. Echidna mothers-to-be probably curl up while laying their small, parchmentlike egg so that it rolls directly into their pouch. Ten days later a hatchling emerges, bald, semitransparent and without hindlimbs. Its early milk is iron-rich and the colour of strawberry milkshake. Once the 'puggles' get too prickly for the pouch their mother leaves them in a burrow while she forages.

Echidnas are often seen during daylight in cooler climates; look for their diggings around termite mounds – they are easy to watch, usually nosing about (their snout, like a platypus' bill, contains electroreceptors), or ploughing open mounds and logs with their huge claws. The scientific name *Tachyglossus* means 'fast tongue' and describes the 17cm-long, sticky, wriggling organ echidnas use to lap up prey. A spooked echidna won't try to run; instead, all four limbs start digging furiously until it submerges like a submarine. If exposed, it rolls into a bristling ball. ∎

Breeding One egg laid 2 weeks after June–September courtship and mating. Fast-growing 'puggle' weaned after about 6–7 months.

Feeding Breaks open termite and ant nests to reach the occupants, preferring the more nutritious termites (ants tend to bite).

Voice Usually silent; may sometimes softly coo or mew; females may vocalise while grooming themselves or young.

Hotspots
Warrumbungle NP, Bruny Island, Kangaroo Island

CARNIVOROUS MARSUPIALS

*The **mulgara** of sandy deserts hunts at night for insects, spiders, lizards and small mammals.*

***Kowaris** inhabit remote stony deserts, sheltering by day in burrows and hunting at night.*

The kultarr club

After dark the bush becomes a hunting ground for a fabulous mixed bag of predatory marsupials, ranging in size from the large Tasmanian devil down to the ferocious long-tailed planigale – which at scarcely 6cm long is probably the world's smallest carnivorous mammal. A diversity of sizes and niches ensures that collectively the marsupial carnivores target almost anything that moves, up to about the size of a wallaby. Being one of the family does not exclude smaller carnivores from being on their larger relatives' hit lists – devils readily steal undefended baby quolls. After the devil, the largest predators are the four species of quoll (formerly known as 'native cats'), which range from cat- to small dog-sized. Quolls prefer wooded habitats, where white spots on their all-dark coats camouflage them perfectly in dappled moonlight (although their bright eyeshine gives them away when spotlit). Quolls are among the most vividly patterned carnivorous marsupials, but more unusual are the desert-dwelling kultarr, which has uniquely long hind legs; and the numbat, because of its highly specialised diet.

All carnivorous marsupials are solitary hunters, typically stalking or chasing prey before pouncing and killing with rapid bites. The choice of victims depends partly on the attacker's size, but the most impressive attacks are made by dunnarts, antechinuses, planigales and other miniature species. These tiny hunters usually prey on insects. Although they are smaller than a mouse, several species will readily tackle one – hugging it tightly and savaging it to death. Yellow-footed antechinuses are seen in suburban gardens, where they often leave the remains of small birds and mammals turned inside out – a common feeding technique among small predatory marsupials.

Bushy-tailed vampires

By reputation, the family's blackest sheep is the brush-tailed phascogale, sometimes labelled a bloodthirsty 'vampire' that 'massacres chooks'. In reality, phascogales are mainly insectivorous and rarely dine on larger prey. Both brush-tailed and red-tailed phascogales resemble squirrels and are the only carnivorous marsupials that are truly arboreal, although quolls and antechinuses also climb ably.

Often unconcerned by spectators, they are entertaining to watch as they dash after insects along trunks and branches of mature eucalypts – often upside down. When threatened, phascogales tap their forefeet against the bark. On the ground

*The **northern quoll** survives in scattered areas of woodland throughout the tropics.*

*The **spotted-tailed quoll** is the largest marsupial carnivore remaining on the mainland.*

Living fast, dying young

Every winter and spring, Australia's forests and heathlands are strewn with small, furry bodies, which scavengers quickly devour. All males of all populations of phascogales and antechinuses (inset: dusky antechinus) lie dead – victims of extraordinary life histories that climax in sudden, en masse die-offs. These small carnivores  are living dynamos, spending nights in nonstop animation as they vigorously demolish prey. The lives of males reach energetic peaks during the brief mating season. They are then so intent on mating that they even stop eating. And each mating lasts up to a dozen energetic hours in some species. The effort is so great that every male succumbs to stress-related infections, ulcers and haemorrhaging, and dies just before its first birthday. Most females make it into their second year of life and raise their young, but few make it to a second breeding season.

*Although probably extinct on the mainland, **eastern quolls** are still abundant in Tasmania.*

they can also be located by sound as they skip lightly over the leaf litter. While brush-tails are still quite widespread, red-tails are now restricted to a small area of south-west WA.

Phascogales and some antechinuses nest in tree hollows during the day; most other carnivorous marsupials shelter in burrows or logs. Most species have shallow pouches – some smaller species lack a pouch entirely and young simply hang from teats and get dragged awkwardly along (inset opposite: numbat). Large litters are normal, many species giving birth to more young than they can raise – eastern quolls can produce 30 infants the size of rice grains, which race to reach one of only six teats (the mother licks up the surplus young for nutrition and cleanliness). After leaving the pouch, young travel on mum's back or are placed in nests, where they develop from blind, hairless infants to playful juveniles – young quolls are often spied chasing each others' tails. Juvenile quolls and phascogales are most conspicuous during summer while dispersing to new ranges.

*Pale-phase **eastern quolls** such as this one interbreed freely with the darker version.*

Most carnivorous marsupials are antisocial, but brush-tailed phascogales occasionally share nests with close relatives or potential mates. In Tasmania, noisy conflicts can emerge as larger spotted-tailed quolls challenge eastern quolls around a carcass, then are harassed in turn when devils arrive. Chocolate-coloured spotted-tailed quolls are easily distinguished from easterns, which are either jet-black or fawn (infants of both colours often appear together in litters). ■

*Highly arboreal, **brush-tailed phascogales** are found in woodlands around Australia.*

Hotspots

Cradle Mountain–Lake St Clair NP Tasmanian devils and two species of quoll. **The South-West** Manjimup for western quolls and red-tailed phascogales. **Kakadu NP** Northern quolls and brush-tailed phascogales common.

*The mouse-sized **common dunnart** is a widespread and fearsome marsupial predator.*

TASMANIAN DEVIL

Recognition Vaguely doglike; stocky with long tail, broad head and massive jaws. Black with white patch on chest and sometimes on rump.

Habitat Most abundant in dry forest and woodland where open grassy areas attract prey.

Behaviour Nocturnal; most active several hours after sunset. Usually forages alone, returning to den during the day in a log, wombat burrow or crevice. Mates promiscuously during March. Climbs well, and forages along roads and tideline.

Breeding Of several young born in April, usually only 2–3 survive to leave pouch in August.

Feeding Hunts mammals of small and medium size, including possums, wombats, pademelons and wallabies; also takes birds and insects, and scavenges for carrion.

Voice Usually silent, although aggression often includes yells, low warning growls and ear-splitting shrieks.

Ferocious wind-up toys

Its sensational name gives Australia's largest carnivorous marsupial a notoriety which is largely undeserved. True, there are the threatening growls, gnashing teeth and blood-chilling screams of a horde of devils devouring a carcass. And even more unnerving is the sight of a dead wombat bulging and heaving as a devil emerges from inside the body covered in gore – they commonly eat large corpses from the inside out.

Their ferocious reputation arises partly from the commotion that accompanies group feeding – more than 20 animals may shove, snarl and aggressively display their teeth as they compete for the best body parts; and heavy scarring on older animals shows that those powerful jaws are sometimes used against each other. But large, rowdy feedings are uncommon and devils are usually shy, solitary foragers. Typically they forage at night, either scavenging or hunting vertebrates, particularly mammals, which they may pursue in an unrelenting lope before pouncing. Their teeth easily inflict lethal bites and are strong enough to dispose of every shred of evidence of death, even bones. Devils are sometimes seen scavenging sheep and cattle remains, and their reputation has been further corrupted by accusations of killing stock.

A devil of a time

Once infants leave the pouch they are left in well-concealed dens – usually logs or burrows – and by November are exploring the outside world. They are weaned onto flesh and in late summer disperse to form new home ranges. Early independence is a dangerous time for young devils – over half may die during their first year, many losing out in competition for food. The best time to see devils is January to February, when newly independent young roam forest roads and are often too inexperienced to avoid detection. They get trapped in car headlights, where they resemble little wind-up toys – running flat-out down the road with their tail stuck up in the air, too panicked to slow down and find an escape route. ■

Hotspots
Freycinet NP, Cradle Mountain–Lake St Clair NP, Mt William NP

NUMBAT

Living works of art

According to the Nyoongar people's Dreamtime, numbats are living artworks. Their mythology tells how Numbat asked Goanna to paint colours and patterns on her, but didn't like the white stripes he designed and threw red sand over them, which merged to create the bright decorations that numbats still display. The Dreamtime story ends with a disgruntled Numbat chasing Goanna with a stick. Today numbats are still seen carrying mouthfuls of sticks, leaves and other soft vegetation which they use to carpet nests. The numbat is high on the wildlife hotlist, but for once no after-dark adventures are necessary – numbats are often seen simply by strolling through woodland on a warm, sunny day. This unusual carnivorous marsupial is specialised to eat termites, and is the only small marsupial that forages during full daylight.

Recognition Slender (45cm overall) with long, bushy tail and tapering snout. Russet with white stripes across rump; black 'mask' through eyes.

Habitat Wandoo woodland and open jarrah forest with high concentrations of termites and hollow logs.

Behaviour Solitary; individuals of same sex have completely separate home ranges; male and female home ranges may overlap. Active in open areas on sunny days, foraging around fallen logs for termites. Darts into shrubbery or hollow logs if disturbed.

Breeding In late summer, 4 furless young are born, just 2 weeks after mating; the young are independent by mid-December.

Feeding Consumes up to 20,000 termites per day by excavating them from soil and licking them up with long, adhesive tongue.

Voice Sometimes clucks softly while foraging.

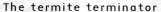

The termite terminator

Tough termite nests are usually left alone, the numbat preferring to sniff out the shallow, fragile galleries around nests, which it digs open and invades with a sticky, flickering tongue half as long as its body. In winter numbats are most active around midday, when termites are busiest – watch for the bristly tail standing out like a banner as they fossick around rotting logs. During summer they prefer midmorning and midafternoon, napping in logs or burrows during the hottest hours. Since the introduction of foxes, hollow logs have become critical for the survival of numbats – they are usually found within a quick scamper of a bolt hole.

Numbats dig tunnels to a nest chamber, where they usually sleep alone; they are only sociable during the summer breeding season. Females may be seen collecting grasses for nursery nests in July, by which time they have been carrying four young on their teats since late summer – nearly six months before! Once they become furred and heavy, infants are left in burrows by day. They start following their mother in September – sunbathing and playing together near the entrance, then gradually ranging further away. ∎

Hotspots
Dryandra Woodland, Perup Forest, Yookamurra Earth Sanctuary

BANDICOOTS

Southern brown bandicoots are commonest in scrubby vegetation along the south coast.

*Once widespread, the **western barred bandicoot** now survives only on islands in Shark Bay.*

Long-nosed bandicoots are common in most treed habitats along the eastern seaboard.

*The **rufous spiny bandicoot** inhabits rainforests of Cape York and New Guinea.*

Bold as brass

Resembling narrow, oversized guinea pigs with a long nose and tail, several of the seven surviving bandicoot species are common nocturnal visitors to suburban gardens – particularly long-nosed, and southern and northern brown bandicoots. They are among the boldest of marsupials, often ferreting around unfazed by the presence of spectators. Typically they dart their noses erratically over the ground – pointed tips quivering like divining rods that sniff out worms, insects and buried bulbs. Bandicoots make themselves unpopular among gardeners by using their foreclaws to drill neat, cone-shaped holes in lawns. They often seem oblivious to their audience until, after skipping slowly nearer, they suddenly bound madly for the nearest bushes. Scooting into dense vegetation is the usual escape strategy for all bandicoots and they usually forage in open areas near thick undergrowth.

Outside suburbia, they are found in most habitats where there is low cover for a quick getaway. The familiar 'backyard' bandicoots are variously grey-brown; barred bandicoots have pale-banded rumps; and the golden bandicoot (inset) is sleek burnished bronze, flecked with black. Apart from telltale diggings, another bandicoot clue is their mutterings as they forage – long-nosed bandicoots are particularly vocal squeakers. All bandicoots hole up during the day in well-hidden nests – shallow beds covered with plant litter. During rains, northern browns even scrape soil over the top as waterproofing.

Bandicoots have astonishingly high reproductive rates, becoming sexually mature at only three or four months – in some cases, before they are fully grown. Northern browns are born just 12.5 days after conception – the fastest gestation of any mammal. Some bandicoots produce seven young in a litter, several times a year; however, only two to four young usually survive until weaning because, as the growing infants jostle in the pouch, one often tumbles out and is lost. Except during breeding, bandicoots avoid each other, maintaining separate home ranges. Males may patrol their turf and aggressively confront intruders – a short tail on a southern brown is likely evidence of such a scuffle. ∎

Hotspots

Mt William NP Spotlight eastern barred bandicoots in their Tasmanian stronghold. **Dryandra Woodland** Southern brown bandicoots common. **Julatten** Northern brown bandicoots easily seen on Mt Lewis at night.

BILBY

Last of the line

One of the Outback's most colourful marsupials lies hidden by day beneath the burning surface of the Red Centre. But as it shuffles from its burrow after dark, it becomes immediately apparent why it is so often described as 'delicately featured' or 'exquisite' – and why a glimpse of a bilby is so highly prized.

During foraging, bilbies bunny-hop with noses twitching to catch the faintest scent of seeds and bulbs, and ears swivelling for whispers of small prey; their 'dainty' forepaws then become powerful tools for unearthing food. Clear signs of bilby feeding grounds are the numerous shallow excavations they make while sifting through soil. If startled, they canter quickly to their burrows, which are often located beside shrubs or termite mounds. Deep burrows offer protection from the deadly sun, but the desert has also been the bilby's saviour. Once, bilbies and four closely related bandicoots thrived throughout much of arid and semiarid Australia; since the European fox was introduced all but the bilby have vanished.

Tasty Easter emblems

The bilby has survived by retreating deeper into the deserts where foxes can't follow, although the foxes must be salivating for the last few – the *Quarterly Gazette* in 1924 described 'curried bilby' as 'a fine meal'! Bilbies are usually found singly or in small family 'colonies'. Several colonies occasionally gather at rich feeding sites, but in general they are gypsies that shift home ranges regularly in search of new food sources. Wherever they wander, bilbies dig new burrows or reoccupy previous ones. Once infants leave the pouch, they are cached in nursery burrows for several weeks – for the first fortnight they have a startling appearance, with gangly, almost furless, bodies and gigantic floppy ears.

Bilbies have won the adoration of children across Australia since they were adopted as native replacements for the environmentally destructive Easter bunny. Ironically, while they are winning hearts, bilbies are continuing to lose the fight to survive and, unless things change, a belief in bilbies – Easter or otherwise – may soon be just another fairy tale. ∎

Recognition Size of a hare (males larger than females) with large, upright ears and an elongated pink nose. Bluegrey (white underneath) with long black-and-white tail.

Habitat Arid and semiarid grassland and open shrubland with stony or clayey soil for burrowing.

Behaviour Strictly nocturnal and often solitary. Family 'colonies' comprised of mated pair, sometimes accompanied by 1–2 recently independent young. Each has a home range on which there are many spiralling, 2m-deep burrows, several of which are visited every night.

Breeding All year-round in favourable conditions; 1–2 infants carried in pouch about 11 weeks before placement in nursery.

Feeding Omnivorous; prefers bulbs, seeds, fruit and fungi when available, switching to invertebrates (eg, termites, ants and larvae) in leaner times.

Voice Usually silent.

> **Hotspots**
> **Karajini NP**, in large enclosures at **Currawinya NP** and **Karakamia** (Perth)

KOALA

Tougher than they look

A classic image of the Australian bush is a koala dozing on a branch framed by eucalypt leaves. Koalas are a favourite with wildlife lovers, partly for their 'furry toy' appearance and also because they are among the easiest marsupials to watch during the day. They often rest conspicuously in a low fork of a large eucalypt, waiting for sunset before climbing into higher branches to munch foliage. At night they may be encountered ambling between food trees, but if startled will gallop to a nearby tree and bound up the trunk. Young are often seen hugging their mother's back or snuggling against her while she dozes – a peaceful contrast to the usually antisocial adults.

Although their ranges may overlap, koalas are usually solitary; interactions become more frequent and spectacular during the summer mating season, and include violent confrontations between males. Dominant males will chase and attack subordinates, and consequently males can often be recognised by battle scars. At dusk throughout the mating season males may be heard bellowing to attract females and warn competitors – their loud, low-pitched roars carry hundreds of metres through the forest.

Toxic tucker

Young koalas are first seen peering from pouches during winter, when they are six months old and becoming weaned. Weaning onto gum leaves is quite a feat – the leaves are nutrient poor, and loaded with toxins and indigestible compounds. Between bouts of thorough chewing, young koalas store half-crushed leaves in their cheek-pouches to release as many nutrients as possible – the accompanying flood of toxins is inactivated in their liver. To ready her offspring for its new diet, the mother produces pap – soft faeces which are eaten by the infant, which thus gains the microbes it needs to digest foliage. Young remain with their mothers throughout spring, continuing to suckle while mastering browsing. They are independent at 12 months and are often then seen dispersing to new home ranges. ∎

Recognition Large (c. 75cm) with no visible tail; large, rounded ears with tufts; and flat, dark nose. Woolly fur pale grey to grey-brown.

Habitat Eucalypt forest and woodland. Common in coastal forests, widespread inland where food trees available.

Behaviour Inactive for up to 20 hours a day; this reduces energy needs and enables survival on poor-quality diet. Moves between trees on all fours, bounding when threatened; can swim well. Individuals have well-defined home ranges.

Breeding Single young (rarely twins) born in summer and remains in pouch 6 months.

Feeding Eats only eucalypt leaves; favours blue, manna and swamp gums in south, red and grey gums in north.

Voice Usually silent; males give deep, snorting bellows during breeding season.

Hotspots
Warrumbungle NP, Grampians NP, Brisbane

COMMON WOMBAT

Going bear-serk

The scientific name *ursinus* refers to the common wombat's vaguely bearlike shape and amble. There are two other wombats: southern and northern hairy-nosed wombat, both extremely rare. The most abundant wombat species is best tracked down by visiting forest clearings after dark, when solitary adults or females with young graze in open areas or unearth roots with their strong foreclaws.

Young wombats sometimes seem to go insane, bursting into playful romps during which they harass mother (or an unlucky grass tussock) with mock-savage lunges, wrestling and biting. These games may be dress rehearsals – wombats are intolerant of others on their feeding grounds, which they defend aggressively and define with scent markings. Growling disputes are sometimes overheard; adult males also threaten others by swinging their head and displaying formidable teeth. Clashes between rock-solid wombats would be dangerous affairs, but briefly gnashed teeth are usually a sufficient deterrent.

Underwater wombats

Wombats can gallop at 40km/h; they also climb if pressed, and bush rumour has them crossing small streams by simply marching into the water and across the riverbed (an orphaned wombat that fell into a swimming pool was found walking apparently unperturbed along the bottom). One hint that you're in wombat country might be when your foot disappears down a burrow. Many mountain stockmen and horses have 'come a cropper' in this way; Banjo Patterson wrote of hillsides 'full of wombat holes, and any slip was death'. Common wombats dig short burrows as night-time refuges and elaborate complexes as daytime rest quarters. They devote much labour to home improvement and maintenance, and may visit a few burrows within their home range each night. When pursued, wombats retreat to burrows and block the entrance with their hefty rump, which is tough enough to crush intruders against the burrow walls. ∎

Recognition Large with a stocky build, short legs and no visible tail; head broad with small ears and hairless nose. Coarse grey-brown fur.

Habitat Sclerophyll forest with adjacent grazing in mountainous areas; also woodland and heath at lower altitudes.

Behaviour Usually solitary. Shelters in burrows during day, emerging after dark to graze; bolts noisily for cover if disturbed. Burrows may be used, usually at different times, by several wombats with overlapping ranges.

Breeding The single young are born year-round (winter in Tasmania), carried in a backward-facing pouch for six months and remain with their mother for almost another whole year, hurrying alongside and emitting urgent hisses if separated.

Feeding Grazes in open on grasses, and also feeds on vegetation such as herbs and tree roots.

Voice Usually silent; mothers and young maintain contact with repeated short hisses *heh-heh-heh*.

Hotspots
Blue Mountains NP, Wilsons Promontory NP, Asbestos Range NP

*The **striped possum** is an aberrant glider restricted to rainforest of the Wet Tropics.*

*The rare **Leadbeater's possum** is restricted to the tall forests of south-eastern Australia.*

*V-shaped incisions in trunks are signs of **yellow-bellied gliders** in tall, wet forests.*

GLIDERS

Flying carpets and rope-dancers

Wildlife-watchers who encounter gliders sailing through the bush may be forgiven for wondering whether their Australian evening has magically transformed into an Arabian night. In flight, flexible membranes between a glider's fore- and hindfeet unfold, to sail them through the air between trees like flying carpets. Gliders come in four styles, from the handkerchief-sized, amber-brown mahogany glider, through the common blue-grey sugar and squirrel gliders, to the tea towel-sized yellow-bellied glider. Common features include deep, soft-pile fur; a long fluffy tail; a pale belly; dark mascaraed eyes; and a dark blaze on the forehead extending to midback (in most species); and a tough, brazen attitude which completely belies their cute-and-fluffy appearance.

Gliders have the distinction of being some of the most social and vocal of possums – a volatile combination which often leads them into fierce chattering and screaming squabbles over territory, food or mates. They also will not hesitate to defy much larger possums, and are often discovered clinging to a tree trunk in a noisy, bristling stand-off with a possum several times their size. The gliders most often seen are sugar (inset) and squirrel gliders, both of which thrive in a wide range of eastern forest and woodland.

Despite their fiery streak, gliders generally manage to live in relative harmony with each other. Each shares a communal nest in a tree hollow with several other individuals and their young. Infants (usually one or two per litter) begin tagging along with their parents in spring on foraging expeditions for insects, pollen, nectar, sap, gum, or occasional small birds. Like many marsupials, gliders are easiest to spot when youthful, inexperienced animals first leave home to disperse. The Latin name for the glider group means 'rope dancer' and they do seem to dance nimbly along branches, often defying gravity to scamper upside-down along the underside of limbs. Two nongliding family members (Leadbeater's and striped possums), are nonetheless both highly agile and have the trademark black dorsal stripe and fluffy, curling tail. ■

*Up to twice the size of sugar gliders, **squirrel gliders** inhabit woodland and dry forest in eastern Australia.*

Hotspots
Gibraltar Range NP Greater gliders around Mulligans Hut. **Great Ocean Road** Yellow-bellied gliders easily seen at Sheoak Creek in Lorne-Angahook SP. **Chiltern Box-Ironbark NP** Sugar gliders common, and good for squirrel gliders.

SUGAR GLIDER

Possum with a secret up its sleeves

Sugar gliders are hot favourites for the 'marsupial most likely to astonish' award – as voted by many unsuspecting wildlife enthusiasts who are quietly dumbstruck when a small possum bounds along a branch, launches itself with its hindfeet and star jumps into the air. A membrane attached at wrists and ankles immediately ripples open on either side between its outstretched limbs, and spreads like a grey cape with which the possum glides between trees. Covering sometimes 50m in a single glide, it 'stalls' by tilting its hindlegs inwards and landing gracefully on the side of the target tree.

Sugar gliders are the gliders most frequently seen; their aerial stunts are best witnessed after dark in open forests as they go in search of food. Sugar gliders are very possessive of feeding sites and aggressively guard food against goliaths such as brushtail possums three times their size. Disputes are easily located as the glider hurls torrents of loud, chattering abuse at the larger trespasser. Their impressive vocal repertoire includes fierce shrieks when two gliders are having a tiff; and high yipping when a predator is seen.

Gregarious gliders

They are very social, sharing tree hollows in groups of several adults (usually a dominant male and several females) and their infants. In cold weather or when food is scarce, individuals may go into torpor. The dominant male scent-marks his territory, drives off rivals and forces young to disperse after eight to 10 months. Twins are usual, and are first seen emerging from the nest in spring. Early attempts to glide are hesitant affairs, perhaps forced by the need to navigate a short gap to be reunited with their mother. The youngster may pace agitatedly back and forth, calling, tensing to jump and balking several times before leaping. By late summer many young are independent and, having perfected their gliding technique, set out to seek new social groups. ■

Recognition Possum with bushy tail longer than 17cm body. Smoky blue, paler underneath, with dark stripe from forehead to midback.

Habitat Most common in open forest with hollow trees for shelter, especially near stands of wattles.

Behaviour Sleeps in leaf-lined nest in hollow limbs during day; forages in canopies and glides between food trees at night. Young start foraging with mother at about 15 weeks old.

Breeding In June–July, 2 young are born then carried for 10 weeks before being left in a group nest.

Feeding Eucalypt sap lapped from incisions chiselled in trunks; also wattle gum, invertebrates ripped from under bark, nectar, pollen and seeds.

Voice Chatters or screams loudly when threatened or fighting; a series of shrill barks warns of predators.

Hotspots
The Kimberley (Mt Hart homestead), **Cradle Mountain–Lake St Clair NP, Grampians NP**

RINGTAIL POSSUMS

Dark lemuroid ringtail possums are the more common of a dark and light colour variation.

Greater gliders *can be seen in tall forests of the east coast; they also have a dark phase.*

Green ringtail possums *are found in rainforest above 300m in the Wet Tropics.*

Curl power

The seven species of possum known as ringtails are endowed with long natural curls – curling tails, that is. Their strong, prehensile tail transforms into a bonus '5th limb' whenever extra dexterity or speed is required. Consequently, few tasty leaves, fruits or flowers are out of their reach, and ringtails are fun to watch as they weave through densely tangled branches, smoothly using their paws and tail in concert to reach, grip and balance. Green ringtails rival even Tarzan in their ability to swing rapidly up vines. Small round ears and short-furred, prehensile tails distinguish ringtails from brushtail possums.

The spectacular exception is the greater glider, which is identified by huge ears, fluffy tail and dark fur (although some individuals are creamy white). It is a ringtail that has taken to the air and is only superficially similar to the 'true' gliders. Many ringtails are dusky brown-grey, but rainforest species are strikingly coloured – Daintree River ringtails may be golden caramel (inset); green ringtails are olive green; and the Herbert River ringtail wears an ebony coat with white front. Most ringtails' nights are spent foraging in the canopy, where a strong light locates the red reflection from their eyes (orange-pink in Herbert Rivers). Lemuroid ringtails can also be detected by their musky scent and by listening for them crash-landing

into foliage as they leap between trees. Ringtails are unlikely to perform for an audience – most species freeze when spotlit, although a group of lemuroid possums may huddle together, and rock ringtails withdraw to a nearby crevice where they sometimes hide their head but forget about their body. Ringtails are often discovered in gardens feasting on fruits, holding a morsel tightly in both forepaws.

Most build nests in tree hollows, although rock ringtails shelter among rocks, and green ringtails simply crouch into a ball on a branch with their head tucked into their chest. In woodlands where hollows are scarce, common and western ringtails make stick nests – dreys – which can be conspicuous in the canopy of trees. Many ringtails are gregarious, and are often spotted in small groups consisting of a mated pair and their infant or, in some species, twins. ■

The **Daintree River ringtail possum** *is endemic to the rainforests of the Wet Tropics.*

> **Hotspots**
> **Julatten** Lemuroid and green ringtails present on nearby Mt Lewis. **Washpool/Gibraltar Range NPs** Greater gliders common. **The South-West** Perup NR is good for rare western ringtails.

COMMON RINGTAIL POSSUM

Bright-eyed and twisty-tailed

Common ringtails are a spotlighter's dream. Illuminated by torchlight, their bright eyeshine is an instant giveaway – two red coals glowing just above a branch, often with one or two smaller pairs gleaming above the first. Even better, they share with most possums a 'freezing' response when caught in a light beam, and remain peering down at the torch wielder – making them among the easiest marsupials to watch.

Sometimes their white-tipped tail is seen curled tightly round a posy of grass and leaves, which the possum is carrying back to its nest as a soft lining. The tail is prehensile and often used to wrap around branches as a climbing aid. If the possum slips, the tail is even strong enough to prevent a fatal plummet to the forest floor. Common ringtails cope well with urban life and pay frequent visits to city residents and their delicious gardens, where they spice up their natural diet by pilfering exotic fruits and flowers.

Paternal possums

Early evening is the best time to look for them, when foraging is at a peak. Older infants may be left in nests in hollow limbs or thickets, or carried on foraging expeditions – twins are often seen jockeying for position on a parent's back. Unusually among possums, at least some male common ringtails are dedicated carers who cart infants around, groom them between feeding spells and babysit them in the nest while the female is away. Males also put in a lot of groundwork before breeding – becoming an attentive consort to their female, following her around and gently grooming her before eventually sharing her nest. Family groups are close-knit; mated pairs forage together and snuggle down together with their young during the day. If one adult is discovered while spotlighting, a quick scan will sometimes locate its partner nearby. Listen also for their characteristic soft, birdlike twittering – common ringtails are quite vocal, and will often call wayward young back to the nest if a predator approaches. ∎

Recognition Small (35cm body) possum with rounded ears. Grey-brown to almost black above, underside white to rufous but 35cm-long prehensile tail always tipped white.

Habitat Treed areas, from rainforest to woodland, with dense shrubs; common in urban parks and gardens.

Behaviour Strictly nocturnal; rests in spherical stick nests in tree hollows or shrubbery during the day. Frequently associates in family groups until young are weaned. Home range of a male often overlaps those of two females.

Breeding Depending on area, births occur April–November; twins are usual, 2 litters sometimes raised a year.

Feeding Forages for leaves, buds and blossom, including eucalypts, but also raids gardens for exotic flowers and fruit.

Voice Quite vocal; a high twittering call is the most common.

Hotspots
Wilsons Promontory NP, Cradle Mountain–Lake St Clair NP, Royal NP

COMMON BRUSHTAIL POSSUM

Waking up the neighbours

Australia's most familiar possum is also one of the largest and certainly the most boisterous. Common brushtails are renowned for the racket they make as they race over suburban roofs. They are among the most vocal of Australian mammals, particularly during their autumn and spring breeding seasons. At these times, males are often easily located as, with loud hoarse coughs, hisses and screeches, they noisily warn other males approaching too closely. Home ranges are also advertised by scent-marking, and many males have rust-coloured stains on their white chest fur from wiping their chest glands incessantly on branches and other signposts throughout their domain.

In the urban environment brushtails readily compensate for the lack of tree hollows by taking up lodgings in roofs, and stomping about on ceilings every evening as they leave to forage. They are often encountered just after dark clambering along the top of fences, sometimes with a young perched on the back or ambling behind, heading towards nearby food trees. Females with large pouch-young are easily recognised in profile by their distended (sometimes wriggling) pouch.

Guerillas in our midst

Unhabituated brushtails will stop dead when spotlit, but quickly become tolerant of human spectators – at camping grounds they can be accomplished raiders, ransacking unattended tents for anything remotely edible. Although common brushtails will travel on the ground between trees, they spend most of the night among branches, climbing slowly or sitting still to eat. If startled they can move quite quickly and bound up a tree trunk with their long, sharp claws. Brushtails prefer mature trees which provide food and large hollows for nesting. Well-used trees may be identified by vertical tracks which have been scratched up the trunk by generations of possum claws – many electricity poles have slippery, claw-proof metal plates around them to prevent possums getting electrocuted. In south-eastern forests, common brushtails share their range with mountain brushtails. ∎

Recognition Large (90cm long, head and tail), robust silver-grey possum (sometimes much darker) with pale belly, long bushy tail and large erect ears.

Habitat Closed and open forest, woodland; also parks and suburbs.

Behaviour Rests by day in shelter such as a hollow tree, roof or log; forages in canopies after dark. Breeds year-round in arid and tropical regions if conditions favourable. Male home ranges overlap those of females.

Breeding Normally a single infant remains pouch bound for 4–5 months before being transferred to the nest.

Feeding Eucalypt and other leaves form bulk of diet, supplemented by fruits and blossoms; forages for scraps around camps and houses.

Voice Hisses, rattles and deep coughs are common during aggressive encounters, particularly during the breeding season.

Hotspots
Atherton Tablelands (Mount Hypipamee NP), **Cradle Mountain–Lake St Clair NP**, **Fitzroy Gardens** (Melbourne)

'SMALL' POSSUMS

Possums from Wonderland

'Small' possums scrambling among branches is one of the rarest highlights of watching Australian wildlife. The five species of pygmy-possum include the world's smallest, the 6cm-long little pygmy-possum. The other two small possums – the honey possum and feathertail glider – are only 1cm larger. Despite appearances, these three groups are not especially close relatives – each forms its own distinct family – and neither is the feathertail closely related to other gliders.

*The **mountain pygmy-possum** lives above the treeline in the Australian Alps.*

Feathertail gliders are common in eastern eucalypt forests; honey possums choose flowering heaths in the south-west; and pygmy-possums range widely from forest understoreys to alpine

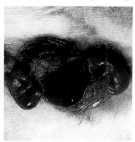

peaks. The tails of feathertail gliders, the smallest gliding mammals, help them steer between trees. During the day, honey and pygmy-possums can be as difficult to wake as the dormouse from Alice's Wonderland. In fact, pygmy-possums were once called 'dormouse possums' for the ease with which they enter torpor when the temperature or food sup-

*Eastern **pygmy-possums** are found from heath to forest in south-eastern Australia.*

plies are low. During tree felling, they are sometimes discovered tucked into tight bundles on a leaf bed within an abandoned bird's nest or hollow limb. Feathertails also use hollows, or weave spherical stick nests shared by a social group of up to 20 animals. Mountain pygmy-possums are unique among marsupials for their ability to hibernate for many months, curled among rocks under the snow. Small possums become most conspicuous on warm nights, darting among branches using their prehensile tails and handlike forepaws. Often their activity is in pursuit of insects, and little pygmy-possums even tackle lizards, but all species also eat pollen and nectar. Honey possums are nectar specialists, often balancing on flower clusters larger than themselves to reach nectar with their long, brush-tipped tongues.

Honey possums emerge after dark to feed on nectar in southern coastal heath.

Depending on the species, female small possums generally carry two to four pouch-young (inset: a pygmy-possum). Male honey possums produce the largest sperm of any mammal, and have testes weighing around 5% of their body weight – signs of a promiscuous mating system; in an odd quirk, females produce the smallest mammalian young. ■

Hotspots
Kosciuszko NP Mountain pygmy-possums active in summer above the snowline. **Kangaroo Island** Better-than-average chance of western pygmy-possum. **Wilsons Promontory NP** Eastern pygmy-possum and feathertail glider in banksia woodland.

*The **feathertail glider** is widespread in eastern forests and is the world's smallest gliding mammal.*

KANGAROOS AND WALLABIES

*Once widespread in the arid zone, the **rufous hare-wallaby** survives only on desert islands.*

*The gregarious **agile wallaby** is the most abundant macropod of tropical savannahs.*

Setting an example

Australia's most famous animals are excellent examples of much that is unique and fascinating about marsupials. The kangaroo's classic upright posture displays the trademark marsupial baby-carrier, the pouch, and when pouch-young peer from their pockets there's no missing them. Plus, their size is often eye-catching – the red kangaroo is the largest of the world's marsupials – and although kangaroos don't usually hop down the main street of Sydney they are still the most visible marsupial family.

Collectively, the 39 species of kangaroo and wallaby (small kangaroos under 25kg) are known as macropods, meaning 'big footed'. They are distributed right across the continent, from bush clearings to dusty Outback roads and inner-city golf courses, often entering open spaces to graze from late afternoon to early morning. Even around midday they don't retire to nests like most marsupials; in arid regions rock-wallabies (inset: yellow-footed rock-wallaby) and common wallaroos (or euros) shelter in caves, and tropical tree-kangaroos sleep in the rainforest canopy. Elsewhere kangaroos simply rest under vegetation, where mobs of reds and greys often remain easy to watch as they doze, groom and socialise. Look for males sparring fiercely over mates; females tipping older joeys out of pouches to groom themselves; and joeys pawing at their mothers, pestering to get back in. All marsupials give birth to tiny, embryonic young, but only in the most conspicuous kangaroos is it easy to watch a female attending to her 'pouch embryo' – its presence is hinted at whenever she pushes her muzzle into her pouch to clean.

Baby boomers

Most large wallabies and all kangaroos are highly sociable, living in tightly knit groups called mobs, the members of which look out for each other. Agile wallabies and several others 'beat a retreat' by thumping a warning with their hindfeet to alert their mob to danger; and black-striped wallabies stick together in a group when fleeing – no matter how panicked, they streak away in coordinated single file. And it is at high speed that kangaroos really impress – taking off like they're on pogo sticks with high bounds on powerful hindlegs, long tails bouncing behind for balance. Hopping may look laboured in a macropod just ambling along, but at high speeds – larger roos can hit nearly 60km/h in a burst – it is more energy efficient than other fast gaits. Some species are distinguished by striking colouration, such as the red kangaroo's bright-rufous or smoky-blue coat, and the euro's

*The **antilopine wallaroo** replaces eastern and western grey kangaroos in tropical woodlands.*

*The **black wallaroo** blends into shadows among the boulders of Kakadu NP's stone country.*

Swimming beans

Naked, blind, weighing less than a gram and smaller than a chilli bean, newborn kangaroos seem hardly capable of the struggle needed to reach the pouch. Their mother gives them every chance; she is often seen spring-cleaning the pouch in the hours before birth, and licking with their tongue down the fur along the path her infant must take. As a sign that birth is imminent, female roos adopt the birth position, sitting with their hindlegs – and, in some species, their tail – stretched out before them. Red kangaroos get comfortable by leaning their back against a tree. Once born, the tiny infant rips itself out of its birth sac and begins the climb to the pouch, 'swimming' through a sea of fur using its forelimbs (it doesn't yet have hindlimbs). Within minutes it reaches the pouch and disappears inside to become attached to a teat. It won't leave for good, until it is too large to fit (inset: eastern grey kangaroo).

Nearly extinct on the mainland, *tammar wallabies* thrive on Kangaroo Island.

Primarily nocturnal and solitary, the *parma wallaby* of subcoastal NSW wet forests is generally rare.

shaggy, rusty-grey hair, and shoulders-back, elbows-tucked stance. Others have distinctive features, such as the hairless, horny tail tips of nailtail wallabies; and the granulated soles of rock-wallabies that aid their propulsion over rock faces.

Most wallabies and roos have another rare ability – females mate soon after giving birth and 'pause' their new embryo's development, a process called embryonic diapause, until the older joey is nearly ready to leave the pouch permanently (or dies). Once conditions are right, its dormant successor is reactivated and born only weeks or even just days later. The new pouch-young attaches to a different teat than that used by its older sibling, who continues to squeeze its nose into the pouch to suckle for several weeks before being weaned.

Out of the pouch, young kangaroos and wallabies stick close to mother, tumbling back in when danger – such as a dingo – threatens, until they are too big to get in or a new joey takes up residence. Mothers communicate with their offspring using soft clucking sounds, warning them of danger and keeping them from straying too far. Within a mob, females may be closely related, and collectively scan for enemies and provide a safe haven for playgroups of joeys. When in oestrus, female eastern grey kangaroos may be courted by a queue of males, which can result in spectacular boxing matches between rival suitors. ∎

The *common wallaroo*, or euro, is found across the continent on rocky hillsides.

Hotspots

Warrumbungle NP A good variety includes eastern grey kangaroos, euros, swamp wallabies and brush-tailed rock-wallabies. **Kakadu NP** Northern specialities, such as the agile wallaby, two rock-wallabies, and antilopine and black wallaroos. **Flinders Ranges NP** Inland species such as the red and western grey kangaroos, euro and yellow-footed rock-wallaby.

The cattle industry hastened the decline of the now-rare *bridled nailtail wallaby*.

LUMHOLTZ'S TREE-KANGAROO

Strange tenants of the canopy

Although ancestral kangaroos left the trees many millennia ago to live on solid ground, tree-kangaroos have recently (in terms of geological time) returned to the canopy. Lumholtz's is the more common of Australia's two species, and distinguished from Bennett's by pale cheeks and forehead. Tree-kangaroos won't win any prizes for arboreal elegance – they climb and clamber awkwardly along branches and vines; and descend from a tree by holding on loosely with the foreclaws, sliding down the trunk like a firepole (if they need to, they can jump up to 20m to the ground). But on the rare occasions tree-kangaroos travel on the ground they hop impressively, despite having shorter hindlegs than those of other roos.

Tree-kangaroos are nocturnal, sleeping and basking high in the canopy before setting out at sunset to feed. They are sometimes spotted perched on a branch grooming, or stuffing their faces with two fistfuls of soft seasonal fruits. Several Lumholtz's tree-kangaroos may sometimes converge on the same fruit-laden tree, but usually they forage alone or with a single young (breeding occurs year-round). Large amethystine pythons often wait on fruiting trees to ambush inexperienced young tree-kangaroos. ■

Recognition Grizzled blackish brown above and cinnamon below; paler cheeks. Long tail.
Habitat Edges and canopy of tropical montane rainforest.
Behaviour Nocturnal; solitary. Tail not prehensile; used as counterbalance.
Breeding Single joey.
Feeding Leaves; some fruit.
Voice Courting males make clucking sounds.

Hotspots
Atherton Tableland, Daintree NP

WHIPTAIL WALLABY

Things that go thump in the night

Whiptails (watch an agitated animal to see where the name comes from; they're also known as 'pretty-faced wallabies') are far more active during daylight than most macropods – feeding peaks at dawn and continues well into the morning before starting again in the late afternoon. Dozens of individuals may associate together, grazing open forests and clearings in mixed groups of adults, juveniles, young-at-foot and a joey in nearly every pouch.

Females in oestrus are simple to spot as they are trailed by several males, dominants threatening other suitors. Like other macropods, whiptail mothers do not help their young into the pouch, although they may tilt forwards and relax the opening. Many joeys are lost by falling out a few days too early, before they have the strength to climb back in; survivors must master the art of reentry – an incoming joey typically dives headfirst then wriggles around until its head resurfaces. Startled whiptails have a distinctive alarm response – they thump the ground with a hind foot, a warning that is readily detected by their companions at night. When the alarm is sounded, the mob scatters instantly, each wallaby zigzagging, a tactic that may leave pursuers floundering behind in indecision. ■

Recognition Pale grey; white hip- and cheek-stripes; white ear tips and dark face.
Habitat Hilly, open forests with grassy understorey.
Behaviour Sociable; mobs up to 50; ranges of subgroups overlap. Often active by day.
Breeding Year-round; single joey carried c. 9 months.
Feeding Mostly grasses.
Voice Coughs in alarm.

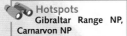

Hotspots
Gibraltar Range NP, Carnarvon NP

RED-NECKED WALLABY

Baby boom

Red-necked wallabies are the most commonly seen large forest wallaby in south-east Australia – their joeys are also very familiar, since the wallabies' sky-high reproductive rate ensures that almost every sighting of an adult female includes a bonus joey visible in the pouch or at foot. Other than mother–young combinations, red-necked wallabies are usually solitary, although lush pastures may attract large feeding groups. Open patches (including camping areas) amid thick understorey are favoured foraging haunts. Over time red-necks can become accustomed to feeding near human activity, sometimes foraging for campers' leftovers.

Red-necked wallabies on the mainland breed year-round, but most births in the Tasmanian subspecies are in late summer and autumn. Wildlife-watchers in Tasmania can therefore witness an exodus of red-necked joeys from their pouches each year around December, when all infants reach the age of emergence together. Their first brave excursions into the world are brief affairs – the joey typically falls out, wobbles to its feet for a few seconds, does a fast about-turn and scrambles straight back into safety.

A year-long suspension

Female red-necked wallabies mate again soon after giving birth – so while courtship and mating can be observed throughout the year on the mainland, in Tasmania most activity occurs in autumn. And, like other roos, females are able to delay the development of the new embryo until after the current joey has left the pouch permanently. This strategy of embryonic diapause allows mothers to keep a 'spare' infant, so that if they lose the active one they can quickly replace it by taking the embryo off pause and fast-forwarding its development to birth. Red-necked wallabies have a remarkably long embryonic diapause; if an older joey survives until it leaves the pouch for good, its younger sibling will have been on hold for a year. ∎

Recognition Large (c. 1m tall). Variable grey-brown above (paler below), with characteristic reddish nape and shoulders; dark nose, paws and big toe.

Habitat Eucalypt communities with moderate to dense shrubbery and adjacent open areas; also coastal heaths.

Behaviour Rests in dense undergrowth during the day and follows habitual runways to feeding sites. Feeds on overcast afternoons during cool weather. Animals scatter when startled. Joeys spend 3–8 months suckling at foot before weaning.

Breeding Single joey born following 1-month gestation spends 9 months in pouch.

Feeding Grazes on grass and herbs; in farmland shelters along vegetated watercourses, emerging at dusk to graze in paddocks.

Voice Usually silent.

Hotspots
Warrumbungle NP, Bunya Mountains NP, Bruny Island

EASTERN GREY KANGAROO

Grey ghosts

Close encounters of the eastern grey kind are best experienced by walking just before dawn on almost any east-coast country golf course, and watching for large, upright silhouettes looming out of the mist. Half-light and fog banks lend atmosphere to the sight of fairways crowded with kangaroos of all sizes, usually grazing or sitting up to watch you – many with joeys peering from pouches.

Spectacular social interactions are occasionally witnessed, especially close to the summer breeding peak. Watch for ritualised aggression: two adult males may circle each other stiff-leggedly on all fours with backs arched, or one male may start ripping up grass and wrestling shrubbery in a show of strength while coughing harshly and eyeing his rival. Challenges occasionally lead to vigorous fights, with contestants rearing up, leaping, kicking and grappling with splayed claws. Stiff-walking and grass-tearing are male threats which eastern greys have in common with other kangaroos; both sexes may also stand to their full height with forelegs outstretched when trying to intimidate another individual. Joeys are sometimes seen play boxing with their mothers.

Roos at rest

Activity declines after early morning when the roos abandon open feeding areas to seek shelter. Around golf courses, groups are often spied reclining beneath trees, their long legs stretched out. Close relationships are not neglected during rest times; look for females with their heads in their pouch, giving joeys a good licking to keep them clean. Older joeys that have left the pouch are often seen standing long sufferingly as their mothers drag their ears sideways while grooming them.

Females in turn must tolerate a lot of physical attention when in oestrus; males express their interest in a female by repeatedly pawing her face and grabbing her tail. The mother–infant bond remains strong at least until weaning and a joey newly out of the pouch is very sensitive to separation – if its mother moves off too quickly it may throw a conspicuous tantrum, nickering urgently after her, and hopping agitatedly up and down. ∎

Recognition Large (upright males 1.6m tall) and solidly built. Thick fur varies from light to dark grey-brown.

Habitat A wide range of wooded areas from mallee and woodland to forest, heath and farmland.

Behaviour Grazes open areas from late afternoon to early morning, usually in subgroups (up to 20 individuals) of a larger mob. Retires to denser vegetation during the day. Swims if necessary to avoid predators.

Breeding A single joey carried in pouch for 9 months and remains at foot until about 18 months old.

Feeding Mostly grazes but also eats herbs and shrubs. May compete with livestock for graze and water.

Voice Mothers and infants – and courting males to oestrus females – often communicate by soft clucking.

Hotspots
Warrumbungle NP, Grampians NP, Mt William NP

RED KANGAROO

True blues and red giants

Red kangaroos are the only 'true blue' kangaroos of the Outback and their range is actually restricted to the arid inland. They are nomads who roam in mobs and follow rains that bring on flushes of green grass. On good grazing grounds, several mobs may aggregate to form a huge, colourful spectacle. Red kangaroos, particularly females, are often blue, and a mob of several hundred rusty-red animals will be peppered with smoky-blue individuals.

Reds are the largest of all marsupials, and mobs are dominated by giant battle-scarred males that can be 1.8m tall when standing upright. Subordinate males usually live in separate mobs, moving up the hierarchy until ready to stage a coup against the current command. When competing for mates, two males may display one of the Outback's most dramatic sights: gripping each other tightly with large foreclaws, they wrestle, cuff and scratch their opponent, or balance on powerful tails and lash forward with their hindlegs.

Although adapted to an arid environment, the red kangaroo is most abundant on the slightly wetter surrounding plains. They are commonly spotlit in small subgroups – look for their bright eyeshine bobbing up and down as they hop, like the mythical min-min light (the Outback's will-o'-the-wisp).

Tough times, tough measures

In times of drought, fewer joeys are present because females have a drastic strategy to increase their own chances of survival. Kangaroo infants are born at an early stage of development, and the demands of supporting a growing joey in the pouch may be life-threatening for females when little food is available. Under such conditions females may cease to provide sufficient nutrients for their infant, so that after only two or three months, up to half of pouch-young are dead. Females, and some males, become temporarily infertile after a few rainless months, but with a gestation of just 33 days, once drought breaks mobs quickly bounce back to be full of joeys again. ■

Recognition Large and powerful. Red or smoky-blue coat, white below. Distinguished by black-and-white muzzle patch and pale stripe between mouth and ear.

Habitat Inland plains and flat, open, grassy woodland where rainfall provides adequate grazing.

Behaviour Social and nomadic; lives in large mobs which usually travel in smaller subgroups. Mobs are often comprised of a dominant male, several females and young. Shelters beneath trees during the day; often seen along Outback roads at twilight, where their lack of road sense makes them dangerous.

Breeding A single joey first leaves the pouch at just over 6 months.

Feeding Forages early morning and night for short grass and herbs, also browses from arid-zone shrubs.

Voice Usually silent, but may scream and hiss during confrontations; mothers and infants make soft clucking contact call.

Hotspots
Uluru–Kata Tjuta NP, Mutawintji NP, Flinders Ranges NP

One of several similar species, the **allied rock-wallaby** *can be seen on Magnetic Island.*

Black-footed rock-wallabies *are camouflaged against rocky cliffs and boulders.*

It's hard to miss the **Mareeba rock-wallaby** *at Granite Gorge, Far North Queensland.*

ROCK-WALLABIES

Colourful kangaroos living the high life

Rocky outcrops, cliffs and gorges are the domain of the 15 species of rock-wallaby, renowned for being the most brightly patterned and colourful subset of the kangaroo family. Some have bold markings – the yellow-footed rock-wallaby (inset) has a fawn coat with white highlights and a banded tail seemingly dipped in yellow or deep-orange paint. Others have highly variable colours to blend into local habitats – the Mareeba rock-wallaby varies from sandy to charcoal, depending on whether it lives among pale- or dark-coloured rocks; and Sharman's rock-wallaby has a coat the same shade as local grasses.

Most species have limited distributions, a result of populations being isolated on their rocky islands. This evolutionary process can be seen in action in the only widespread species, the black-footed rock-wallaby: it has several isolated subspecies and forms that may eventually evolve into separate species.

Anyone exploring high slopes of plateaus and canyons has a chance to glimpse a rock-wallaby – they are nocturnal, but often bask on secluded ledges early and late in the day. By day they may also be startled from rocky shelters – listen for loose pebbles rattling as the wallabies bound away. Passing through remote gorges an audience of sometimes dozens of rock-wallabies may watch from safety above. In the late afternoon, entire colonies descend to graze and browse around the foot of their retreats.

Rock-wallabies leave another striking impression: their incredible agility, highlighted as they hurtle across even the steepest, most chaotic jumbles of rocks. Built for speed and power over rugged surfaces, their thick, roughly granulated footpads provide extra grip (like heavy-duty off-road tyres); and fine balance is provided by their upswept tail. Without doubt, rock-wallaby young get a rough ride. Once out of the pouch, their habitat is so difficult to traverse that while other joeys

travel beside their mothers, rock-wallaby infants are kept hidden in rocky retreats until they find their footing. Clumsy infants are be easy targets for wedge-tailed eagles, which are sometimes seen swooping over colonies and even tackling adults. ∎

> **Hotspots**
> **Flinders Ranges NP** One of the few places where yellow-footed rock-wallabies are easily seen. **MacDonnell Ranges NP** Black-footed rock-wallabies at Standley Chasm and Heavitree Gap. **Carnarvon NP** Supports many brush-tailed rock-wallabies. **The Kimberley** Short-eared rock-wallabies at Lake Argyle.

Yellow-footed rock-wallabies are widely distributed on rocky ranges in the arid zone.

PADEMELONS

Wallabies on fire

Wildlife-watchers hoping to stumble upon pademelons should be on the lookout for small wallaby-like animals darting about in densely tangled undergrowth of rainforests and wet eucalypt forests in eastern Australia. When caught in torchlight they should be immediately recognisable by their glowing patches of rich, fire-coloured fur: all three pademelon species possess dusky grey-brown coats (paler underneath), over which each species has its own characteristic pattern of flame-orange highlights. Red-necked pademelons have warm reddish-orange capes across their neck and shoulders; red-legged pademelons have

Tasmanian pademelons are widespread and common in wet forests and gullies.

bronze cheek-stripes which match their gloves and socks; and Tasmanian (red-bellied) pademelons have soft rusty-gold undersides. All species are common in their respective ranges, but the Tasmanian pademelon once also occurred in Victoria and South Australia.

Pademelons make runways in grasses, fernery and other thick low vegetation, from which they emerge to feed in nearby grassy clearings at dusk – they are also sometimes active at other times of day, but usually keep to deeper thickets. They are most likely seen between evening and early morning, hopping or shuffling slowly along with noses low to the ground (inset: red-necked pademelon), not usually straying far from the shelter of the forest's edge.

Pademelons share their realm of wet forests and dense riverside vegetation with another group of small macropods, the potoroos. Competition between the two for food is unusual, since potoroos prefer underground foodstuffs, such as fungi and bulbs, while pademelons graze and browse. Rivalry between pademelons is also rare, as they are essentially solitary, although several individuals may be seen feeding together on lush pastures. When animals meet, confrontations can arise over good food patches and a group sometimes erupts briefly into a melee of hissing, growling, skirmishing bodies.

Females are often encountered with a single infant in tow, hopping alongside or straying off to explore before being brought to heel by a few soft clucks. Other pademelon vocalisations are rarely heard – a better sound to listen for at night in the hope of locating pademelons is their rustling through leaf litter. ■

Red-legged pademelons are common in rainforest from northern NSW to Cape York.

In the south of its range the **red-legged pademelon** feeds deeper in forest and is darker in colour.

Red-necked pademelons graze rainforest edges in coastal NSW and southern Queensland.

Hotspots
Washpool/Gibraltar NPs Easily seen red-necked and red-legged pademelons. **Bunya Mountains NP** Abundant red-necked pademelons. **Mt Field NP** Excellent for Tasmanian pademelons.

QUOKKA

Recognition Hare sized; short tail and short, rounded ears. Grizzled grey-brown above.
Habitat Dense heathland.
Behaviour Nocturnal (except Rottnest population). Rests in social groups inside thickets.
Breeding Single joey born year-round on mainland; late summer on Rottnest.
Feeding Herbs and foliage.
Voice Usually silent.

Hotspots
**Two Peoples Bay NR,
Rottnest Island.**

Wildcat wallabies

Visitors to Rottnest Island don't need to be quiet and cautious to have a quokka experience – in fact if helps if they are as conspicuous as possible. They can then expect to be ambushed by bands of small, shaggy wallabies so eager to beg a few scraps of food they will often hop to within touching distance. With their bouncy inquisitiveness and stumpy tails, it is hard to believe that European seafarers who saw them almost 350 years ago called them 'wild cats'. Far from being fierce hunters, 'normal' quokkas browse on low vegetation and themselves fall easy prey to introduced predators; as a result, they have disappeared from most of their original range.

Luckily for wildlife-watchers, it is almost impossible to escape from quokkas on 'Rotto', where they gather around freshwater pools, and hide under bushes and scrub beside roads, ready to waylay passers-by. They are most active during the cooler hours, sheltering around midday inside mazes of passages that they have tunnelled through dense undergrowth. Within their social groups, the Rottnest quokkas can often be observed having minor tiffs over food and resting places; elsewhere in the south-west, quokkas are most often observed foraging singly at night. ■

SWAMP WALLABY

Recognition 80cm; shaggy, brown-black above; yellowish or rust below and on cheeks.
Habitat Wooded areas with thick, low undergrowth.
Behaviour Usually solitary and nocturnal. Forages near cover.
Breeding Single joey at any time of year.
Feeding Usually browses on shrubs.
Voice Usually silent.

Hotspots
**Warrumbungle NP,
Wilsons Promontory NP**

Black creature from the lagoon

An unidentified creature splashing loudly as it approaches you through shallow water at the edge of a marsh or pool at night can be disconcerting. But a quick pan with a torch will most likely illuminate a small, almost black wallaby, frozen knee-deep and well camouflaged against the dark water – unless it is facing you to reveal its distinctive gold or orange front.

Swamp wallabies live in forests around swamps, streams and wet gullies, and are commonly found on damp, misty hillsides. Generally darker than other wallabies within the same range, they are probably better described as 'brush' wallabies because of their preference for hiding in dense fernery or other low, almost-impenetrable undergrowth during the day. After dark they may be encountered foraging – mostly alone, although several are sometimes spotted feeding together and females often have a joey. Unlike almost all other wallabies, they don't usually graze, preferring to browse on leafy shrubs; this and several anatomical features set them apart from all other macropods. Observers who know their plants may be horrified to watch swamp wallabies munching hemlock and other poisonous species known to kill other animals; swamp wallabies apparently suffer no ill effects. ■

POTOROOS, BETTONGS AND RAT-KANGAROOS

Truffles, burrows and broomsticks

Potoroos, bettongs and rat-kangaroos together comprise the potoroids – a family of energetic wallaby-like creatures about the size of rabbits. Potoroids are closely related to macropods, but few display the sociable nature of their bigger relatives. Most of the eight species forage alone after dark for insects, bulbs and, especially, native 'truffles' – the fruiting bodies of underground fungi that grow on eucalypt roots. Potoroids' exquisite noses can distinguish between different kinds of truffle, even those deeply buried. When foraging they home in on promising patches of earth then eagerly excavate morsels which are then clutched in both forepaws and demolished in seconds. Shallow diggings are often found about 1m from the bases of mature eucalypts in dry habitats.

On the odd occasions when individuals congregate at a rich feeding site, a hot-tempered brawl usually develops, accompanied by growling, grunting and chases – such conflicts can be a good way to locate potoroids. Potoroids avoid open pastures, preferring to stay within dashing distance of cover, although individuals can become habituated and easily seen around camping grounds.

Land clearing, foxes and cats have taken a heavy toll of potoroids: two species are already extinct; the burrowing bettong

survives on only a few islands off the coast of Western Australia and South Australia; and the ranges of the others have shrunk drastically – though the Tasmanian bettong (inset) remains reasonably common. Bettongs tend to inhabit drier, wooded habitats, while wetter forests and heaths are better for finding potoroos. To distinguish between them, look for the short, chubby face of bettongs and the longer, narrower head and nose of potoroos.

Burrowing bettongs are unique among kangaroos and their kin because they live underground. Some potoroids weave cosy stick beds, collecting and carrying the nesting material in their coiled tail tips – look for them hopping along with their long tails sprouting a bunch of twigs at the end like a broomstick. ∎

The **musky rat-kangaroo** of Wet Tropics rainforests is often abroad during the day.

Now extinct on the mainland, **burrowing bettongs** survive on islands off Western Australia.

Small populations of **brush-tailed bettongs** survive only in south-western woodlands.

The **long-footed potoroo** is a rare and little-known species of south-eastern forests.

Hotspots

Dryandra Woodland Habituated brush-tailed bettongs at camping grounds. **Julatten** Musky rat-kangaroos common here and elsewhere on the Atherton Tableland. **Mt Field NP** Camping grounds are good places to seek long-nosed potoroos at night.

*Able to hover while feeding, **eastern tube-nosed bats** are common in Queensland's coastal forests.*

*The **black flying-fox**, found around tropical coasts, is the largest of Australia's flying-foxes.*

FRUIT-BATS

Winged foxes on juice

Dozing fruit-bats wrap their wings around themselves – in contrast to microbats, which fold their wings neatly by their sides. Hanging by their feet from branches, they resemble miniature foxes draped in long cloaks. A single tree may be festooned with hundreds of suspended fruit-bats, swaying in the canopy like toys on a mobile, chattering and waiting for nightfall. At dusk, spiralling columns of bats disappear swiftly towards feeding grounds. When those wings unfurl, many of Australia's 12 fruit-bats reveal a more glaring difference from microbats – their size.

Largest and most familiar are the flying-foxes, the black flying-fox has a colossal wingspan that can reach 1.6m; other group members, including blossom-bats, are only mouse sized. Fruit-bats are plant-juice specialists, and most inhabit tropical forests with a year-round menu of nectar, flowers and fresh fruits. Flying-foxes may travel 50km in a night to reach feeding trees, crowding into the canopy and squabbling for feeding territories. Yellow-spotted eastern tube-nosed bats feed upside down, hugging tropical fruits sometimes larger than themselves. Blossom-bats lap nectar with long, absorbent, brush-tipped tongues (inset: common blossom-bat).

Fruit-bat colonies are often noisy places. Bare-backed fruit-bats shelter in caves (the only fruit-bat to use caves); blossom-bats roost in foliage, hollows and under bark; and flying-foxes often form massive, conspicuous colonies (camps) of many thousand individuals in paperbark and mangrove stands along coasts or rivers. Camps can be located by their strong odour and noisy social activity, but be stealthy – in some species of flying-fox, old males act as sentries to warn the camp against intruders. Commotion reaches a crescendo in the early morning and evening, particularly during the autumn breeding season, when males vigorously defend arenas on branches where they preen and display. Single infants are born and carried for some weeks before being left in maternity camps. When learning to fly they accompany adults on foraging excursions and are left en route in nursery trees to be collected on the way home. ■

*Widespread east and north, **little red flying-fox** camps have up to one million occupants.*

> ### Hotspots
> **Daintree NP** Camps of spectacled flying-foxes, plus eastern tube-nosed bats and smaller fruit-bats in rainforest. **Kakadu NP** Look for black and little red flying-foxes near Cahills Crossing. **Bundjalung NP** Good for grey-headed flying-foxes and others.

*The **spectacled flying-fox** is a rainforest specialist found only in tropical Queensland.*

MICROBATS

Acrobats

High-energy skydives, twists and other aerial displays are the microbats' forte in their lively pursuit of prey. Their slick performances screen nightly across Australia and the cast includes 59 species, differentiated from fruit-bats by their taste for meat (usually insects) and their talent for echolocation – microbats navigate by emitting ultrasonic beams that echo off their surroundings and are received in large, elaborate ears. Close-up, microbats have tiny eyes and leathery wing membranes spread across thin, elongated fingers. Some species have intricate, leafy noses crumpling their faces.

In the bush their stunts are most visible silhouetted against the sky at last light on warm nights; in suburbia, look for flickering shadows chasing insects around streetlights. Many emit cricket-like *tik-tik-tik*s spaced about one second apart as they forage.

Hunting techniques vary. Sheathtail-bats have long, narrow wings for lightning-fast manoeuvres above the canopy, while leafnosed-bats flutter slowly like large moths through undergrowth, hovering and dodging after prey. The southern myotis hunts over freshwater, even skimming the surface for insects and small fish – infants follow their mother for several weeks after weaning, rehearsing their technique. The pale, big-eyed ghost bat – Australia's largest predatory bat – silently takes small mammals and birds, and even seizes other bats in midair; wrapping its wings around victims, it bites them to death then carries them to a habitual feeding site – look for heaps of left-over fur and feathers below ledges in caves in the north of Australia. Ghost bats often cohabit with their potential victims: many microbat colonies roost on the ceilings of caves, hanging upside-down in the depths or in 'twilight zones' near the entrance.

Visitors who brave the caves after dark will hear them flapping, vocalising and scuttling – even up vertical walls – as they prepare to leave. Giant colonies of many thousands of bats (such as those of little bentwing-bats – inset) sound like rushing wind as they billow forth, some in the north flying straight into the jaws of swooping ghost bats and lunging pythons. ■

*The carnivorous **ghost bat** is widespread in tropical Australia; Mt Etna has a large roost.*

***Southern freetail-bats** feed above forest canopy and along tree-lined creeks in the south.*

***Lesser long-eared bats** are widespread and commonly found – even in urban areas.*

***Gould's long-eared bat** hunts in forests throughout the south-east and south-west.*

Hotspots
Mt Etna NP Huge nursery colonies (100,000+) of bentwing-bats run the gauntlet of ghost bats and pythons. **The Kimberley** Several species roosting among Aboriginal rock art at Tunnel Creek NP. **Litchfield NP** Orange leafnosed-bats emerge from behind Tolmer Falls at dusk.

RODENTS

Broad-toothed rats inhabit the alpine and subalpine zones of south-eastern Australia.

*The **spinifex hopping-mouse** is widespread in spinifex dunes across arid Australia.*

Mitchell's hopping-mouse shelters during the day in burrows in mallee country.

Daytime shenanigans

Australia's 57 species of native rodent feature many rare and colourful characters. While all possess basic mouse- or ratlike forms, many outshine their foreign relatives in appearance in hue. Highlights include the tiny ash-grey mouse and the shaggy black-footed tree-rat – a rabbit-sized animal with long ears and long, feathery tail. Hopping-mice are favourites because of their slender, 'kangaroo-like' hindlegs; long, tufted tail; large, delicate ears; and huge eyes – complemented in some species by apricot to deep-orange coats.

But there are many little-known species just as fascinating – such as the rock-rats of northern Australia, which have fat tails that readily break off – it is not clear why – so that many rock-rats are missing part or all of their tail. In an illustration of the frontiers still open in Australian biology, and of the threats to Australian wildlife, a new species of rock-rat, the Carpentarian rock-rat (inset), became known to biologists only in the late 1980s. Extremely restricted in distribution and in danger of extinction due to habitat degradation, it could easily have vanished without anyone knowing.

Native rodents may be seen in every corner of Australia including hopping through woody undergrowth and desert sand dunes, swimming in lakes and rivers, and scampering in tree tops. Like most marsupials, most rodents are nocturnal, but there is some daylight action. When a mild wet season on the plains of the Northern Territory is followed by rains during the Dry, populations of dusky rats skyrocket to Pied Piper proportions and the overcrowding provokes intense daytime squabbling and other social dramas. Another exception to the nocturnal rule is the amphibious water-rat, which may be seen dog-paddling sleekly with partly webbed hindfeet in estuaries and freshwater at sunset, or even in broad daylight.

Most rodents are herbivores or omnivores, but water-rats explore shorelines for fish, crustaceans, good-sized insects and even occasional waterbirds. They return to favourite feeding platforms to eat; the best way to find their territories is to look for waterside rocks or other 'tables' littered with leftovers. The giant white-tailed rat – Australia's largest rodent – similarly leaves piles of empty seedcases on logs, and is sometimes glimpsed during the day stalking crabs through mangroves.

Signs and clues

Other rodents also leave evidence of their presence. Pebble-mound mice are famous for their stone constructions, but several other species are also talented architects. The rare

*The **smoky mouse** is a rare inhabitant of coastal forests and uplands in the south-east.*

Builders of the first pyramids

Australia's northern rangelands are dotted with miniature low pyramids, some over 8m wide and built by 'hand' using thousands of pebbles. The identity of the tiny builders remained a mystery for many years until the first pebble-mound mouse was captured near its stonework. Pebble-mound mice (inset: western pebble-mound mouse) are superstrong and capable of carrying stones half as heavy as themselves. Beneath the piles lie labyrinths of communal burrows and chambers – like most native mice, pebble-mound mice are highly social, with several sharing each complex. Mounds still in use can be recognised by the crater-like depression and entrance hole at the summit, kept tidy by the many industrious inhabitants.

The **eastern chestnut mouse** is found in woodland and heath along most of the east coast.

Heath rats depend on mosaics of burnt and unburnt heathland in southern states.

greater stick-nest rat chews branches into required lengths and creates stick houses up to 1m high, each carpeted with soft vegetation and housing several individuals (successive family members often renovate the home). To avoid daytime heat, the many arid-zone native mice and hopping-mice dig elaborate communal burrows up to 3m deep, with several surface pop holes. They may hide entrances under shrubs, but piles of dug-out debris near holes are dead giveaways. If an opening becomes blocked by sand, a dusky hopping-mouse may squeak loudly until another arrives and helps dig it out.

One of Australia's boldest rodents is the orange-brown Cape York melomys, which may be followed easily by torchlight through the rainforest – it also breaks into nearby houses and noisily runs amok. While spotlighting for Cape Yorks, watch for the long, curling tail of prehensile-tailed rats in the trees; if pinned in a light beam they characteristically panic and dash madly back and forth along branches. Tree-rats of northern Australia are sometimes spotlit perched in the canopy munching fruit, or bounding over the ground between trees with their brush-tipped tail waving.

Sometimes active by day, **water-rats** feed in both fresh and brackish water.

Native rodents usually have three to six young, which are typically dragged along – or run to keep up – while clinging tenaciously to teats. Older young may remain in nests: young water-rats stow away in tunnels in riverbanks or logs; tree-rat offspring are hidden in hollows; and young native mice hole up within their community's underground maze. ■

Hotspots

Karajini NP Look on rocky slopes or ask rangers how to see handiwork of the western pebble-mound mouse. **Kakadu NP** Localised and endemic species plus dusky rats fleeing monsoonal floods. **Julatten** Mainly arboreal rodents of the rainforest canopy, including giant white-tailed rat.

The **Cape York melomys** is an agile climber in rainforest with a dense understorey.

AUSTRALIAN SEA-LION

An insatiable curiosity

One of the most striking attributes of sea-lions is an often intense fascination for human visitors – to onlookers, at least, they are perhaps the most inquisitive of Australian mammals. Vessels near colonies often attract an escort of frolicking animals. Youngsters especially flash up to the boat, then catch your eye before leaping away, twisting and tumbling smoothly underwater with frequent looks back.

Visitors walking near colonies may also become sea-lion magnets. Older pups and juveniles will often take to the water, swim over to visitors and bob up in the shallows, craning their necks forwards before approaching in a mob, hesitating and jostling each other forwards. Close to their target, the lead youngster will spook and crash back into the others, scattering them seawards – but within moments they regroup for another advance. Younger pups – glossy black until their first moult – sprawl together on the sand, using each other as pillows as they wait for their mothers to return from foraging trips to nurse them.

Bull fighting

Female sea-lions gather in large numbers at popular pupping sites to give birth – usually on protected, rocky patches of beach. Soon after pupping, females come into oestrus and males start arriving to mate, sometimes swimming many kilometres from their usual colonies. Younger bulls arrive first, attempting to sneak a mating before the 'heavies' show up – prime males weighing 300kg that stake out areas around groups of cows and defend their turf fiercely from rivals. Titanic threats and battles on the beach include bulls rearing up open mouthed (displaying their sharp teeth), chest thrusting and chasing each other, snapping and roaring. Breeding season is dangerous for both new pups and wildlife-watchers. Many infants are caught in the firing line, either savaged or trampled to death by bulls. Cows guarding pups, and bulls guarding cows, can become aggressive to human intruders – and its startling how fast a charging sea-lion can lumber towards you. Outside breeding time, bulls bask placidly side by side, ignoring spectators and each other. ∎

Recognition Ears very small, snout short. Older males 2m long, very bulky; dark brown to black. Females slimmer (1.5m long); pale silver-grey.
Habitat Sandy and rocky beaches of mainland coasts, scattered islands; and the surrounding seas.
Behaviour Hauls out for 2–3 days between oceanic foraging trips lasting a few days. Colonies contain dozens to hundreds of individuals.
Breeding Single pup born after a 14-month gestation; nursed for over a year. Breeding season lasts c. 5 months, although starting time varies between colonies due to an unusual breeding cycle of 17–18 months.
Feeding Dives to catch fish, squid, crayfish and seabirds such as penguins underwater.
Voice Usually silent. Bellows of breeding males most obvious.

Hotspots
Leeuwin-Naturaliste NP, Kangaroo Island, Seal Island (Perth)

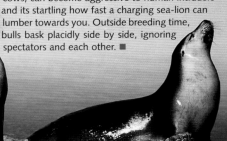

NEW ZEALAND FUR-SEAL

Underwater ballet

Visitors to southern coasts may notice sleek, dark-furred bodies scattered among rocks by the shore, or porpoising through the ocean with small fish leaping frantically ahead of them. Fur-seals were once known as 'sea-bears'; although satiny when wet, their dense, warm coats become very furry as they dry. A juvenile basking on its back in the water, holding its back flippers with its front while rocking back and forth conjures a cartoon image of a playful bear cub clutching its toes.

New Zealand fur-seals are common and more often encountered than the slightly bulkier Australian (or more correctly, Australo-African) fur-seal, which breeds on only a few islands in Bass Strait. The New Zealand fur-seal breeds in several more accessible and widespread mainland locations. Their colonies are crowded with animals lying about, shuffling to and from the sea, or dozing upright with noses held high in a characteristic posture that lends them an aloof air. Around colonies where diving is permitted, you can view an underwater scene that can resemble centre stage during a swirling, high-energy dance, with streams of inquisitive seals cavorting, looping and rippling in circles around divers. But it's when fur-seals accelerate into high-speed chases after fish that their agility really shines – onshore they may be slugs, but underwater they're action heroes.

Recognition Adults brown-grey; smaller than sea-lions, with pointier snout. Coarsely maned males up to 2.5m long; females slimmer (1.5m long).

Habitat Cool or temperate seas, breeding on rocky coasts and islands.

Behaviour Social, often in dense colonies; rests and nurses pups on land for c. 2 days between fishing trips.

Breeding A single pup born November–January is weaned by next breeding season.

Feeding Pursues prey underwater; fish eaten mainly in winter, squid and octopus more in summer; also eats crayfish and little penguins.

Voice Often silent; obvious vocalisations while breeding are males' growls and barks during territorial conflicts.

Hard-won harems

During spring and summer more aggressive displays take place on beaches, and New Zealand fur-seals become intensely territorial when breeding. Males put on ritualistic shows of force that include stretching to their full height, shoving each other and roaring threats, which sometimes lead to bodily attacks – nonterritorial males and savvy human spectators usually keep away during this time. The few most dominant males are easy to pick – they are the giants guarding territories, complete with a handful of females (inexperienced and geriatric 'bachelor' males can be found loitering hopefully at the colony's edges). A male's reign is usually over within two to three years, but defeat must be a physical relief – defending a territory is an exhausting activity during which he doesn't eat for several weeks. ■

> **Hotspots**
> **Kangaroo Island, Leeuwin-Naturaliste NP, Phillip Island** (Australian fur-seals)

DUGONG

Recognition Resembles a bulbous, dark grey or brownish dolphin with no dorsal fin.
Habitat Sheltered, shallow tropical and subtropical waters with seagrass meadows; usually inshore but occasionally visits reefs.
Behaviour Forages and rests throughout the day. Usually solitary or in small herds. Herds may approach shore on high tides to graze, retiring to deeper water on ebbing tides.
Breeding A single calf born September–April accompanies the mother at least 18 months.
Feeding Grazes exclusively on the leaves, rhizomes and roots of seagrasses by uprooting them with its large, spreading upper lip.
Voice Very vocal; barks associated with territorial aggression, and birdlike calls with friendly interactions and displays.

Hotspots
Hinchinbrook Island, Shark Bay MP, Brisbane (Moreton Bay)

King Neptune's herds

Wisps of seagrass floating to the surface of shallow coastal waters are a subtle sign that herds of large marine animals are grazing the aquatic meadows below. The dugong (sometimes known as 'sea cow') feeds entirely on seagrasses torn from the seabed and is the only Australian sea mammal that is exclusively herbivorous. Dugongs have fired the imagination of seafarers for centuries, and are believed to have evoked legends of sirens and mermaids. Up close it is difficult to see how – their body shape resembles a plump dolphin, but their face is dominated by a wide, bristly piglike snout.

Glass-calm days are best for viewing dugongs. Herds (sometimes numbering several hundred) are then visible beneath the surface, swimming slowly over shallow banks and surfacing in unison to breathe every 80 seconds or so. Calves bob up beside their mothers, and beneath the surface swim 'piggyback' above her, which affords them protection from sharks attacking from below. Like dolphins, dugongs often raise their triangular whale-like tail flukes as they dive, but they are easily distinguished from dolphins inshore by their lack of a dorsal fin.

Siren song

They may not resemble the classic Disney mermaid, but dugongs' voices can be siren sweet and fill the water with chirping, trilling and twittering calls, earning them the nickname 'sea canaries'. Unfortunately these sounds are not usually audible at the surface. Some new evidence suggests that male dugongs may form leks (small territories a few metres wide) within which they remain during the breeding season, on display for potential mates. Dozens of lekking males fill a shallow bay, stirring up the sand as they apparently patrol their turf and skirmish with their neighbours.

Mating can be a violent affair; many females bear parallel scars on their backs from the short tusks of overzealous males. In isolated areas where they aren't hunted or hassled by vessels, dugongs are inquisitive and will approach to investigate boats and divers. ■

BOTTLENOSE DOLPHIN

High jinks on the high seas

When bottlenose dolphins want to joyride, there's no stopping them. They burst out of the waves towards the nearest boat, twisting onto the bow to swim rippling in the slipstream. Here they may tilt and gaze directly at spectators, playing up to the image that a dolphin's life is one long exhilarating game.

In reality the ocean is no fun park and a dolphin's life is rarely carefree. They must constantly be on the alert against attacks by large sharks and killer whales; in some areas, about half of all calves fall prey to sharks. But there's safety in numbers and bottlenose dolphins are therefore usually encountered in groups (pods). Females with calves tend to form large nursery parties, within which calves are often seen splashing around together in high-spirited playgroups as they practise their social and hunting skills. In quiet conditions their excited whistling is clearly audible. Dolphins are best located in calm seas, when their dorsal fins are most visible – look out for feeding groups, leaping in all directions in pursuit of prey.

Sex games

Group membership is fluid, with temporary parties joining together and dispersing as individuals come and go. In contrast to myths about their peaceful nature, bottlenose dolphin societies are rife with aggression and the power-plays that come with being an intelligent social species. Males usually form teams of two or three who work together to score mates and often remain as a stable alliance for many years. Each alliance competes against others for receptive females and their contests may escalate into battles in which dolphins ram each other sky-high.

Relationships are complex; for example, two rival alliances occasionally join forces to steal a female from a third. Males can be recognised by their heavily scarred, ragged fins, and alliances by tightly synchronous surfacings of members. Spectacular somersaults and breaches are usually males displaying their fitness. Bottlenose dolphins are promiscuous, and sexual behaviour is used in a variety of contexts, including threat and to reinforce 'friendship' bonds between alliance partners. ■

Recognition Robust, stream-lined body (to 3m long) with large, curving dorsal fin. Dark to light grey.
Habitat Oceans, bays and river mouths; inshore, including coastal urban areas.
Behaviour Usually in small parties, leap-feeding or chasing fish at the surface, riding bow waves (especially calves), or resting. Preceding a deeper dive, usually surfaces several times displaying dorsal fin (shark fins are straight and remain slicing through the surface).
Breeding A single calf, usually born in summer and weaned when c. 4 years old.
Feeding Using sight and echolocation, hunts a wide range of fishes, including eels, plus cuttlefish and squid.
Voice A large repertoire of communication and navigation sounds, including ultrasonic beams.

Hotspots
Melbourne (Port Phillip Bay), **Shark Bay MP** (Monkey Mia), **Moreton Island** (Tangalooma)

HUMPBACK WHALE

Recognition Robust 14–19m body; flat, knobbed head; small dorsal fin on obvious 'hump'. Dark grey above.

Habitat All oceans, migrating to tropical and subtropical coastal waters. Females calve in sheltered bays.

Behaviour Encountered in small groups or alone. Often breaches, spy-hops and raises flippers or tail. Inquisitive – may approach vessels and eyeball spectators.

Breeding A single calf is born every 2–3 years and becomes independent after about 11 months.

Feeding Gulps of water are forced through baleen plates to sieve over 1000kg of krill (tiny crustaceans) and small fish daily.

Voice Complex, mournful, ever-changing 'songs' are sung by males during the breeding season.

Hotspots
Fraser Island (Hervey Bay), **The Coral Coast**, **The Kimberley** (Broome)

Making a splash

Few animals can create a impression that rivals the spectacle of a breaching humpback whale. It happens suddenly, whether on the horizon or only a boat's length away – a huge whale erupts from the sea, towering into a backwards arch, flippers flung like giant wings. Risen almost fully, the humpback seems to pause, water sluicing down its sides; then it avalanches back into the ocean, smashing the surface into shards.

Humpbacks are the most visible – and acrobatic – baleen whales in Australian waters. They feed around Antarctica over summer and are seen near Australia from autumn as they migrate up the east and west coasts, either alone or in groups of two or three, to mate and give birth in warm waters over winter. Their return journey down the coasts during spring brings them inshore where they enter bays to doze, sometimes with 10m-long flippers waving lazily in the air. Their calves frolic nearby, lunging skywards and hitting the water like demolition balls, but risk a walloping from a huge flipper if they pester their mother.

Song contest

Like all large whales, humpbacks leave visible 'blows' as they exhale – white fountains of vapour which hang clearly suspended for several seconds in calm air. Humpbacks usually blow several times at 20 to 30 second intervals before diving for three minutes to nine minutes, sometimes longer. When diving deeply, humpbacks roll forward and arch their backs to reveal the characteristic 'hump', often hoisting their colossal tail-flukes gracefully into the air as they disappear.

Tails are also used in aggression; it's usual to witness lobtailing (slapping) during violent confrontations between males. More often, males are simply heard; they emit haunting, melancholy moans, which rise ethereally from the depths. These 'songs' – the longest and most intricate of any animal – are followed by all local males, and are constantly evolving as the males adopt seasonal changes to phrase and theme. Singing is perhaps a display of fitness to receptive females (some vessels deploy hydrophones to broadcast the serenades to receptive whale-watchers). ■

SOUTHERN RIGHT WHALE

Whales with the right stuff

Right whales were a whaler's dream and so-named because they were the 'right' whales to hunt – many of these same qualities make them a dream for whale-watchers today. They swim slowly and are easy to approach – in fact their curiosity sometimes brings them right up to vessels – and they tend to rest and calve in shallow inshore waters where they are visible from shore. Although they do not show off as much as humpbacks, they can still put on an energetic performance that includes breaches, lob-tailing and flipper-slaps. They also headstand, floating vertically upside down with tail hoisted like a sail which blows the whale along through the water.

Once abundant, southern rights were almost completely wiped out during the whaling years and now only a few hundred visit southern coasts from autumn to spring. They are usually encountered alone, in mother–calf pairs, or in small groups that individuals periodically join and leave.

Throwing a right

Killer whales – the famous 'wolves of the sea', which hunt in highly organised 'packs' – sometimes prey on southern rights and other large whales. When under attack, right whales may form a circle with their tails facing outwards to batter their assailants. Right whale calves often practise these defensive and aggressive moves during play – smashing the surface with their flippers and flukes, and improving their strength and agility by breaching sometimes dozens of times an hour.

Adult males also sometimes use aggression to compete for females; it has been suggested that the rough callosities on their head may be used as weapons to lacerate each other. However, males are usually peaceful and several will even take turns to mate with a female. Most reproductive contests happen inside the females as sperm competition; as a result, male right whales have the world's largest testes – weighing almost a tonne – which produce massive amounts of sperm. They also own a penis almost 2.5m long, which is surprisingly mobile and with which they occasionally probe and investigate vessels, to the entertainment of onlookers. ■

Recognition Broad, 13–18m body with smooth, finless back; massive head (¼ total body length) has yellow-white callosities inhabited by crustaceans. Usually black, sometimes with white patches.

Habitat Oceans. Calves inshore during winter or spring then returns to deep waters half-way to Antarctica.

Behaviour Usually seen in small groups (up to 12) with characteristic wide, V-shaped blow. Travels on surface for 5–10 minutes between dives of 10–20 minutes. Sometimes breaches, headstands, lobtails or flipper-slaps. May fluke-out when diving, showing smooth fluke edges.

Breeding Bears a 1-tonne infant every 3–4 years in the lower latitudes of its range.

Feeding Krill and other small invertebrates are skimmed from near the surface and strained through baleen plates. Feeds mostly in subantarctic waters.

Voice Moaning and roaring, usually heard after dark in breeding waters.

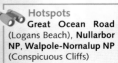

Hotspots
Great Ocean Road (Logans Beach), **Nullarbor NP, Walpole-Nornalup NP** (Conspicuous Cliffs)

DINGO

The dog that doesn't bark

Recognition Sandy or golden red, with black, black-and-tan and almost white variations; usually has white chest, paws and tail tip.

Habitat Alpine areas, woodland and forest bordering grassland to savannah, desert and semidesert with drinking water.

Behaviour Common. Usually lives in packs of 3–12 individuals, foraging from late afternoon to early morning and resting during day. Scavenges around camping grounds. Hybridises with dogs in many areas. Can survive for long periods without drinking.

Breeding About five pups whelped in winter in an underground den are weaned at 3–4 months.

Feeding Hunts prey from large insects, birds, lizards, rodents and rabbits to livestock, feral pigs, wallabies and kangaroos; also takes carrion.

Voice Range of vocalisations, including yelping, yodelling, purring and howling (doesn't usually bark).

As night closes in on remote camping grounds, travellers may hear the Outback's most penetrating call-to-arms – the howling of dingoes firing up for the hunt. Their soaring voices carry over several kilometres and often a distant summons is answered by another unnervingly close at hand. The dingo's hunting styles reflect those of its wolf ancestors; dingoes often hunt cooperatively and perform excited prehunt rituals to rev themselves up for the intense teamwork needed to catch large prey. Hunting tactics depend on the available prey – a skilled pack can bring down water buffaloes and kangaroos, but dingoes often forage alone and scavenge – watch for them trotting beside Outback roads searching for roadkills.

As with most wildlife encounters, the dingo experience is often unexpected – a prickling on the back of the neck has led many a camper to turn around and find a dingo staring silently at them. Although often seen alone, dingoes usually belong to a small, closely bonded group whose members roam throughout their territory and meet every few days. The best time to hear them howling is winter, when social activity intensifies for breeding. Often only a pack's dominant pair produces pups, but the entire pack helps raise the youngsters – who consequently overdose on care and attention.

Native or feral?

Dingoes are among Australia's newest 'natives'; they arrived with Asian sailors as recently as 3500 years ago, and Aborigines recruited them as hunting dogs and as furry insulation on cool nights. While fast becoming the first Australians' best friend, dingoes are efficient predators that probably influenced the disappearance from the mainland (dingoes did not reach Tasmania) of large marsupial carnivores, such as devils and thylacines.

Dingoes are excellent predators of rabbits, but also attack livestock – usually when native prey is scarce – and many farmers treat them as vermin. Attempts at control have included 'The Longest Fence in the World' – built across Australia to keep dingoes from eastern farmlands (it failed completely). ∎

Hotspots
Myall Lakes NP, Fraser Island, Uluru–Kata Tjuta NP.

FERAL MAMMALS

Feral peril

Unfortunately, nearly everywhere you go in Australia there are feral mammals. Wild horses ('brumbies') trample alpine and Outback hills; rabbits strip vegetation and erode the soil with their burrows in all but the wettest areas; goats denude rocky Outback areas; pigs rip up the ground, destroy waterholes and eat ground-dwelling fauna. Some species, especially deer, have restricted distributions but others are widespread. Outback areas in particular often have high numbers of several species. In all, 20 species of feral mammal have become established.

*The **fox** is a deadly nocturnal predator that has seriously affected native mammals.*

Foxes and cats are most often indicted for decimating Australia's mammals. Foxes are absent from large areas, but cats have been able to expand across the country, partly because, unlike foxes, they do not need to drink – they gain sufficient water from their prey. Cats probably came to Australia a few hundred years before foxes, but their current abundance may have been aided by the introduction of rabbits, which make up a large part of their diet in drier areas. Where cats are present but foxes absent, medium-sized mammals are often still common. The abundance of mammals in Tasmania compared to nearby Victoria is striking.

*Introduced **pigs** cause extensive damage to habitat and prey on small animals.*

Eradicating ferals is not only difficult, it can pose thorny conservation issues. Remove cats – trapping (inset), shooting and poisoning are all used – and predation rates on native mammals may actually increase, as foxes, which often eat cats, are forced to rely more on native mammals. If rabbits are removed, cats and foxes prey more on natives; and native predators are also deprived of a major food source. Australia has the only wild one-humped camels in the world – should they be eradicated? Similarly, Bali banteng (wild cattle) thrive in Gurig NP but are endangered in their native range. Brumbies of the Australian high country have a place in the region's culture, yet damage the alpine grasslands.

*There are an estimated 100,000 **one-humped camels** roaming the arid interior.*

But remove ferals, and native fauna and flora bounces back. Swamp buffaloes once infested the wetlands of Kakadu NP, but their elimination has seen spectacular bloomings of yellow lilies return. And the Earth Sanctuaries illustrate how native mammals can proliferate in the absence of their exotic predators. ■

*Swamp **buffaloes** caused extensive damage to Kakadu's wetlands until culling started.*

Hotspots
Kangaroo Island No foxes or rabbits; several species rare or extinct on mainland thrive; abundant small mammals. **Kakadu NP** No foxes or rabbits; wetlands returning to natural state after eradication of swamp buffaloes.

BIRDS

IN the absence of large, diurnal mammals birds are Australia's most conspicuous vertebrates, and of the 750 or so species on the official list some 300 are endemic – the highest total for any country. Around 575 species breed in Australia and another 65 or so (the exact figure is constantly debated) are regular migrants.

A flip through any field guide will quickly show parrots, seabirds and honeyeaters as strong suits; birders steadily discover more vagrant waders and Asian migrants reaching these shores, and meet the challenge of seabirding on the high seas. However, it isn't necessary to go to extremes to see a good variety: should you have the inclination, it is reasonably easy to clock up over 200 species during a weekend's birdwatching in many parts of the country.

Worlds apart

Unique birds will be encountered everywhere and Australia has recently been recognised as the centre of evolution for a major group of the world's passerines (perching or songbirds). Some groups that evolved here, such as ravens, are now distributed worldwide while others, such as lyrebirds and pardalotes, are restricted to Australia.

Several families widespread on other continents, such as the woodpeckers, do not occur here, while others, including the old-world warblers, thrushes, larks, starlings and sunbirds, are represented by only a few species. And several Australian families have evolved to fill niches occupied by other families elsewhere: in a classic example of convergent evolution, the sittellas and tree-creepers both resemble and behave like the nuthatches and creepers, respectively, of the northern hemisphere.

Colour and sound

While spectacular parrots and cockatoos are often conspicuous, many other common birds add splashes of colour to the bush – the exquisite fairy-wrens are often singled out as favourites, but noisy and quarrelsome flocks of honeyeaters feeding in flowering trees can hardly be overlooked; and animated groups of babblers and apostlebirds usually keep the observer entertained with their antics.

Other species are songsters; the calls of whistlers, songlarks and Australian warblers are among the many whose voices ring through the bush in spring. The superb lyrebird, with its astonishing vocal mimicry, and the bowerbirds, whose elaborately decorated bowers are used to attract mates, are always high on the list of must-see Australian birds.

Australian birds are known by a hodgepodge of names, colloquial (jacky winter, willie wagtail), onomatopoeic (kookaburra), Aboriginal (budgerigar), academic (cisticola) and ecological (spinifexbird). Many, such as fairy-wren and shrike-tit, were inspired by their superficial similarity to unrelated groups in the northern hemisphere.

Some species are always elusive and for this very reason are keenly sought by birdwatchers. But there are also many that are easily seen. And, whether handfeeding crimson rosellas at Wilsons Promontory, marvelling at wetlands thick with waterbirds in Kakadu, being enthralled by wheeling flocks of pink-and-grey galahs at Mungo Lakes or mesmerised by the presence of a cassowary at Paluma Range, one thing is certain – experiences featuring Australian birds will be firmly etched into the memory. ■

SOUTHERN CASSOWARY

Recognition Large (up to 1.5m tall), stocky and glossy black. Bare, blue head and neck with pendulous red wattles; prominent casque.
Habitat Rainforests and rainforest edges, occasionally visiting adjoining gardens, fields and woodlands.
Behaviour Usually solitary, associating only to breed and when males attend broods. Males look after chicks for 9 months after hatching; probably sedentary, requiring a large home range in which to feed. Swims and jumps well.
Breeding 3–4 eggs laid on the forest floor during dry season. Only males incubate and care for young.
Feeding Omnivorous; mainly fallen fruit, but also fungi, snails, frogs, fish, birds' eggs, rodents and carrion.
Voice Generally silent; a low, hollow booming is uttered to attract a mate and in alarm.

Hotspots
Atherton Tableland, Mission Beach, Paluma Range NP

The rainforest phantom

The largest animal native to Australian rainforests is also one of the world's largest birds, but cassowaries are notoriously hard to see and a search often ends in frustration. Perhaps no other bird looks less birdlike than the cassowary: even the heaviest rain runs off its thick, hairlike plumage; and a prominent, horny casque, or helmet, tops its bare head and neck.

There is much speculation about the function of the casque, the most popular theory being that it protects the birds as they run through the forest, although it may also be used to signal dominance and as a shovel to search for food.

Cassowaries are nearly silent when walking through the densest undergrowth and an observer can easily walk right past an adult standing motionless only metres from the path. The first indication of its presence is often a low rumbling from somewhere in the vegetation; closer inspection may reveal nothing until suddenly the cassowary rises to its full height and hisses. Generally, it will then quietly walk away, but the inside toe of each foot is equipped with a 10cm-long spike and an adult can deliver a lethal kick when cornered (signs in Cairns warn against jogging near cassowaries).

Traffic hazards

Cassowaries leave telltale piles of droppings from which the seedlings of their favourite fruit trees sprout. The relationship between cassowaries and rainforests trees is important, as cassowaries are the only birds that disperse the seeds of many species – they swallow the fruits whole by tossing them into the back of their throat and excrete the seeds intact. The decline of cassowaries will possibly be followed by a decline of their habitat.

The trick to seeing a cassowary is to look along roads through rainforest in the early morning and evening; the unfortunate corollary of this is that traffic casualties are one of the main causes of falling cassowary populations. Although found only in northernmost Queensland, it is known as the 'southern' cassowary because there are also two species in Papua New Guinea. ∎

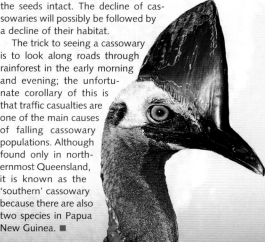

EMU

Single fathers

Australia's largest bird is a ratite, one of the group of flightless birds that includes kiwis, cassowaries and the ostrich. Ratites evolved in Gondwana and survive only in the southern continents. Emus are common and typically seen in small groups picking their way slowly across Outback plains, looking for anything edible. Intensely curious, they can be attracted from some distance away by remaining quiet and waving an article of clothing in the air; Aborigines exploited this curiosity to lure them within spearing range.

As in all ratites, only male emus incubate and attend the chicks; females abandon the male after laying their clutch, and more than one female may lay in one nest. The downy chicks are boldly striped upon hatching and can walk within 24 hours, following the male around for the first five months of life.

Three toes, six senses

Restricted to movement on the ground, adult emus can nonetheless cover 13.5km in a day and one was recorded moving 540km in nine months. Emus and cassowaries differ from most other birds in having only three toes on each foot, one of which is greatly enlarged. When startled, emus can stride at speeds of up to 50km/h and are frequently seen, neck stretched straight out, running next to – and occasionally veering into – moving vehicles. Large flocks sometimes converge on areas with plentiful feed after isolated storms, although how they know where rain has fallen is a mystery – it has been suggested they can sense lightning from great distances or detect vibrations from thunder through the ground.

Emus can become tame in picnic and camping grounds where they scavenge; they shouldn't be encouraged, but it can be difficult to refuse an insistent, 2m-tall bird. They are not welcomed by farmers in some areas and have been persecuted in strategically planned 'emu wars' in which even the Australian Army was called in. ∎

Recognition Large (1.9m tall) with long neck, powerful legs and rudimentary wings; loose, grey-brown plumage with bare, blue neck fringed black.
Habitat Most common on semiarid plains, but occurs in all habitats except waterless, heavily timbered or densely settled areas.
Behaviour Nomadic in response to drought and rains; populations in south-west migratory. Swims well, occasionally visiting ocean beaches; Usually drinks daily but can go several days without if succulent plants available. Raises tiny wings to cool off.
Breeding 5–11 dark green eggs laid in shallow scrape during cooler months.
Feeding Omnivorous; seeds, fruits, shoots, large insects. Swallows stones to grind food in gizzard.
Voice Deep guttural grunts; females also utter a resonant booming.

Hotspots
Innes NP, Mutawintji NP, Warrumbungle NP

MEGAPODES

A testing ordeal

Australia's three species of megapode (Australian brush-turkey, malleefowl and orange-footed scrubfowl) are large, ground-dwelling birds that all look very different but share a remarkable strategy for incubating their eggs. 'Megapod' comes from the Greek for 'huge footed'; males use their feet to scratch leaf litter into massive piles, leaving the surrounding area bare;

females lay their eggs in the mound and as the vegetation starts to decay it generates enough heat to incubate them. The male adds or removes material to maintain a constant 33°C and for up to nine months of the year his entire life is consumed with the care of the giant incubator.

If the male brush-turkey gets it right he will win the lion's share of females, but competition is rife and his mound must be defended against young upstarts. Even females are viewed with some suspicion: they are treated roughly during mating and chased away once laying is completed. Malleefowl and scrub-fowl are less competitive, both pairing for life.

Maintaining the correct temperature and humidity in the mound are essential if the embryos are to develop and hatch – a newly established mound can rise to over 40°C. Consequently, the female always tests the temperature before laying by plunging her head deep into the mound; the male also does this during routine maintenance. The bare head of the brush-turkey was once considered to be its thermometer, but this wouldn't work for those species of megapode with feathered heads and it is now suspected that the tongue or palate is used to determine a mound's internal temperature.

Once the rate of decay reaches equilibrium it is a relatively simple matter to add or remove material to heat or cool the mound as needed – malleefowl rake layers of sand off their mound (inset) to cool the eggs in the hot, dry inland.

Chicks of all species hatch deep inside the piled-up debris and must struggle to the surface, where they rest long enough to recover before running off into the scrub to fend for themselves. The young can fly within a day, but chicks are not often seen and lead a secretive life during their vulnerable first few months. ■

*The **Australian brush-turkey's** long yellow wattles and bare red head are unmistakable.*

***Malleefowl** are found in tall, dry, southern scrublands from NSW to WA.*

*Brightly coloured legs and feet distinguish the **orange-footed scrubfowl** of tropical forests.*

> **Hotspots**
> **Wyperfeld NP** Good chance of seeing malleefowl at mounds. **Lamington NP** Brush-turkeys abundant around camping grounds. **Daintree NP** Brush-turkey and orange-footed scrubfowl side by side.

WATERFOWL

A bill for every occasion

Swans, geese and ducks, known collectively as waterfowl, are some of the world's most familiar birds. All species have a broad, flattened bill (although there are many variations on the theme) and webbed feet; and all are accomplished swimmers that feed in or near water. Being such a dry continent, Australia's waterfowl are represented by only 19 native species, but their behaviour allows them to thrive in the unpredictable cycles of drought and flood. When the dry inland is transformed into extensive

Plumed whistling-ducks flock on shrinking northern wetlands during the Dry.

wetlands after heavy rains, massive numbers, particularly of grey teal, pink-eared ducks, hardheads and Australasian shovelers, arrive to breed as the flood peaks. Depending on the species, nests are built in tree hollows, on stumps, in wetland vegetation or on dry land at the margins. Then it's a race to raise chicks before the water dries out again – a drying wetland will often contain thousands of half-grown ducklings concentrated in dwindling ponds and drains. During drought many waterfowl return to permanent coastal wetlands, where they will also breed, if not quite in the same numbers.

Waterfowl in the tropics experience a similar but more predictable cycle of dry and wet annually. During the Dry, the few permanent wetlands on the vast coastal floodplains attract immense, noisy flocks of magpie geese and whistling-ducks (inset: plumed whistling-ducks). Strikingly patterned radjah shelducks are readily picked out among them, but tiny pygmy-geese are much more difficult to locate floating among the lilies on deep water. With the arrival of the Wet the flocks disperse to breed.

No Australian species appears to be have a specialised diet, but the way in which they feed varies greatly. Dabbling, the 'typical' method of upending and sifting through the mud, is practiced most often by black duck and teal; these species have the classic duck bill. The wood duck and Cape Barren goose have shorter bills ideally suited to grazing short, tender grass; other ducks, such as shovelers and the pink-eared duck, filter tiny plants and animals through rows of plates in their large bills; and the musk duck dives deeply, collecting aquatic insects, crayfish and molluscs which are then crushed in its broad, powerful bill. ■

*The **Cape Barren goose** competes with sheep for grazing on southern islands.*

*Look for the tiny **green pygmy-goose** among waterlilies on tropical billabongs.*

*Most abundant in the south-east, the **chestnut teal** wanders inland when droughts break.*

Hot spots

Kakadu NP Famous for its dry season flocks of tropical waterfowl. **Bool Lagoon GR** Large concentrations of waterbirds, particularly in summer. **Rowles Lagoon CP** Many waterbirds, including the rare freckled duck.

MAGPIE GOOSE

Recognition 90cm; pied; legs and face red; head knobbed.
Habitat Freshwater wetlands; floodplains and grasslands.
Behaviour Feeds mostly dawn and dusk. Outside breeding season roosts communally.
Breeding 1–9 eggs laid in late Wet; both sexes incubate.
Feeding Seeds in Wet, bulbs in Dry; also grazes.
Voice Loud resonant honk.

Hotspots
Townsville Common, The Kimberley, Kakadu NP

Two's company, three's even more secure

Vast, honking flocks of magpie geese (they are close relatives of ducks, geese and swans, but are actually in a family of their own) are one of the spectacles of the Top End – hundreds of thousands congregate in Kakadu alone. Their abundance made them a popular food for Aboriginal people, who climbed to the tops of trees to strike down bloated, low-flying birds as they returned from feeding at dusk. During the dry season they dig for the nutritious bulbs of rushes with their strongly hooked bill in the baked clay of the drying floodplain.

With the arrival of the Wet, the geese establish breeding colonies, sometimes containing thousands of nests, in water about 1m deep. Many males have two mates, the females between them laying up to 16 eggs in the same nest of trampled rushes. Predators, especially crocodiles, take a heavy toll of the fluffy, cinnamon-headed goslings, but trios are better able to defend them from predators and consequently suffer fewer losses than pairs. After a perilous crossing to the relative safely of the shallow wetland edges, the geese and their young feed on the seeds of wild rice and other grasses. Magpie geese are unusual among waterfowl in that the parents drop morsels of food in front of the chicks. ■

BLACK SWAN

Recognition To 1.4m. Black except for white-banded red bill and white wing tips.
Habitat Most wetlands.
Behaviour Flocks of hundreds; flies in V-formations.
Breeding Nests are in water; 4–7 eggs April–September.
Feeding Upends for water plants; occasionally grazes.
Voice Musical bugling, often in flight and at night.

Hotspots
Myall Lakes NP, Coorong NP, Moulting Lagoon

Wetland bugler

To the first European settlers, the presence of black swans really drove home the feeling that everything in this strange, new land was the opposite of their homelands. Equally at home on fresh or brackish water, black swans manage to live and breed even on ornamental lakes in the centre of cities – as long as there is enough space to take off. With a 2m wingspan they must patter across the surface while flapping hard to become airborne.

On large expanses of water swans usually nest in colonies on islands, the fluffy grey cygnets accompanying their parents until almost fully grown. But on small wetlands they can be very territorial. Neighbouring males reinforce territorial boundaries by swimming parallel to each other, necks arched and wing ruffles raised, each trying to outbluff the other – but at times violence appears to be the only means by which disputes are resolved.

Large concentrations containing thousands of swans gather to moult in spring and summer at favoured lakes and bays. During this flightless period swans need the security of a large expanse of water with a plentiful supply of water plants, although at times they graze nervously on nearby pasture. ■

SHORT-TAILED SHEARWATER

Long-distance seafarer

The short-tailed shearwater makes one of the longest migratory journeys of any bird, arriving in south-eastern Australia in September after migrating from the north Pacific. The rather fanciful alternative name 'muttonbird' comes from the tradition on certain islands of harvesting the fat chicks for food. Muttonbirds nests in burrows, usually on offshore islands, where tiger snakes also prey on the chicks and may remain in the burrow as a hazard to the harvesters.

During the day the adults either remain deep in their nest burrows or feed far out to sea, where dense flocks may form hundreds of metres wide and several kilometres long. Towards dusk thousands of birds returning to the colony gather in the offing, where they can easily be seen from coastal vantage points shearing low over the water in the troughs between the swell.

After dusk they fly into the colony, crash-landing in the soft vegetation, and the air is filled with an eerie wailing as birds above and below ground start calling to each other. The best time to visit a colony is in October when courting birds are excavating, or February to April while the young are in the burrows. ■

Recognition Short-tailed seabird. Sooty grey-brown, with paler underwings; dark bill.
Habitat Lives at sea, coming ashore only to breed.
Behaviour Flocks leave in April. Uses burrow for years.
Breeding 1 egg laid in burrow in late November.
Feeding Dives for krill, small squid and fish.
Voice Wails or croons on land.

Hotspots
Bruny Island, Ocean Beach, Great Ocean Road

AUSTRALIAN PELICAN

Photogenic predators

In some seaside locations pelicans have learned that boat ramps can be a ready source of food when fishermen clean their catch; in some towns they have even become a minor tourist attraction. They spend a lot of time resting, pulsating the naked pouch under their bill to cool off. But when they're not posing for cameras pelicans are voracious predators. Fish, their most important prey, are snatched by solitary pelicans or surrounded by groups that dip their bills simultaneously into the school. Pelicans have an eclectic diet: one was seen herding and eating ducklings then snatching and swallowing the mother; and (this is absolutely true) even small dogs are sometimes taken. Such large birds need large bodies of water to take off from and to land on, pattering along the surface to become airborne and water-skiing to a halt as they land.

When large inland lakes flood, pelicans flock to the resultant islands and form breeding colonies, sometimes containing thousands of birds. However, this strategy has its risks: stocks of fish becoming depleted in the three months before the young fledge (many chicks perish in some years); falling water levels allowing predators access to colonies; and rising water flooding the nests. ■

Recognition 2.5m wingspan; black and white; pink bill and pouch; yellow eye-ring.
Habitat Most water bodies.
Behaviour Usually in flocks; soar in V-shaped formations. Chicks form crèches.
Breeding 2–3 white eggs laid on rough platform on ground.
Feeding Mainly fish. Sometimes hunts cooperatively.
Voice Sometimes grunts.

Hotspots
Coorong NP, Lake Eyre NP, The Lakes NP

SEABIRDS

All at sea

Many birds feed at sea, but a large group of species that spend most of their lives far from land earns the title of 'seabirds'. Some 80 species have been recorded in Australian waters and there is no better place in the world for birdwatchers to get to grips with this challenging group. Among them are the largest of flying birds, the albatrosses; some of the most abundant, the storm-petrels; and some of the greatest travellers, the long-distance migratory shearwaters.

Red-tailed tropicbirds are best seen at breeding sites, such as Lady Elliott Island.

Seabirds are characterised by a special tube-like growth above the bill through which salt is secreted ('tubenoses' is an alternative name), enabling them to spend weeks or even months at sea without drinking freshwater. Seabirds also have legendary powers of flight, and most have long, narrow wings that maximise their gliding efficiency – there are few sights more graceful than an albatross effortlessly cruising down the wind.

Landlubbers should watch from headlands during 'albatross weather', when winter gales strike the southern coasts. Black-browed albatrosses and other species are then regularly seen inshore and may even be seen feeding on dead cuttlefish. Another group of seabirds usually feeds in continental waters – and therefore can often be seen from shore; it includes the Australasian gannet, and its various, mainly tropical, relatives, the boobies, frigatebirds and tropicbirds.

*Although the **Australasian gannet** breeds on islands it is readily seen from shore.*

Gannets are often seen just beyond the breakers along the southern coast, plunge-diving from as high as 20m, wings folded back along the body, to capture fish several metres below the surface. Boobies, such as the brown booby (inset), and frigatebirds can usually be seen by taking a Barrier Reef cruise. Frigatebirds force other birds, such as terns, to disgorge their catch then snatch it before it hits the water. Frigatebirds and tropicbirds can also be seen on breeding islands.

*The **darter**, also called the snakebird, swims with only its head and neck above water.*

Most cormorants, the darter and Australian pelican are members of the seabird group that spend most or all of their lives in freshwater. Although other cormorants visit coastal waters and build nests of seaweed on coastal cliffs, black-faced cormorants are Australia's only exclusively marine cormorant. ■

*Male **lesser frigatebirds** inflate their throat pouch to attract females to a nest site.*

> **Hotspots**
> **Great Ocean Road** Albatrosses and other seabirds often close inshore. **Great Barrier Reef** Boobies, frigatebirds and tropicbirds easily seen on breeding islands. **Lord Howe Island** Close encounters with breeding tropicbirds, boobies and shearwaters.

LITTLE PENGUIN

Penguins in the spotlight

Although it resembles other penguins in general appearance, the little penguin (or 'fairy penguin') is the world's smallest and the only one coloured blue. Several other penguin species that breed on subantarctic islands regularly come ashore on southern coasts to moult, but the little penguin is the only one that breeds in Australia. All penguins have highly specialised feathers – thick, insulating and waterproof; feed by pursuing prey underwater; and, like other seabirds, excrete excess salt. But the little penguin is the only penguin that occupies burrows, to which it returns at night after fishing trips.

Little penguins can occasionally be seen by day, swimming close inshore or further out at sea, but the show is more reliable and spectacular at a nesting colony. There are several colonies – most famously at Phillip Island, near Melbourne – with regulated viewings of the penguins leaving the surf and moving up the beach in small groups

Shared parental duties

While one parent incubates the other goes to sea for up to 10 days, the changing shift accompanied by much braying as the birds greet each other in the burrow. Once the chicks hatch, the parents return each night to satisfy their growing appetites. Feeding is messy: partially digested fish is regurgitated into the chick's mouth. By the time the young leave the burrow the parents will have lost considerable weight because of the strain of parental care.

Once rid of their offspring, adults go to sea for a six-week stint before returning fat and ready to moult. The mainstay of the little penguin's diet is bait fish; in some years low stocks – possibly because of overfishing – result in poor breeding success. In recent years unexplained mass die-offs of pilchards have severely affected some little penguin populations. ■

Recognition Small (40cm) blue, blue-grey or almost black penguin with white underparts and cheeks; bill black, feet pink.

Habitat Temperate continental seas including bays and harbours. Breeds on dunes, offshore islands and rocky cliffs.

Behaviour Most nocturnal penguin, usually seen in daylight only when swimming with head and bill raised; 'flies' underwater by flapping flippers. Moulting birds are unable to maintain their waterproofing and must fast onshore.

Breeding 2 eggs laid July–November in burrow or cavity under rocks or vegetation.

Feeding Feeds on small schooling fish, squid and crustaceans. Catches prey by diving and snatching it underwater.

Voice Yaps both at sea and on land; also various growls and braying on land.

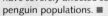

Hotspots
Phillip Island, Bruny Island, Kangaroo Island

HERONS AND EGRETS

Pied herons are common on tropical lagoons. Only the elusive little bittern is smaller.

The largest of the white egrets, the *great egret* develops showy wing plumes when breeding.

Living on the edge

The herons, egrets and bitterns are a cosmopolitan family distinguished by long legs, toes and necks, and dagger-shaped bills. Australia's 15 species range in size from the 30cm little bittern of reed beds to the great-billed heron, standing 1.5m high, of tropical mangroves. The name egret is used for several all-white species that can be difficult to tell apart – bill and leg colour are clues. Most bitterns are solitary, well-camouflaged inhabitants of dense reed beds, although the black bittern is an elusive exception that also lives in rainforest. All species hunt fish, frogs, rodents and other small animals. The long neck can be folded in a tight S-shape (and is invariably held thus in flight), and strikes with speed and accuracy to grab – or sometimes harpoon – prey.

Most species typically feed while standing at water margins, although striated herons sometimes snap up tadpoles and insects from an overhanging perch. At least one representative of the family utilises every aquatic habitat, including mudflats and mangroves; several species can feed side by side without direct competition – identifying the specialisation of each can be absorbing. All hunt by standing stock-still for long periods before striking; other techniques include running, stirring mud with their feet or flapping their

wings to startle prey. The nankeen night heron is nocturnal and cattle egrets snap up insects disturbed by livestock. In a reversal of the usual trend, cattle egrets introduced themselves to Australia and now range across the continent. Eastern reef egrets hunt primarily along the tideline and two colour varieties, slate grey and pure white, live side by side and apparently interbreed.

During courtship several species of egret and heron grow long, plumes, and patches of bare facial skin become intensely coloured (inset: cattle egret). Usually silent, herons often make guttural territorial calls at the nest – most species nest communally and heronries can be noisy places. Most species also roost communally, flying sometimes great distances in V-shaped flocks at dusk.

The closley related ibises and spoonbills hunt by feeling for prey – ibises probing with their bills and spoonbills sweeping their bills from side to side. Unlike herons and egrets, they fly with their necks extended. ■

Roosting in trees by day, the *nankeen night heron* emerges at dusk to hunt.

Straw-necked ibis commonly congregate in flocks with other species to feed in paddocks.

Hotspots

Kakadu NP Up to 11 species, especially concentrated at waterholes during the Dry. **Daintree NP** Breeding great-billed herons, Australia's largest, plus the black bittern. **Great Barrier Reef** Both colour phases of the eastern reef egret.

BIRDS OF PREY

Sibling rivalry

Birds of prey, or raptors, can be found in all terrestrial habitats. Their bills and talons are obvious features, adapted to hunting and a carnivorous diet. Most are especially visible when hunting and are often seen patrolling near roads. Goshawks (inset: brown goshawk) use stealth to surprise small birds and can be difficult to see, but nankeen kestrels, brown falcons and black-shouldered kites perch conspicuously on poles and dead trees, or hover over grasslands; harriers quarter fields at near-stalling speed and drop onto prey; and eagles may be seen soaring high on thermals. In arid areas, raptors are often found near water where trees are available for nesting, and because water attracts prey.

Along most of the coastline the primarily fish-eating raptors (osprey, brahminy kite and white-bellied sea-eagle) are easily seen; and rainforests are home to the Pacific baza, a crested hawk that plucks insects and frogs from the foliage. Apart from the cosmopolitan peregrine falcon, other spectacular bird-killing falcons include the grey falcon of the inland and the immensely powerful black falcon. Black kites gather in large numbers at unsavoury locations, such as abattoirs and rubbish tips. Fires also attract kites and falcons that feed on fleeing animals and freshly roasted insects. In wheat-farming areas small raptors will gather around grain silos because they attract mice. When mice reach plague proportions, birds such as letter-winged kites go into feeding and breeding overdrive.

All raptors, whether they lay just two eggs or as many as five, start incubating as soon as the first egg is laid. This means that the eggs hatch asynchronously, resulting in a disparity in the size of the young. Naturally aggressive, the oldest chick eats its fill before allowing younger birds to feed. The availability of prey is thus a major factor in determining just how many chicks will fledge. If prey is plentiful the appetite of the older chicks may be satiated long enough to allow their younger siblings to feed. If not, the growth of the oldest chick quickly outstrips that of later-hatched young, which eventually perish, often to be eaten by big brother or sister. In species that lay only two eggs the younger chick is almost always systematically attacked and killed unless prey is exceptionally abundant. ■

Ospreys feed primarily on fish and can be seen around most of the mainland coastline.

This juvenile **black-shouldered kite** will moult into pristine grey, black and white plumage.

The inland **black-breasted buzzard** has the unusual habit of breaking eggs with a rock.

Whistling kites are widespread scavengers and hunters; look for them along highways.

Hotspots
Kakadu NP High diversity of species easily seen; rare red goshawk present. **Bundjalung NP** Coastal species easily seen. **Townsville** High diversity of raptors in surrounding habitats.

WHITE-BELLIED SEA-EAGLE

Recognition Large (2m wing-span) white raptor with slate-grey back, wings and rump; grey bill, and yellow legs and feet. Tail wedge-shaped.

Habitat Coastal waters, estuaries and lagoons, extending inland along large rivers, lakes and swamps; sometimes far from land or sea.

Behaviour Usually seen singly or in pairs. Follows dolphin pods and also hunts over land, sometimes following farm machinery; recorded attacking a seal to rob its catch. Prey eaten in flight or taken to perch.

Breeding 1–2 eggs laid in a substantial stick nest in a tree or on a cliff near water.

Feeding Fish a staple, but also takes reptiles, birds and mammals. Robs birds and eats carrion, including fish, whales and seals.

Voice Far-carrying, 'goose-like' honking, and yelps.

> **Hotspots**
> **Fraser Island, Kakadu NP, Bundjalung NP**

Consummate fish hunter

The white-bellied sea-eagle is the largest of three primarily fish-eating raptors that coexist along tropical and subtropical Australian coasts. The others, the osprey and brahminy kite, are not as widespread in Australia, but all three are distributed across South-East Asia and the osprey is almost cosmopolitan. Its pure-white head and neck glowing in sunlight, the sea-eagle is conspicuous whether patrolling the beach on broad wings or sitting quietly on an exposed branch scanning for a prospective catch.

An opportunistic carnivore, the hunt is skilled and graceful. Sometimes apparently flying into the sun so its shadow won't give it away, the bird swoops in a long, fast glide and at the last moment throws forward its huge, hooked talons to grasp the prey. Fish, eels, turtles and seasnakes basking just beneath the surface are common targets and, once hooked, few victims get away. The sea-eagle's long, bare legs ensure feathers don't get waterlogged or matted with gore, although sea-eagles sometimes almost submerge when striking. Aloft again, the birds sometimes juggle large fish in their talons so that they point forwards, thus reducing drag in flight.

Cartwheels in the sky

And they are not averse to a bit of piracy: sea-eagles will harass other birds, including gulls, gannets and other raptors, until they regurgitate their catch; recalcitrants may become victims themselves. Sea-eagles often take fruit-bats and large chicks from their nests, and are known to hunt waterbirds such as coots by harassing them until they tire, then striking.

Sea-eagles pair for life and often use the same nest year after year. Nests and young are vigorously defended against potential predators, and a nest that has been disturbed will normally be deserted in subsequent seasons. Courtship is a spectacular display in which members of a pair chase each other through the air, mimicking each other's movements and from up high, joining talons to cartwheel in a free fall before breaking apart to climb and repeat the performance. ∎

WEDGE-TAILED EAGLE

A versatile predator

Wedge-tailed eagles are most often seen soaring near Outback highways where there's a chance of a roadkill to pick over. Groups of a dozen or more sometimes gather at a large kill, although it is rare for more than two to feed at once.

When seen perched on a kangaroo carcass, a wedgie's true size becomes apparent. But Australia's largest predatory bird can just as comfortably kill its own food – that includes the largest and fastest kangaroos, with pairs or groups of eagles cooperating to bring down such large prey. Wedgies pursue and kill other birds, and drive mammals down steep slopes to injure them; sick or injured sheep also fall prey, which once led to their persecution by farmers; and eagles follow tractors, cattle and even dogs in search of flushed prey. However, their main food in many areas is now the introduced rabbit.

Roller coaster ride

High densities of rabbits can support a number of breeding pairs in a relatively small area and, ironically, the introduction of this pest has probably allowed the eagle's population to rise. Australia is fortunate that such a large raptor remains abundant, although the long-term effects of rabbit control, such as the spread of calicivirus, on eagles and other large birds of prey remain to be seen – they may well plummet.

The effortless soaring is deceptive. While power and speed is evident when hunting, the flying ability of wedge-tailed eagles is also showcased in spectacular aerial courtship displays: males execute a series of stoops and climbs while calling to the female, who occasionally turns on her back in flight and presents her claws. Their huge nests are often built in trees commanding a wide view of the area; in arid areas where tall trees are scarce, the accumulations of sticks may be built at head height or even on the ground. Nests are used repeatedly and added to each breeding season, sometimes by successive generations – they can measure up to 2m wide and 3m deep. ∎

Recognition Huge raptor (2.5m wingspan) with long, diamond-shaped tail; completely black or dark brown with black flight feathers and tail; strongly feathered 'trousers'.

Habitat Widespread from forested mountains to open plains and desert; most common in open habitat.

Behaviour Often seen soaring at great heights singly or in pairs. Pairs mate for life and defend a large home range. Hunt mostly at dawn and dusk, spending much of the day soaring or perched.

Breeding 1–3 eggs laid in a huge stick nest, usually June–August; only one chick normally survives.

Feeding Carnivorous, feeding on vertebrates, especially rabbits and hares, but also large lizards, birds (often taken in flight), macropods, sheep and carrion.

Voice Usually silent; repeated whistle *seet-you, seet-you* near nest.

Hotspots
Flinders Ranges NP, Nullarbor NP, Sturt NP

BLACK-NECKED STORK

Stately but deadly

Arguably Australia's most striking waterbird, the black-necked stork features prominently in tourist promotions across the tropics. Commonly called the 'jabiru' (a name popularly thought to be of Aboriginal origin, it is actually a South American Indian name for a similar stork species), it is Australia's only member of the stork family and a favourite of nature photographers.

Spending much time standing quietly in water, when hunting the black-necked stork strides purposefully, occasionally sweeping its heavy, 30cm-long bill through the shallows. Prey is caught with a sudden forward thrust of the bill and swallowed with a backward flip of the head – a writhing eel wrapped around the bill sometimes complicating the process. Occasionally, in more open areas such as estuaries, jabirus prance around with wings spread as they pursue fish – putting on a surprising burst of speed when necessary.

Showers at the nest

Not unexpectedly for such a large bird, black-necked storks occur at low population densities and are usually solitary or sometimes in pairs (sexes can be told apart by eye colour – females have yellow eyes, males black). They usually share wetlands with many smaller waterbirds, and an abundance of fish trapped in a drying pond may attract a number of stork families to feast on this short-lived bonanza. Even in these situations individuals hunt independently.

Although mostly foraging alone, black-necked storks form long-term pair bonds and partners may come together at night to roost on the ground at the edge of wetlands. The large stick nests of black-necked storks are often conspicuously placed in a large tree, sometimes as high as 25m but also low over water in large wetlands, and generally well away from disturbance. Both parents incubate and care for the young. Once the young are about one month old they are left unattended in the nest, although on hot days the parents regurgitate water over them for a welcome drink and cooling shower. ■

Recognition Very large (1.4m tall) with heavy, black bill and long red legs. Superficially black-and-white, but head and neck iridescent green-blue.

Habitat Waterways, including swamps, floodplains, lakes, river estuaries and mudflats; also sometimes on adjoining land.

Behaviour Usually seen singly or in pairs, groups may form at times. Both sexes build nest, incubate eggs and feed young. Flies with head and neck extended, shape and colouration giving a gaunt 'skeletal' look.

Breeding 2–4 eggs laid in a large stick nest used for many years in succession.

Feeding Snaps up fish (especially eels), large insects, crustaceans, molluscs, frogs, reptiles such as water pythons, and occasionally small mammals.

Voice Usually silent; bill-clappering at the nest.

Hotspots
Kakadu NP, Lakefield NP, The Kimberley

BROLGA

Ballet on the plains

Aboriginal folklore tells of a dancer who rejected the attentions of a magician. Spurned, he changed her into a crane, which to this day can be seen gracefully dancing on the plains.

Although more common during the breeding season, when it is an integral part of courtship, dancing maintains the pair bond and can be seen at any time of year. Pairs shake their spread wings, bowing and bobbing their heads while throwing grass and other items into the air. Throwing their heads back and trumpeting wildly, they step forward then back, occasionally leaping into the air and floating back to the ground on outstretched wings. It is a stately spectacle and indigenous Australians aren't the only people to hold the crane family in awe. All crane species dance, and worldwide are protected and respected as symbols of longevity and fidelity.

Flocks of thousands

Pairs mate for life, and brolgas nest during the wet season in the extensive shallow wetlands that develop after heavy rains. The nests are generally mounds of vegetation in shallow water built high enough to ensure the eggs remain dry, although they are also built on dry land, in which case they are often no more than a few pieces of stick and grass. The plentiful sedge tubers and insects found in shallow wetlands provide ample food for the adults and two chicks, as well as cover for the young when threatened. Brolga chicks are covered in soft, grey down and can leave the nest a day or two after hatching, hiding and remaining motionless when danger threatens.

During the drier months large flocks, some numbering thousands of birds, may form at dwindling wetlands where they dig in the drying mud for their favourite tubers. In some areas flocks make themselves unpopular by feeding in fields, causing damage to newly planted crops. Australia's other crane species, the very similar sarus crane, has pink legs and more extensive red on the neck; mixed flocks sometimes occur. ■

Recognition 125cm tall; upright stance. Soft grey overall with black wing tips; bare red skin on head and dewlap.

Habitat Shallow wetlands, floodplains, grassland, farmland, ploughed fields and even Outback towns.

Behaviour Feeds by walking slowly with head down, snapping up insects and digging for tubers. Flies with neck and legs outstretched. Adults perform broken-wing display to distract predators from the nest. A flock of 12,000 was once recorded.

Breeding 2 eggs laid early spring (south) or early Wet (north); both sexes incubate.

Feeding Omnivorous; chiefly seeds, including cereal crops, shoots, tubers and insects; also small vertebrates.

Voice A far-carrying, exuberant, trumpeting *kawee-kreee-kurr-kurr-kurr-kurr*; pairs call in unison.

Hotspots
Townsville Common, Atherton Tableland, Mary River NP

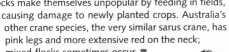

*Like most migratory waders, **great knots** are easier to identify in breeding plumage.*

***Pied oystercatchers** can be seen on sandy beaches along almost the entire coastline.*

***Inland dotterels** are very well-camouflaged where they nest in the open in stony deserts.*

SHOREBIRDS

Tied to the tides

A clan of gregarious birds known collectively as shorebirds, or waders, exploits the rich food resources in the zone between land and sea – a world ruled by the continual ebb and flow of the tides. Spreading across intertidal mudflats at low tide, many species can feed side by side because each employs a different technique. Plovers hunt by sight, taking items from the surface, while red-necked stints rapidly jab their bill into the mud. Curlew sandpipers probe the mud while the longer-billed godwits reach even deeper; and the large eastern curlew (inset) can probe further than any other – to a depth of 20cm.

As the tide rises, waders retreat to quiet beaches, saltmarshes and mangroves to roost and await the next ebb. Roosting flocks often contain thousands of birds and 20 or more species. Sorting through the flocks to identify each species often presents a challenge to even the most experienced birdwatcher. A few species, such as the red-kneed dotterel and banded stilt, are usually found on inland waters; fewer still, such as the Australian pratincole and inland dotterel, have abandoned life by the water almost completely.

But most shorebirds, especially the sandpipers, godwits and stints, visit Australia only during the austral summer, returning between April and August to their breeding grounds in the high latitudes of Mongolia, Siberia and Alaska. As summer days shorten, they start to eat virtually round the clock, some birds doubling their body weight and putting on enough fat to sustain them through the migration on which they are about to embark.

These long-distance migrations have become famous: as autumn advances, immense flocks in freshly grown breeding plumage gather in Australia's north. Their restlessness is obvious: flocks chatter and occasionally rise into the air only to settle again; a small group might break away, gaining height and calling, until suddenly many more will rise and join them as they head purposefully northwards. The

journey is completed in stages, but as much as 5,000km is covered nonstop to mainland Asia and a total of 10,000km is travelled each way – an astonishing journey for a red-necked stint weighing all of 25g. ∎

*The strident kek-kek-kek of the widespread **masked lapwing** is often heard at night.*

> **Hotspots**
> **The Kimberley** Immense flocks of many species assemble at Roebuck Bay. **Coorong NP** Large numbers of small shorebirds. **Cairns Esplanade** High diversity of species easily seen.

COMB-CRESTED JACANA

Role reversal

A bird that walks on water. Or so it seems – the jacana's weight is evenly spread on long, splayed toes that enable it to walk across floating vegetation. Its progress often pushes lilies under the surface, completing the illusion and earning it the folk name 'Jesus Christ bird'. Female jacanas are larger than males and each defends a territory from other females during the breeding season. Within this territory are a number of smaller territories belonging to males; the female mates with each, then leaves him to incubate the eggs and raise a brood of chicks on his own. Should the males enter into territorial disputes, the female quickly intervenes.

The flimsy floating platform that passes for a nest is often waterlogged and eggs are regularly rolled through the water to drier sites. Chicks, looking like balls of fluff on outsize legs and feet, can walk soon after hatching and follow the father around on their floating universe. When danger threatens he tucks the chicks under his wings and transports them to safety, but in a tight spot they have a trick of their own – jumping into the water and remaining submerged until the coast is clear. ∎

Recognition Brown back; black nape and breast; white underparts; orange-red comb.
Habitat Freshwater wetlands.
Behaviour Aggressive when breeding; at other times can be gregarious.
Breeding 3–4 eggs are incubated 28 days by the male.
Feeding Seeds, water plants, insects and larvae.
Voice High *pee-pee-pee*.

Hotspots
The Kimberley, Fogg Dam CR, Townsville

BUSH STONE-CURLEW

The nocturnal wailer

The eerie, wailing calls of the bush stone-curlew are a common night sound in northern Australia. Calls coming from a dark and unfamiliar bush caused consternation among early European settlers and stories about fearsome creatures known as bunyips seemed credible. And with a habit of frequenting cemeteries stone-curlews can still scare those taking a short cut at night. Their large eyes, often sleepily hooded by day, are adapted for hunting insects and other small animals at night.

The bush stone-curlew has disappeared from much of southern Australia where farming has destroyed its habitat; the introduced European fox has also contributed to the decline of this ground-nesting bird. Even though they are common in the parks of northern cities, finding stone-curlews requires a keen eye. Their plumage offers almost perfect camouflage amid dead timber and dry grass, and they often freeze or slowly slink away; they sometimes lie flat on the ground to avoid detection. However, when their young are threatened, parents spread their wings and run hissing at the intruder.

Another species, the beach stone-curlew, is a boldly marked inhabitant of tropical beaches and mudflats, where it catches crustaceans with its large, chisel-like bill. ∎

Recognition 55cm; long legs; yellow eyes; brown streaked upperparts, whitish below.
Habitat Woodland, scrub, and, in north, urban parks.
Behaviour Stands or sits among timber during day. May flock when not breeding.
Breeding 2 eggs laid on ground; incubated 25 days.
Feeding Mainly invertebrates.
Voice Mournful *wer-loooo*.

Hotspots
Townsville, Elsey NP, Litchfield NP

*The widespread **buff-banded rail** is resident and easily seen on some Barrier Reef islands.*

*The **purple swamphen** is the largest Australian rail and common on many waterways.*

*Distinguish the **dusky moorhen** from swamphens by sooty-black (not blue) plumage.*

CRAKES AND RAILS

The bold and the secretive

Although the crakes and rails make up one of the most widespread bird families, many of Australia's 14 species are often cautious and secretive, and are among the most elusive of birds.

The three exceptions to this rule, the purple swamphen, dusky moorhen and Eurasian coot, are common and familiar inhabitants of urban parks; they are also among the largest members of the family. But some of their smaller relatives have been the bane of many a birdwatcher's life. Often the only signs of their presence are unfamiliar clicks, trills and chattering deep in the reeds; and these quick-moving skulkers are usually first seen flashing across exposed patches of mud. It's all a matter of finding the correct place, conditions and time – and then several species can appear together in abundance.

When drying swamps expose mud around reed beds in the south-east and south-west, spotless, Baillon's (inset) and Australian spotted crakes will feed in the open (especially on overcast days), searching the mud for molluscs, insects and tender shoots. In the tropics white-browed crakes will forage in the open among floating water lilies, as long as noise and movement are kept to a minimum. Taking secretiveness to extremes, the Lewin's rail is rarely seen, despite probably being quite common. Its presence is usually revealed by characteristic clicking calls (not unlike tapping two coins together) and can be attracted by imitating this call, although it rarely ventures from cover.

In contrast, large social groups of dusky moorhens and purple swamphens are often animated and noisy, giving a complex array of signals relating to territorial disputes (both to threaten and appease opponents), group socialisation and mating. One of their more obvious displays is tail-flicking, which flashes the contrasting white undertail feathers. Tail-flicking may alert other birds to danger, as well as signal to a potential predator that it has been detected. Some moorhens, such as young birds and those retreating from a fight, tail-flick more often than others – this suggests that tail-flicking is also an indicator of social status, with the dominant and more confident birds flicking less. ■

Hotspots

Coorong NP Small, cryptic species may be seen when water levels have fallen. **Julatten** Normally secretive, rainforest-dwelling bush-hen and red-necked crake quite easily seen. **Maria Island NP** Tasmanian native-hens common.

*Look for the **Tasmanian native-hen** in paddocks and coastal flats, where it is common.*

GULLS AND TERNS

Maintaining the pecking order

The silver gull is one of Australia's most familiar coastal birds and a seaside picnic usually attracts a crowd. The 'seagull' was always widespread, but today's birds have taken to life in the cities, where they compete with pigeons for hand-outs in city parks, attend sporting fixtures and roost on factory roofs – a messy habit which has led wildlife authorities to use trained falcons to discourage them. Highly gregarious and quarrelsome, the social skills of the silver gull are constantly tested. A pecking order is maintained with a complex series of postures and calls. Dominant birds often stand upright with neck stretched, plumage ruffled and head and bill turned downward, calling occasionally. It might be followed by a strong upward arching of the neck with much calling, or a lowering of the head and downward arching of the neck while uttering a soft purr. These threats are often all that is needed to force a retreat from lower-ranked birds, which respond by hunching forward and low, keeping their bill pointed down. The other two gulls – the Pacific and kelp gulls – are much larger, similar in appearance to each other, and inhabit southern coasts.

*The ubiquitous **silver gull** is a common sight in coastal areas, although it also breeds inland.*

Less familiar but more diverse are the gulls close relatives, the 21 species of tern – best described as slender gulls with pointed wings, forked tails and, often, black caps. The large crested tern

is by far the commonest and a familiar sight in all harbours, estuaries and beaches. It frequently roosts with gulls and makes a useful yardstick when trying to identify other terns. Several terns, such as the sooty tern, are largely pelagic and return to land only to breed; another, the whiskered tern, is mostly found on inland waters. Noddies are mainly tropical terns and, in a negative image of their cousins, have a dark body and silver cap. Most gulls, terns and noddies are gregarious and usually nest in colonies on islands, although little and fairy terns often nest on mainland beaches. Silver gull colonies can contain tens of thousands of birds, and those of sooty terns, some of which are on popular Barrier Reef islands (inset), can hold more than 100,000 pairs – with a corresponding noise level. Courting male and female terns fly in zigzag unison above the colony, such ritualised displays helping to identify mated pairs. ■

Crested tern *at the nest. Tern chicks are precocious and can walk soon after hatching.*

Roseate terns *are found around tropical coasts. In flight the typically forked tail is visible.*

Black noddies *feed at sea and nest on tropical cays in sometimes huge colonies.*

Hotspots

Great Barrier Reef Breeding colonies of tropical terns on many islands. **Coorong NP** Large numbers of terns, with three species breeding. **The Lakes NP** Many species, including little and fairy terns – Australia's two smallest.

PIGEONS AND DOVES

Powerful flight, powerful thirst

White-headed pigeons are large fruit-eaters common in rainforests along the east coast.

*Watch for the **emerald dove** feeding on the rainforest floor in northern and eastern coastal areas.*

*The **common bronzewing** is common and the most widespread of Australian pigeons.*

The large and cosmopolitan family that includes pigeons and doves is well represented in Australia. Among the 24 recorded native species (a further three have been introduced) are several colourful fruit-doves of tropical rainforests, plus many unique and distinctive inland-dwelling forms. The forests and woodlands of eastern and northern Australia support the greatest diversity, but wherever there is water at least one species can be found in any part of the continent.

A regular supply of drinking water is essential to pigeons and they will fly considerable distances to drink daily. Unlike most other birds, pigeons drink by immersing their bill into the water and sucking, which reduces the time that they might otherwise be exposed to potential predators. During hot weather, particularly in the north, large numbers may be seen landing near waterholes in the late afternoon then cautiously walking to the water's edge (watch for lines of partridge pigeons doing this in Kakadu NP).

Strong flight is one of the survival secrets of this widespread family; ground-dwelling species are notorious for bursting into flight almost at the feet of an observer and should a predator grab one it will often end up with nothing more than several loose feathers. Several species engage in display flights when courting, or fly in large flocks between roosts and feeding areas. Pied imperial-pigeons migrate long distances from islands of the south-west Pacific to breed on Australian tropical coasts during the Wet. And most nomadic of all is the flock bronzewing, which wanders the Outback in vast flocks searching for suitable feeding and breeding habitat. Most pigeons also have a short 'turnaround time' for breeding, dispensing with all but the minimum of nesting materials and raising fast-growing young.

But sometimes not even these traits guarantee survival. In a sad parallel of the fate of the North American passenger pigeon, flocks of the flock bronzewing once regularly comprised tens of thousands of birds (those of the passenger pigeon numbered, incredibly, in the millions); now flocks rarely number more than a few hundred. Hunting, introduced animals and land-use changes have taken a massive toll. Thankfully the flock bronzewing has survived – unlike the passenger pigeon – and is now secure.

Glowing colours that blend in

The first Europeans often referred to pigeons in this country. In 1606 the crew of the Portuguese explorer Torres was the first to

*Spilled grain attracts small flocks of **crested pigeons** along roads over most of inland Australia.*

Coo are you?

The calls of pigeons and doves are probably one the most widely recognised of all bird calls. Variations on the simple and familiar 'coo' sound form the

basis of most calls uttered by this group. For example, the common bronzewing utters a single coo while the rose-crowned fruit-dove strings together a series. Wonga pigeons pitch their coos high while white-headed pigeons prefer them low. The pied imperial-pigeon forces its coo out almost as a bellow, in contrast to the hoot of the banded fruit-dove. And the diamond dove has a soft and gentle coo while the wompoo fruit-dove can deliver a guttural shout. But whether the end result is an *oom*, *cook-a-wook*, *hoo-hoo-hoo-hoo-hoo-hoo* or *wallock-a-woo*, it serves the same functions – advertising territories and for mates.

Spinifex pigeons inhabit sandstone outcrops and tend to run rather than fly.

describe an Australian bird, the pied imperial-pigeon; in the 17th century Dutch explorers recorded bronzewings along the coast of Western Australia; Dampier's crew ate well on small plump 'turtle-doves' in 1688; and James Cook's crew feasted on the large topknot pigeon while stranded in north Queensland. But although a significant part of Australia's birdlife, several species can be difficult to see. For example, the calls of the brilliantly coloured fruit-doves can be conspicuous (inset opposite: wompoo fruit-dove), but the birds themselves blend into the greens of the foliage and often feed high in the canopy. The trick is to locate the source of the calls – listen for fruit falling from where the birds are feeding then carefully search the canopy for movement (you can avoid a strained neck by lying on your back and looking up, although it's not advisable if leeches are present!). You can also grab better views by watching for pigeons sunning themselves on exposed branches in the early morning; winging above the forest canopy; or by taking to a canopy walkway such as those at Dorrigo and Lamington NPs.

The many and varied species of the inland are a bit easier to see, although the rich brown and reddish tones of desert pigeons also make them blend in beautifully. The ochre red of the spinifex pigeon perfectly matches the Outback's sand, while the more sombre greys of the common bronzewing and crested pigeon are offset with iridescent wing mirrors that shine in the sun. ■

*The **peaceful dove's** doodle-oo call is a haunting and familiar bush sound.*

*The **wompoo fruit-dove's** wallock-a-woo is a giveaway when it skulks in foliage.*

Hotspots

Lamington NP High diversity of rainforest pigeons and canopy walkway. **Daintree NP** Various rainforest pigeons plus spectacular flights of pied imperial-pigeons. **Watarrka NP** (Kings Canyon) Desert pigeons including the spinifex pigeon.

Pied imperial-pigeons migrate in their thousands of to northern coastal rainforests in summer.

Restricted to Cape York, male **palm cockatoos** *use tools to proclaim their territory.*

The **red-tailed black-cockatoo***, the largest black-cockatoo, can be seen throughout the tropics.*

Gang-gang cockatoos are easily located in south-eastern forests by their creaking call.

COCKATOOS

Knocking on wood

Noisy and gregarious, most cockatoos are common and hard to overlook. Australia is the centre of cockatoo evolution, with 14 species found here – of which 11 are endemic. There are two distinct groups. The so-called black-cockatoos are large, black birds that essentially inhabit moister forests; the five species feature splashes of red, yellow or white on the head and tail. Other cockatoos are mostly white and/or pink, and tend to occur in more open, drier habitats. The anomalous cockatiel looks more like a 'conventional' parrot but has the signatory crest of its larger cockatoo relatives.

Naturally there are some exceptions to these generalisations. For example, red-tailed black-cockatoos are widespread in tropical woodland and parts of the inland; and in the wet forests of the south-east lives the gang-gang, a cockatoo whose steely-grey plumage and, in the male, red head and crest, don't quite fit either category. However, all cockatoos (except the cockatiel) are large-bodied, slow-flying birds with a powerful, hooked bill and an erectile crest, often in a colour that contrasts with their general colouration.

Variations in bill shape reflect differences in diet: the elongated bill of the long-billed corella (inset) is used to dig up bulbs while the palm cockatoo uses its massive bill to crack open palm nuts and extract the contents. The palm cockatoo is perhaps the most extraordinary cockatoo of all: it is one of the few animals known to make and use tools. Sitting atop a broken trunk, the male drums on the bark with a grevillea nut or a specially trimmed twig, making a noise that can sometimes be heard from 100m away. This behaviour probably serves to maintain the pair bond as well as advertise territory. Like other species, it also has a distinctive call and cockatoos are among the noisiest birds of the bush: flocks of red-tailed black-cockatoos wing their way across the landscape with a 'creaking gate' sound; sulphur-crested cockatoos make a deafening screeching; and the various corellas make a turkey-like gobbling.

Sociable creatures

Cockatoos are highly social and flocks can form containing thousands of birds. In some species, flocks disperse at the start of the breeding season, but in others they are maintained throughout the year. All cockatoos require tree hollows in which to nest, although their size dictates the suitability of a site; the logging of old-growth forests has caused the disappearance of many suitable trees and may have a detrimental long-term effect on some

Playing the galah

While most cockatoos are content to sit quietly chewing in a shady tree, galahs and corellas (inset: little corellas) seem to have too much energy to let an opportunity to enjoy life pass them by. Flocks are frequently seen swinging upside-down from telegraph wires and television antennas. Sliding down tensioned support

wires is another favourite activity, while in rural areas the slowly rotating blades of windmills often can't be ignored, the birds alighting on a blade until they are tipped off their Ferris wheel – only to fly up again for another ride. Flocks have been seen to fly deliberately and repeatedly into a 'willy-willy' (a whirlwind of dust),

swirling around the vortex before being slung out. And galahs have even been seen sliding on their backs down a slide in a children's playground. No wonder the phrase 'playing the galah', meaning to act the fool, has entered the vernacular.

So common as to be taken for granted, the **galah** is nonetheless a striking bird.

species of black-cockatoo. The black-cockatoos usually lay one or two eggs; the young remain in the nest for three months and are fed by the parents for a further four months. The smaller galah lays as many as five eggs; after fledging, galahs leave their young in a crèche some distance from the nest. All adult cockatoos feed their young by locking bills with a chick and regurgitating food into its bill with a jerking movement. Large groups of young galahs can become quite noisy because of the constant loud begging of fledglings, which goes on even while their parents are actually feeding them.

Little corellas form huge flocks recognisable from a distance by their turkeylike gobbling.

Compulsive communicators

Cockatoo social displays can be raucous affairs. Every morning before flying to their feeding trees, palm cockatoos gather in groups and give shrill-whistled greetings accompanied by displays in which they lunge upside-down on their perches, wings spread and crest erect. The distinctive crests of all cockatoos are used in communication whenever the birds are excited or alarmed; for example, the colourful crest of the Major Mitchell's cockatoo is fanned when a mate is greeted; in aggressive encounters; and to signify ownership of a nest site. Cockatoos are also renowned for piercing calls, which are likely to convey information including the caller's identity and whereabouts, or the appearance of a threat such as a wedge-tailed eagle – which may then be mobbed by the flock. When feeding on the ground, flocks of some cockatoos, especially sulphur-crested cockatoos are popularly supposed to station sentinels in tall trees to watch for danger. ■

Their exquisite markings make the **Major Mitchell's cockatoo** a prized sight in the inland.

Hotspots

Blue Mountains NP High diversity of cockatoos, many easily seen. **Keep River NP** Large flocks of red-tailed black-cockatoos. **MacDonnell Ranges NP** Desert cockatoos easily seen.

The **cockatiel** looks like no other cockatoo (except for the crest), but is a common inland bird.

SULPHUR-CRESTED COCKATOO

Blue cockatoos

The sulphur-crested cockatoo is one of Australia's most wide-spread birds. An often accomplished mimic when hand raised, cockies kept by publicans sometimes pass into folk-lore owing to some colourful language learnt over a lifetime that can span many decades. In the wild these birds are often found along timbered watercourses, which flocks favour as roost sites. At sunrise they depart with much screeching and, after drinking, fly often long distances to a feeding area.

Of an evening the flocks return and, after a drink, again assemble in a frenzy of screeching and jockeying for position in the crowded trees. The screeching continues until well after dark. Such behaviour can readily be appreciated at many camping grounds, where the tall trees, open spaces and nearby water that attract campers also make for ideal roost sites.

Town and country cockies

During the day, flocks feed on the ground searching for seeds or digging for bulbs. There are many anecdotal accounts that a few birds will remain perched high in nearby trees watching for danger. A screech from these 'sentinels' alerts the entire flock, sending it screeching into the air; but there is little hard evidence that these sentinels are any more than birds having a rest.

During the middle of the day the flock rests perched in cool trees, chewing bark and nibbling leaves; flowering eucalypts seem to be particularly favoured when available and undoubtedly supplement the diet – the ground beneath these trees soon becomes littered with sprigs of leaves and blossom. The sulphur-crested cockatoo is becoming increasingly common in urban areas, where it is likely that wild populations are augmented with escaped (or released) pets. Some flocks have taken up the unpopular habit of chewing on wooden balconies, doors and window frames in their idle hours.

Sulphur-cresteds often associate with other white species, such as corellas, and white goshawks sometimes fly among flocks. ∎

Recognition Large and completely white plumage except fanlike, yellow crest. Under-wings and undertail washed pale yellow; grey or dark grey bill, legs and feet.

Habitat Rainforest, forest and woodland, farmland, timbered watercourses in arid areas, and parks and gardens.

Behaviour Noisy and conspicuous, in pairs and small groups to large flocks. Often seen feeding in association with other cockatoos on grain spilt along roadsides. Mobs predators, including people, raptors, large lizards and snakes.

Breeding 2–3 eggs laid in a large tree hollow are incubated 30 days by both sexes.

Feeding Mainly seeds, such as from grasses, but also fruit, flowers, roots and insect larvae. A pest of commercial grain and oilseed crops.

Voice Harsh, raucous screech while perched or in flight.

Hotspots
Mutawintji NP, Royal NP, Grampians NP

RAINBOW LORIKEET

A colourful native holds its own

One of the most brilliantly coloured of Australia's birds, and featured heavily in tourist promotions, the rainbow lorikeet is so abundant and common that it is almost taken for granted by residents of the east coast. Never scarce, in recent decades it has proliferated in urban areas because of the increased planting of Australian native shrubs and trees; and its pugnacious nature ensures it holds its own against introduced birds, such as common mynas, that compete for nest hollows.

Rainbow lorikeets can easily be seen in even the largest coastal towns and cities; at Currumbin in south-east Queensland hundreds of rainbow and scaly-breasted lorikeets are fed daily by tourists at a wildlife park. A distinct form of the rainbow lorikeet inhabits northern Australia and the Top End – it is sometimes known as the red-collared lorikeet because of its most obvious plumage difference.

Noisy blossom feeders

Rainbow lorikeets do nothing quietly and wherever they occur are hard to overlook, advertising their presence with constant screeching and chattering. Flocks often leave trees in which they are feeding to wheel around noisily before settling again. The noise of feeding birds often attracts other lorikeets flying overhead and consequently large numbers sometimes gather. In the late afternoon, flocks gather at communal roosting sites (vast numbers assemble in the centre of Cairns), pairs and individuals coming and going with much quarrelling and jostling for position – the din doesn't subside until well after dark.

Pollen and nectar are the principle components of lorikeets' diet and are harvested with a large, rounded tongue equipped with brushlike hairs. Because lorikeets rely on flowering plants they tend to be nomadic, wandering in search of resources. In some areas they feed on ripening apples and pears, and cause damage in orchards. When feeding on fermented fruit they can become intoxicated and roll about drunkenly on the ground.

Several other lorikeet species inhabit the drier eucalypt woodlands, sometimes feeding together in mixed flocks. ■

Recognition Brilliant colours: bright green back and tail; blue head and belly; breast fiery orange or red; eyes and bill scarlet.

Habitat Coastal rainforest and woodland, particularly where trees are flowering; common in some urban areas.

Behaviour Noisy and conspicuous flocks are generally seen flying swiftly overhead or feeding in flowering shrubs and trees. Stops feeding to preen or idly strip leaves during the heat of the day. Interbreeds with scaly breasted lorikeet.

Breeding 2–3 eggs laid in a tree hollow are incubated for 23 days; chicks fledge at 60 days.

Feeding Pollen and nectar of flowering trees and shrubs; also raids orchards, vineyards and flower gardens.

Voice Noisy: a sharp rolling screech while perched or flying; also a shrill chattering while feeding.

Hotspots
Jervis Bay NP, Royal NP, Litchfield NP (red-collared subspecies)

PARROTS

*The **varied lorikeet** feeds and travels in noisy flocks throughout tropical woodlands.*

*Smallest of the lorikeets, a red face is diagnostic of the **little lorikeet** of eastern woodlands.*

*The **purple-crowned lorikeet** of drier southern woodlands often feeds with other small lorikeets.*

Terra Psittacorum

With 39 of the world's 180 or so species of parrot (plus the various closely related cockatoos) found in Australia, it's not surprising this continent was called *Terra Psittacorum* – the Land of Parrots – by early naturalists. Only South America can match such diversity and not a corner of Australia, or any terrestrial habitat, is without parrots. Some, such as the budgerigar, can be found throughout most of the continent while others, such the eclectus and red-capped parrots, have very restricted ranges.

Parrots are the quintessential arboreal birds, roosting, feeding and nesting in trees. Their feet are arranged with two toes pointing backwards and two forwards, thus enabling them to grasp food and climb with great agility, sometimes assisted by their powerful, hooked bill. But as with all rules there are exceptions, and in Australia evolution has led these conspicuous and often bold birds down some unusual byways. Ground-dwelling, migratory and nocturnal parrots have all evolved: the ground parrot, an inhabitant of thick button-grass heathland, is usually seen only when unwittingly flushed by walkers; the endangered orange-bellied parrot, whose population numbers only 100 or so birds, migrates from Tasmania to spend winter on the mainland; and the elusiveness of the night parrot of the far inland has given it an almost mythical reputation among birdwatchers.

Australian parrots fall into several distinct groups. The six species of lorikeet are noisy, fast-flying jewels that feed on nectar and pollen with their brushlike tongues. These nomadic birds are found in coastal and subcoastal forests, and common species include the rainbow, purple-crowned and musk lorikeets (inset). Rosellas also number six species and are among the most familiar of Australian birds, commonly visiting parks and gardens. The 'grass-parrots' of the genus *Neophema* are among the smallest – and most exquisite – Australian parrots; outstanding examples include the turquoise and scarlet-chested parrots. Anomalous groups include the equally spectacular (and common) red-winged and king-parrots.

Urban life and other traits

Many species have adapted well to life in urban areas, the biggest factor limiting the survival of many being the lack of hollows in which to nest. Rainbow and musk lorikeets feed on nectar in trees flowering in urban streets, while crimson rosellas visit gardens to feast on the fruit and seeds of shrubs. Some species, notably red-rumped parrots and eastern rosellas, thrive in neglected parklands; and even the endangered superb parrot,

*Male (left) and female **eclectus parrots** from the rainforests of Cape York.*

*The **Australian king-parrot** is a striking inhabitant of eastern wet forests and rainforests.*

which normally inhabits riverine woodland, can regularly be found in country towns within its limited distribution.

Most parrots nest in hollows or cavities; boxes placed high in trees are often utilised while some birds are more innovative, or desperate, nesting in cavities in the walls of buildings. They are equally creative with natural resources: besides tree hollows, they will lay their eggs in burrows, rock crevices, vegetation and on the ground. Some, like hooded and golden-shouldered parrots, excavate tunnels in termite mounds. Often the nests are unlined, although tree hollow nests may be carpeted with woodchips chewed from inside the cavity; varied lorikeets sometimes add chewed leaves. Females incubate the eggs and males feed them while they sit. Most young hatch within 23 days, and are naked and awkward until they grow their plumage.

*You'll probably need to look no further than a city park for the **eastern rosella**.*

Parrots and cockatoos are the only birds that routinely use their feet to hold and manipulate their food, although a few other birds may pull food toward themselves. Cockatoos are almost invariably left-footed, in the same way that most humans are right-handed (having a preference indicates greater specialisation of each half of the brain), but with parrots 'footedness' isn't so clear cut and many are ambidextrous. Many individuals favour one foot ahead of the other; rosellas, for example, tend to use their right foot far more than their left, but even then some individuals are clearly left-footed. Parrot-watching is nearly always entertaining, but watching for an individual's footedness is an added dimension. ■

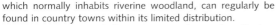

*The **red-rumped parrot** is an unobtrusive ground-feeding species of the south-east.*

👓 Hotspots
Warrumbungle NP Parrots of the east coast meet parrots of the inland. **MacDonnell Ranges NP** Desert parrots amid spectacular scenery. **Coffin Bay NP** Good place to see several species of grass-parrot.

*Most brilliant of grass-parrots, the **scarlet-chested parrot** is a bird of the remote inland.*

CRIMSON ROSELLA

Recognition Crimson overall with blue 'cheeks', wings and tail; black scalloping on back. Immatures dull green with crimson undertail, forehead, face and breast.

Habitat Rainforest, wet eucalypt forest and woodland to above the snowline in summer; gullies, urban parks and gardens.

Behaviour Probably mates for life. Rests in foliage of trees during heat of day. A large group has been recorded mobbing a southern boobook owl, but possums, bees and introduced birds may oust rosellas from nest hollows.

Breeding 4–6 eggs laid in a tree hollow September–January; chicks incubated 20 days by female only.

Feeding A wide variety of seeds, buds, blossom, nectar, fruit and nuts, taken from the ground or foliage; also insects and larvae.

Voice Mellow, piping or bell-like *kwik-kweek*; contact call in flight is *cussik-cussik*.

Hotspots
Blue Mountains NP, **Dandenong Ranges NP**, **Hattah-Kulkyne NP** (yellow subspecies)

Bold beauty

Among Australian parrots, at least, beauty does not necessarily equate rarity, and the crimson rosella is both striking and abundant. It invariably attracts attention in leafy suburbs of major cities such as Canberra, Melbourne and Sydney, but is most spectacular when seen among the tree ferns and other greenery of the rainforest. In many forest picnic areas crimson rosellas have become very tame and are easily approached; bold individuals that have overcome their fear of humans can be fed by hand. Adult crimson rosellas are usually seen in pairs or small groups, but larger flocks of the dull-green immatures form after the breeding season, wandering locally in search of food.

Crimson rosellas eat a wide range of fruit and seeds, and may gather in large numbers to feed on the berries of introduced *Cotoneaster*, *Pyracantha* and hawthorn. At times they can make a nuisance of themselves by raiding orchards, although the damage caused is probably offset by the amount of weed seeds, particularly from thistles, they consume. Nonetheless, they remain unpopular with some orchardists.

Variations on a theme

In the river red gum forests along the Murray River is a rosella with all the blue markings of a crimson rosella but otherwise coloured yellow instead of red. Similarly, around Adelaide another version ranges in colour from soft orange-yellow to orange-red. The yellow and Adelaide rosellas, as they were previously known, are now recognised as subspecies of the crimson rosella, and these isolated, relict populations are probably a legacy of a drying Australian continent. Only around Albury, on the NSW–Victoria border, do two subspecies come into contact, and the young produced by crimson–yellow rosella matings look similar to the Adelaide rosella. The name 'rosella' is peculiar to Australia; it was probably derived from Rose Hill, a suburb of Sydney where these birds were common.

Crimson rosellas sometimes fight with other parrots over nest holes, and are themselves attacked by aggressive, territorial species such as wattlebirds and magpies. ∎

BUDGERIGAR

Abundant nomad that follows the rain

The budgie is the most popular caged bird in the world, familiar to millions of people, and in the domestic environment has been bred into an astonishing range of colours. However, the wild budgerigar is a native of Australia and bears only a superficial resemblance to its tame counterpart. Smaller and sleeker, the ancestral budgerigar is normally available only in one colour – bright green.

Even though found across the inland, predicting where wild budgerigars can be seen with any certainty is difficult. Epitomising the true nomad, flocks wander widely in search of seeding grasses. Rainfall is one of the key factors controlling their lives: they are rarely seen more than a few kilometres from water, and rain often precedes the arrival of flocks into Outback areas where they may have been absent for years.

Pet-shop noise

Inland rain will often trigger breeding, particularly if it falls in spring. The birds become even more animated than usual, forming pairs and commencing courtship feeding; mating may take place within days of rain. Breeding is often in colonies and a number of pairs may occupy hollows in a single branch. Young budgerigars can be sexually mature within two months of leaving the nest, so in good seasons immense flocks can form. During prolonged droughts flocks will move to the periphery of their range and may even be found in coastal regions. Budgerigars are usually heard well before they are seen; large flocks in particular are characterised by an incessant 'pet-shop' warbling and chattering.

A flock of budgerigars is an impressive sight, whether they are feeding among seeding grasses, resting quietly in a tree in the middle of the day or wheeling in tightly co-ordinated twists and turns. Early in the morning and then again late in the afternoon, the flocks travel to waterholes to drink. When a large flock gathers to drink, all available space at the water's edge may be occupied, so birds will alight on the surface to drink quickly while floating. ■

Recognition Small (20cm); bright yellow-green with yellow head, face and back; finely barred black on head, nape, back and wings.

Habitat Drier areas, particularly lightly timbered grassland, shrubland with plentiful grass, spinifex, woodland and timbered watercourses.

Behaviour Generally in noisy and conspicuous flocks that may number thousands of birds. Visits water early and late in the day. Flight is swift and flocks often fly erratically but remain a tight unit.

Breeding 4–6 eggs laid in small tree hollow in August–December, or opportunistically after rain.

Feeding Eats small grass seeds almost exclusively. Gathers seeds from ground but also from standing heads.

Voice Musical chattering and scolding while feeding; incessant warbling often given in flight.

> **Hotspots**
> **Uluru–Kata Tjuta NP, Connells Lagoon CR, Mungo NP**

NIGHTBIRDS

Hoots, barks and falling bombs

Owls, nightjars and frogmouths are nocturnal hunters characterised by highly sensitive eyesight, excellent hearing and specialised feathers that allow silent flight. Otherwise, however, their features are very different. Owls are similar to diurnal birds of prey, with a hooked bill, strong feet and talons; frogmouths and nightjars are strong fliers that take insects on the wing. A total of nine owl species breed in Australia, split fairly evenly between the so-called barn owls and hawk owls.

The largest predator in tropical rainforests, the **rufous owl** *commonly preys on fruit-bats.*

Owls the world over have a prominent place in folklore, but few Australian owls sound like their northern equivalents. One that vaguely does is the powerful owl, the largest of the Australian hawk owls. Powerful owls require a huge territory to ensure an adequate supply of possums as food. In the tropics the powerful owl is replaced by the rufous owl, the biggest nocturnal predator of the rainforest. The calls of the southern boobook (Australia's smallest owl) and barking owl definitely do not sound like other owls: the boobook sounds like it is written and is one of the signatory night sounds of the bush; the most common call of the barking owl is a two-syllable doglike yapping, although it also utters a blood-curdling scream. The five members of the barn owl group are characterised by feathers which form a disk on their face (inset: grass owl), thereby funneling sound into their ears. The call of sooty owls sounds like a falling bomb.

The **southern boobook's** *two-note call is a common night sound throughout Australia.*

Similar to the barn owl, the **masked owl** *is widespread but often difficult to find.*

Hearing an owl is one thing, but finding one is quite another. They are sometimes seen sitting quietly among dense foliage during the day, where they are sometimes mobbed by small birds. And barking owls not infrequently call during the day, enabling them to be tracked down and sighted. But by far the best method of 'owling' is patient spotlighting. Nightjars are perhaps even more difficult to see, although they are common in suitable habitat. Unlike owls, their legs and feet are relatively weak and nightjars roost and nest on the ground, where their camouflage renders them almost invisible. The owlet-nightjar is another variation, looking like a cross between a small owl and a nightjar – there's always a chance of spotting one peering out of a tree hollow during the day. ■

The only cosmopolitan owl, the **barn owl** *is found right across the continent in more open habitats.*

> ### Hotspots
> **Yarra Ranges NP** A variety of common forest owls. **Julatten** Several owl species, including the barking and lesser sooty, plus the Papuan frogmouth. **Border Ranges NP** Large forest owls common, plus the marbled frogmouth.

TAWNY FROGMOUTH

Mistaken identity

One of Australia's most common nocturnal birds is often incorrectly referred to as an owl; it actually belongs to an only vaguely related group, the frogmouths. The tawny frogmouth is familiar to many people because of its habit of roosting on large, exposed branches, but it is frequently confused with the southern boobook (an owl), because the latter's *mopoke* call is so commonly heard. Frogmouths in fact sound completely different: a low, pulsating, resonant *oom-oom-oom* that can continue for over half an hour. Both males and females call, most often in the hours just after sunset and before sunrise, and mostly in the spring–summer breeding season.

Frogmouths have weak legs and feet and take their prey from the ground by scooping it into their wide, shovel-like bills. They are superbly camouflaged, roosting in a stiff, upright posture that imitates a broken branch; when approached they smooth down their feathers to accentuate their wooden appearance and watch the intruder through narrowed eyes.

Tawny territory

The call probably mostly functions in warning others off the territory. The smallish territories are most likely permanent; moreover, they often return to the same roost day after day. Members of a pair often roost side by side; if you find one perched alone, its partner is likely to be quite nearby. After dark, frogmouths start to hunt by dropping onto prey from a perch, flying to a new vantage point at regular intervals. Many tawny frogmouths are hit by cars when they hunt around roadside lights, and are among the birds most commonly rehabilitated by wildlife care groups.

From a young age, the downy young also adopt the classic upright posture when disturbed, but when pressed, open their mouths widely, revealing a bird that seems almost all bill. Two other frogmouths – the marbled and Papuan – are restricted to tropical and subtropical rainforest; like the tawny frogmouth they are superbly camouflaged. ■

Recognition Medium-sized (40cm) with large head, broad bill and upright posture. Grey or brownish with subtle camouflage markings; large yellow eyes.

Habitat Forest and woodland with open areas; also tree-lined watercourses, mallee, parks and gardens.

Behaviour Nocturnal; uses habitual roosts. Pairs form permanent bonds, share nesting duties and typically roost in a row with young. Young are covered in fluffy down and snap at intruders – showing bright yellow bill lining.

Breeding 1–3 eggs are laid August–November on flimsy platform of sticks; incubated 29 days.

Feeding Large insects, mostly taken from the ground, but also moths at streetlights, molluscs, crustaceans, frogs and occasionally small mammals.

Voice Monotonous, soft *ooo* repeated for several minutes at a time.

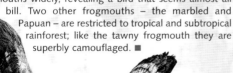

Hotspots
Brisbane Ranges NP, **Royal NP, Carnarvon NP**

Buff-breasted paradise-kingfishers migrate to the Wet Tropics in summer to nest.

KINGFISHERS AND A BEE-EATER

Eat to the beat

Nearly all kingfishers and the closely related rainbow bee-eater are brightly coloured, and all are voracious predators of insects and other small animals. Flocks of rainbow bee-eaters are animated affairs with much musical trilling and aerial acrobatics as they pursue flying insects – largely bees, wasps and other potentially dangerous sorts. Prey is caught with the tip of the bill, and upon landing is bashed against the perch with a sound that may be audible from several metres away. If the prey is a bee or wasp, the bee-eater, with eyes closed, rubs it against the branch to discharge the sting and venom. Often there is one more beating before the insect is tossed back and swallowed.

Australia's 10 species of kingfisher include one of the world's largest – the laughing kookaburra – and one of the smallest – the little kingfisher. Many kingfishers also beat their prey to death against a perch, although they are generally sedentary hunters that sit for long periods then drop onto insects, reptiles and small mammals on the ground. However, two – the little and azure kingfishers – dive into water after tadpoles, crustaceans and small fish. This behaviour is learned, rather than innate, and young 'fishing' kingfishers learn by experience how to judge depth and distance. But diving is not without its dangers: the feathers of kingfishers are not waterproof and many young birds drown. Most kingfishers are usually easy to locate, and many advertise their territories with far-carrying calls. More difficult to observe are those which inhabit heavily vegetated streams, and the little kingfisher is one of the species most sought-after by birdwatchers. The beautiful azure kingfisher (inset) is somewhat easier to see along the streams of the east coast, although first views are often just a flash of rich colour.

All kingfishers and bee-eaters nest in holes and their short legs are ideally suited to moving about in narrow spaces. Bee-eaters and some kingfishers excavate tunnels in earthen banks, while others use tree hollows. One exception is the spectacular buff-breasted paradise-kingfisher, a wet season migrant that digs nest chambers into termite mounds that litter the rainforest floor. ■

Forest kingfishers are common in woodlands of eastern and northern Australia.

The sacred kingfisher, widespread except inland, can be recognised by buff underparts.

Migratory in southern Australia, rainbow bee-eaters are resident in the tropics.

Hotspots

Kakadu NP Bee-eaters and seven species of kingfisher easily seen. **Daintree NP** Rainforest species, including the migratory buff-breasted paradise-kingfisher. **Uluru–Kata Tjuta NP** Home of the desert-dwelling red-backed kingfisher.

KOOKABURRAS

≡ *Blue-winged*

▇ *Laughing*

Setting the boundaries

The call of the laughing kookaburra is one of the most distinctive and common sounds of the Australian bush – around just about any picnic ground within forests of the east and northern coast there will be a resident group or two. The boisterous laugh is most often heard at dawn and serves to reinforce a group's territorial boundaries. Usually one bird will start with a rapid, rolling *kook-kook-kook* from a prominent perch; as other birds in a group join in the chorus becomes louder and wilder, eventually dying down to a few final chuckles.

The closely related blue-winged kookaburra of the tropics (main photo) has an even more raucous, although less laughterlike, call. In both species, calls by one group are often answered by those in adjoining territories. Group dynamics are important to the success of a kookaburra clan. Breeding pairs are apparently monogamous and capable of rearing young, but a pair is often assisted by other residents of their territory, who are invariably offspring from earlier broods.

No laughing matter

The chicks hatch asynchronously; the older, more aggressive, chicks are fed first and attack younger siblings, with the result that the last hatched often die. As the best habitat is generally already occupied, individuals must wait until there's a vacancy in a neighbouring group before leaving home. There are usually more male than female helpers because females tend to find breeding vacancies more readily than males. The dominant pair quickly attack any helpers that initiate calling – they are probably a threat to their dominance. As breeding approaches, the dominant male shadows the female, guarding her from the attentions of helper males – but sometimes they slip through his guard and sneak a clandestine mating.

Kookaburras are famous for eating snakes, but old photos of kookaburras holding large specimens should probably be treated with scepticism – such large reptiles were probably fed to the birds by the photographer. ∎

Recognition Large (45cm), stout-billed kingfisher. Brown upperparts with a russet, black-striped tail; brown-streaked head and white underparts; dark patch behind eyes; and silver-blue 'shoulders' (blue-winged is slightly smaller with more extensive blue on wings and rump; a striped crown and no eyepatch; males have blue tail).

Habitat Open forest and woodland.

Behaviour Generally hunts alone but close to family group. Perches like a typical kingfisher, pouncing on prey from a conspicuous perch. Laughing call given with head thrown back while flicking tail. Often becomes tame in picnic grounds.

Breeding 1–5, usually 3, eggs laid in a tree hollow September–January; incubated by all group members.

Feeding Large invertebrates (insects, worms, crustaceans and snails) and small vertebrates, such as frogs, fish, reptiles, birds and rodents.

Voice Distinctive, loud and far-carrying 'laughter', often in a group chorus.

Hotspots
Grampians NP, Royal NP (laughing); **Kakadu NP** (blue-winged)

NOISY PITTA

Recognition Bright green above with turquoise 'shoulders'; black head and throat with chestnut crown; underparts buff with crimson vent and black central stripe.

Habitat Tropical and subtropical rainforest, adjacent scrub and sometimes gardens.

Behaviour Usually solitary but sometimes in pairs. Vocal in spring and summer, often calling at night. Bounds quickly along ground; usually flies only a short distance, flashing white 'windows' in wings. Nest often built between tree roots.

Breeding 3–5 eggs are laid in a bulky domed twig nest with a side entrance.

Feeding Turns over leaf litter in search of invertebrates, particularly snails (which are cracked open on an anvil) and worms.

Voice Most commonly heard call is a loud and far-carrying *walk-to-work* whistle.

Pitta patter

Dumpy with a short tail – nothing to write home about so far, but add some vivid reds, blues and greens and you have the jewels of the rainforest, the pittas. You don't have to be a birdwatcher to get enthusiastic about pittas, but birders seek them out avidly and many are avowed 'pitta tickers'. Of the four species found in Australia, the noisy pitta is the most common and widespread, and in fact, probably the easiest pitta to see anywhere in the world. The red-bellied pitta is a wet season visitor; the rainbow pitta is endemic to the Top End; and the blue-winged pitta is a vagrant to the northwest. Pittas are largely ground-dwelling birds and even in full view their striking colours somehow blend in with the rotting leaves and dappled sunlight on the forest floor.

Knocking on wood

Sound is the trick to finding pittas and they are usually heard well before they are seen. Their distinctive whistle-like calls carry far through the forest and with a good imitation they often approach – whether territorial or simply curious. However, they can fly in quietly and still be difficult to locate among tangled vines and branches; or worse still, perch in the canopy where they are almost impossible to pick out silhouetted among the leaves. Listen for them scratching through fallen leaves and bounding across the ground when feeding; and there's another clue – a persistent knocking sound.

Snails are deemed irresistible by pittas and while getting to the soft bodies of large rainforest molluscs might pose a problem for most birds, pittas have a solution. Snails are picked up and transported to an anvil (usually a rock, but pieces of wood and even discarded beer bottles are used) where they are held by the rim while the spire of the shell is bashed until the bird can reach the flesh inside. Some anvils are worn smooth by generations of use and surrounded by piles of weathered snail shells. ■

Hotspots
Border Ranges NP, Atherton Tableland, Iron Range NP

SUPERB LYREBIRD

Bush symphonists

The two lyrebird species (Albert's and superb) are large (the world's largest songbirds), ground-feeding birds unique to Australia. Both are subtly coloured, but perform stunning displays and vocalisations. Male superbs, especially, perform an complex display to attract mates, often conducted from atop a mound of leaf litter that it scratches together. In display, the male's long tail, which usually trails behind, is thrown over the head, the broad, curved outer feathers forming the arms of a 'lyre' around a fan of quivering white filamentous feathers. Simultaneously, he mimics a series of the commoner sounds of the bush – black-cockatoos, kookaburras, rosellas, whipbirds and more – and blends them with his own rich buzzing and clicking calls into a symphony that can last up to 20 minutes.

The mimicry is perfect, but the game is given away by the stream of calls of multiple species; the rare imitations of barking dogs, chainsaws, and even camera motor-drives and flutes; and the distinctiveness of its own calls. Females also sing, but less often, less strongly and with less mimicry.

Dialects and repertoires

Lyrebirds sing at any time of the year but are heard much more often during the winter breeding season, at which time forested valleys can ring with the calls of several males. The superb lyrebird's sedentary nature has resulted in distinct song 'dialects' arising throughout its range. Young birds learn their song from nearby males, so birds within a particular valley will often structure their song in a similar way (lyrebirds introduced to Tasmania still mimic species found only on the mainland); should the next valley be out of earshot, lyrebirds there might have a slightly different repertoire.

Lyrebirds have very weak powers of flight, and with strong legs and large feet usually run from danger. Normally wary, lyrebirds are most often seen as they dart across a forest road, but in some parks individual birds become tame and they, and sometimes their displays, can be easily watched. ■

Recognition Large ground bird (1m long, including long tail); male has white, filamentous plumes. Upperparts dark brown with rufous wings; underparts grey-brown.

Habitat Dense eucalypt forest and rainforest, especially fern gullies; also in adjacent woodland and sometimes gardens.

Behaviour Generally solitary; males and females establish separate territories, females incubating and caring for the chick. Young males may sing outside breeding season. Keeps head still while raking through leaf litter, snatching morsels darting for cover.

Breeding A single egg laid May–October in large, domed nest of sticks on or above the ground.

Feeding Invertebrates, such as insects and their larvae, earthworms and crustaceans, exposed by raking over the leaf litter and soil.

Voice Expert mimicry during displays can contain up to 15 different sounds, interspersed with whistles and clicks.

Hotspots
Washpool NP, Royal NP, Dandenong Ranges NP

'WRENS'

*Few birds rival the brilliance of the male **splendid fairy-wren** of the inland.*

*The **variegated fairy-wren** ranges across the country in habitats from heaths to spinifex.*

White-winged fairy-wrens *nest among low shrubs across most of arid Australia.*

*The **striated grasswren** is one of 10 species of grasswren specialised to life in Australia's most arid areas.*

Fairies at the bottom of the garden

A varied group with a superficial resemblance to the wren of Europe includes the fairy-wrens, emu-wrens and grasswrens. Among them are some of Australia's most, and least, familiar birds; some with colouration to rival the parrots for brilliance. Nearly anywhere, including gardens, with an understorey of shrubs or other thick cover will be found at least one species (in places several live side by side). All share the habit of cocking their long tail. Male fairy-wrens and emu-wrens are richly coloured (females are predominantly brown – inset), with blue usually dominating (although the red-backed fairy-wren is attired in red and black). In contrast, the earthy tones and pale streaking of grasswrens help disguise them in spinifex tussocks.

Most wrens are inquisitive and respond to squeaking or 'pishing' noises by hopping through the vegetation to look at the intruder; if they are breeding they may also run along the ground, fluffed up and trailing their tail, in a terrific imitation of a mouse – this 'rodent run' display may distract potential predators from the nest or fledglings. White-winged and superb fairy-wrens show little fear and sit in the open, while others invariably keep some vegetation between them and the observer.

Several species of grasswren are distributed in inland areas. The isolation of some species makes them among the hardest of Australia's birds to see, and thus all the more attractive to hardcore birders. There are even tours that attempt to find all the grasswrens – an industry unlikely to run out of material in the near future, as re-examination of isolated populations has indicated that some are actually distinct species (such as the newly named short-tailed grasswren of the Flinders Ranges).

Wrens live in small family groups. It was long thought that male fairy-wrens established harems, as a coloured male is often seen with a group of brown birds. In fact, just one of these brown birds is the coloured male's mate; most of the others are male offspring from previous broods that have remained at home to assist their parents in raising young, and have moulted into a female-like eclipse plumage at the end of the breeding season. ■

Hotspots

Hattah-Kulkyne NP Three species of fairy-wren, an emu-wren and a grasswren. **Shark Bay MP** Black-and-white subspecies of the white-winged fairy-wren on Barrow Island plus the thick-billed grasswren. **Bundjalung NP** Three species of fairy-wren plus the southern emu-wren are all easily seen.

SUPERB FAIRY-WREN

Adultery and nepotism

One of the most familiar small birds of south-eastern Australia is the superb fairy-wren – often simply known as the 'blue wren'. Family parties of mousy-brown birds led by a brilliant male hop about with tails cocked, and during the breeding season loudly proclaim their territories from strategic points. It was once assumed that males tend a harem of females, but families actually consist of a breeding pair assisted in raising the young by offspring, usually 'uncoloured' males, from previous broods – breeding females drive off mature female offspring. Helpers share in the feeding of chicks and other duties, but this does not appear to increase the chicks' survival rate. It does, however, decrease the demands on the breeding pair, enabling them to nest again more rapidly – a useful strategy given that predation of nests is high and few broods survive to fledging.

Saying it with flowers

Having helpers may also free up the coloured male of a group for outside activities. Recent studies have shown that adultery is rife among breeding fairy-wrens. Coloured males seek out and mate with females in neighbouring territories, enticing them by performing displays involving the carrying of a yellow petal. Evidently it's a winning combination, because, in one study at least, more than two-thirds of superb fairy-wren offspring were sired by males outside the parental group. And it appears that it is males with helpers that are the most successful philanderers.

Why helpers help is more complex. It appears that they have nowhere else to go, as suitable habitat for new territories is in short supply. If they can't breed themselves it pays to stay home and assist their parents; as a bonus they remain on a safe territory, which they may one day inherit. But it is no free ride and helpers risk attack by the breeding male if they do not perform their share of duties. With the passing of summer, most coloured males moult into brown plumage (but always retain their blue tail), although a few, usually older birds, will moult directly back into their blue plumage. ∎

Recognition Breeding males bright blue with black saddle and rump, brown wings and white belly. Females and nonbreeding males brown with blue tail.

Habitat Low, dense cover near open areas in forest, woodland, heath, saltmarsh, parks and gardens.

Behaviour Usually seen in groups on or near the ground. Tail usually cocked, but held flat when birds flee in 'rodent run' along the ground. Breeding males and females pugnacious and attack their own reflections in shiny objects.

Breeding 3–4 eggs are laid in a well-hidden, domed nest in a low, dense shrub.

Feeding Feeds on invertebrates, such as insects, larvae and spiders, from on or near the ground.

Voice A rolling series of short high notes, accelerating to a gushing trill.

Hotspots
Wilsons Promontory NP, Asbestos Range NP, Royal NP

Little wattlebirds are very common when southern heathlands and woodlands are in flower.

Another common heath bird, the **spiny-cheeked honeyeater** *ranges from coast to coast.*

Big and bold, the **blue-faced honeyeater** *is common in eastern and tropical Australia.*

HONEYEATERS

'Sweet-toothed' birds

Parrots and cockatoos may decorate the Australian bush, but it is dominated by a diverse group of nectar-loving birds called honeyeaters. No matter where you are, at least one species appears on the local bird list and in some areas as many as 20 have been recorded. Among the 71 Australian species at least one occupies every terrestrial habitat; various forms include the large wattlebirds and friarbirds, the colonial miners, and the nomadic desert-dwelling chats.

Most honeyeaters are avid nectar feeders, although all species include insects in their diet and some consume large quantities of fruit. They are important pollinators of Australian plants – a role in which they perhaps rival even insects. Diagnostic features are a generally downcurved bill housing a long, flexible tongue with delicate brushlike structures, which gather the nectar as the bird probes blossoms. Honeyeaters and the flowers on which they feed have long co-evolved, with features such as the shape and colour of flowers adapted to attract certain

honeyeaters, and the shape and length of the birds' bills adapted to raid specific flower types. For example, red is more attractive to birds and thus most bird-pollinated flowers are red; and such plants produce far more nectar – to make it worthwhile for birds to visit – than typical insect-pollinated species. The eastern spinebill (inset) has an extremely long bill with which it extracts nectar from long tubular flowers inaccessible to other birds. And the completely bald head of the noisy friarbird allows it to feed on nectar-saturated blossoms without getting its feathers matted.

Some species are very mobile, their movements generally reflecting the flowering patterns of plants. The black honeyeater of the arid zone often arrives in an area as emu-bushes start to flower. Others cope with spasmodic periods of little or no flowering by switching to other sources of carbohydrate, such as lerp (a sugary, protective coating produced by sap-sucking psyllid insects), manna (a saplike substance exuded by trees) and honeydew (exuded by insects). Insects are also actively sought, either by searching through leaves and under bark or by hawking (snatching in flight).

The tinkling call of the tiny scarlet honeyeater is a common sound in the streets of east coast towns during spring; the brightly coloured males are well camouflaged while feeding among red *Callistemon* (bottlebrush) blossom. Most honeyeaters are much more subtly coloured in shades of grey, brown and olive, but a few, such as the dandy New Holland honeyeater, sport bold patterns of black and white with yellow highlights.

The distinctive call of the **bell miner** *is far easier to detect than the bird itself.*

Fighting for resources

Patches of flowering woodland in south-eastern Australia can attract as many as 15 different species of honeyeater, and hundreds of indivduals competing for nectar in a relatively small area. During times of heavy nectar flow there is relatively little conflict, because there is plenty of food to go around, but at other times competition can be fierce. Pugnacious by nature, honeyeaters spend an inordinate amount of time defending their patch. Flowering trees become a hive of activity as larger species, notably friarbirds and wattlebirds, attempt to exclude all comers from the best feeding areas. The smaller species are often forced to the perimeter of the patch, but at times species such as the white-naped, New Holland (inset) and yellow-faced honeyeaters swamp the trees. The larger species continue to chase these smaller invaders, but, for a while at least, individuals may feed in peace as the larger occupants busily chase others.

*Noisy and gregarious, the **yellow-throated miner** is abundant away from the east coast.*

The colonial mentality

While some honeyeater species typically nest in pairs, many, such as the blue-faced honeyeater, breed either cooperatively (a pair being helped by other birds, typically offspring from an earlier brood) or in colonies. The miners are very aggressive, chasing off as many other species as they can from their territories and mobbing predators (even people). Bell miners ('bellbirds') take colonial living to extremes: colonies defend territories to the exclusion of almost all other small birds, and 'farm' psyllid insects to 'harvest' the sugary lerp they produce.

*Staccato bursts give away **Lewin's honeyeater** in dense gullies and rainforests of the east coast.*

Honeyeaters generally build cup-shaped nests into which are laid two or three pinkish buff eggs. Some nests are easily located, for example, the large untidy bark nest of the noisy friarbird is suspended in outer foliage, but the nests of smaller honeyeaters are often well hidden in dense shrubs. Members of miner colonies are often related and assist each other in feeding young.

Chats are aberrant, ground-dwelling honeyeaters – often brilliantly coloured – that owe their name to a superficial resemblance to the 'true' chats of Eurasia. Chats are renowned for being highly nomadic, and mixed flocks of crimson, orange and white-fronted chats periodically appear in areas from which they have been absent for years. The yellow chat is the most localised species and much sought after by birdwatchers. ■

*Huge aggregations of **yellow-tufted honeyeaters** occur in flowering eucalypt woodlands.*

Hotspots

Chiltern Box-Ironbark NP A high diversity of species, including the endangered regent honeyeater. **Bundjalung NP** Very high densities of honeyeaters in coastal heathland during winter. **Eungella NP** Only location for the rare Eungella honeyeater.

*The golden-backed honeyeater is a race of the widespread **black-chinned honeyeater**.*

*The male **red-capped robin** is difficult to confuse with any other inland bird.*

***Flame robins** migrate from higher altitudes in winter and form loose feeding flocks.*

*Endemic to Tasmania, the **dusky robin** frequents forest edges and cleared country.*

*The **eastern yellow robin** is a bird of forests and gullies. The western species has a greyish breast.*

ROBINS

Same only different

Homesick British settlers erroneously deduced that the plump, red-breasted birds in the Australian bush were relatives of the familiar European robin. In fact, Australian robins are not related, and occupy niches filled by groups not widely represented in this country, such as thrushes, warblers and flycatchers. But like their namesake, most species wait on an exposed perch – often perching sideways on a trunk, holding their body parallel to the ground – and pounce on insects and other small animals.

A flash of red among the blackened trunks in a recently burnt eucalypt forest is likely to be a scarlet robin hunting for invertebrates exposed in the now-open understorey. In the mallee, scarlets are replaced by red-capped robins, perhaps the most striking species; in woodlands the hooded robin takes over; and in the tropical rainforest it is grey-headed robins. More active hunters include the lemon-bellied flycatcher of the tropics, which darts out to snatch insects in flight or beats through the foliage, picking prey off leaves; and the rose robin, which pursues insects through foliage. At the other end of the spectrum are the ground-dwelling, thrushlike scrub-robins, which toss aside leaves and other debris in their search for insects. Among the best known of forest birds are the three species of yellow robin: inquisitive and confiding, they make themselves known around picnic areas, even landing on tables in search of a handout.

Most robins are sedentary, but the flame robin is a notable exception: it moves out of the high forest country during winter to more open areas at lower altitude, where they congregate at sites with abundant food – they can be seen perched conspicuously on every available vantage point. A few robins build untidy bowl-shaped nests of twigs, but most species camouflage their nests by decorating the exterior. Strips of bark hanging horizontally are favoured by the eastern yellow robin (inset) while the nest of the rose robin is beautifully decorated with pieces of lichen. Robins often become foster parents when cuckoos lay an egg in their nest; once hatched, the alien chick pushes out its foster siblings so it alone is raised by the duped robins. ■

Hotspots
Hattah-Kulkyne NP Arid-country robins plus the southern scrub-robin. **Atherton Tableland** A number of rainforest robins easily observed. **Kakadu NP** Tropical robins along watercourses and in mangroves.

FANTAILS AND FLYCATCHERS

Bold, hyperactive and confiding

Flycatchers are small bush birds that busily hunt insects by gleaning, hawking and frenetic chases. Many species are boldly, rather than colourfully attired (although the yellow-breasted boatbill is a bright exception) and a handful of aptly named species in their own distinct subgroup – the fantails – attract attention by distinctively fanning their tail. The best-known fantail is the bold willie wagtail, a familiar garden bird which regularly builds its delicate, cobweb-bound nest close to houses and sheds. When breeding, willie wagtails become very pugnacious, taking on all comers and even harassing kookaburras, eagles and cats that pass through their territory. The acrobatics of another common species, the grey fantail, as it twists and turns through clouds of newly hatched insects, can't be matched. Bold and confiding, this species will often flutter and snatch insects swarming around the head of an observer.

The constant wagging of the tail isn't just a way of dissipating nervous energy. Even though all employ different feeding techniques – the rufous fantail actively searches through foliage, the

grey fantail chases prey and willie wagtails spend much time on the ground, pursuing prey by sight – fanning the tail often flushes insects and is probably more efficient than simply waiting for one to move. Other flycatchers are scarcely less frenetic. The restless flycatcher (inset) of open forests hovers 1m or so above the ground with tail fanned and wings quivering, all the time giving harsh rattles, rasps and grinding *churr*s – it was once believed that this display enticed worms from the ground.

The rainforests contain the greatest number of flycatchers, some of them among the more commonly encountered birds in this habitat. The pied monarch of north Queensland actively searches under loose bark and leaves, occasionally fluttering through the foliage to flush insects. But perhaps the most unusual flycatcher of all is comparatively large, highly vocal and almost magpie-like in appearance: a common urban inhabitant, the magpie-lark is a primarily ground-dwelling flycatcher, invariably seen in pairs that duet with a distinctive *pee-wit* call while half opening their wings. ∎

Hotspots
Lamington NP All of the southern rainforest flycatchers occur here. **Daintree NP** Rainforest flycatchers easily observed. **Roebuck Bay** Mangrove grey fantails and shining flycatchers.

The **yellow-breasted boatbill** of tropical rainforests actively chases insects from a perch.

The **magpie-lark** is a large, ground-feeding flycatcher that often associates with magpies.

Far less frenetic than other species, the **northern fantail** frequents tropical forest edges.

One of Australia's most widespread birds, the **willie wagtail** is common and approachable.

White-breasted woodswallows, found all over bar the south-west, often sit together on wires.

*The **black-faced woodswallow** hawks for insects in open country over most of Australia.*

*Although cryptic at times, the **grey butcherbird** is a common urban bird.*

WOODSWALLOWS, BUTCHERBIRDS AND CURRAWONGS

Melodious predators

The relatedness of the small woodswallows and the larger, mainly black-and-white butcherbirds and currawongs at first seems un-likely, but there's an obvious clue in that all have blueish bills with black tips. All are carnivorous, the woodswallows hawking for flying insects and the larger species taking a wide variety of prey, from insects to rodents and birds. Currawongs and, especially, butcherbirds have a prominent tip to their bills (inset: grey butcherbird), to assist in the tearing apart of prey. Despite their rapaciousness, currawongs can become quite tame and readily approach picnickers for handouts, while the Australian magpie readily adapts to urban areas and is a common sight in parks and gardens. Butcherbirds often skulk in dense foliage, where they ambush prey, although pied butcherbirds are conspicu-ous inhabitants of inland areas.

Magpies and butcherbirds are famous songsters, and there are few finer ways to be awak-ened than by the exquisite calls of the pied butcherbird at dawn. The loud calls of currawongs are also distinctive, particularly the piercing yodels of pied currawongs – listen for the strong differ-ences in regional dialects of this widespread eastern species.

Strong and graceful fliers, all six woodswallows are either nomadic or migratory birds of woodland and open plains; large chattering flocks often appear overnight in inland areas. Flocks may also be seen soaring in circles, feeding on flying insects or, where wingless grasshoppers are common, hopping about on the ground. Extremely gregarious, they often sit in rows along a branch, each bird touching its neighbour. When roosting at night, large huddles form in protected nooks such as under large branches or in tree cavities. Sometimes, for no obvious reason, the huddle will 'explode' with birds flying in all directions before settling once again – it is thought that other birds may use them as early warning systems. Nesting is usually colonial and flocks will cooperate with the defence of a threatened nest, mobbing potential predators such as currawongs and kookaburras. ■

*Usually found in treed areas on the eastern seaboard, **pied cur-rawongs** can become tame.*

> **Hotspots**
> **Mutawintji NP** Large flocks of inland woodswallow species at times. **Nitmiluk NP** Black-faced woodswallows associating with hooded parrots. **Cradle Mountain–Lake St Clair NP** Tasma-nia's endemic black currawong in abundance.

AUSTRALIAN MAGPIE

Morning caroller

A marvellous songster common in both urban and rural areas, the Australian magpie is among the most widespread and recognisable birds in the country. Its familiarity has made it a popular choice as a logo among sporting clubs – and its fierce reputation probably doesn't hurt the sporting image either. Australian magpies are not related to the 'true' magpies of the northern hemisphere (which are actually members of the crow family). Unlike its namesake, the Australian magpie is an adept songster with a melodious repertoire that is familiar to all Australians as part of the dawn chorus.

Magpies typically live in groups, in which the breeding pair and a number of helpers share in the feeding of nestlings and, importantly, the defence of their territory. Groups jealously guard territorial boundaries, as premium habitat is often in short supply and competition for it is fierce. Larger groups are at a distinct advantage because they can more effectively repel intruders and even manage to expand their empire should their neighbours prove unequal to the task. Magpies will also attempt to drive white-winged choughs, similar-sized ground feeders, from their patch.

An overdeveloped sense of duty

If all territories are at maximum carrying capacity, many young magpies are forced to live in large, nomadic flocks of nonbreeding birds. Such flocks often wander widely in areas lacking the vital prerequisite of a breeding territory – trees in which to nest – and are often seen feeding in newly ploughed paddocks.

During the breeding season a surge of hormones in some birds can result in the overzealous defence of the nest. Some pairs will attack anything they perceive to be a threat, including humans. Driving people from their territory seems to be more prevalent in urban areas, perhaps as magpies there have overcome their natural fear of humans. Attacks involve powerful, repeated swoops, which sometimes make contact and occasionally draw blood – waving your hands overhead is usually enough to prevent a direct strike. ∎

Recognition Robust with stout, pointed bill; white nape and 'shoulders'; subspecies vary from all-white back and tail to black back.

Habitat Almost anywhere with trees (except rainforest) adjoining open ground, including parks, gardens and golf courses.

Behaviour Usually seen in family groups, although large, nonbreeding flocks numbering hundreds can gather on paddocks. Flies swiftly and powerfully, driving other birds and magpies away. Groups compete with song. Can become tame around people.

Breeding 2–3 eggs laid July–December in an untidy stick nest, usually high in a tree.

Feeding Mainly eats insects and other invertebrates, occasionally small vertebrates. Takes prey mainly from the ground, probing soil for larvae.

Voice Loud flute-like warbling, usually at dawn; also a single *sheow*. Young call insistently when begging.

Hotspots
Wilsons Promontory NP (white-backed form), **Myall Lakes NP** (black-backed form), **Caranbirini CR** (Papuan form)

VICTORIA'S RIFLEBIRD

A spectacular display

Most birds of paradise are renowned for their vibrant plumage and courtship displays. Three species inhabiting the tropical and subtropical rainforests of the east coast are known as riflebirds – the males' colouration resembles the uniform of 19th-century British riflemen. Victoria's riflebird was named after a former Queen of Australia and is the most easily seen species. Victoria's riflebirds are comparatively sombre (for birds of paradise) – males are entirely velvet black, their plumage shot with iridescence (male paradise and magnificent riflebirds look very similar). But their displays are extraordinary.

Males display from prominent perches in response to the presence of a female: sunlight catches the iridescence of the fanned body plumes as the male throws his fully spread wings forward and downward until the tips meet over his head while the stiffened tail is cocked over the back. Slowly, then with increasing momentum, the body pivots backward and forward while each wing in turn is half closed then extended and the lowered head, bill open to show its bright yellow interior, moves from side to side within the arch of the wings. Displays often attract an excitable group of females and immature males in female-like plumage – the young males are probably learning the intricacies of courtship.

Recognition Male velvety black with long, down-curved bill; iridescent blue-green cap and gorget; 'oily' green belly. Females and immature males grey-brown above with buff underparts.

Habitat Mountain rainforest and adjoining foothills, gullies, wet forest and gardens.

Behaviour Usually seen singly or in pairs, although loose groups may gather in fruiting trees. Males perform on large limbs or an upright stump. Probe crevices for prey with long bill. Flight direct and undulating.

Breeding 2 eggs October–January in a nest well hidden in dense foliage. Young raised by female alone.

Feeding Omnivorous; rainforest fruit, sometimes held with foot and peeled, and insects, their larvae and spiders.

Voice Typically a loud, strident *yaa-aas*, often from a prominent perch.

Tea with the Queen

Riflebirds spend much time in the canopy, where they can be difficult to see – look for them searching for prey among ferns and orchids, spiralling up tree trunks and picking through suspended leaf litter. Listen for their harsh call and the distinctive paperlike rustling of their feathers as they fly, especially when they chase other birds from fruiting trees on which they are feeding. At several places in north Queensland, riflebirds – and various species of honeyeater – visit tea-houses adjoining rainforest for hand-outs. After searching the dimly lit rainforest canopy for this species it can be quite a thrill to share your Devonshire tea with a gloriously coloured male. ■

Hotspots
Paluma NP, Atherton Tableland, Daintree NP

BOWERBIRDS

Avian opera houses

Many birds have elaborate plumage and courtship displays to attract a mate, but some bowerbirds not only have brilliant colouration, they take courtship rituals to unrivalled lengths. Males of many species build and decorate elaborate structures of vegetation – bowers – to attract females, and to ensure their song and dance routines are appropriately accommodated.

Three types of bower are constructed by Australia's nine species of bowerbird (all but one of which are endemic). The most basic model, called a stage bower, is simply a cleared arena decorated with leaves a shade lighter than the surrounding vegetation. More complex are avenue bowers comprised of stems and twigs woven together vertically into two parallel walls with a cleared area at either end. Most species make avenue bowers, which can be highly decorated with odds and ends. Many bowerbirds also 'paint' the inner walls of the avenue with a mixture of saliva and vegetable matter, applied with the bill. However, none surpasses the maypole bowers made by the golden bowerbird. These amazing structures consist of a pair of slender trees about 1m apart, connected by a horizontal branch which serves as a display perch. Each upright support is piled with twigs into massive cones, which can stand 3m high.

The decorations used on bowers differ between species. Spotted and great bowerbirds accumulate piles of stones, shells, seeds and metallic objects. Satin bowerbirds will take just

about anything, as long as it is blue (inset): blue flowers, fruit and feathers are often supplemented by artificial items, such as blue straws, pens, clothes pegs and bottle tops; so strong are these preferences that should a red item be placed in his bower the male will quickly remove it. Golden bowerbirds augment their stately twin towers with less garish taste, using pale-green moss, pale-coloured flowers (often orchids) and fruits as decoration.

After mating, the female assumes all the responsibilities of nesting, including nest building, incubation and feeding the young. Female bowerbirds are usually secretive and the nests of many species are difficult to find. ∎

The male **regent bowerbird** *is one of the most spectacular of subtropical rainforest birds.*

Satin bowerbirds move out of rainforests into more open country when not breeding.

Female **satin bowerbirds** *show none of their mates' showy plumage or behaviour.*

The **great bowerbird***, common in tropical Australia, builds a typical avenue bower.*

Hotspots

Lamington NP The three southern rainforest species all easily seen here. **Atherton Tableland** Rainforest species endemic to the Wet Tropics, including the golden bowerbird. **Nitmiluk NP** Great bowerbirds frequently seen at their bowers.

*The **zebra finch's** nasal call is a common background noise in any inland setting.*

***Double-barred finches** are found in grassland and woodland near water in eastern and northern Australia.*

*A striking bird of the east coast, the **red-browed finch** calls with a high-pitched seet.*

***Painted finches** come to drink at waterholes late in the day in the arid inland.*

FINCHES

Colourful seed-eaters

The small, seed-eating Australian grass-finches are gregarious, engaging and often beautiful birds. The tropical woodlands and grasslands support the greatest diversity; two other species are adapted to the arid zone; two more are restricted to the cool southern heaths and forests; and the blue-faced parrot-finch inhabits tangles on rainforest edges.

Like most seed-eating birds, finches must drink regularly. As waterholes are haunts for predators and there is safety in numbers, drinking flocks are often large and sometimes contain a number of species. Once an individual has mustered the courage to approach the water, others quickly join it. Many of the dry-country species, such as the zebra and long-tailed finches (inset) and the diamond firetail, drink by suction, a trait which enables them to drink their fill quickly

at even the smallest puddle then retreat to safety. Finches inhabiting wetter coastal habitats tend to drink in a more conventional way, taking short, single sips.

All Australian finches build untidy domed nests of grass, often conspicuously, but inaccessibly, in spiny shrubs. Others hide them in grass or reeds, while Gouldian finches usually nest in small hollows in trees, sometimes dispensing with nesting material altogether. A few species occasionally nest colonially and several pairs of Gouldian finch, for example, may nest in the same hollow branch. Zebra finches are notable for often building their nests in the base of large eagles' nests and even in the cowling of stationary aircraft. Australian grass-finches probably mate for life and, once bonded, pairs are almost inseparable.

Courtship dancing is common and elaborate, and although displays differ slightly between species the same general pattern is followed. Displays commence with both birds hopping between branches with heads and tails twisted towards each other. This is followed by a song and dance routine by the male with, in some species, a length of grass used as a prop. The plumage is fluffed out and the male bounces up and down, singing as he does so. If the male has suitably impressed his mate she will invite him to mate by quivering her tail. ■

Hotspots

Gregory NP High diversity of tropical savannah species, including the endangered Gouldian finch. **Kakadu NP** Large numbers of tropical finches, particularly near waterholes during the Dry. **Warrumbungle NP** Southern and woodland finches common.

YELLOW-BELLIED SUNBIRD

Flower piercers

One of the most delightful birds of tropical Queensland is without doubt the yellow-bellied sunbird, Australia's only representative of this otherwise widespread family. This tiny, bright and engaging bird is common in parks and gardens throughout its range, and could otherwise be mistaken for a small honeyeater except for the male's brilliant iridescent throat. As brilliantly coloured as many Australian birds are, iridescence – in which colours change depending on the observer's position – is quite rare.

The sunbirds are at times referred to as hummingbirds because of their iridescence, but hummingbirds are entirely unrelated and don't occur in Australia. Extremely active, they often mix with honeyeaters as they dart among the foliage searching for insects and nectar-laden flowers. They hover in front of small flowers sipping nectar or at cobwebs, picking-off spiders. Nectar is even taken from blooms longer than their bill – by piercing the base of such flowers they can tap into a nectar source that would otherwise be beyond their reach.

Recognition Small (11cm) with long, down-curved bill. Olive above with yellow belly; male has iridescent blue-black throat and breast.
Habitat Woodlands, rainforest edges, vegetated watercourses, mangroves, orchards, parks and gardens.
Behaviour Usually alone or in pairs; occasionally in small flocks. Very active and often unafraid of humans, even entering buildings to build nests or hunt. Pulls apart large spiders while hovering in front of webs.
Breeding 2–3 eggs are laid in a suspended ball of fibre and bark, mainly August–March.
Feeding Mainly nectar-eating, but also takes insects, larvae, spiders and other invertebrates on flowers, by probing among foliage and in flight.
Voice Short, shrill *tsee-tsee-tsee-tsee-tss-ss-ss*; also a double noted *dzit-dzit*.

Suspended domestic duties

Although they favour low shrubs it can be difficult to get more than a glimpse of darting yellow as sunbirds hurry about. They are far easier to see when nesting, which can take place at any time of year. The nest is usually conspicuously placed and the simple act of hanging some rope or wire from the eaves is often all the encouragement that is needed for a pair to build their pendulous nest outside a window. Pairs constructing nests will accept offers of nesting material, such as plant fibre, feathers or cotton wool, flying off with the material trailing behind them.

Normally territorial, males gather in small groups to attract females before the breeding season. Males spend much time trilling and chasing each other before taking up a prominent position and, with bills pointed skyward, show off their iridescent blue throat. The arrival of a female may also prompt a male to puff out his throat and sing. ∎

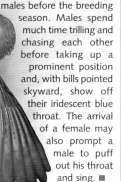

Hotspots
Townsville, Mission Beach, Hinchinbrook NP

MORE CREATURES
GREAT AND SMALL

Where reptiles still rule

Although for most visitors to Australia mammals and birds are the peak attractions, several other groups of vertebrate are prominent in nearly every habitat. The hundreds of species of reptile include the world's largest, the saltwater crocodile; more species of lizard than any other continent (as many as 40 species can share the same dune system); the highest number of species of python and blind snake; and a wealth of turtles – both the great marine turtles that rarely touch land and a peculiarly Australasian group, sometimes called freshwater tortoises, that has become highly diversified in the country's few large or permanent waterways. In this driest of continents the presence of so many frog species is paradoxical; in reality they are a relic of wetter times and show how already specialised animals can adapt further to a changing environment. And under the ocean's surface another world awaits, where whole groups of invertebrate not found on land – including the spectacular corals – live side by side with an astonishing array of marine fish from tiny, camouflaged blennies to the massive whale shark with a host of colourful reef species in between.

Nameless hordes

Space permits us to describe only a few groups and species here, and many common and obvious creatures miss out. This is especially true of the many thousands of species of spectacular and extraordinary invertebrate found in Australia. For example, tropical forests abound with large and colourful butterflies, including birdwings and the bright blue Ulysses butterfly; primitive relics of Gondwanan forests such as peripatus get only a mention; and the stunning diversity of spiders, ants (of which

Australia probably has more species than any other continent), bushflies, mosquitoes and other biting invertebrates will have to remain anonymous. Indeed, many thousands of species of invertebrate are still unknown to science: an average eucalypt in an average forest is likely to host dozens of undescribed species.

Armed and not so dangerous

Much is made of Australia's venomous animals, but you'll find few references to them here. Danger certainly lurks in the bush and underwater, and a few species of snake and spider – to name only two groups – have justified their reputation frequently enough. But your chances of a one-on-one encounter with a dangerously poisonous animal are low and you can be confident that you stand virtually no chance of coming to harm, provided you use common sense (see the Wildlife-Watching chapter for further details). For many species their toxin is a means of subduing prey and they are not keen on using it without good reason – leave them alone and they'll leave you alone. Rather, the few potentially dangerous species and the far greater number of their harmless kin, such as the dozens of nonvenomous snake species and hundreds of spiders in shapes, sizes and colours to rival the showiest butterflies, can be appreciated for what they are and for the vital role each plays in maintaining the health of the environment. ■

SALTWATER CROCODILE

Recognition Massive body and tail with broad, rough snout. Normal maximum length 5m. Brown or dull grey above with darker mottling.
Habitat Billabongs, swamps, major rivers and estuaries; also bays and open sea, sometimes far from land.
Behaviour Basks on mud banks during day, often with mouth open. Cools off and hunts in water. Flooding and overheating of nests destroys many eggs. Females remain with hatchlings for up to 3 months.
Breeding 50–60 eggs laid in nest of vegetation and soil during the Wet hatch after 75–106 days.
Feeding Carnivorous; eats mostly crabs, fish and turtles, but large salties take dingoes, livestock, feral pigs, wallabies, buffaloes and humans.
Voice Young squeak when ready to hatch.

Hotspots
Kakadu NP, Mary River NP, Daintree NP

Lethal weapons

Commonly known as 'salties', the saltwater (or estuarine) crocodile is Australia's – and the world's – largest living reptile: males can grow up to 7m in length and weigh over a tonne. Its common names are owed to its habit of swimming out to sea and between islands – hence their wide distribution through South-East Asia. Once hunted extensively in Australia, salties are now fully protected and becoming common again – during spotlighting forays in the Top End their reflected eyeshine will show just how common. Lying still on a muddy bank their bulk is deceptive – they can move fast and once in the water are deadly predators. A hunting crocodile waits with only eyes and nostrils above the surface. Once prey is sighted it submerges and swims towards it, finally lunging with immense power and speed to drag its victim under. Crocs drown their prey by rolling over and over, but cannot swallow underwater and after the 'death roll' must surface to eat.

In the hotseat

During the Wet, females lay their hard-shelled eggs in a nest of rotting vegetation piled up near permanent water, and guard them aggressively against foraging goannas and the like. The temperature of the nest during incubation determines the sex ratio of the offspring – an average of 31.6°C will produce predominantly males, while slightly lower or higher temperatures will produce mainly females. The young call from inside the egg when hatching, prompting the mother to excavate the mound and even gently carry hatchlings in her mouth down to the water. The young are born only 30cm in length and to reach maturity must dodge predatory birds, fish and larger crocodiles. To find a mate, a male must compete against older, territorial males which sometimes inflict fatal injuries. And while travelling overland to reach a new waterhole, crocs sometimes die from dehydration. Should it survive these trials a croc can live 50 years and some very large specimens are estimated to be 80 years old. ■

FRESHWATER CROCODILE

Feeling the pressure

In contrast to its saltwater cousin, the freshwater crocodile (sometimes known as Johnston's crocodile) is relatively small and poses no real threat to humans. In fact, it is a rather retiring animal, although it's not a good idea to tangle with any croc, large or small – a freshie of any size can inflict a nasty bite. During warmer months freshwater crocodiles often float at the water's edge, with only their eyes and nostrils exposed. Special sense organs associated with their needle-like teeth (a feature which helps tell them apart from salties) detect pressure changes in the water made by the movement of prey. Combined with binocular vision, freshwater crocs can thus accurately locate prey, even at night – a quick snap and it's gone, swallowed whole. To maintain a constant body temperature, freshwater crocodiles must frequently move between water and land. This is especially evident early in the Dry, when the water temperature cools and waterholes contract (this is the best time to see them). As the temperature increases later in the Dry, freshwater crocs must avoid overheating; this can present a major challenge if they become confined to warm, shrinking waterholes that become increasingly overcrowded.

Temperature-controlled sex

During the dry season large males compete to mate and subsequently females lay about a dozen hard-shelled eggs in a nest of excavated sand on the bank of a waterhole. As with salties, the temperature of the nest determines the gender of most hatchlings: temperatures around 32°C cause males to hatch; any higher or lower favours the birth of females. But regardless of temperature, only approximately 30% of the eggs originally laid ever hatch and less than 1% of hatchlings survive to maturity. Life is tough for newly hatched freshies, which fall prey to other crocs (of both species), goannas, large fish, and birds such as sea-eagles. Freshwater crocs are seen far less frequently than salties, but despite a naturally low survival rate their population is increasing. ■

Recognition Slender croc (up to 3m) with smooth, narrow snout. Grey or grey-brown above, with irregular dark mottling on back and flanks. **Habitat** Freshwater rivers, streams, billabongs, swamps and lakes.
Behaviour Females explore sandy banks at night during Dry to select nesting sites. Females may help hatchlings from eggs and guard them for several weeks. Has been timed running at 18km/h in short bursts on land.
Breeding 5–25 eggs buried in sand are incubated 65–95 days and hatch at the start of the Wet.
Feeding Youngsters eat small aquatic prey, such as insects, frogs, spiders and prawns. Adults take fish, lizards, rats, bats and birds.
Voice Young crocs squeak loudly when ready to hatch.

Hotspots
Litchfield NP, **Kakadu NP**, **Lakefield NP**

TURTLES

*The 50cm **broad-shelled river turtle** lives in the Murray-Darling system.*

*Necks of tropical **northern snake-necked turtle** can be 25cm long.*

***Northern snapping turtles** are common in tropical rivers and lagoons.*

*Eastern subcoastal rivers are home to the **saw-shelled turtle**.*

An ancient success story

Turtles, tortoises and sea turtles have changed little over the past 100 million years. At least 20 species of freshwater turtle (also known as 'tortoises', although no land tortoises live here) and six of sea turtle occur in Australia. Freshwater turtles are common in most river systems and lakes in all mainland states, and just about any reasonably sized body of water will support one or more species. The best time to see them is during the middle of the day when they bask by floating in sunlit patches of water, or climb onto logs and rocks. If a waterhole dries out, they migrate overland to a more suitable location or bury themselves in the mud until rains come again.

While freshwater turtles have clawed feet with strong webbing (except for the unique pitted-shelled turtle, which has paddles), sea turtles' limbs are all modified as paddle-like flippers. These exclusively marine reptiles live their entire adult lives

*Known only from Top End rivers, the **pitted-shelled turtle's** flippers, soft shell covering and a 'pig nose' make it unique. Hatchlings (inset) emerge after the start of the Wet.*

at sea and only return to land to nest. Sea turtles are common throughout the Great Barrier Reef, but perhaps your best chance of seeing one is when females haul themselves onto beaches to dig a nest. Nesting seasons are well defined, and you also may be lucky enough to see the miniature hatchlings as they race from their nest to the sea. ■

Hotspots

Kakadu NP Six freshwater species, including unique pitted-shelled turtle, plus nesting sea turtles. **Great Barrier Reef** Sea turtles nest on islands such as Heron, Curtis, Lady Elliott and Lady Musgrave. **Fraser Island** Abundant freshwater species in lakes.

GREEN TURTLE

Beach babies

One of the best nature experiences is watching a female sea turtle slowly climb out of the waves onto a sandy beach then dig a hole in which to lay her eggs. At other times of the year, the same beach may become alive with tiny hatchlings making their first run towards the water. There they will live the rest of their lives and only females will emerge to repeat the breeding cycle. The green turtle is the world's most wide-spread and Australia's most common sea turtle. And the Great Barrier Reef is its most important nursery – at Raine Island, 10,000 females may lay their eggs in a single night. After hatching, a green turtle is rarely seen for the next five to 10 years, by which time it will have grown to around 40cm. At this stage it spends much of its time among coral reefs, mainly feeding on molluscs, sea jellies, crustaceans and sponges.

The long haul

It takes 30 to 50 years for green turtles to grow to maximum size and start breeding. A couple of weeks after mating, females weighing 100kg or more haul themselves ashore after dark at high tide during a full or new moon. With their flippers they scrape a pit in sand above the high-water mark then lay about 100 leathery eggs the size of ping-pong balls. After covering the eggs, the females return to the sea. Sun warming the sand makes a natural incubator, and two or three months later (depending on how sunny it is) tiny replicas of their parents (below) emerge from the eggs and climb to the nest's surface. At nightfall, a mass of hatchlings suddenly breaks through the sand and dashes to the water, running the gauntlet of crabs, gulls and frigatebirds on land, and large fish such as sharks in the water. ■

Recognition Rarely exceeds 1m. Almost circular or heart-shaped shell. Olive green above marked red- to dark brown; creamy white below. Bill powerful but not hooked.
Habitat Tropical seas, in open water and around reefs; occasionally strays into cooler waters.
Behaviour Only sea turtle that basks near shore. Light above the horizon at night appears to guide the newly hatched turtles to the sea (artificial lights can lure them to their deaths). Very few live to breeding age.
Breeding Eggs laid from late October until mid-February hatch after 60–90 days.
Feeding Adults are the only primarily vegetarian sea turtles, eating green, red and brown seaweeds, mangrove roots and leaves, and seagrass.
Voice Silent.

Hotspots
Great Barrier Reef (especially Heron Island), **Coral Coast**

LIZARDS

*Common in arid country, **shingle-backs** are slow-moving skinks.*

*The 25 monitor species range up to to 2m long: above, **Gould's goanna**.*

*The **thorny devil** is a harmless, ant-eating desert dragon.*

Bearded dragons often bask on roads in eastern Australia.

Fragile tails and walking pine cones

A warm, dry climate is perfect for lizards and nearly 500 species live in most terrestrial habitats across Australia. Many are common, although the north and inland have the highest diversity, and several different types can normally be seen by walking almost anywhere on a warm, sunny day. Lizards range in size from tiny, cryptic geckoes that shelter under bark to the perentie, a desert-dwelling goanna (monitor lizard) that exceeds 2m in length. Some, such as water dragons, water skinks and some goannas, spend much of their life in or near freshwater. The legless lizards have only vestigial back legs and can easily be mistaken for snakes (legless lizards have a broad, fleshy tongue while all snakes have a forked tongue). Skinks comprise

Eastern water dragons typically lounge on rocks or branches overhanging rivers, dropping into the water to escape danger. Juveniles (inset) receive no parental care.

the largest family and several examples are among the most familiar of Australian lizards. The various blue-tongued lizards, so-called because of their broad, blue tongue, are large and common; and the shingle-back has an extraordinary pine cone-like skin. Small, quick-moving 'droptail' skinks can be found just about anywhere scuttling through leaf litter; their folk name refers to their habit of dropping the end of their tail as an enticing decoy to any would-be predator.

Art gecko and scrounge lizards

In colouration if not in size, the most spectacular Australian lizards belong to the gecko family. These fragile-looking reptiles typically have soft, velvety skin and bulbous eyes; most are active only at night, when they hunt small animals. Many

*Usually arboreal, the **spiny-tailed gecko** is widespread from forests to spinifex country.*

*The **mangrove monitor** lives in forests and mangroves of Cape York and the Top End. An agile climber, it also swims well enough to take fish underwater; other prey includes a wide range of small vertebrates.*

geckoes live in trees, sheltering under bark and in hollows, while some forage on the ground and retreat into burrows during the day. The most familiar species, the house gecko, has adhesive toe pads and is commonly seen clinging to the ceiling of tropical houses as it attempts to catch insects attracted to lights. One of the most unusual is the 30cm northern leaf-tailed gecko, a tree-dwelling rainforest species whose colouration perfectly matches lichen-encrusted bark. 'Goanna' is probably a corruption of 'iguana', and refers to Australia's 25 species of monitor lizard. Goannas are the giants of the lizard world and large species, such as Gould's goanna and the 2m-long lace monitor, can often be spotted at camping grounds sleeping in a tree or rummaging around for food. Two of the best-known species - the frilled lizard and the thorny devil - belong to the dragon family. The thorny devil is brightly coloured and slow-moving, but well armed with stout spines. ■

*The **beaded gecko** is a ground-dwelling species that shelters in a burrow or ants' nest.*

*Found from Cape York Peninsula to the central coast of NSW, the **northern leaf-tailed gecko** is superbly camouflaged on lichen-covered trunks.*

Hotspots

Lamington NP Rainforest dragons, large skinks and leaf-tailed geckoes. **Kakadu NP** Many skinks and dragons (frilled lizards common), plus goannas and geckoes. **Hattah-Kulkyne NP** Dragons, goannas, shingle-backs, blue-tongues and a multitude of small geckoes and skinks all easily seen.

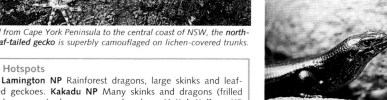

*The **land mullet** is a smooth-scaled rainforest skink reaching 65cm in length.*

FRILLED LIZARD

Recognition Up to 80cm including long tail. Almost black to pale grey-brown or yellowish, with darker blotches. Lower frill yellow, orange, pink or rust red. Males have black chest.

Habitat Tropical woodland, foraging on ground during the Wet, otherwise remaining in trees.

Behaviour Climbs well, living high in trees above level of grass fires during the Dry; shelters in hollow limbs or termite mounds.

Breeding Up to 24 eggs laid during the Wet take about 4 weeks to hatch.

Feeding Carnivorous; forages on the ground for invertebrates, such as hatching termites, plus small vertebrates such as lizards. Earthworms form high percentage of diet when rains arrive.

Voice When threatened, accompanies raising of frill with hissing.

The biggest frill of all

Among Australia's many unusual and famous animals is an extraordinary member of the dragon family, the frilled (or frill-necked) lizard. Images of this lizard with mouth agape and large neck frill extended – plate-sized in some specimens – adorn countless tourism promotions in the Top End, and this reptile is a must-see for wildlife-watchers. The frilled lizard is common enough, but it is rarely seen outside the wet season. From late October until May, however, they forage on the ground, mate and lay eggs, and are a common sight by the roadside, sitting semierect and looking uncannily like a bit of dead wood as they bask in the morning sun. When relaxed, the distinctive frill lies in folds around the neck and shoulders, and if approached the lizard may flatten itself to the ground to look inconspicuous. But if the threat persists it erects the impressive and colourful frill, opens its mouth, hisses and makes short charges at the enemy. If this fails and its bluff is called, it jogs off on its hindlegs to the nearest tree and scales the trunk – on the side away from the observer.

Built-in thermostat

The famous frill also seems to be used in territorial displays by males during the breeding season (males often wage fierce battles for territory and mates). And it assists in the regulation of body temperature; for example, to warm up rapidly the lizard holds its raised frill to the sun, whereas dropping the frill reduces the area exposed and thus cools it off. During the Wet, frilled lizards spend much time foraging on the ground, taking advantage of insects hatching or displaced by rising floodwaters, and searching for a mate. With the coming of the first rains females dig a burrow in soft soil and lay their eggs, but after covering them up they show no more interest in their offspring. The newly hatched frilled lizards have a poorly developed frill but are superbly camouflaged. ■

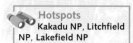

Hotspots
Kakadu NP, Litchfield NP, Lakefield NP

AMETHYSTINE PYTHON

Purple pythons

The python family is found worldwide across the tropics and subtropics and contains the largest living snakes. In Australia the family is represented by 15 species, of which the amethystine (or scrub) python is the largest (and one of the world's largest species) – an exceptional specimen measured 8.5m in length and individuals 5m or longer are not uncommon. Most pythons are slow moving and primarily ground dwelling. The amethystine python, so-called because in certain lights its otherwise camouflaged body shows a purple or violet sheen, is primarily active at night, especially during the warmer months of the wet season. However, during the cooler dry season they often move out of dense forests and can be spotted basking in the morning sun on rocky ledges, flat out on trees or even floating on vegetation at the edge of lakes. Check fruiting trees that possums and tree-kangaroos visit – amethystines often lay in wait for prey at such sites.

Heat-seeking constrictor

All pythons are nonvenomous, instead killing their prey by constriction. As it slowly searches the forest floor at night a series of heat-sensitive organs below the jawline, called labial pits, helps the snake detect 'warm-blooded' prey. Striking fast, it grips prey with numerous sharp, backward curving teeth, then throws its muscular body in coils around the victim and exerts tremendous force, tightening each time the prey exhales until the life is literally squeezed out of it. After suffocation, the prey is eaten whole, head first. Pythons can unhinge their lower jaw to engulf prey many times their own body's circumference, slowly swallowing and forcing the victim down into the stomach with muscular ripples. Females lay about a dozen eggs, which are often sticky and form clusters. They stop feeding before laying and remain tightly coiled around the eggs during incubation (this behaviour probably makes pythons unique among Australian snakes). At this time female pythons are able to raise their body temperature – by shivering – to assist incubation. ■

Recognition Long and slender. Golden brown or olive with dark brown blotches and bars on upperparts; creamy white underneath; head plain or blotched.

Habitat Widespread in rainforest, savannah woodland, vine thicket, regrowth and even scrubby vegetation on coral cays.

Behaviour Apparently gather in open valleys during winter to sunbathe and mate. Juveniles probably spend more time in trees than adults. Can go for long periods without eating.

Breeding About 12 sticky eggs are laid and guarded by the female until hatching.

Feeding Carnivorous, feeding mostly on mammals such as bandicoots, possums, flying-foxes, rats, mice and macropods including tree-kangaroos and pademelons.

Voice Silent.

Hotspots
Iron Range NP, Daintree NP, Atherton Tableland

SNAKES

*The **bandy-bandy** is an inoffensive burrowing snake.*

A serpentine rogues' gallery

Snakes are some of the most recognisable animals – everyone instantly reacts to that notorious legless form that so often incites hysteria and violence. But among Australia's 130 species, the majority of which are completely harmless, is a fascinating diversity of shapes, sizes, colours and behaviour. Most Australian snakes are rarely encountered and it's normal to walk in the bush for hours or days without seeing one. All snakes are generally solitary and seen in close proximity only when mating or emerging from hibernation. Warm, sunny conditions, such as the start of spring, are best for seeing snakes during the day, while nocturnally active species are most mobile on warm, humid nights.

*The **white-lipped python** inhabits islands of Torres Strait.*

*The **green python** of Cape York Peninsula's rainforests is an arboreal species, almost identical to an unrelated species in South America. Juveniles (inset) are remarkably different from adults.*

***Arafura filesnakes** spend their entire lives in tropical billabongs.*

Australia does have an unusually high proportion of venomous species, including 25 considered dangerous to humans. Known as the elapids, they have short, effectively hollow fangs – like hypodermic needles – at the front of their mouth through which venom is injected. Australian elapids live in most habitats and include eight of the world's ten deadliest snakes: infamous names include the taipans; the death adders, which lie motionless while wriggling their tail-tip to attract prey; tiger snakes, some of which share the nesting burrows of muttonbirds; and the marsh-dwelling red-bellied black snake.

The rough and the smooth

Although some snakes bear live young while others lay eggs, none shows much interest in their offspring; instead, large litters are one of the secrets of their success as a group. Seasnakes are a group of 30-odd highly venomous but normally inoffensive

***Carpet pythons** vary in colour across their wide distribution.*

Masters' snake is a small, lizard-eating species from dry parts of southern Australia.

*An agile climber, the **slaty-grey snake** is a tropical forest species that eats mainly frogs but occasionally lizards. This venomous snake is often found near houses and is aggressive when cornered.*

snakes commonly encountered in tropical waters. Like all snakes they breathe air, but seasnakes have a strongly compressed, paddle-like tail and live a wholly marine existence. They dive to feed on fish and when basking near the surface are often snatched by sea-eagles. The worm like blind snakes live underground, where they feed mainly on termites, and are usually seen only at night after rain. Another, generally tropical, group includes several arboreal (eg, the brightly coloured tree snakes) and aquatic species. Some are mildly venomous, but their fangs are at the back of their mouth and they are not considered dangerous to people. Australian pythons range in length from the 50cm pygmy python to the 8m amethystine python. Pythons are mainly nocturnal and kill by constricting the ability of its prey to breathe until it suffocates. A family of two specialised, nonvenomous species, known as filesnakes because of their rough, granular skin, feed on fish and are never found out of water. ■

*The arboreal **brown tree snake** is common in eastern and tropical Australia.*

*Camouflaged in a variety of colours, **death adders** are distinguished by their triangular head. Their alarming habit of remaining motionless when walkers pass nearby has earned them the nickname 'deaf adder'.*

Hotspots
Kakadu NP Arafura filesnakes in billabongs, olive pythons follow dusky rats fleeing floodwaters. **Lamington NP** Rainforest pythons, elapids and tree snakes. **Flinders Island** Black tiger snakes cohabiting with muttonbirds.

Western brown snakes are found across almost the whole continent west of the Divide.

FROGS

***Green tree frogs** are a familiar sight in Outback buildings.*

***Verreaux's tree frog** is a variable species of south-eastern Australia.*

***Water-holding frogs** emerge from burrows after heavy rains inland.*

*The **crucifix toad** burrows in black-soil plains of the Darling Basin.*

Wetland-dwellers from rainforests to deserts

Frogs are almost totally dependent on freshwater to breed and its availability is therefore the most significant constraint on their distribution. Not surprisingly, the frog fauna of this very dry continent is impoverished when compared to some parts of the world, but among the 200 species are many colourful and unusual examples. During warm, wet conditions frogs are not difficult to track down, especially at night when males congregate and frantically call to attract a mate. The best places to look are around farm dams, streams and rivers. Many species are common and any national park with a watercourse near the camping ground should also hold a few different types. The east coast offers the most suitable conditions and therefore the highest diversity – more than 25% of species inhabit the Wet Tropics alone. However, even seemingly unlikely areas, such as deserts and sand dunes, may be home for some unique forms. And visitors to the Queensland coast can hardly miss Australia's only member of the toad family, the introduced cane toad. This common pest has been blamed for the decline of many small animals.

*The **dainty green tree frog** is common in rainforests, woodland and adjoining gardens on the eastern seaboard. Mating among frogs (inset) is known as amplexus.*

Famous and familiar, great and small

The largest family, the Myobatrachidae, is unique to the Australian region and its members therefore commonly known as 'southern frogs'. Among this diverse group are burrowing species of the arid zone, such as the bizarre turtle frog and the colourful crucifix toad, whose short breeding cycles coincide with infrequent rains. Other well-known examples include the

Skin flaps complement the camouflage of the **New Guinea tree frog** of the Wet Tropics.

Peron's tree frog of south-eastern Australia is often found well away from water. On humid nights it descends from the trees to hunt on the ground. Listen for its long, rattling call.

large, rainforest-dwelling barred frogs; the striking corroboree frog of the high mountains; and the amazing gastric brooding frogs, whose tadpoles develop in the stomach of the female to be regurgitated as miniature replicas of adults.

The most distinctive family is probably the tree frogs, most of whose members are easily identified by large adhesive pads on the tips of their fingers and toes. Able to scale even vertical glass surfaces, these efficient climbers range from various green species found throughout eastern Australia to the giant tree frog, a rainforest giant which measures up to 14cm. Scientists also classify several burrowing frogs in this family, the most famous example being the water-holding frog, which Aborigines squeeze for a refreshing drink. The narrow-mouthed tree frogs, or microhylids, are confined to areas of high rainfall in north-east Queensland and the Top End. They are only a few centimetres in length and probably lay eggs in moist leaf litter, thus avoiding the need for a free-swimming tadpole stage. ■

The **striped burrowing frog** is seldom found far from water along the eastern seaboard.

The **giant tree frog** of tropical Queensland is Australia's largest – easily recognisable by a vibrant white stripe along its lower 'lip'.

Hotspots
Lamington NP Barred river frogs on rainforest tracks and abundant tree frogs. **Eungella NP** Home of the rare northern gastric brooding and torrent tree frogs. **Kakadu NP** Millions of frogs calling and spawning on floodplains early in the wet season.

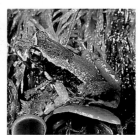

The **tinkling frog** is known only from mountain rainforests in Far North Queensland.

WHALE SHARK

The mother of all fish

Reaching 12m or more in length, the whale shark is the largest of all fish – rivalled only by the basking shark – and surpassed in size by only the great whales. But for all the impressive statistics (it weighs a tonne for every metre of length and you could almost park a small car in its mouth), these gentle giants have no interest in humans. Like all sharks, whale sharks have teeth – over 300 rows of them – but they are small and the shark's diet is largely zooplankton – the tiny creatures that drift around with ocean currents. As it swims along it sucks huge volumes of water into that cavernous mouth, where modified gill rakers effectively filter out crustaceans and small fish. Should a whale shark accidentally swallow something large or distasteful it can evert its stomach to empty it – a feature that lends some credence to the tale of Jonah, the Biblical prophet who was swallowed then regurgitated by a large fish. Divers nonetheless must avoid getting in the path of a cruising whale shark and the 5m arc of its powerful tail stroke.

Recognition Up to 12m (possibly 18m) with a very broad head and enormous mouth. Upper surface bronze-brown with paler spots and vertical bars. Prominent ridges along body length.
Habitat Tropical and temperate waters of Atlantic, Indian and Pacific Oceans; in Australia mostly in tropical waters.
Behaviour Usually solitary, but congregates at prey concentrations. Swims near the surface when feeding, sometimes hanging vertically to swallow water and prey. Remains calm in the presence of divers.
Breeding Females retain egg cases within their body and bear hundreds of 60cm-long, free-swimming young.
Feeding Filter-feeds on plankton, including crustaceans, and small schooling fish such as pilchards and anchovies; occasionally takes squid and tuna.

A slow-motion feeding frenzy

Whale sharks are long lived, although nobody knows just how long and much of their biology is still a mystery. It is believed that individuals migrate in search of concentrations of zooplankton; and in the waters surrounding Ningaloo Reef, off the north-west coast, a remarkable gathering takes place every autumn. The dramatic spawning of coral, usually around March to April, triggers an explosion of feeding and breeding among the creatures of the plankton. Tiny krill swarm in huge numbers, adding their own spawn to the mix and attracting other plankton, such as juvenile crabs and shrimps, that feed on the eggs. They, in turn, lay on a banquet for well over 100 whale sharks – mostly immature males about 7m to 8m long. Timing is important to maximise your chances of seeing the Ningaloo phenomenon, but it is possible to encounter these fish at any time of year. Several dive operators launch diving/snorkelling expeditions out of Exmouth. ∎

> **Hotspots**
> **Ningaloo MP** (Coral Coast)

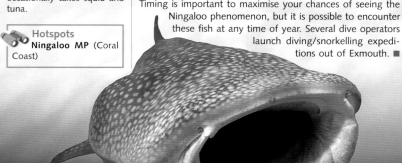

SEA DRAGONS

≣Leafy sea dragon
Weedy sea dragon

Well-developed paternal instincts

Enter the sea dragons, delicate fish at home in the cold marine waters of southern Australia – and nowhere else. Sea dragons are related to sea horses and pipefishes, and like them lack scales. Instead, a bony armour of rings and plates protects them as they forage in the turbulent waters of rocky reefs. Superbly camouflaged, they swim slowly through the forests of green-brown kelp, sucking up shrimps and other tiny crustaceans with their toothless, tube-like snout. Sea dragons spend more time horizontal than vertical and, unlike sea horses, don't have a prehensile tail with which to anchor themselves to weed. But they do share a rare trait – male 'pregnancy'. Whereas sea horses have an egg pouch, male sea dragons carry their mate's fertilised eggs under their tail attached to the skin like a ball into a socket.

Recognition Weedy: grows to 45cm; red, orange and yellow with pale spots. Leafy: grows to 35cm; yellow-brown with pale horizontal stripes and large leaflike appendages.

Habitat Weedy: seagrass meadows in shallow estuaries to kelp gardens on deep off-shore reefs. Leafy: high-energy offshore reefs from 4 –30m in depth.

Behaviour Usually swims slowly among or around seaweed, relying on camou-flage to avoid detection. Young hatch almost fully formed, but are sustained by egg yolk until their snout develops and they can begin feeding.

Breeding Males carry a brood of 200 or more eggs for about 2 months from early summer.

Feeding Carnivorous; preys mainly on small crustaceans such as myscid shrimps.

Masters of disguise

The weedy, or common, sea dragon (below) is the larger of the two species, but despite its lurid colouration it is difficult to see – small, leaflike lobes borne on dorsal and ventral spines give it excellent camouflage. Propulsion is by trans-parent pectoral and dorsal fins, but when swimming its stiff form and bright colours lend it a mechanical appearance – all that's missing is the wind-up key. Weedy sea dragons are widespread across southern Australia in estuaries, bays and offshore reefs. Many divers get their first glimpse in Sydney Harbour, Botany Bay or Westernport Bay; the best places to start looking are where thick kelp gives way to clear sand.

The camouflage of the leafy sea dragon (above) is even more spectacular. Sprouting a mass of kelplike 'fronds' from its undulating body, it almost per-fectly resembles its seaweed habitat. Not surpris-ingly, leafy sea dragons are not easy to find and many divers have missed an opportunity by ignor-ing a 'fragment of weed'. Leafy sea dragons are restricted to the offshore waters of South Australia and Western Australia, where they usually inhabit high wave energy environments, such as rocky reefs covered in brown kelp, that belie their delicate appearance. ■

> **Hotspots**
> **Botany Bay, West-ernport Bay** (weedy); **Victor Harbor, Kangaroo Island** (leafy)

CORAL REEF LIFE

Yellowfin goatfish are so-called because of their long chin barbs.

Potato cod grow to 1.4m and lurk near caves and crevices.

Freckled hawkfish generally sit among the outer branches of coral.

Stingrays are normally inoffensive, but can deliver a painful sting.

Clone zones

Coral reefs astound us with their abundant fauna in endless colours, and myriad shapes and forms. The basis of all coral reefs are the so-called hard corals, created by tiny self-cloning polyps that lay down generation after generation of resilient limestone skeletons. While temperate Australian reefs should not be forgotten, the Great Barrier Reef is spectacular. Almost 400 species of coral have been recognised on this reef alone, their popular names describing the many forms a colony or individual polyp can take: staghorn, brain, encrusting and mushroom. Most corals grow towards the sunlight because their health depends on tiny single-celled plants (zooxanthellae) that live inside each polyp's tissue. At night the reef's true colours come to life as coral polyps extend their feeding tentacles.

Clark's anemonefish is always associated with large sea anemones that adhere to coral reefs. *Sea stars* (inset) shelter by day among the coral, emerging at night to feed.

Complex kaleidoscopes of life

Plantlike soft corals, sea whips, gorgonian fans and feather stars add texture and complexity to the underwater stage, but stealing the limelight are the hundreds of species of colourful fish, from tiny fairy basslets to huge potato cod that reach 1.4m in length. As many as 200 fish species may inhabit a single reef and more than 1500 species have been identified across the expanse of the Great Barrier Reef. Thousands more species of invertebrate, such as sea urchins, sea anemones, molluscs and crustaceans, add to the panoply: there are sea stars of every colour, outlandishly vibrant nudibranchs, large green-lipped clams and painted crayfish.

Each reef is an intricate network of niches – shallow, deep, exposed, protected, light and dark – and each is filled by a

Longfin bannerfish *hunt for invertebrates on coral reefs, usually singly or in pairs.*

Sweetlip emperors *are carnivorous bottom dwellers that grow to 90cm and forage mainly at night. This species is female when it first reaches maturity and later changes sex to male.*

diverse array of creatures. There are bottom dwellers, surface feeders, schooling fish and solitary hunters. Life on the reef is a relentless struggle to find food and avoid being eaten. But it's not always a lonely struggle, and reefs are great places to study cooperative behaviours and harmonious relationships among different species. Colourful and easily observed examples are the anemonefishes that swim immune among the forest of poisonous tentacles of sea anemones. The protective advantage to the fish is apparent, but just what the anemone gets out of the deal, if anything, is not yet understood.

Timing is a key feature of reef life as tides rise and fall and day becomes night. It's now that plankton levels are at their highest, stimulating the coral polyps to unfurl their delicate tentacles to capture a passing meal and displaying their dazzling colours. With the warming of waters in spring, the moon becomes ringmaster for a spectacular event on the Great Barrier Reef – synchronised mass spawning – as an astounding array of corals simultaneously release their eggs and sperm into the sea. ■

Although in places decimated by collectors, giant clams *are still abundant over most reefs.*

Gaudy colouration warn that the spiny fins of the **spotfin lionfish** *are venomous. Their delicate, gauzy 'plumes' make them a favourite among divers – as long as they stay a safe distance away.*

Hotspots
Heron Island Coral cay with many excellent dive sites. **Hastings Reef** Colourful fish, giant clams, lagoon rays. **Lord Howe Island** The world's most southerly coral reef.

Nocturnal **spiny squirrelfish** *can be found by day sheltering under ledges in coral reefs. Listen for them 'talking' to each other with clearly audible 'clicks'.*

RESOURCE GUIDE

The following information isn't meant to be comprehensive; so if something's not here it doesn't mean it's not worth checking out. We've simply put together what we feel are some key references and contacts as a starting point to help you find what you're looking for.

RECOMMENDED READING

Field guides

Mammals First stop is *The Mammals of Australia* by R Strahan. It's comprehensive and illustrated with colour photos, but it's weighty and doesn't cover cetaceans. *A Photographic Guide to Mammals of Australia* is Strahan's lighter-weight field guide and L Cronin's *Key Guide to Australian Mammals* is also portable. *Tracks, Scats and Other Traces: A Field Guide to Australian Mammals* by B Triggs, is the definitive guide for interpreting signs and markings.

The Sierra Club Handbook of Whales and Dolphins by S Leatherwood and R Reeves, is the whale-watcher's Bible; it's comprehensive, accurate, and practical in a handy, large-pocket size. *Collins Eyewitness Handbooks: Whales, Dolphins and Porpoises* by M Carwardine, is a good, practical field guide with a comprehensive collection of illustrations, text and checklists of important features to identify each species, plus distribution maps and lots of information on natural history. *Whales and Dolphins of New Zealand and Australia: An Identification Guide* by A Baker, is a large pocket-sized ID book of cetaceans around Australasia. It's accurate, but ID notes are in a separate chapter and require cross-referencing.

Birds Three field guides cover all species except those of Australia's island territories and a few vagrants. *The Slater Field Guide to Australian Birds* by P Slater, P Slater & R Slater, is the only pocket-sized guide and is highly recommended. *The Field Guide to the Birds of Australia* by G Pizzey & F Knight, is more up-to-date and has a clear layout, although it is somewhat weighty. The popular *Field Guide to the Birds of Australia* by K Simpson & N Day, is patchily illustrated, but improves with each reprint. The only portable guides for seabirds and waders are the standard texts: *A Field Guide to Seabirds of the World* by P Harrison, and *Shorebirds: An Identification Guide to the Waders of the World* by P Hayman, J Marchant & T Prater.

Serious birders will benefit from *The Complete Guide to Finding the Birds of Australia* by R & S Thomas. It gives the low-down on every species likely to be seen and is particularly good for those short of time. J Bransbury's *Where to Find Birds in Australia* is a bit long in the tooth, but still offers comprehensive coverage. Among the few regional identification guides available, *Birds of Queensland's Wet Tropics and Great Barrier Reef* by L Nielsen (which includes information on where to stay), and *Field Guide to Tasmanian Birds* by D Watts, are recommended. Other useful regional guides include *Finding Birds in Australia's Northern Territory* by P Wilkins et al, and *Where to Find Birds in North East Queensland* by J Weineke.

Reptiles and amphibians *Reptiles and Amphibians of Australia* by H Cogger, is the standard tome; every known species is covered – most with distribution maps and colour photos. More portable are *A Photographic Guide to Snakes and Other Reptiles of Australia* by G Swan; and *A Field Guide to Australian Frogs* by J Barker, G Grigg & M Tyler – an excellent guide to all known species that includes colour photos, distribution maps and keys based on obvious features.

Invertebrates *Name That Insect: A Guide to the Insects of Southeastern Australia* by T New, is an introduction to Australian insects. *A Field Guide to Australian Butterflies* by R Fisher, identifies more than 200 of the 385 or so species, and includes colour photos. *Butterflies of Australia* by I Common & D Waterhouse, is the standard reference, but too heavy to carry around. *Australian Ants: Identification and Description* by S Shattuck, offers a complete listing of Australia's ants.

Marine life Among several excellent Great Barrier Reef field guides are *Marine Fishes of the Great Barrier Reef and South-East Asia*, by G Allen; and *Indo-Pacific Coral Reef* by G Allen and R Steen, which covers other marine creatures as well as fish. The *Reader's Digest Book of the Great Barrier Reef* gives an insightful overview of this World Heritage site. For temperate waters, *Australian Marine Life: The Plants and Animals of Temperate Waters* by G Edgar, describes the most commonly seen plants and animals. *Australia's Seashores* by F Haddon, is a useful reference for beachcombing and Lonely Planet's Pisces series gives information on diving and snorkelling in Australia, with a range of titles on the Reef and southern waters.

Background reading

A readable and concise description of the development of Australia's environment and wildlife is given in *Nature of Australia: Portrait of the Island Continent* by J Vandenbeld. Lavishly-illustrated, *The Greening of Gondwana* by M White, is a fascinating account of plant evolution and the fossil record. T Flannery's *The Future Eaters*, is a controversial and thought-provoking look at how the Australian environment has influenced life on the continent, and its ramifications for human settlement. *This Tired Brown Land* by M O'Connor, offers a provocative and political argument on ecological sustainability and population growth in Australia. There are many general books covering Australia's national parks, although few have a wildlife focus. *Kakadu National Park Australia* by I Morris, is one of the best.

Large newsagents usually stock *Nature Australia*, *Geo* and *Australian Geographic* – all are readable and authoritative quarterly magazines that cover Australian and international wildlife and conservation issues. *Australian Birding* is the best Australian magazine for birdwatchers, although *Wingspan*, published by Birds Australia, is also worth reading. Many of the naturalists' and research organisations listed elsewhere in this section publish regular journals, newsletters and/or magazines – most are available only by subscription.

Natural history booksellers

Nationwide book retail chains usually stock the big-selling field guides. For a bigger variety and specialist titles, try bookshops at museums, zoos, national park authorities, and Birds Australia (see listings in this section). Before your trip it's worth checking out the comprehensive range available from international mail-order natural history bookshops; several have a web catalogue and online ordering service.

Andrew Isles Natural History Books 115 Greville St, Prahran, VIC 3181 (☎ 03-9510 5750, fax 9529 1256, ✆ books@AndrewIsles.com, 🖳 www.AndrewIsles.com).
American Birding Association (ABA) PO Box 6599, Colorado Springs, Colorado 80934, USA (USA & Canada ☎ 800-634 7736, International ☎ 719-578 0607; USA & Canada fax 590 2473, International fax 578 9705; ✆ abasales@abasales.com 🖳 www.americanbirding.org /abasales).
Natural History Book Service (NHBS) 2–3 Wills Rd, Totnes, Devon TQ9 5XN, England (☎ 1803-865 913, fax 865 280, ✆ nhbs@nhbs .co.uk, 🖳 www.nhbs.com).

Subbuteo Pistyll Farm, Nercwys Nr. Mold, Flintshire CH7 4EW, North Wales (☎ 1352-756 551, fax 756 004, ✉ sales@subbooks.demon .co.uk, 🖳 www.subbooks.demon.co.uk).

ECOTOURS

Although ecotourism has become a buzzword, the industry is little regulated and not all ecotours are informative or environmentally sound. The following operators we feel know their stuff and will offer enlightening and interesting wildlife-watching experiences.

National
Australasian Ornithological Services PO Box 385, South Yarra, VIC 3141 (☎/fax 03-9820 4223, ✉ mahert@patash.com.au). Bird tours specialising in difficult skulkers and nocturnal species.
AWT Adventure Tours PO Box 1687, Cairns, Qld 4870 (☎ 07-4031 5058, fax 1323, ✉ enquiries@awttravelaustralia.com.au, 🖳 awttravelaustralia.com.au/index.htm). Wildlife tours including specialist tours on birdwatching and photography.
Emu Tours PO Box 4, Jamberoo, NSW 2533 (☎ 02-4236 0542, ✉ emutours@ozemail.com.au, 🖳 www.ozemail.com.au/~emutours). Nature tours with a birdwatching focus.
North West Safaris PO Box 211, East Kew, VIC 3102 (Melbourne ☎ 03-9852 3398; Adelaide 08-8280 7149) Ex-Alice Springs wildlife-watching trips to the Kimberley, Great Victoria Desert and more.

New South Wales and Australian Capital Territory
Andy Burton's Bush Tours 12/8 Cambridge St, Cammeray, NSW 2062 (☎ 02 9954 0893, ✉ andyburton@s055.aone.net.au). Tours ex-Sydney specialising in the east's flora and fauna (particularly birds).
Australian Birding Itineraries PO Box 243, Woden, ACT 2606 (✉ jleonard@spirit.com.au, 🖳 www.spirit.net.au/~jleonard/john.htm) Personalised bird tours around Canberra and throughout Australia.
Environment Tours GPO Box 3268, Canberra, ACT 2601 (☎ 02-6249 1560, fax 02-6247 3227, ✉ ianf@pcug.org.au) Natural history tours throughout Australia with a specialisation on the south-east.
Wild Scenes PO Box 138, Macarthur Square, NSW 2560 (☎ 02-4621 3986, fax 4628 5799, 🖳 www.wildscenes.com.au). Tours in NSW; special interests catered for, including participation in wildlife research.

Northern Territory
Denise Goodfellow 15 Somerville Gardens, Parap, NT 0820 (☎/fax 08-8981 8492, ✉ goodfellow@bigpond.com). Wildlife guiding in the Top End. Denise's specialty is birds, especially mangrove species.
Kimberley Birdwatching (see listing under WA). Also operate bird tours into the NT featuring Kakadu NP.
Kirrama Wildlife Tours PO Box 1400, Innisfail, Qld 4860 (☎ 07-4065 5181, fax 5197, ✉ kirrama@znet.net.au, 🖳 www.gspeak.com.au /kirrama). Bird-focussed tours across northern Australia.

Queensland
Australasian Birding Services Box 7999, Cairns, Qld 4870 (☎/fax 07-4032 3387, ✉ birdo@internetnorth.com.au) Andrew Anderson specialises in bird tours in the Cairns area, Australia, Papua New Guinea and elsewhere.
Australian Natural History Safari Thylogale Nature Refuge, North Qld 4871 (☎/fax 07-4094 1600, ✉ anhs@tpgi.com.au, 🖳 www.anhs .com.au). David and Diane Armbrust pick up from around Port

Douglas and Mossman before heading to their own private patch of rainforest and then on the Mt Lewis SF and the Mitchell River.

Bird & Bush Tours PO Box 6037, TMC, Townsville, Qld 4810 (☎/fax 07-4721 6489, @ b.b.t@ultra.net.au, 🖳 www.ultra.net.au/Xbbt.) Ian Clayton specialises in small group birdwatching tours to sites in the north, far north and western Qld.

Cassowary House PO Box 387, Kuranda, Qld 4872 (☎ 07-4093 7318, fax 9855, @ sicklebill@internetnorth.com.au, 🖳 www.cassowary -house.com.au). One of the best wildlife spots in Qld, operates as a B&B where you see cassowaries, riflebirds, musky rat-kangaroos and more, as well as organising specialist birdwatching tours locally and further afield.

Chris Dahlberg's Specialised River Tours Daintree Village, Qld 4873 (☎/fax 07-4098 7997, @ chrisd@internetnorth.com.au, 🖳 www .ozemail.com.au/~fnq/daintree/dvta01.html). Informative cruises on the Daintree River.

Kirrama Wildlife Tours (see details under NT). Klaus and Brenda Uhlenhut conduct extended tours to Iron Range and the Gulf country from a base at Cairns and come highly recommended. Also run tours to NT.

Wait-a-While Environmental Tours PO Box 6647, Cairns, Qld 4870 (☎ 07-4033 1153; fax 5999; @ morrisson@iig.com.au 🖳 www.iig .com.au/~cns01789). Natural history tours specialising on the Atherton Tableland and Daintree NP including spot-lighting.

South Australia

Atriplex Services PO Box 74, Morgan, SA 5320 (@ atriplex@river land.net.au 🖳 www.riverland.net.au/ atriplex). Guiding to many areas of the Murray Mallee and Riverland.

Tony's Birding (☎ 08 8337 5959, @ twitcher@senet.com.au). Bird-watching tours from Adelaide through a variety of habitats including the mallee.

Tasmania

Close to Nature Tours National Park, TAS 7140 (☎ 03-62 881 477, fax 478). Mt Field NP specialists, departing from Hobart.

Inala (☎/fax 03-6293 1217, @ inala@tassie.net.au, 🖳 www.inalabruny .com.au). Flora, fauna and specialist birding tours to Bruny Island and other Tasmanian destinations.

Victoria

Bronz Discovery Tours PO Box 83, West Collins St, Melbourne, VIC 8007 (☎ 03-9670 6988, fax 6185). Tours in Victoria (eg, the high country) and throughout Australia as well as specialist sea voyages including Wilsons Promontory and the Bass Strait Islands.

Gippsland High Country Tours PO Box 69, Bruthen, VIC 3885 (☎ 03-5157 5556, fax 5539). Small group tours to alpine areas including the Snowy River, Alpine and Errinundra NPs; and partic-ipation in wildlife research.

Surefoot Explorations PO Box 124, Cowes, VIC 3922 (☎ 03 5952 1533, @ info@surefoot.com.au, 🖳 www.surefoot.com.au) Bird tours from the Great Dividing Range to the Bass Strait with access to private land as well as public areas like NPs.

Western Australia

For information on a range of ecotours of the south-west, contact the Living Windows hotline (☎ 08-9721 7778).

Cape to Cape Eco Tours (☎ 08-9752 2334). Run tours of the south-west, including Perup Nature Reserve.

Coate's Wildlife Tours PO Box 64, Bullcreek, WA 6149 (☎ 08-455 6611, country WA/interstate ☎ 1800 676 016, fax 6621, ✆ coates@ iinet.net.au, ☐ coates.iinet.net.au). Tours in WA including islands and reefs; also specialist wildflower and birdwatching tours.

Falcon Tours (☎ 08-9336 3882, ✆ falcon@highway1.com.au). A wide selection of expert WA birding tours, including Two People's Bay NR.

Kimberley Birdwatching PO Box 220, Broome, WA 6725 (☎/fax 08 9192 1246). Birding and wildlife tours in the Kimberley region.

Sea Lion Charters 24 Bryant St, Green Head, WA 6514 (☎ 08-9953 1012). Seasonal tours to sea-lion breeding islands, north of Perth.

Southern Ocean Charters (☎ 08-9841 5068) Whale-watching trips and deep-sea fishing trips with opportunities to see pelagic seabirds.

PARKS AUTHORITIES

National Parks Australia (☎ 02-6250 0221, ☐ www.environment .gov.au/bg/protecte/anca/index.htm).

ACT Environment ACT (☎ 02-6207 9777, ☐ www.act.gov.au/environ)

NT Parks & Wildlife Commission (☎ 08-89 995511, ☐ www.nt.gov .au/paw).

NSW National Parks and Wildlife Service (Information Line ☎ 1300 36 1967 or ☎ 02-9585 6333, ☐ www.npws.nsw.gov.au).

Queensland Queensland Parks & Wildlife Service (Information Line ☎ 07-3227 8197, ✆ nqic@env.qld.gov.au, ☐ www.env.qld.gov.au) Great Barrier Reef Marine Park Authority, Townsville (☎ 07-4750 0700, ☐ www.gbrmpa.gov.au).

SA National Parks & Wildlife SA (☎ 08-8204 1910, ✆ environment shop@deh.sa.gov.au, ☐ www.denr.sa.gov.au/parks/parks.html)

Tasmania Tasmanian Parks and Wildlife Service (Information Line ☎ 03-6233 6191, ☐ www.parks.tas.gov.au).

Victoria Parks Victoria (Information Line ☎ 13 1963, ☐ www.parkweb .vic.gov.au).

WA Conservation and Land Management (Information Line ☎ 08-9430 8600, ✆ wa.naturally@calm.wa.gov.au, ☐ www.calm.wa .gov.au).

NATURALISTS' ASSOCIATIONS

There are literally hundreds of local and national organisations catering to the interests of amateur and professional naturalists. Here's just a few.

Australian Entomological Society c/o Dr David Evans Walter, AES Secretary, Dpt Entomology, University of Queensland, St Lucia, Qld 4072 (✆ d.walter@mailbox.uq.edu.au, ☐ www.uq.edu.au/entomol-ogy/aes/intro.html).

Australian Mammal Society c/o Alison Mathews, Membership Officer, PO Box 1967, Hurstville, NSW 2220 (fax 02-9585 6606, ✆ alison .matthews@npws.nsw.gov.au, ☐ ikarus.jcu.edu.au/mammal).

Birds Australia 415 Riversdale Rd, Hawthorn East, VIC 3123 (☎ 03-9882 2622, fax 9882 2677, ✆ raou@raou.com.au, ☐ www.birds australia.com.au). Research and conservation, with regional branches and special interest groups. Also observatories offering accommodation, short courses, and participation in research.

Bird Observers Club of Australia POB 185 Nunawading, VIC 3131 (within Australia ☎ 1300 305 342; outside Australia ☎ 613-9877 5342, fax 03-9894 4048, ✆ boca@ozemail.com.au ☐ www.birdobservers .org.au) Branches in each state with opportunities for birdwatching trips and other activities.

Entomological Society of Victoria 56 Looker Road, Montmorency VIC 3094 (☎ 03-9435 4781, 🖥 home.vicnet.net.au/~vicento/vicent.htm).
Field Naturalists Club of Victoria Locked Bag 3, PO Blackburn, VIC 3130 (☎ 03-9877 9860).
Gould League of NSW PO Box 16, Gladesville, NSW 2111 (☎ 02-9817 5621).
Marsupial Society of Australia GPO Box 2462, Adelaide, SA 5001 (☎ 08-8374 1783).
NT Field Naturalists Club PO BOX 39565, Winnellie, NT 0821 (🖥 birds.rhyme.com.au/ntfnc.htm).
NSW Field Ornithologists Club PO Box Q277, QVB Post Shop, NSW 1230 (☎ 02-9698 7263, 🖥 www.geocities.com/RainForest /Vines/7708).
Queensland Frog Society PO Box 7017, East Brisbane Qld 4169 (☎ 07-3366 1806, 🖥 www.qldfrogs.asn.au).
Queensland Ornithological Society Inc PO Box 97, St Lucia, Qld 4067 (☎ 07-3870 8076, 🖥 www.uq.edu.au/~anpwooda/pages /qosi-q.html).
SA Herpetology Group c/-SA Museum, North Terrace, Adelaide, SA 5000 (☎ 08-8204 8772).
SA Ornithologists Association c/- SA Museum, North Terrace, SA 5000 (☎ 08-8337 5959, ✉ twitcher@senet.com.au).
Tasmanian Field Naturalists Club GPO Box 68A, Hobart, TAS 7000 (☎ 03-6344 1076, 🖥 www.tased.edu.au/tasonline/tasfield /homepage.htm).
WA Naturalists Club PO Box 8257, Perth Business Centre, WA 6849 (☎ 08-9228 2495, fax 2496, ✉ wanats@iinet.net.au, 🖥 www.wanats .iinet.net.au/wanatur.html).

WEBSITES

The following websites offer useful background information on wildlife, wildlife-watching and wildlife research.

www.acfonline.org.au The Australian Conservation Foundation – Australia's leading environment group.
www.atcv.com.au Australian Trust for Conservation Volunteers – Volunteer opportunities to help Australia's environment and wildlife.
www.ausbird.com Birdwatching Australia – A state-by-state directory of everything to do with birdwatching: tours, clubs, guides, accommodation and references.
www.csu.edu.au/biodiversity.html Australian Biodiversity Index – Links to flora and fauna indexes, and to wildlife organisations.
www.iinet.net.au/~foconnor Frank O'Connor's Birding Western Australia – Great information on birding sites, with lists and photos, and details of bird tours.
www.jcu.edu.au/school/tbiol/zoology/herp/herp2.html The Australian Herpetological Directory – Information on Australian herpetologists and herpetological research.
www.ozemail.com.au/~amcs The Australian Marine Conservation Society – A national conservation group dedicated to the study and protection of the marine environment.
www.upstarts.net.au/site/non_commercial/whales.html Whales of Australia – Where to go, what you'll see and whale conservation.
www.zip.com.au/~palliser The Australian Pelagic Home Page – Information on pelagic birdwatching, photography and whale-watching including a directory of tour operators around Australia.

GLOSSARY

adaptation – trait that helps an organism survive or exploit an environmental factor.

aestivation – slowing-down of body functions during drought.

aquatic – living in freshwater.

arboreal – tree-dwelling.

Australasia – Australia, New Zealand, New Guinea and nearby islands.

avian – characteristic of birds.

baleen – horny plates suspended from upper jaw of some whales to filter plankton from water.

benthic – bottom-dwelling, eg, marine life.

biodiversity – faunal and floral richness characterising an area.

birder – alternative name for birdwatcher.

brigalow – dense acacia scrub of the inland.

brood – group of young animals produced in one litter or clutch.

browse – to eat leaves and other parts of shrubs and trees.

camp – a roost of bats, especially flying-foxes.

carnivore – a meat-eating animal.

carrion – dead or decaying flesh.

Centre – see Outback.

cetacean – whale or dolphin.

class – a major division of animal classification, eg, mammals.

contiguous – adjoining, eg, woodland spanning two adjacent reserves.

convergent evolution – similar adaptations among unrelated animals, eg, kangaroos and hopping mice.

courtship – behaviour (often a ritualised display) associated with attracting a mate.

crèche – young birds or mammals gathered for safety.

crepuscular – active at twilight, ie, evening or before dawn.

crustacean – crabs, lobsters and shrimps etc.

dasyurid – a member of the carnivorous marsupial family.

detritus – particles of dead animals and plants.

diapause – the temporary suspension of development in an embryo.

dispersal – movement of animals across a geographic area.

display – behaviour transmitting information from the sender to another, eg, threat, courtship.

diurnal – active during daylight.

dorsal – upper (top) surface, ie, the back on most animals.

down – loose, fluffy feathers that cover young birds and insulate plumage of adults.

echolocation – the emission of high-pitched sounds and using the echoes to navigate (eg, whales) or hunt (eg, bats).

edge – transition zone between two habitats, eg, savannah and forest. Also called ecotone.

endemic – found only in a certain area.

epiphyte – plant growing on another for support, eg, orchid on a tree.

eucalypt – any tree of the genus *Eucalyptus*.

eyeshine – light reflected from animals' eyes in torchlight.

family – scientific grouping of related genera, eg, bandicoots.

feral – running wild, eg, pigs.

filter feeding – straining food from water, eg, baleen whales.

fledgling – young bird able to leave the nest, ie, to fledge.

flukes – tail fins of whales and dolphins.

frugivore – a fruit-eating animal.

genus – taxonomic grouping of related species (*plural* genera).

gestation – period during which young mammals develop in the womb before birth.

gibber – stony desert.

glean – to feed by gathering, eg, along branches or among foliage.

Gondwana – ancient supercontinent which broke apart to form Australia, South America, etc.

graze – to eat grass.

guano – phosphate-rich excrement deposited by birds and bats, accumulated over generations.

gumtree – see eucalypt.

habitat – natural living area of an animal; usually characterised by a distinct plant community.

harem – group of females which mate with one male.

hawk – to fly actively in search of prey, eg, insects.

helper – animal, usually from a previous brood, which helps parents raise young.

herbivore – a vegetarian animal.

hierarchy – order of dominance among social animals.

home range – the area over which an individual or group ranges over time.

host – organism on (or in) which a parasite lives; bird which raises the young of parasitic cuckoos.

immature – stage in a young bird's development between juvenile and adult.

insectivore – an insect-eating animal.

introduced – not native to Australia; exotic.

invertebrate – an animal without a spinal column or backbone, eg, insects, worms.

iridescence – metallic sheen that changes according to the viewpoint of the observer.

joey – young marsupial, especially of macropods.

juvenile – animal between infancy and adulthood (mammals) or with first feathers after natal down (bird).

kelp – thick, leathery brown seaweed of southern oceans.

larva – stage of development after hatching in invertebrates, fish and amphibians (*plural* larvae).

littoral – inhabiting the shore of a lake or ocean and adjacent shallow waters.

leaf litter – decaying vegetable matter on the ground beneath living vegetation.

loaf – to laze about.

localised – found only in a small or distinct area.

macropod – kangaroo, wallaby or tree-kangaroo.

mallee – a distinctive arid-zone eucalypt form with many trunks.

mandible – lower jaw or bill.

marine – living in the sea.

marsupial – mammal bearing live but undeveloped young which are suckled in a pouch.

migration – regular movement, often en masse, from one location to another, eg, shorebirds.

mob – (*noun*) group of kangaroos; (*verb*) to harass a predatory animal, eg, small birds mobbing an owl.

monogamy – having one reproductive partner.

monotreme – primitive egg-laying mammal, eg, platypus.

moult – to shed and replace all or selected feathers or fur, usually in response to seasonal or behavioural changes, eg, courtship.

mulga – low acacia trees dominating parts of the arid zone.

natal – pertaining to birth.

nestling – young bird until it leaves the nest (*see* fledgling).

niche – specialised ecological role played by an organism.

nocturnal – active at night.

nomad – animal that wanders in response to seasonal change.

oestrus – period when female mammal is ovulating and therefore sexually receptive.

omnivore – an animal that eats both plant and animal matter.

order – grouping of one or more similar families.

Outback – the vast, dry, largely unpopulated inland of Australia. Often also called the Centre.

parasite – plant or animal that obtains nourishment from another, usually to the detriment of the host.

pelagic – living in or above open oceanic waters.

photosynthesis – process with which plants convert sunlight, water and carbon dioxide into organic compounds.

plankton – tiny animals and plants that live suspended in water.

pod – group of whales, dolphins or seals.

polygamy – having access to more than one reproductive mate.

polyp – sedentary sea animal that forms hard coral.

pouch-young – marsupial young unable to live outside pouch.

precocial – able to walk, run, swim and/or feed itself shortly after birth.

prehensile – flexible and grasping, eg, tail, fingers.

primitive – earlier-evolved (*not* inferior or poorly adapted).

quarter – to systematically range over an area in search of prey, eg, by a raptor.

race – *see* subspecies.

raft – a group of birds, eg, muttonbirds, resting on water.

raptor – bird of prey, eg, hawk.

relict – remnant of formerly widespread species, community or habitat, now surrounded by different communities.

resident – an animal that remains in an area for its entire life cycle.

riparian – living near or in rivers or streams.

rodent – any species of rat or mouse.

roost – area where mammals or birds gather to sleep, sometimes in large numbers (*also verb*).

savannah – vegetation zone characterised by a grassy understorey with scattered trees and shrubs.

scavenger – animal that feeds on carrion or scraps left by others.

scent gland – concentration of cells that secrete chemicals conveying information about the owner's status, identity, reproductive state etc.

sclerophyll forest – evergreen forest dominated by hard-leaved trees such as eucalypts.

sedentary – remaining in one area for all or part of its life cycle.

selection – process whereby traits that don't further an organism's reproductive success are weeded out by environmental or behavioural pressures.

spawn – eggs of fish and amphibians, usually laid in water (*also verb*).

speciation – the evolutionary process through which species are formed.

species – organisms capable of breeding with each other to produce fertile offspring; distinct and usually recognisable from other species, with which the majority don't interbreed.

spur – a horny growth on monotremes, eg, platypus, and some birds, eg, lapwings.

spy-hop – (whales) to hold head vertically above water to check bearings, threats, etc.

stoop – powerful dive of a raptor.

subalpine – habitat and climate below the treeline on high mountains.

subspecies – population of a species isolated from another population (eg, by landforms) that has developed distinct physical traits (*also called* race).

subtropical – the habitats and climate between tropical and temperate zones.

talon – hooked claw on raptor.

temperate – moderate in climate, ie, not too hot, not too cold.

termitarium – earthen mound constructed by a termite colony (*also called* termitary).

terrestrial – living on the ground.

territory – feeding or breeding area defended against others of the same species.

Top End – the northern part of the Northern Territory.

vagrant – animal far outside normal range.

ventral – lower (under) side of an animal.

vertebrate – an animal having a backbone, ie, bony fish, amphibians, reptiles, birds and mammals.

waders – shorebirds, eg, sandpipers.

warm-blooded – maintaining a constant body temperature by internal regulation, eg, birds and mammals.

warren – network of holes used as a shelter and nursery.

waterfowl – swans, geese and ducks.

Wet Tropics – coastal region between Townsville and Cooktown, characterised by very high summer rainfall and rainforests.

woodland – habitat where dominant trees grow well-spaced, with an open canopy.

wreck – animals beach-cast after a storm, eg, seabirds.

zooplankton – animal plankton.

zooxanthellae – symbiotic algae living in coral polyps.

PHOTO CREDITS

Kelvin Aitken/ANT Photo Library **260** bottom, **263** top & bottom, **328** bottom Matt Alexander **66** top, **198** bottom, **237** bottom David Andrew **38** top Jon Armstrong **75** inset, **156** left, **177** Michael Aw **5** column 3 & 7, **79** inset, **128**, **152** top, **215**, **330** column 1- 3 & insets, **331** top left & inset GB Baker/ANT Photo Library **238** column 3 JP & ES Baker/ANT Photo Library **92**, **98** top Ross Barnett **5** column 1 & 4, **15**, **47**, **72**, **102**, **106** left & middle, **152** bottom, **153**, **154**, **258** top Daniel Birks **124** left, **236** top & bottom Rob Blakers **69**, **73**, **94** top & bottom **176**, **182** left Tom Boyden **7** column 1, **59** inset, **70** bottom, **115**, **145**, **147** left, **148** left, **250** column 3, **268** top, **271** column 2, **273** bottom, **274** column 2, **276** column 1, **282** column 4, **286** column 2, **287** column 3, **291** top, **292** column 4a & 4b, **295** top, **316** bottom David Byrant **40** bottom, **41**, **79** main, **225**, **331** bottom right & right middle Dale Buckton **311** column 1 J Burt/ANT Photo Library **103**, **143** Bethune Carmichael **192**, **193** Bob Charlton **5** column 2, **44** top, **46** top, **78** top & bottom, **131** left, **262** top, **266**, **274** column 1, **285** column 3 & 4 Rohan Clarke **71** inset, **231** column 4, **234** column 4, **257** column 1, **302** column 4, **318** column 1, 3 & 4, **321** top right, **324** column 1 & 3, insets, **327** top left Sara-Jane Cleland **6** column 2, **144**, **168**, **198** top, **203**, **290** top Martin Cohen **7** column 2, **43**, **44** bottom, **46** bottom, **57**, **71** main, **147** middle & bottom right, **227** background, **229** top, **240** column 1, 3 & 4, inset, **242** bottom, **250** column 1, **254** column 1, **255** inset, **256** column 3, **257** column 4, **261** bottom, **265** column 2 & inset, **307** column 2, **314–315** foreground, **317** bottom, **319** bottom, **321** inset, right middle & top left, **322** bottom, **323** top, **324** column 4, **325** top right & bottom right, **326** column 2 & insets, **327** right middle, bottom right & inset Robyn Coventry **322** top David Curl **6** column 4 & 5, **54** top, **58** bottom, **59** main, **61**, **112** top, **113**, **114**, **116** bottom, **122** top right, **148** right, **230** inset, **232** bottom, **233** bottom, **235** bottom, **237** top, **238** inset, **239** top, **243** inset, **244** column 2, **249** top, **265** column 3 & 4, **270** inset, **278** top, **280** top & bottom, **281** bottom, **296** column 4, **297** bottom, **299** bottom, **305** column 1, **307** inset, **309** top, **311** column 3, **316** top, **318** column 2 & insets, **320** column 3 Grant Dixon/ANT Photo Library **180** Rob Drummond **284** column 3 & inset, **286** column 4, **288** column 3, **293** column 3, **302** column 2, **303** top, **306** column 1 & 2 Jason Edwards **27**, **45**, **49**, **50** bottom, **60**, **62** top, **91**, **98** bottom, **108** left, **122** bottom right, **156** right, **157**, **160** left, middle & right, **161** top & bottom, **170**, **171**, **172**, **175**, **183**, **184** left & right, **199**, **210** bottom, **213**, **214** top & bottom, **218**, **219**, **223** left, **228** bottom, **229** bottom, **230** column 1 & 2, **231** inset, **233** top, **234** column 1, **235** top, **238** column 2, **241** top, **243** column 1, 2 & 4, **244** column 1 & 3, **247** top, **253** column 3 & 4, **254** column 2, **255** column 1-4, **256** column 1, 2 & 4, inset, **257** column 2 & inset, **260** top, **261** top, **264** top, **269** top, **270** column 1, **271** column 4, **274** column 4, **275** top, **276** column 2 & 3, **277** column 2 & inset, **278** bottom, **279** top & bottom, **282** column 3, **284** column 2 & 4, **286** column 3, **287** column 4 & inset, **288** column 1, 2 & 4, inset, **289** column 4, **292** column 2 & 3, inset, **293** column 1, 2 & 4, **296** column 1 & 3, inset, **297** top, **298** column 2, 3 & 4, **300** top, **302** inset, **304** column 1 & inset, **305** column 3, **306** column 3, **307** column 3, **308** column 1- 3, inset, **311** inset, **312** column 3 & inset, **313** top, **320** column 4, **323** bottom, **324** column 2, **325** top left, right middle & inset **326** column 1, 3 & 4, **327** top right, **329** top Greg Elms **55** inset, **216**

Hugh Finlay **58** top Matt Fletcher **62** bottom, **123** top right Simon Foale **86** left, **228** top, **329** bottom P German/ANT Photo Library **238** column 4 Christopher Groenhout **126**, **186** Dan Harley **90**, **134**, **202**, **205** middle, **206** right, **251** column 4 & inset Martin Harvey/ANT Photo Library **270** column 3, **301** bottom John Hay **5** column 5, **6** column 3, **54** bottom, **107** left, **118** top, **166**, **210** top, **212** top, **247** bottom, **248** bottom, **264** bottom Chris Howe **107** middle Richard I'Anson **5** column 6, **6** column 1, **51** main, **52**, **55** main, **63** main & inset, **64**, **65**, **67** main, **75** main, **76**, **83**, **88**, **100** top, **104**, **116** top, **121**, **122** bottom middle, **123** bottom right, **132** top, **136**, **140**, **150**, **158**, **159**, **167**, **169** right, **174** top & bottom, **194**, **196** top, **200** bottom, **205** top & bottom left, right, **208**, **221**, **222** top, **223** bottom Dennis Jones **245** inset, **246** bottom, **248** top, **252** top, **259** top & bottom, **277** column 4, **289** inset, **314-315** background, **317** top, **320** inset Ralph & Daphne Keller/ANT Photo Library **238** column 1, **246** top, **273** top, **307** column 1, **309** bottom, **310** bottom Mark Kirby **106** right, **138** Chris Klep **155**, **226–227** foreground Diana Mayfield **74** top, **222** bottom IR McCann/ANT Photo Library **257** column 3 Gareth McCormack **66** bottom, **81**, **173**, **182** right Ted Mead/ANT Photo Library **96** top, **178** Chris Mellor **51** inset, **86** right, **95**, **119**, **122** top middle, **164**, **181**, **190**, **244** inset, **245** column 2, **251** column 3, **252** bottom, **275** bottom, **284** column 1, **287** column 2, **289** column 1, **290** bottom, **298** column 1, **299** top, **301** top, **312** column 4, **320** inset (small), **321** right bottom Frédy Mercay/ANT Photo Library **105**, **243** column 3 John Moverley **96** bottom, **282** column 1 & 2, **304** column 4, **305** column 2 & 4, inset, **306** column 4, **311** column 2, **312** column 1 & 2 Natfoto/ANT Photo Library **310** top Frank Park/ANT Photo Library **234** column 3, **302** column 1 and 3 David Paton/ANT Photo Library **262** bottom C & S Pollitt/ANT Photo Library **239** bottom Peter Ptschelinzew **50** top, **70** top, **77**, **123** left, **132** bottom, **223** middle Mitch Reardon **6** column 6, **39**, **42** top & bottom, **53**, **68**, **100** bottom, **107** right, **108** right, **112** bottom, **118** bottom, **120**, **124** right, **162**, **196** bottom, **206** left, **212** bottom, **230** column 3 & 4, **231** column 1 & 2, **232** top, **234** column 2, inset, **241** bottom, **242** top, **244** column 4, **245** column 1, 3 & 4, **249** bottom, **250** column 2 & 4, inset, **251** column 1 & 2, **253** column 2, **254** column 3, **258** bottom, **265** column 1, **268** bottom, **269** bottom, **270** column 2, **271** column 1 & 3, inset, **272** top & bottom, **274** column 3, inset, **276** column 4 & inset, **277** column 1 & 3, **281** top, **282** inset, **283** top & bottom, **285** column 1, **286** column 1 & inset, **287** column 1, **289** column 2 & 3, **291** bottom, **292** column 1, **294** top & bottom, **296** column 2, **300** bottom, **304** column 2 & 3, **307** column 4, **308** column 4, **311** column 4, **320** column 1 & 2 Otto Rogge/ANT Photo Library **110** Paul Sinclair **56**, **67** inset, **74** bottom, **141**, **142**, **146**, **179**, **188**, **191**, **200** top, **204** AP Smith/ANT Photo Library **93**, **254** inset Duncan Sutherland **147** top right, **231** column 3, **254** column 4 Jan Taylor/ANT Photo Library **220** BG Thomson/ANT Photo Library **240** column 2 Keith K Vagg/ANT Photo Library **303** bottom P & M Walton/ANT Photo Library **97** Dave Watts/ANT Photo Library **253** column 1 & inset, **295** bottom Cyril Webster/ANT Photo Library **298** inset, **313** bottom MA Weston **285** column 2, **306** inset Alan Wiggs **80** Astrid Witte & Casey Mahaney **139** Len Zell **38** bottom, **40** top, **130**, **131** right, **285** inset, **319** top, **328** top, **330** column 4, **331** top right

INDEX

LONELY PLANET

You already know that Lonely Planet produces more than this one wildlife guide, but you might not be aware of the other products we have on this region. Here is a selection of titles that you may want to check out as well:

Available wherever books are sold

Australia
ISBN 1 86450 068 9
US$24.95 • UK£14.99 • 180FF

Islands of Australia's Great Barrier Reef
ISBN 0 86442 563 5
US$14.95 • UK£8.99 • 110FF

Outback Australia
ISBN 0 86442 504 X
US$21.95 • UK£13.99 • 170FF

Australia Road Atlas
ISBN 1 86450 065 4
US$14.99 • UK£8.99 • 109FF

Walking in Australia
ISBN 0 86442 669 0
US$21.99 • UK£13.99 • 169FF

Cycling Australia
ISBN 1 86450 166 9
US$21.99 • UK£13.99 • 169FF

Diving & Snorkeling Australia: Southeast Coast & Tasmania
ISBN 1 55992 059 9
US$14.95 • UK£7.99 • 110FF

Diving & Snorkeling Australia's Great Barrier Reef
ISBN 0 86442 763 8
US$17.95 • UK£11.99 • 140FF

Diving & Snorkeling Victoria Australia
ISBN 1 86450 072 7
US$16.99 • UK£10.99 • 149FF

New South Wales
ISBN 0 86442 706 9
US$19.99 • UK£12.99 • 149FF

Northern Territory
ISBN 0 86442 791 3
US$16.95 • UK£10.99 • 130FF

Queensland
ISBN 0 86442 590 2
US$17.95 • UK£11.99 • 140FF

South Australia
ISBN 0 86442 716 6
US$16.95 • UK£10.99 • 130FF

Tasmania
ISBN 0 86442 727 1
US$16.95 • UK£10.99 • 130FF

Victoria
ISBN 0 86442 734 4
US$17.95 • UK£11.99 • 140FF

Western Australia
ISBN 0 86442 740 9
US$15.99 • UK£9.99 • 119FF

Melbourne
ISBN 1 86450 124 3
US$14.99 • UK£8.99 • 109FF

Sydney
ISBN 0 86442 724 7
US$15.95 • UK£9.99 • 120FF

Sydney Condensed
ISBN 1 86450 045 X
US$9.95 • UK£5.99 • 59FF

Melbourne City Map
ISBN 1 86450 009 3
US$5.95 • UK£3.99 • 39FF

Sydney City Map
ISBN 1 86450 015 8
US$5.95 • UK£3.99 • 39FF

Out to Eat - Melbourne
ISBN 1 86450 142 1
US$14.99 • UK£9.99 • 99FF

Out to Eat - Sydney
ISBN 1 86450 141 3
US$14.99 • UK£9.99 • 99FF

Australian phrasebook
ISBN 0 86442 576 7
US$5.95 • UK£3.99 • 40FF

Healthy Travel Australia, NZ & the Pacific
ISBN 1 86450 052 2
US$5.95 • UK£3.99 • 39FF

Sean & David's Long Drive
ISBN 0 86442 371 3
US$10.95 • UK£5.99 • 90FF

RESEARCH

All the authors who worked on this book are professional biologists or experienced naturalists. They visited all the parks that are reviewed (with the exception of the Other Sites, although they went to many of these too). Some of our authors work under cover; others aren't so secretive. None of them accept freebies in exchange for positive write-ups. And none of our guidebooks contain any advertising.

In their research, the authors draw on their experience, their contacts and their personal observation. They have not necessarily been able to see everything in the parks they visited, and they certainly have not gone on every ecotour. Instead, they have used their expertise to judge what to bring together in as accurate a picture of a place as possible.

In this book, taxonomy and species names of mammals, birds, reptiles and frogs follow the CSIRO List of Australian Vertebrates by Malcolm Stanger, Mark Clayton, Richard Schodde, John Wombey and Ian Mason (1998).

We welcome feedback to help us improve new editions. All information is passed onto the authors for verification on the road. The best information is rewarded with a Lonely Planet guidebook.

Send all correspondence to the Lonely Planet office closest to you:

Australia PO Box 617, Hawthorn, Victoria 3122
USA 150 Linden St, Oakland, CA 94607
UK 10A Spring Place, London NW5 3BH
France 1 rue du Dahomey, 75011 Paris

Map Legend

HYDROGRAPHY

Reef
Coastline
River, Creek
Lake
Intermittent Lake
Salt Lake
Canal
Spring, Rapids
Waterfalls
Swamp

ROUTES & TRANSPORT

Freeway
Highway
Major Road
Minor Road
Unsealed Highway
Unsealed Major Road
Unsealed Minor Road
Walking Track
Ferry Route
Train Route & Station
Cable Car or Chairlift
Route Number

MAP SYMBOLS

✪ **CAPITAL** National Capital
● **CAPITAL** Regional Capital
● **CITY** City
◉ Town Town
◉ Village Village

● Point of Interest
● Geographic Feature
● Hydrographic Feature
● Reserve/Wildlife Park
✈ Airport
⌂ Cave
Cliff or Escarpment
◄ Gate
⛪ Lighthouse
☀ Lookout
▲ Mountain or Hill
Ⓟ Parking
) (Pass
ⓘ Tourist Information

BOUNDARIES

International
Regional

AREA FEATURES

Beach
Park
Urban
Aboriginal Land

ABBREVIATIONS

CA   Conservation Area
CP   Conservation Park
CR   Conservation Reserve
CWP   Conservation & Wildlife Park
FP   Forest Park
FR   Forest Reserve
MP   Marine Park
NP   National Park
NR   Nature Reserve
NrP   Nature Park
RP   Recreation Park
RR   Regional Reserve
SF   State Forest
SP   State Park
SR   State Reserve
WPA   Wilderness Protection Area

Note: not all symbols displayed above appear in this book

ABOUT LONELY PLANET GUIDEBOOKS

Lonely Planet published its first book in 1973 in response to the numerous 'How did you do it?' questions Maureen and Tony Wheeler were asked after driving, busing, hitching, sailing and railing their way from England to Australia.

Written at a kitchen table and hand collated, trimmed and stapled, *Across Asia on the Cheap* became an instant local bestseller, inspiring thoughts of another book.

Eighteen months in South-East Asia resulted in their second guide, *South-East Asia on a shoestring*, which they put together in a backstreet Chinese hotel in Singapore in 1975. The 'yellow bible', as it quickly became known to backpackers around the world, soon became the guide to the region. It has sold well over half a million copies and is now in its 10th edition.

Today an international company with offices in Melbourne (Australia), Oakland (USA), London (UK) and Paris (France), Lonely Planet has an ever-growing list of books and other products, including: travel guides, walking guides, city maps, travel atlases, phrasebooks, diving guides, wildlife guides, healthy travel guides, restaurant guides, world food guides, first time travel guides, condensed guides, travel literature, pictorial books and, of course, cycling guides. Many of these are also published in French and various other languages.

In addition to the books, there are also videos and Lonely Planet's award winning Web site.

Some things haven't changed. The main aim is still to help make it possible for adventurous travellers to get out there – to explore and better understand the world.

At Lonely Planet we believe travellers can make a positive contribution to the countries they visit – if they respect their host communities and spend their money wisely. Since 1986 a percentage of the income from each book has been donated to aid projects and human rights campaigns.

> **Lonely Planet gathers information for everyone who's curious about the planet – and especially for those who explore it first-hand. Through guidebooks, phrasebooks, activity guides, maps, literature, newsletters, image library, TV series and Web site we act as an information exchange for a worldwide community of travellers.**

LONELY PLANET OFFICES

Australia
PO Box 617, Hawthorn, Victoria 3122
☎ 03 9819 1877 fax 03 9819 6459
✆ talk2us@lonelyplanet.com.au

USA
150 Linden St, Oakland, CA 94607
☎ 510 893 8555 or ☎ 800 275 8555 (toll free)
fax 510 893 8572
✆ info@lonelyplanet.com

UK
10a Spring Place, London NW5 3BH
☎ 020 7428 4800 fax 020 7428 4828
✆ go@lonelyplanet.co.uk

France
1 rue du Dahomey, 75011 Paris
☎ 01 55 25 33 00 fax 01 55 25 33 01
✆ bip@lonelyplanet.fr
🖳 www.lonelyplanet.fr

World Wide Web: 🖳 www.lonelyplanet.com *or* AOL keyword: lp
Lonely Planet Images: ✆ lpi@lonelyplanet.com.au